Publications of the John Gower Society

IV

JOHN GOWER AND
THE STRUCTURES OF CONVERSION
A READING OF THE CONFESSIO AMANTIS

This book examines the significance of John Gower's re-creations of the cultural past in the *Confessio Amantis* through the stories and teachings of the confessor, Genius. Although the poem has many of the attributes of a compilation, Gower reforms material to create a range of 'wise' responses to important moral questions, intended to sharpen his readers' judgment and nurture their capacity to deal wisely with the contingencies and temporal uncertainties of the moral life.

Olsson analyses the poet's conversions of old to new as an effort to inspire the moral renewal of the age. He contends that the poet sees the past as the key to the regeneration of his world. In this reading, the past, an ever-new and renewable repository of wisdom, also holds a promise for Amans, who, in a controversial turn in the poem, learns that he is an old man, unfit to serve in Venus's court. Thus the author perceives Gower to offer through his re-creations of the past a strong, responsive and balanced moral vision to an age or an individual seemingly victimised by change.

KURT OLSSON is Professor of English and Dean of the College of Letters and Science, University of Idaho, and author of numerous articles on Gower; this is his first book.

Publications of the John Gower Society

General editors R. F. Yeager and A. J. Minnis

ISSN 0954–2817

I

A Concordance to John Gower's *Confessio Amantis*
edited by J. D. Pickles and J. L. Dawson

II

John Gower's Poetic: The Search for a New Arion
R. F. Yeager

III

Gower's *Confessio Amantis*: A Critical Anthology
edited by Peter Nicholson

John Gower and the Structures of Conversion

A Reading of the Confessio Amantis

Kurt Olsson

D. S. BREWER

First published 1992 by D. S. Brewer, Cambridge

D. S. Brewer is an imprint of Boydell & Brewer Ltd
PO Box 9, Woodbridge, Suffolk IP12 3DF, UK
and of Boydell & Brewer Inc.
PO Box 41026, Rochester, NY 14604, USA

ISBN 0 85991 314 7

British Library Cataloguing-in-Publication Data
Olsson, Kurt
    John Gower and the structures of conversion:
A reading of the "Confessio Amantis".
    – (Publications of the John Gower Society)
I. Title II. Series
821
ISBN 0–85991–314–7

Library of Congress Cataloging-in-Publication Data
Olsson, Kurt, 1941–
    John Gower and the structures of conversion : a reading
of the Confessio amantis / Kurt Olsson.
        p.   cm. – (Publications of the John Gower Society,
ISSN 0954–2817 ; 4)
    Includes bibliographical references and index.
    ISBN 0–85991–314–7 (alk. paper)
    1. Gower, John, 1325?–1408. Confessio amantis.
    2. Conversion in literature.   3. Ethics in literature.
I. Title.   II. Series.
PR1984.C63048   1992
821'.1 – dc20   91–36625

The paper used in this publication meets the minimum requirements
of American National Standard for Information Sciences –
Permanence of Paper for Printed Library Materials, ANSI Z39.48–1984

Printed in Great Britain by
St Edmundsbury Press Ltd, Bury St Edmunds, Suffolk

CONTENTS

FOR MY PARENTS

ACKNOWLEDGMENTS

I am pleased to thank the Curators of the Bodleian Library, Oxford, and the Syndics of Cambridge University Library for kindly allowing me to quote from manuscripts in their collections. I also wish to thank the librarians and staff of these libraries and the British Library for the help they have provided. Portions of my argument have been adapted from earlier articles: "Natural Law and John Gower's *Confessio Amantis*," *Medievalia et Humanistica*, n.s. 11 (1982): 229–61; and "Aspects of Gentilesse in John Gower's *Confessio Amantis*, Books III–V," in *John Gower: Recent Readings*, ed. R. F. Yeager (Kalamazoo, Michigan, 1989), 225–73. I gratefully acknowledge the Medieval and Renaissance Society and the Board of the Medieval Institute, respectively, for permission to reprint this material. Grants from the American Philosophical Society, the National Endowment for the Humanities, and the University of Idaho Research Council have also allowed me to pursue certain key aspects of the project.

I am indebted to many teachers, colleagues, and friends who have nurtured my interest in Gower and provided me with wise counsel at various stages of my research: to Theodore Silverstein, who years ago introduced me to Gower and subsequently directed my dissertation; to Jerome Taylor, also a reader of that thesis; to V. A. Kolve, Robert Kellogg, Leo Damrosch, Siegfried Wenzel, and Robert Yeager, who advised me on materials that figure significantly in this study. I am particularly grateful to other friends – Hoyt Duggan, Wayne Fields, the late Herbert Lamm, and my father, Karl Olsson – for reading the manuscript in one or more of its versions and for stimulating this inquiry through many conversations. The project would not have been possible without the wonderfully cheerful support of my wife Charlene and daughters Katherine, Annika, and Brita. Moreover, for their love and encouragement, I owe a special debt to the two people to whom the book is dedicated, Sally and Karl Olsson.

A NOTE ON THE TEXT

Most quotations of foreign language material appear only in translation in the text; I have used published translations whenever these have been available to me. Quotations of Gower's Latin prose and verse, however, are presented in the original language, with a translation immediately following. Book and line numbers of quotations from the *Confessio* are from the Macaulay edition; in the case of quotations of the Latin epigrams, I cite book, section within the book, and line numbers. The following abbreviations of Chaucer's works are used in the text and notes.

Bo	*Boece*
ClT	*Clerk's Tale*
FranT	*Franklin's Tale*
Gent	*Gentilesse*
KnT	*Knight's Tale*
LGW	*Legend of Good Women*
MLT	*Man of Law's Tale*
ParsP	*Parson's Prologue*
ParsT	*Parson's Tale*
Ven	*Complaint of Venus*
WBT	*Wife of Bath's Tale*

CHAPTER ONE

THE *CONFESSIO* AND COMPILATION

One of John Gower's undoubted claims to join the company of important late fourteenth-century English poets, including Chaucer, Langland, and the Gawain-poet, lies in the vast knowledge he made available to his public. In three long, encyclopedic poems, he gathered and arranged material from a great number of ancient and medieval sources and, with a consistent stylistic grace, made that material accessible in his chosen language, whether it was French, as in the *Mirour de l'Omme*, Latin, as in the *Vox Clamantis*, or English, as in the *Confessio Amantis*. Gower was not content, however, merely to generate cultural thesauri. Well-attuned to the major issues of his day and versed in the current idioms of the court, the legal profession, the schools, and the Church, he drew the old and new together to the end of reshaping the values of Ricardian England. No small task facing the reader of his works, and especially of the *Confessio*, the most complex of the poems, is to discover how, in that process, he not only retrieved and transmitted, but redefined his culture.

The natural starting point for such an enterprise is to resort to the famous epithet that Chaucer invented for him. Chaucer's "Moral Gower" became "olde Morall Goore" to a later generation, and so he endures to this day in various refinements of that perception. Indeed, there seems little point in trying, as Rosemary Woolf has done, to cancel Chaucer's term by turning the tables, making Chaucer the "moral" and Gower the "kindly" poet.[1] The weight of tradition is against it, and the poetry also is.

The appeal of this catch-phrase lies partly in its imprecision. All poetry is in some sense moral, of course, and that is how it was perceived in medieval literary theory. If the *pars philosophiae* to which the *Confessio* belongs is *ethica*, the same might be said of virtually all poems, ancient and medieval, introduced in medieval *accessus ad auctores*. Giovanni del Virgilio put it succinctly when, in writing of Ovid's *Metamorphoses*, he remarked, "As for the part of philosophy to which it belongs, I say that it belongs to ethics, that is, moral philosophy, for all poets deal with behavior."[2] Nevertheless, though one rarely finds a medi-

---

[1] Rosemary Woolf, "Moral Chaucer and Kindly Gower," in *J. R. R. Tolkien, Scholar and Storyteller: Essays in Memoriam*, ed. Mary Salu and Robert T. Farrell (Ithaca, N.Y., 1979), pp. 221–45.

[2] Fausto Ghisalberti, "Giovanni del Virgilio, espositore della *Metamorfosi*," *Il Giornale Dantesco* 34, n.s. 4 (1933) 19; trans. Judson Boyce Allen, *The Ethical Poetic of the Later Middle Ages: A Decorum of Convenient Distinction* (Toronto, 1982), p. 53 n. 14.

eval critic who claims for a poem a content field other than ethics, the term moral seems especially applicable to Gower because the poetry it describes is, on the surface, so much more "ernest" than "game." This feature has led many critics to judgments such as D. W. Robertson's indictment of Gower's "plodding seriousness,"[3] but recently there has emerged in the criticism a new, and very different assessment of the poetry. When Gower seems to be most earnest, the argument runs, he may very well be engaging in a deeper and most sophisticated "pleie." Anthony Farnham has remarked on Gower's "keen awareness of the didactic value of misdirected seriousness," and others have followed this lead in perceiving what Farnham describes as the poet's "almost perverse comic sense."[4] Gower is not merely a humorless champion of ethical causes. Indeed, the best grounds for showing him to be a truly moral poet lies in the comedy of his English poem, for it is there that he most fully reveals his deep awareness of the complexities of human behavior and offers his keenest insight into it. This poem is as effectively moral in its "game" as it is in its earnestness, and in both things together Gower will challenge and ultimately reward the careful reader.

Gower makes a "refined" love – a love associated with *gentilesse* – the subject of his book. As Derek Pearsall has remarked, Gower is not, in a technical sense, a court poet, but "of the qualities that go to the making of 'courtly poetry', whether we associate it with the royal court or not, he has all that is essential."[5] Genteel, sophisticated, and "well-mannered," he fashions his work to courtly tastes,[6] giving a clear indication of that interest in a famous passage opening the original version of the poem, where he describes a meeting with Richard II on the royal barge on the Thames. On that occasion, he writes, the king

> bad me doo my besynesse
> That to his hihe worthinesse
> Som newe thing I scholde boke,
> That he himself it mihte loke
> After the forme of my writynge.   P.49*–53*

Whether Gower specifically sought to tailor his new poem to this royal patron's interests must remain a matter of conjecture, but it is clear that he chose a subject that could win Richard's regard, especially if we believe the testimony of Jean Froissart, who in 1395 gave a volume of his own poems to Richard and

---

3   D. W. Robertson, Jr., *Chaucer's London* (New York, 1968), p. 170.
4   Anthony E. Farnham, "The Art of High Prosaic Seriousness: John Gower as Didactic Raconteur," in *The Learned and the Lewed: Studies in Chaucer and Medieval Literature*, ed. Larry D. Benson, Harvard English Studies, 5 (Cambridge, Mass., 1974), pp. 164–65.
5   Derek Pearsall, *Old English and Middle English Poetry* (London, 1977), pp. 208–209.
6   Although Gower's poetry, like Chaucer's, "appears to have been written, on occasions, with an aristocratic courtly audience in mind . . . its more significant readers appear to have been career diplomats, civil servants, officials and administrators who were attached to the court and the government" (V. J. Scattergood, "Literary Culture at the Court of Richard II," in *English Court Culture in the Later Middle Ages*, ed. V. J. Scattergood and J. W. Sherborne [London, 1983], p. 38).

"shewed hym howe it treted of maters of love; wherof the kynge was gladde and loked in it, and read it in many places."[7] Gower's meeting with Richard on the Thames may have been nothing more than a "casual contact," but his account of that meeting itself suggests that he envisions his readers as people drawn to the "language" of court as inspiring certain preferred modes of behavior. Whatever the specific issues of patronage or readership, this poem explores and celebrates courtly values.

But the *Confessio* also does much more. Gower works with topoi originally devised by poets of the French court, and this is perhaps no more in evidence than in his portrait of the poem's central character, Amans. The eight books of the English poem recount the confession of this lover to Genius, the priest of Venus, who for his part not only shrives the lover, but teaches him about the vices and many other things, sometimes by means of narrative "ensamples," sometimes by means of plain exposition, "withoute frounce" (7.1594).

Gower's doctrine is "translated" not merely out of French *dits* written in his own century, but out of such works as were more certainly familiar to English courtly audiences: the Bible, the *Roman de la Rose*, political treatises such as Aegidius Romanus' *De regimine principum*, books of vices and virtues, encyclopedias *de proprietatibus rerum*, occasional "tretes amoireux & moralitez & de caroll,"[8] as well as collections of tales and "histories" written by authors ranging from Ovid to Godfrey of Viterbo. Gower orders and reorders what he gathers from these books, fitting that material not only to the structure of a gentle lover's confession, but to other frames of perception as well: in the Prologue and epilogue, a tract for the times; in one of the eight books, an outline of an ideal education for a prince, cast in the "forme of Aristotles lore"; in excursus interspersed throughout the poem, treatises on a wide variety of historical, doctrinal, and scientific subjects. Still other frames of perception are provided by the poem's apparatus: at the head of each of the poem's major divisions, Latin poetic epigrams; and in the margins of the text, Latin prose summaries. Each of these fields in the text and apparatus has unique formal

---

7 *The Chronicle of Froissart*, trans. Sir John Bourchier, Lord Berners, ed. William Paton Ker (London, 1901–03), 6:147. Though we know little about Richard's reading, we do know that a number of French romances, a two-volume Bible, and a copy of the *Roman de la Rose* were presented to him in 1379. By 1384–84, however, these books were no longer in his possession. See D. W. Robertson, Jr., *Chaucer's London*, p. 208; Edith Rickert, "King Richard II's Books," *The Library*, 4th ser., 13 (1932–33): 144; Richard F. Green, "King Richard II's Books Revisited," *The Library*, 5th ser., 31 (1976): 235–39; Scattergood, "Literary Culture," pp. 32–33.

8 Such are the works listed in the inventories of books owned by members of the aristocracy in fourteenth-century England. See Scattergood, "Literary Culture," pp. 33–36; A. I. Doyle, "English Books In and Out of Court from Edward III to Henry VII," in *English Court Culture*, ed. Scattergood and Sherborne, pp. 163–81; A. I. Doyle and M. B. Parkes, "The Production of Copies of the *Canterbury Tales* and the *Confessio Amantis* in the Early Fifteenth Century," in *Medieval Scribes, Manuscripts, & Libraries: Essays Presented to N. R. Ker*, ed. M. B. Parkes and A. G. Watson (London, 1978), pp. 163–210, esp. pp. 177, 208.

attributes, and each provides its own structure or structures of meaning. The "game" or "lust" of the *Confessio* rests in part on the writer's shifting repeatedly from structure to structure to interpret his matter, and on his not allowing readers to settle comfortably into a single mode of perception or to light on a single thematic "center" as sufficient for explaining the poem. Sometimes inside these structures, and sometimes crossing their boundaries, meanings conflict with each other and with the meanings hinted at in the announced *ordinatio* or topical arrangement of the work.

Gower's use of topics evolves out of medieval strategies of compilation which, over the past several decades, have been examined and discussed by many scholars. M. B. Parkes, in a seminal article, placed *compilatio* in the setting of what has since become a popular distinction, Bonaventure's notion of the four ways of making a book. The scribe (*scriptor*) simply writes the words of others, "nihil addendo vel mutando"; the compiler (*compilator*) joins together the words of others, but none of his own; the commentator (*commentator*) writes the words of others as well as his own, but those of others make up the principal part, and his are annexed in order to clarify those words; the author (*auctor*), finally, writes the words of others as well as his own, but his words form the principal part, and those of others are annexed in order to confirm his own.[9]

This distinction is less important as a prescription – it is doubtful, for example, that Gower had read Bonaventure – than as a description of issues of invention, judgment, and statement that concerned virtually all medieval writers of books. The roles of authoring, compiling, and even commenting are obviously variable and relative to each other, and a question about any of them is often a question of degree. One of the great medieval compilers, Vincent of Beauvais, testifies that in putting together the *Speculum maius* he adds little or nothing of his own to what he gathers from others, for his end is not to feature his own words, but to collect and arrange those of others.[10] At the same time, he does not entirely avoid assertion,[11] but offers "sentences" that may effectively become a comment on material compiled. Even when a compiler merely

---

[9] Bonaventure, *Commentarius in librum primum sententiarum*, prooemium, q. 4, S. *Bonaventurae opera omnia* (Quaracchi, 1882–1902), 1:14; quoted by M. B. Parkes, "The Influence of the Concepts of *Ordinatio* and *Compilatio* on the Development of the Book," in *Medieval Learning and Literature: Essays Presented to R. W. Hunt*, ed. J. J. G. Alexander and M. T. Gibson (Oxford, 1975), pp. 127–28; this paraphrase is adapted from the translation of A. J. Minnis, *Medieval Theory of Authorship: Scholastic Literary Attitudes in the Later Middle Ages*, 2nd ed. (Philadelphia, 1988), p. 94.

[10] Vincent of Beauvais, "Apologia totius operis," cap. 4, ed. Anna-Dorothee v. den Brincken, "Geschichtsbetrachtung bei Vincenz von Beauvais: Die Apologia Actoris zum Speculum Maius," *Deutsches Archiv für Erforschung des Mittelalters* 34 (1978): 470. On the "Libellus Apologeticus," see J. B. Voorbij, "The Speculum Historiale: Some Aspects of Its Genesis and Manuscript Tradition," in *Vincent of Beauvais and Alexander the Great: Studies on the Speculum Maius and Its Translations into Medieval Vernaculars*, ed. W. J. Aerts et al., Medievalia Groningana, fasc. 7 (Groningen, 1986), pp. 18–20.

[11] Minnis, *Authorship*, pp. 191–94, 200.

quotes authors verbatim, however, he also "asserts," or engages in a form of authoring, specifically as he fits their words to new contexts, to a new *ordinatio* of parts.

My purpose in introducing the term *compilatio* in this study is not to defend it as a genre, or to pursue at great length its history or the history of terms that surround it in medieval treatises, or even to suggest that Gower himself is an exemplary *compilator*.[12] It is rather to use it as a means of identifying issues and strategies that become central to Gower in the work; the procedure of compilation impinges significantly on how he understands history and organizes moral experience itself.

Alastair Minnis has provided a very important start to the discussion of *compilatio* in Gower's poems, and my debt to his inquiry will be evident in the pages of this book. His statement that "Gower was a compiler who tried to present himself as an author"[13] usefully points out that Gower works between roles of authoring and compiling, and it correctly asserts that Gower privileges authorship. I disagree with the statement, however, to the extent that it also carries an imputation of failure, an implication that the poet succeeds in neither role. Gower writes to an authorial end, but he does not, through some incapacity, become a *compilator* by default. As we shall see, his activities of compilation do not weaken, but energize his authorship.

A pair of marginal glosses on the *Confessio* suggest the order of Gower's roles as a writer, including, by their own example, his activity as a commentator. In the revised version of the opening to the poem, a marginal comment at P.22 explains, very simply, that "Iohannes Gower presentem libellum composuit et finaliter compleuit" 'John Gower composed and finally completed the present book.'[14] This statement is innocent enough: what gives it moment is that the poet, with these words, replaces a gloss at P.34* of the first version suggesting that the poem is chiefly a compilation, its maker a *compilator*: "Iohannes Gower, . . . tanquam fauum ex variis floribus recollectum, presentem libellum ex variis cronicis, historiis, poetarum philosophorumque dictis . . . studiosissime compilauit" 'from various chronicles, histories, and sayings of poets and philosophers, John Gower . . . most diligently compiled the present book, as a honeycomb gathered from various flowers.'

Some of the terms Gower uses in this passage – not only *recollectum* and *compilauit*, but *fauum* and *floribus* – commonly appear in prefaces to late medieval compiled books. Such is the case, for example, in one of Gower's known sources, Brunetto Latini's encyclopedic *Tresor*:

---

[12] On *compilatio* as a genre, see Alastair J. Minnis, "Late-Medieval Discussions of *Compilatio* and the Role of the *Compilator*," *Beiträge zur Geschichte der Deutschen Sprache und Literatur* 101 (1979): 386–87.
[13] Minnis, *Authorship*, p. 210.
[14] All quotations from Gower are from the edition of G. C. Macaulay, *The Complete Works of John Gower*, 4 vols. (Oxford, 1899–1902).

And I do not say that the book is drawn from my poor wit or my scanty learning; but it is like a honeycomb gathered from different flowers, for this book is compiled exclusively from the marvellous sayings of authors who before our time treated of philosophy, each according to the part of it that he knew.[15]

Of these terms, the most important is *flores* 'flowers': it is, of course, a root term for the popular medieval genre of *florilegia*, and it stands alone in many book titles: *Liber florum, Manipulus florum, Flores paradysi, Parva flores*. It is, indeed, "the most common medieval name for a collection of extracts."[16]

Having introduced the *Confessio* in this way, Gower does not repeat the statement, or reintroduce its terminology, but neither do other compilers once they have prefaced their collections. Furthermore, though the poet cancels this gloss in later versions of the work and turns our attention to his generic office as a writer, or perhaps to his office as an author, he does not divert our attention from compilation for very long. In the course of the confession, Genius, in keeping with his task of defining the "vices dedly" and shriving the "contrite" lover, also gathers from a wide range of sources tales that he thinks are aptly designed to "amende" the penitent. Genius is a *compilator* who often names his sources, but even when he does not, he reminds us that his stories are "found": "Ovide telleth in his bok" (1.333), "In Metamor it telleth thus" (1.389), "in the tale of Troie I finde" (1.483), "I finde ensample in a Croniqe" (1.759), "I finde in the bokes write" (1.2458), "Among the bokes of latin / I finde write" (2.3187–88). Gower's point, of course, is not merely to show that Genius is one of those "who these olde bokes rede / Of suche ensamples" (2.2140–41); by such references the poet opens his work out to the field of books, to a literary heritage.

Gower's process of compiling draws its support chiefly from practices of late medieval writers, but its roots lie in antiquity. The analogy between gathering extracts and culling flowers is itself drawn from a famous letter of Seneca:

We should follow, men say, the example of the bees, who flit about and cull the flowers that are suitable for producing honey, and then arrange and assort in their cells all that they have brought in.[17]

Seneca does not introduce the terms compiling and authoring in this analogy: he is in effect describing a long process of composing, effectively authoring, that includes both gathering and reforming what one has read, until the "separ-

---

[15] Brunetto Latini, *Li Livres dou Tresor*, 1.1.5, ed. Francis J. Carmody, University of California Publications in Modern Philology, vol. 22 (Berkeley and Los Angeles, 1948), pp. 17–18; trans. Minnis, *Authorship*, p. 192.

[16] Richard H. Rouse and Mary A. Rouse, *Preachers, Florilegia and Sermons: Studies on the Manipulus florum of Thomas of Ireland*, Texts and Studies, vol. 47 (Toronto, 1979), p. 113; see also Henri-Marie Rochais, Philippe Delhaye, and Marcel Richard, "Florilèges spirituels," *Dictionnaire de spiritualité*, fasc. 5 (Paris, 1964): 435–512.

[17] Seneca, *Ad Lucilium Epistulae morales* 84.3, trans. Richard Gummere, Loeb (London and Cambridge, Mass., 1962–1967), 2:277.

ate elements are united into one substance." In his perspective, one must transform what has been collected: "whatever we have absorbed should not be allowed to remain unchanged." And thus he describes the entire process:

> We also, I say, ought to copy these bees, and sift whatever we have gathered from a varied course of reading, for such things are better preserved if they are kept separate; then, by applying the supervising care with which our nature has endowed us, in other words, our natural gifts, – we should so blend those several flavours into one delicious compound.[18]

The medieval compiler is concerned with form in two senses: the one is the surface structure, the *forma tractatus*, or the physical division of the work into books and chapters; the other is a deeper structure, the *forma tractandi*, or the manner of treating the subject, the flow of his thought.[19] Seneca, it appears, is more broadly concerned with the style, the "blend" of the entire work, or, in medieval terms, the *forma tractandi*, and that is perhaps because he is more concerned that things gathered in reading be fully assimilated. One "sifts" and "keeps" those things "separate" in an intermediate stage of the composing process.

Sifting and keeping things separate are, however, ends of medieval compilers; a product of their ordering material topically is the *forma tractatus*. This form provides a critical division of the text, and it is to it that Parkes refers when, in discussing the influence of practices of *compilatio* on vernacular literature, he remarks that "the process of *ordinatio* at the higher level may be detected in the general schemes of the *Decamerone*, the *Confessio amantis*, *Les Cent Balades* and the incomplete *Canterbury Tales*." [20] Such a scheme is marked in the *Confessio* by a marginal comment at 1.59: Gower "varias eorum passiones variis huius libri distinccionibus per singula scribere proponit" 'proposes to write of [lovers'] various passions one by one in the various distinctions of this book,'[21] The distinctions, we soon learn, are the "vices dedly."

Interposed between the late medieval idea of physical division of the book and the Senecan notion of uniting separate elements into one substance is the practice of Macrobius, who in the introduction to his own "literary storehouse," the *Saturnalia*, uses the Senecan metaphor to describe his purpose. Claiming that the education of his son Eustachius is his chief care, Macrobius has striven to unify the material he has gathered:

> things worth remembering have not been heaped together in confusion, but a variety of subjects of different authorship and divers dates

---

[18] Ibid., 84.5, p. 279; on the importance of Seneca's statement to medieval florilegists, see Rouse and Rouse, *Preachers*, pp. 115–17.

[19] On this distinction, and the usefulness of both senses of form in determining the intent of an author, see Rouse and Rouse, *Preachers*, p. 38.

[20] Parkes, "*Ordinatio*," p. 130.

[21] Trans. Minnis, *Authorship*, p. 189.

have been arranged to form, so to speak, a body, in such a way that the notes which I had made without any plan or order, as aids to memory, came together like the parts of a coherent whole.[22]

Macrobius uses Seneca's metaphor of the bees to describe "a kind of mental fermentation which serves to season the whole," and testifies that the gathered material is "sometimes set out plainly in my own words and sometimes faithfully recorded in the actual words of old writers, as each subject has seemed to call for an exposition or a transcript."[23]

Unlike Seneca, Macrobius also stresses "the actual process of arrangement." Arrangement aids the memory, and most notably it serves the reader:

> if ever you have occasion to call to mind some historical fact, buried in a mass of books and generally unknown, or some memorable word or deed, it will be easy for you to find it and produce it, as it were, from a literary storehouse.[24]

The *ordinatio* of this work serves an end of making gathered material easily accessible. The need "to call to mind" or "to find" something buried provides an even stronger impetus in late medieval collections. As Rouse and Rouse have noted, Thomas of Ireland's emphasis in the preface to *Manipulus florum* is on sorting, cataloguing, and storing ideas. The work itself is "written not to be read, but to be used – that is, to be searched."[25] Like many other books devised to aid in the writing of sermons, it presents quotations from the Fathers under topics arranged in clear alphabetical order, thereby directing readers back through topics and memorable words to the whole works or *originalia*.[26] Such a compilation is designed for a specific purpose. It is a resource, a reference book: its function "is not to lead people back to the faith or to inspire new ideas; it is to be useful, to serve the reader well."[27]

Especially valuable to this type of book is an apparatus of what Rouse and Rouse have termed "finding devices."[28] Parkes illustrates, once again from a case in vernacular literature: "The most spectacular example is the Ellesmere manuscript of the *Canterbury Tales*. Here we find almost all the trappings of *ordinatio*: sources and topics are indicated in the margins, and the word '*auctor*' is placed alongside a sententious statement. The text is well disposed in its

---

[22] Macrobius, *Saturnalia*, 1, preface, 3, trans. Percival Vaughan Davies (New York, 1969), p. 26.
[23] Ibid., 6, 4, p. 27.
[24] Ibid., 2, p. 26.
[25] Rouse and Rouse, *Preachers*, p. 3.
[26] Ibid., pp. 36–37.
[27] Ibid., pp. 115–17.
[28] See Rouse and Rouse, "*Statim invenire*: Schools, Preachers and New Attitudes to the Page," in *Renaissance and Renewal in the Twelfth Century*, ed. Robert L. Benson and Giles Constable (Cambridge, Mass., 1982), pp. 201–25, passim; idem, *Preachers*, pp. 27–34.

sections, and each section is carefully labelled by means of full rubrics."[29] This apparatus quickly and efficiently guides readers to what they seek, and it lends to the entire work an appearance of other books expressly written to be searched.[30]

The best manuscripts of Gower's poem have a like apparatus. By the page headings, marginal notations, "chapter" or section divisions in the form of Latin epigrams, the poem becomes a resource easy to consult, and it is hardly surprising that to this day – because that apparatus has been reproduced in the major printed edition – the work continues to be used as a reference tool by those seeking information about medieval attitudes toward many different subjects.

One must take care, however, not merely to equate Gower's *Confessio* with works of the sort described by Rouse and Rouse as "searchable tools," even if they share certain features in the layout of their manuscript pages. Its *ordinatio* certainly serves a number of other distinct purposes. The topics of the confession organize the analysis of Amans's moral condition: they are aids to the fictive characters. Amans knows that he cannot on his own retrieve his history as a lover or moral agent. As he sets out to confess, he admits to Genius his fear that

> schal I moche thing foryete:
> Bot if thou wolt my schrifte oppose
> Fro point to point, thanne I suppose,
> Ther schal nothing be left behinde.   1.224–27

Genius, for his part, makes sure that he proceeds clearly from point to point. After treating the sins of the senses, he introduces the form of confession:

> Mi Sone, as I thee schal enforme,
> Ther ben yet of an other forme
> Of dedly vices sevene applied.   1.575–77

The vices and their species become discrete topoi of discovery, helping the "penitent" Amans remember all that is required for a complete confession. The device of the lover's confession "precludes the narrating of events in chronological order," John Burrow observes, but its "reference-grid" of topics makes possible an "unusual fulness and penetration" of psychological analysis.[31] As these topics allow the lover to frame, recover, and reorder his past, they may also "turn" his perspective to spiritual issues and make possible his repentance, conversion, and reaffirmed commitment to "vertu moral."

---

[29] Parkes, "*Ordinatio*," p. 134.

[30] Rouse and Rouse point out that "virtually every twelfth- to fourteenth-century aid to study that has a prologue" uses "expressions like *sine labore, facilius occurrere, presto habere,* and *citius* or even *statim invenire*" ("Statim," p. 207).

[31] J. A. Burrow, "The Portrayal of Amans in 'Confessio Amantis,'" in *Gower's Confessio Amantis: Responses and Reassessments,* ed. A. J. Minnis (Cambridge, 1983), p. 8.

These same topics also organize Genius's teaching, of course: a compiling of doctrines is, like a confession, an exercise in recovering and organizing a past. Gower remarks, at the outset of the *Confessio*, that he is concerned not to lose the heritage presented in books, not to forget: he is sensitive to the past as a source of "ensamples," and thence of an *ordinatio* for the present. In the fiction, as the lover wants to proceed "fro point to point" so as to avoid forgetting "moche thing," so the priest, as *compilator* and teacher, is given a ready-made structure to ensure his own recollection. The topics of the "vices dedly," so important to other medieval *compilationes*, enable Genius to find tales and lore whereby he might preserve the past, enlarge his pupil's knowledge, stabilize perception of a world that "neweth every dai," and give the lover a device for wisely ordering moral experience, where meanings are not always certain or easily secured.

The point remains, however, that this very *ordinatio* allows us also to read the work as a compilation. As, inside the fiction, it is important to Genius that the lover be secure in the *ordinatio* of the confession, that he understand where, in the order of things, the priest now leads him, so it is also important to Gower that readers not miss the *forma tractatus*: he thus partitions his topics not only in the English text, but in the headings and margins as well.[32] While this order serves a full confession in the fiction, it also serves readers by providing access, at virtually any juncture of the work, to subjects that interest them. The grid manifests Macrobius' principle for his own literary storehouse: "things worth remembering have not been heaped together in confusion," but have been fit to an order. Topics guide the poet to discovery, or help him remember; ultimately, they guide readers to memorable words or deeds that would otherwise remain "buried in a mass of books."

Unlike the *Manipulus florum* and other compilations of its kind, Gower's book is not a collection of excerpts. The English poet has advanced further along in the Senecan model of composition:

> A true copy stamps its own form upon all the features which it has drawn from what we may call the original, in such a way that they are combined into a unity. Do you not see how many voices there are in a chorus? Yet out of the many only one voice results. . . . In that chorus the voices of the individual singers are hidden; what we hear is the voices of all together.[33]

Gower aspires to be clear, and in that effort he tends to level out the different stylistic features of the authors he consults, thereby making the entire work, in transcript and exposition, speak in "one voice." It is perhaps consistent with this strategy that he should be seen as conservative in every respect: because he sets out to transmit the doctrine of others in what he describes as a plain style, his work has been judged derivative and threadbare. That might suggest that

---

[32] See, for example, the marginal comments at 1.9, 1.59, and 1.576.
[33] Seneca *Epistulae* 84.9–10, trans. Gummere, pp. 281, 283.

the *Confessio* is a work better searched than read. At least it should not be read continuously: such is the opinion of J. A. W. Bennett, who in his edition of selections, advises us to read the work in small doses: "medieval readers," he contends, "would perhaps have been satisfied with a tale or two at a time."[34] Though Bennett never explains why medieval readers might have been so satisfied, or we so justified in following them, one might suppose that the *ordinatio* allows the practice: it creates the appearance of a *compilatio* that its writer has designed to be read piecemeal.

The curiosity of this work that fits so well into the larger genre of compilation, however, is that, in certain respects, it does not fit at all. The explicit *ordinatio* often seems unequal to its task. Material drawn into the structure of the *Confessio*, even after Gower's revision, often appears to spill over the distinction or topic introduced to contain it. Gower's tales often do more, and sometimes do less, than elucidate the particular vice they are supposed to elucidate. To illumine a subtopic of Wrath, for example, he recounts the story of Canace that he had found in Ovid's *Heroides*. The purported topic and *moralitas* of this famous revision should center the narrative not on Canace, but on her melancholic father. To judge by modern critical readings, however, Gower's tale appears to be about Canace, and its subject appears to be incest. Not only does the story seem to have missed its topic, but it also diverges from its source: the narrative has lost its "history," the culture that originally gave it meaning. About Gower's telling, and especially its treatment of incest, Rosemary Woolf remarks, "Gower has skilfully and deliberately worked against the moral pattern of his original, worked against the didactic teaching of his age, and furthermore worked against the moral assumptions of all other medieval stories on the same type of subject."[35] In the *Confessio*, Gower often changes what he inherits from others, and he does not always do so to tighten its fit with a new *moralitas*, or to affirm a truth latent in his source; "the more aggressive *compilare* 'to pillage' " better describes his mode of gathering than does "the rather neutral *colligere* 'to collect.' "[36] On this occasion, he oversteps what tradition, the original narrative, and his announced *ordinatio* allow.

Even that is not the end of the difficulty. What Genius here ventures on the subject of incest contradicts what he says about it elsewhere in the *Confessio*. We can never be sure, before we read the entire work, that Gower has really supplied his doctrine on a given subject in a single tale, excursus, or piece of

[34] J. A. W. Bennett, *Middle English Literature*, ed. and completed by Douglas Gray (Oxford, 1986), p. 415.
[35] Rosemary Woolf, "Moral Chaucer and Kindly Gower," p. 227.
[36] Rouse and Rouse, *Preachers*, p. 41; the terms that Papias links with "compilare" suggest this distinction: "furari, depopulari, expoliare, depilare" (*Vocabulista* [Venice, 1496; rpt. Turin, 1966], s.v. "compilare," p. 72); see also Isidore of Seville, *Etymologiae* 10.44, s. v. "conpilator," ed. W. M. Lindsay (Oxford, 1911); on the basis of a unique statement of Nicholas of Lyra, Minnis suggests that the terms may also reflect a genre difference: the *compilatio* has an *ordinatio*, but the *collectio* does not ("Compilatio," p. 417).

dialogue, neatly placed within the limits of an announced topic: at another point in the work he might present another, sometimes opposed, and equally tenable reading of that subject, and often without a "finding device" to alert us to it. This makes the poem a snare for the unwary reader, and it obviously limits the work's usefulness as a compilation. Whereas we might be satisfied in reading a tale or two at a time, we cannot be certain that any such reading can provide what the poet actually thought or ultimately wished to convey on that subject.

Gower, in fact, often rewrites stories to disjoin meanings in his text, sometimes when the original would seem to have served his announced topic better. If it is a task of the compiler to organize received material in a new structure and to display that material coherently and accessibly, the poet would seem to have failed in the task. This feature of the work, however, is part of a larger design. In one sense, to be sure, Gower creates an impression that he seeks to imprint his own authorship and sense of coherence on what he gathers; as in the Senecan model of voices in a chorus, he gives a performance where "out of the many only one voice results." In another sense, however, he works to separate, to create for the work an impression of *compilatio*, and he does so by authoring divergent outlooks. Indeed, as he breaks his own voice out into many voices in this fiction of a compilation, he does by very different means what Chaucer does through his pilgrims in the *Canterbury Tales*.

One might expect discord in actual *compilationes* as the writer quotes authors who have very different, sometimes apparently contradictory, outlooks on common subjects. Such a problem Vincent of Beauvais faced in composing his *Speculum*, but he "did not attempt to make his *auctores* agree with one another, to make them all speak with one voice."[37] Like other writers of compilations in the thirteenth century, he seeks not to bring "sentences" into concord (*ad concordiam redigere*), but merely to recite those sentences, leaving to the reader's judgment (*lectoris arbitrio*) which one ought to be preferred.[38]

Vincent's perception of his task forms a double response to a dominant literary activity of the twelfth century, when the authors of the *Gloss*, the *Sentences*, and the *Decretum* sought to "organize inherited written authority in systematic form."[39] For Gratian in composing the *Decretum*, *ordinare* means reconciling differences, and Stephen of Tornai sees in the great decretist the activity that distinguished the period: to gather "sentences" in one place, and to bring their contradictions into agreement (*in concordiam revocare*).[40] Vincent in his *apologia* directly addresses that impetus in twelfth-century writers: in his role as an *excerptor*, he will not reconcile the different opinions of his authors. By leaving to the judgment of the reader which sentence ought to be preferred,

---

[37] Minnis, *Authorship*, p. 158; on Vincent, see Minnis, "*Compilatio*," pp. 387–90, 404–408.

[38] Vincent of Beauvais, "Apologia totius operis," cap. 8, ed. v. den Brincken, p. 477.

[39] Rouse and Rouse, *Preachers*, p. 4.

[40] *Die Summa des Stephanus Tornacensis*, ed. J. F. von Schulte (Giessen, 1921), p. 5; quoted by Minnis, "*Compilatio*," p. 397.

however, Vincent creates a work which, in a certain respect, resembles the kind of texts to which twelfth-century writers were responding. Peter Abelard, in the Prologue to his *Sic et non*, notes that the Fathers "may have reported the opinions of others rather than stating their own conclusions. For instance, in many places the writer of Ecclesiastes introduces contradictory views of differing origin; hence his name is interpreted as meaning 'one who causes debates' [*tumultuator*]." Often the Fathers "have left a question-mark hanging over the problems into which they were enquiring, rather than settling them conclusively. St. Augustine, that highly respected teacher . . . tells us that he has done exactly that when writing his *On the Text of Genesis*."[41] And Jerome "said that he often dictated indifferently his own views or those of other men, so that he might leave it to the reader's discretion [*lectoris arbitrio*] as to whether they should be approved or rejected."[42]

In the *Sic et non*, Abelard himself follows a procedure modelled by early canon lawyers who, on practical grounds, understood the urgency "of bringing discordant or apparently discordant canons into concordance."[43] The sayings of the Fathers which Abelard has gathered are "surrounded by some degree of uncertainty," and perusing them "may encourage inexperienced readers to engage in that most important exercise, enquiry into truth, and as a result of that enquiry give an edge to their critical faculty. For consistent or frequent questioning is defined as the first key to wisdom. . . . By doubting we come to enquiry, and by enquiry we perceive the truth."[44]

The conflict of authorities is central for Abelard; for Vincent it is not. Abelard models strategies for reconciling differences; Vincent does not. What happens in the fourteenth century, in Gower's poem, is effectively a combination of the procedures of these writers. The *Confessio* has all the trappings of the *compilatio*. The magnitude of the undertaking is encyclopedic, and there is, even within its superficially clear *ordinatio partium*, a seemingly random, often highly imaginative introduction of material, frequently generating conflict where we cannot anticipate it. Gower is, at one level, a *tumultuator*, one who causes debates. Inside the fiction, such a practice could betray a moral condition in Amans, perhaps even in Genius: in tradition the term applies *in malo* to Cain, the type of unregenerate man, or the soul which, "alienated from the peace of the sons of God, is confused in itself [*in seipsa tumultuatur*]."[45] More relevant for the moment is its application, *in bono*, to authorship of the sort Abelard sees exemplified in the writer of Ecclesiastes. Gower as *tumultuator*

---

[41] Peter Abelard, *Sic et non*, prologus, 88–93, trans. A. J. Minnis and A. B. Scott, in *Medieval Literary Theory c.1100–1375: The Commentary Tradition* (Oxford, 1988), p. 90; ed. Blanche Boyer and Richard McKeon (Chicago, 1976–77), pp. 92–93.

[42] Ibid., 132–33, trans. Minnis and Scott, p. 92.; ed. Boyer and McKeon, p. 94.

[43] Richard McKeon, "Rhetoric in the Middle Ages," in *Critics and Criticism, Ancient and Modern*, ed. R. S. Crane (Chicago, 1952), p. 283.

[44] *Sic et non*, prologus, 188–89, 333–39, trans. Minnis and Scott, pp. 94, 99; ed. Boyer and McKeon, pp. 96, 103.

[45] William of St. Thierry, *De natura corporis et animae* 2, PL 180:725.

seeks to generate an uneasiness, to the end of giving edge to our critical faculty. He also does more: his method is not precisely that of the dialectician, but he works towards concord in a program that continually introduces new authors, new issues. He does not allow us a security at any single juncture of this exercise, and that is to his point of making us wise: out of the discord he generates, we might come to a greater, extra-textual understanding. The form of the *compilatio* is suited to this imaginative play or "game," for it does not allow us to settle prematurely into a superficially "correct" judgment. The conflict is enriched, moreover, because Gower does not merely oppose doctrine to doctrine, but also frames each opinion in a structure of perception that lends to that opinion an appearance of truth. It is now also important to note that these structures are not merely the formal divisions of the *Confessio*, but also frames of perception generated within and across arguments.

Gower introduces and even generates discordant "sentences" not to distance readers from wisdom, but better to ensure their achieving it. We have already remarked that he uses the *distinctio*, a division of a term into an array of its possible meanings, to organize the contents of the separate books of the *Confessio*: the "seven vices dedly" or the various *passiones* of lovers are, in that sense, distinctions. Inside this announced *ordinatio*, however, Gower also evolves other distinctions for major recurrent concepts in the poem, including, for example, *kinde* or nature, love, honesty (*honestas* or *honestum*), *gentilesse*, profit, grace, and fortune. He does not display or develop the latter distinctions in any explicit order, but introduces new meanings as the context allows. The concepts and meanings often do not appear in Gower's immediate source for a given passage, but are taken instead from other *originalia*, or from medieval dictionaries, collections of distinctions, and other compilations.[46] These shifts

---

[46] Of the earliest dictionaries, the most important are Papias, *Elementarium doctrinae erudimentum* (mid-eleventh century), Hugutio of Pisa, *Magnae derivationes* (late-twelfth century), William Brito, *Summa Britonis* (ca. 1270), and John Balbus, *Catholicon* (ca. 1286); see Lloyd W. and Betty A. Daly, "Some Techniques in Medieval Latin Lexicography," *Speculum* 39 (1964): 229–39.

The distinction collections which began to appear in the late twelfth century guided readers to key scriptural terms, a range of figurative meanings for those terms, and biblical illustrations of those meanings. They were, as Rouse and Rouse have remarked, "the earliest of all alphabetical tools, aside from dictionaries," written to assist preachers in composing sermons (*Preachers*, pp. 7–9, 69, 75). Included among the popular late twelfth- and early thirteenth-century distinction collections are Peter the Chanter, *Summa Abel*; Peter of Poitiers, *Distinctiones super Psalterium*; Prepositinus of Cremona, *Summa super Psalterium*; Alan of Lille, *Distinctiones dictionum theologicalium*; Peter of Capua, *Alphabetum in artem sermocinandi*; and the anonymous collections *Angelus* and *Distinctiones monasticae*. With the distinction collections of the Franciscan Maurice of Provins and the Dominicans Nicholas de Gorran and Nicholas de Biard in the mid- to late thirteenth century, the entries become increasingly more elaborate, and interest shifts to broad moral topics. Rouse and Rouse write that "At times, the entries seem not so much to be scriptural terms in want of definition, as to be topics in search of scriptural discussion; so that their collections are in fact part distinctions, in the traditional sense of the term, and part biblical subject concordance, though with no

of meaning have the effect of weaning readers away from the false security of a single-valenced argument, or from a facile morality and illusory wisdom, and they represent a certain mode of writing that Abelard also observed in the works of the Fathers: "very often the same words have different meanings, when one and the same word [*vox*] has been used to express now one meaning [*significatio*], now another." [47] Like the Fathers, Gower is not always explicit about his *significationes*, though the context will often disclose them; nor does he ever openly reveal how they are interrelated, but we ignore this feature of the *Confessio* at our peril.

In the course of this study, then, we shall consider major concepts that cross the boundaries of the poem's many structures, identify the range of meanings assigned to each, and observe how, as interlocked in argument, these meanings vary in relationship to each other. Although such distinctions will prevent the reader from settling on one passage of the *Confessio* as providing the key to the poem's "meaning," they also provide a system of cross-references and the basis for an interdependence of structures within the poem. The challenge to the interpreter of the work – and a major task in this study – is to note these structures and *distinctiones* and to see how Gower points his readers toward wisdom through them. As we shall now discover, Gower begins in the Prologue to articulate his rationale for approaching wisdom in this way.

attempt at being exhaustive" ("Biblical Distinctions in the Thirteenth Century," *AHDLMA* 41 [1974]: 34). By the fourteenth century, "the term *distinctiones*, having lost any precise connotation, survived as a catch-all title meaning little more than 'alphabetical compendium for preachers' " ("Biblical Distinctions," p. 37). Later collections, of considerable use to preachers, include John Bromyard, *Summa praedicantium*, Pierre Bersuire, *Dictionarium seu Repertorium morale*, and Thomas Hibernicus, *Manipulus florum*. For fuller discussions of this history, see Rouse and Rouse, "Biblical Distinctions," pp. 27–37, and André Wilmart, "Un répertoire d'exégèse composé en Engleterre vers le début du XIIIe siècle," *Mémorial Lagrange* (Paris, 1940), pp. 307–46, especially "Note sur les plus anciens recueils de distinctions bibliques," pp. 335–46.
[47] *Sic et non*, prologus, 11–13, trans. Minnis and Scott, p. 87; ed. Boyer and McKeon, p. 89.

CHAPTER TWO

THE PROLOGUE: FORTUNE, GOVERNANCE, AND COUNSEL

The three middle sections of the five-part Prologue of the *Confessio*[1] picture a world racked by division: "regnes ben divided" (P.127), priests make "werre and strif / For worldes good" (P.248–49), and the people suffer and worsen the dreadful "fortune / Which hath befalle in sondri londes" (P.500–01). To readers of Gower's earlier major poems, this is a familiar subject. The poet, habitually a compiler of what he has already written, collects, reorganizes, and modifies observations from those earlier works to generate a new lament over a world that "is changed overal" (P.119), a world which, through a "defalte of bondes" (P.502), like a tun "Tobrekth" (P.505).

The contents of the Prologue lend some support to the notion that "Gower's three major works are one continuous work,"[2] but in each work the poet alters his teaching to suit a world that "neweth every dai"; in each poem he understands his readership differently, and for each work he devises a poetic structure that accommodates these other changes. One of the things that further separates the *Confessio* from the earlier poems is Gower's more focused interest in the very problem of temporality and contingency. The poet adapts "old" ideas to a new *ordinatio* in the Prologue, but he also carefully selects and arranges his topics to inform one part of an extended, complex *redditio*, a "reciprocal representation," of which the confession of Amans becomes the other part. The analogy between these parts – each of which is concerned with the recovery of a past – will reveal a basic difference between the *Confessio* and the earlier works: the poet's changes reach beyond specific content and language or "Stile," beyond a new commitment to sustained narrative, to a reperception of the role of memory in organizing experience.

The first section of the Prologue contains a tribute to old books and, implicitly, a defense of Gower's gathering their treasures in this poem. Books are the means by which distantly separated times are connected: just as those who precede us wrote for our benefit, we write "of newe som matiere, / Essampled of

---

[1] As we have noted, the Prologue and each of the books of the *Confessio* are subdivided in the manuscripts, as they are in Macaulay's edition, by Gower's Latin poetic headings; in this study I shall refer to these subdivisions as sections, occasionally as chapters.

[2] John H. Fisher, *John Gower: Moral Philosopher and Friend of Chaucer* (London, 1965), p. 135.

these olde wyse" (P.6–7) for the benefit of those who follow us. The two generations of writers share a task of "showing forth" such as we associate with epideictic rhetoric: "to magnifie / The worthi princes that tho were" (P.44–45), and to represent also "tho that deden thanne amis / Thurgh tirannie and crualte" (P.48–49). Such magnification of good and evil exemplars in Gower's practice, as in that of all other exempla-writers, is not intended to refine historical sensibilities so much as to recover a "mesure" that has been lost. The task is suited to Gower's status as an author, especially as that term is etymologically understood in the period. *Auctor* is thought to derive from *augere*, to increase.[3] As Conrad of Hirsau explains, "The author [*auctor*] is so called from the very 'increasing' [*augendo*], because by his pen he amplifies the deeds or sayings or thoughts of men of former times."[4] Gower, as an *auctor* or person worthy of credit, consideration, and belief,[5] presents to his readers exemplars, or figures "magnified."

These figures, or the exempla in which they appear, might be thought to mediate between a divine order – or an established truth – and actual experience. Presumably the exemplum contains principles which, because they are made familiar in a human exemplar, can effectively "rule" or measure experience. In "daies olde" – a better age than Gower's own – books containing such examples were "levere" and "Wrytinge was beloved evere / Of hem that weren vertuous" (P.38–39). Books steady and sharpen one's moral perception, one's capacity to understand. As Gower, in *compilatio* and represented confession, seeks to recover the past, so too he perceives in books a means to secure what would otherwise be lost. This premise about the book he shares with other writers such as Pierre Bersuire: books are necessary because our memory is very unstable or "slippery" (*labilis*); they allow us to call to mind what otherwise would be forgotten. They are also necessary because we are mortal; they allow us to transmit to posterity what we have discovered in our pursuit of knowledge.[6] Thus Gower seeks to "wryte of newe som matiere" that will become,

> Whan we ben dede and elleswhere,
> Beleve to the worldes eere
> In tyme comende after this.   P.9–11

Books secure a knowledge of "tyme passed" and present, and that knowledge makes it possible to order, respectively, the present and future.

The problem in Gower's present world can thus be identified and its solution sought by the instrument of an old book that describes a former age blessed

---

3 See, for example, the citations in A. J. Minnis, "The Influence of Academic Prologues on the Prologues and Literary Attitudes of Late-Medieval English Writers," *Mediaeval Studies* 43 (1981): 343 n. 2; see also *Authorship*, pp. 10–12.

4 Conrad of Hirsau, *Dialogus super auctores*, ed. R. B. C. Huygens (Leiden, 1970), p. 75; trans. Minnis and Scott, *Medieval Literary Theory*, p. 43.

5 M.-D. Chenu, *Toward Understanding Saint Thomas*, trans. A.-M. Landry and D. Hughes (Chicago, 1964), p. 130.

6 Pierre Bersuire, *Dictionarium*, s. v. *liber* (Lyons, 1516–17), 2: fol. 231v.

with health and "richesse" when "pes, which ryhtwisnesse keste, / With charite tho stod in reste" (P.109–10). These words, modified from those of the Psalmist, point to instances of strife, duplicity ("lawe hath take hire double face" P.130), and hatred as causing the present division of realms. A collation of books that allows the poet to displace the Psalmist's mercy and truth with charity also serves to focus our attention on love, the one virtue "which is al the chief / To kepe a regne out of meschief" (P.149–50). Conversely, we can lay the blame for our present wretchedness upon a loss of charity: "thurgh lacke of love / Where as the lond divided is, / It mot algate fare amis" (P.892–94).

This doctrine gleaned from ancient writings is significant, of course, but it is not Gower's whole point for the *Confessio*; were that the case, his exercise of then writing eight books of confession and ours of reading them would become otiose.[7] Books give Gower topoi such as these, but not his invention, his "newe som matiere." While the poet composes his work as a compiler might, he also seeks to provide, in his own credible and "authentic" statement, a basis for the analysis and solution of given moral questions; he becomes an author, even while he uses the *auctores*.[8]

The pattern of discovery in the *Confessio* is, I believe, much like one that Ernst Gombrich describes in the field of pictorial art: the artist "begins not with his visual impression but with his idea or concept," proceeding thence through "rhythms of schema and correction" to representation. "The schema is not the product of a process of 'abstraction', of a tendency to 'simplify'; it represents the first approximate, loose category which is gradually tightened to fit the form it is to reproduce."[9] The topos in Gower's Prologue is a "loose category," and from it the poet advances to representation not in one, but in multiple instances or arguments.

Indeed, the Prologue provides a *sufficientia* or rationale for Gower's multiplying instances, for engaging in the larger exercise of *compilatio*. Its topoi include not only assertions about division and love, but statements about fortune, governance, and counsel that will frame the confession to follow. The Prologue, written in a plain style, is designed to advise the "wyse man," and, therefore,

> it to wisdom al belongeth:
> What wysman that it underfongeth,
> He schal drawe into remembrance
> The fortune of this worldes chance.   P.67–70

Gower would thus have the wise person reflect on "this worldes chance," which, paradoxically, "noman in his persone / Mai knowe, bot the god al one"

---

[7] Such is the argument of Michael D. Cherniss, *Boethian Apocalypse: Studies in Middle English Vision Poetry* (Norman, Okla., 1987), pp. 104, 113.
[8] On this distinction, see M.-D. Chenu, "Auctor, Actor, Autor," *Archivum latinitatis medii aevi (Bulletin du Cange)* 3 (1927): 83.
[9] E. H. Gombrich, *Art and Illusion: A Study in the Psychology of Pictorial Representation*, 4th ed. (London, 1972), p. 64.

(P.71–72). No one should recognize the uncertainty and contingency of his knowing better than the wise man, and Gower repeatedly sharpens that awareness by focusing on a fortune that leaves us always in doubt: "The hevene wot what is to done, / Bot we that duelle under the mone / Stonde in this world upon a weer" (P.142–43). This uncertainty is not itself contingent, but in the very nature of earthly existence:

> And evere goth the whiel aboute,
> And evere stant a man in doute,
> Fortune stant no while stille,
> So hath ther noman al his wille.   P.561–64

Gower, in this Prologue, relies heavily on Boethian terms to describe the world and human perception of it, but it would be a mistake to dismiss the Prologue as a statement of already familiar doctrine, worthy only of passing interest. The poet addresses the problem of contingents and the human incapacity ever to achieve a certitude of moral knowledge in ways foreign to Boethius' *modus procedendi*, and we must take care not to lose sight of the difference.

Gower's end, in adopting the strategy of the compiler, is to promulgate wisdom. If, as is often supposed in the period, "sapientis est ordinare,"[10] then Gower is a wise man in ordering such diverse material and in effecting wisdom in his readers through the *ordinatio* of his poem. As with all sayings of this kind, however, it becomes meaningless if we fail to distinguish among degrees of significance in the ordering: it takes much less skill to order an alphabet of tales than to order genres, arts, themes, authors, and stories as Gower has done. Even more important than Gower's own exercise of ordering gathered material, however, is his exercise of making readers wise, that is, of giving them strategies for ordering their complex experience meaningfully. And herein lies a test of his wisdom in writing, of ours in reading.[11]

Although, for purposes of analysis, we may wish to keep separate an author's ordering of a book and a person's ordering of a life, the two processes are related in Gower's perception of experience. The wise person orders parts to a whole, things to an end.[12] A wise prince, writer, or moral agent, however, must order

---

[10] Minnis draws on C. W. Dunn's application of this phrase to Jean the Meun, "the greatest medieval compiler of *auctoritates* on love" (*Authorship*, p. 197); for Thomas Aquinas' uses of the phrase, see Minnis, *Authorship*, pp. 146–47, and "*Compilatio*," p. 391; several relevant passages in Aquinas are referred to in the next two notes.

[11] The rich complexity of this issue involves a recognition of a pre-existent knowledge in the wise writer and reader: "It does not befit a wise man that he should be induced to act by someone else, but that he should use his knowledge to induce others to act" (Thomas Aquinas, *In duodecim libros metaphysicorum Aristotelis expositio*, 1, lect. 2.42, trans. John P. Rowan, *Commentary on the Metaphysics of Aristotle* [Chicago, 1961], 1:19; ed. M. R. Cathala, rev. Raymund M. Spiazzi [Turin, 1971], p. 13).

[12] Thomas Aquinas, *In decem libros ethicorum Aristotelis ad Nicomachum expositio*, ed. Raymund M. Spiazzi, 3d ed. (Turin, 1964), p. 3; idem, *Liber de veritate catholicae fidei contra errores infidelium seu "Summa contra gentiles,"* 1, prooemium, cap. 1.2, ed. L. C. Pera, P. Marc, and P. Caramello, 2 vols. (Turin, 1961), 1:1–2.

things that may be otherwise than they are. Prudence and the artistic faculty both originate in the "opinativa parte animae," that part of the soul which deals with contingency.[13] In the midst of "this worldes chance," where, "Als fer as evere a man may knowe, / Ther lasteth nothing bot a throwe" (P.566–67), the order which the morally wise discover may be tentative and "uncertein," not so much an "imposed" and secure response to fortune as a schema that will be subject to "correction," a correction that, in its turn, will lead to the formation of new schemata, in a cycle of adaptations to change.

Gower recognizes an absolute Wisdom, but he also knows the difference between the agencies of Wisdom and wisdom, or of uncreated Sapience and the wisdom of creatures. The poet's task, even in a Prologue that "to wisdom al belongeth" (P.67), is to begin to order human wisdom concerning a world that "stant evere upon debat" (P.567). Human wisdom in ethical matters can only be approximate: in the field of ethics, amidst the "vncerteyne," "changeable," and "varyant" particulars of experience, familiar truths become useful instruments, accepted conventions through which we approach Wisdom.[14] Old books are sources of new invention or discovery; with the contingent things he inherits even from them, Gower exercises a deliberative playfulness which, while it never denies to Christian orthodoxy its prerogative and Truth, shows us how to deal with a "world which neweth every dai" (P.59). His task as an author, as well as compiler, is not merely to seek order, but to do so while also reflecting, even generating the "uncertein."

Other aspects in the formation of this idea in the Prologue will have a direct bearing on the confession. Some of these aspects surface in the three middle sections of the Prologue, each of which is devoted to an estate – "de statu regnorum," "de statu cleri," "de statu plebis." In these sections, Gower is not content merely to catalogue faults, status by status. He does not indict princes, for example, as the cause of the division of realms, but instead merely offers advice:

> unto him which the heved is
> The membres buxom scholden bowe,

---

[13] ". . . utrumque enim est in opinativa parte animae, et circa contingens aliter se habere" (Thomas Aquinas, *Summa theologiae* 1a2ae, 57.4, trans. W. D. Hughes, Blackfriars ed., 23:52–53).

[14] Basing his discussion on Aegidius Romanus' *De regimine principum*, Charles Runacres has helpfully discussed the relationship between the contingent particulars of ethics and Gower's use of particulars in his stories, in "Art and Ethics in the 'Exempla' of 'Confessio Amantis,' " ed. Minnis, *Gower's Confessio: Responses*, pp. 106–34; for another useful discussion of ethical knowledge as understood by Aegidius, see Judson Boyce Allen, *Ethical Poetic*, pp. 14–18. The terms to describe particulars are taken from the Middle English translation of Aegidius attributed to John Trevisa, in the selections edited by Herbert Ellsworth Childs, *A Study of the Unique Middle English Translation of the De regimine principum of Aegidius Romanus* (MS. *Digby 233*) (Ph. D. thesis, University of Washington, 1932), p. 196 (hereafter Childs); see Aegidius Romanus, *De regimine principum* 1.1.1 (Rome, 1607; rpt. Aalen, 1967), p. 4.

> And he scholde ek her trowthe allowe
> With al his herte and make hem chiere.   P.152–55

This principle of obedience and governance provides a hint of what Gower proposes as a response to fortune. The poet sees in the power of those who rule a means to stand firmly "upon a weer," provided that they,

> With good consail on alle sides
> Be kept upriht in such a wyse,
> That hate breke noght thassise
> Of love.   P.146–49

The topic of counsel is repeatedly introduced in the *Confessio*: in the Prologue, it is a doctrine flagged by a marginal gloss – "Salomon. Omnia fac cum consilio." –

> For good consail is good to hiere.
> Althogh a man be wys himselve,
> Yit is the wisdom more of tuelve;
> And if thei stoden bothe in on,
> To hope it were thanne anon
> That god his grace wolde sende
> To make of thilke werre an ende,
> Which every day now groweth newe.   P.156–63

This perception becomes both an example and a metaphor. It provides an example of how the wise man, who like every other man, "evere stant . . . in doute," deals with uncertainty. Counsel itself is opinion and therefore also uncertain: the wise person elicits multiple, varied, even opposed opinions "on alle sides," and strives to harmonize them or give them an *ordinatio*, however tentatively. This case also becomes a metaphor for the value of looking for counsel in books, of seeking from them the wisdom to end division. Implicitly, Gower's statement is a defense of compiling, of creating a thesaurus of instances. As "the pouer / Of hem that ben the worldes guides" (P.144–45) is kept upright by good advice, so every person achieves an analogous power by drawing from books "consail on alle sides." The authors of books thus provide a storehouse of advice when they meet their obligation to record, and thence preserve, those things "Wherof the world ensampled is" (P.47).

In the literal argument of the Prologue, Gower finds a model of counsel in the "presthode" of a former time. Old books, in imaging clerics as they once were, provide examples of what priests ought to be: in a time past, "thei weren tho / Ensample and reule of alle tho / Which of wisdom the vertu soughten" (P.195–97). Ideally priests are the living counterpart to books, and superficially this is because they are learned: in a former time "the poeple ensample tok" from them because

> Her lust was al upon the bok,
> Or forto preche or forto preie,

> To wisse men the ryhte weie
> Of suche as stode of trowthe unliered.   P.229–33

More profoundly, however, priests are the counterpart of books and have a special prerogative to offer counsel because they mediate between God and man. Clearly, whereas the "ensample" in a book links a truth to experience indirectly, as through a fiction, the priest mediates directly, in reality. Priests are thus

> The Mirour of ensamplerie,
> To reulen and to taken hiede
> Betwen the men and the godhiede.   P.496–99

To follow Gower's logic, then, the age especially needs books – including old books – because priests no longer provide an effective store of "ensamplerie." To be sure, there are still "somme in special / In whom that alle vertu duelleth" (P.432–33), but most, according to Gower's indictment, ignore the godhead, set their wit on "erthly werkes," and become mirrors of "ensamplerie" only in a negative sense. Their "propre duete" is "To make pes betwen the kynges / After the lawe of charite" (P.256–57), but instead, they "magnifie" all seven vices by their conduct. In this breach of charity, they teach division.

The effect of such division is manifested in the "comune." Gower does not refer to "tyme passed" in treating the commons as a status, but rather uses the uncertainties in their present to lead to a final, bookish measure of why the world "is al miswent." Each of the two preceding sections ends with the poet asking for God's help: concluding the section on temporal kingdoms, Gower hopes that God will "Amende that wherof men pleigne" (P.183), and ending his treatment of "holy cherche," he commends the few good priests and prays that "alle these othre god amende" (P.494). Gower offers no such security, or assured hope, in his treatise on the people. This section centers on Fortune and the "uncertein," and it locates that fortune in the human being. In the preceding sections Gower has identified the problem of uncertainty: now he places the burden of "that wherof men pleigne" squarely on man himself, for "of his propre governance / Fortuneth al the worldes chance" (P.583–84). To "magnifie" this observation, Gower takes his measure, as he does most typically in the Prologue, from the chief book neglected by priests: the Bible, providing a store of values, stabilizes perception. Nebuchadnezzar's vision of the human statue, recounted in Daniel, reveals not only "how the world schal change / And waxe lasse worth and lasse" (P.628–29), but how, as the "ymage bar liknesse / Of man" (P.908–09), man, divided in himself, brings on "Thende of the world" (P.883). This image, a "loose category" that the poet had used to another end in the last book of the Vox Clamantis, will in the Confessio achieve its fullest meaning and stature as a "representation" only in the perspective of the conclusion of the poem.

At this point, however, the poet seeks to offer provisional explanations of division; Nebuchadnezzar's dream can be more fully understood, in the context of the Prologue, by means of another device Gower introduces, an allegorical lineage which, in retrospect, also allows us to perceive an order in sections 2–4 of this part of the work. Sin is the "moder of divisioun" (P.1030), and division, in her turn, is the "moder of confusioun" (P.852). The fact that all persons stand "upon a weer" in their perception is now complicated by Gower's further point that the human being has failed in proper governance, has succumbed to "Senne," division, and confusion, and has thence permitted a horrible domin-ance of "worldes chance." The poet, rejecting the argument that the cause of the great adversity besetting the world is "fortune" or the "constellacion," has come to assert that "man is cause of that schal falle" (P.528). Man, by failing to accept counsel and thence to achieve "propre governance," suffers the conse-quences of a divided "reign."

This general statement mirrors "causes" in Amans's own topsy-turvy world. In the exemplum of the lover's psychological "querele," Gower corrects schema deriving from his loose categories of fortune, governance, and counsel. As men are generally confused by "the fortune of this worldes chance," so Amans is bewildered by the fortune of his love and more generally is perplexed that "as the whiel aboute went / [Love] yifth his graces undeserved" (1.50–51). In part, the issue involves the lover's limited knowledge of contingent things: "the certain noman knoweth" (P.140). In part, however, it involves a confusion that originates in Amans's internal debate, where, on the pattern of the body politic introduced in the Prologue, the members will not obey the head, and neither will the head regard the members or "her trowthe allowe" (P.154). This division originates in sin, of course, and Amans's cure thus depends on confession and a priest, and on what the priest teaches: counsel derived from books.

In the fiction of the confession, Genius is a double "Mirour of ensamplerie." He is, as a compiler, a repository of bookish "ensamples" that draw "truths" down to the level of particular human experience, and he is also, as a priest, a living mediator "Betwen the men and the godhiede." We cannot be entirely sure about this Genius or his priesthood, however, for at the very least we must question whether one whose obligation is "to taken hiede" of Venus can bring a lover's warring faculties to accord or, for that matter, champion a "lawe of charite" that can reconcile Amans to his true nature. Are we therefore right to surmise that Genius is an exemplar of the sinful priest, mirroring the status of the "presthode" in these last days? Is he himself a fallen reader who cannot discover apt "ensamplerie" in books? Is he really a mediator, or rather an earth-bound teacher who is attracted more to the lover and his values than to the Christian "godhiede" and His truth? We cannot be sure, for there are multiple sides to his character. In imagination, he is not restricted to the fantasies generated in Amans's love-quarrel, but free enough also to present to his charge aspects of the Christian ideal of regenerated man. Indeed, we might assume that with that knowledge he might help change for the better a lover who "stant evere upon debat" within himself. The point is that his counsel is unsure: what "truths" he voices in one aspect of his character may be challenged by what he voices in another aspect. He represents divided counsel, or unresolved "consail on alle sides."

While this priest will form a subject of later chapters in this study, it is important to introduce the issue of his counsel at this juncture because on a larger scale it and the question of opinion and a falsely secure "wisdom" pervade, indeed become the game of the entire *Confessio*. At the end of the work, Gower prays that God "this lond in siker weie / Wol sette uppon good governance" (8.2986–87). The "siker weie" of good governance is the end sought for the lover; it should be the end sought by wise readers. Achieving it depends upon a clear perception of uncertainty, a capacity to sift through divergent counsel, and a readiness to accept the gift of good governance. The virtue of a book of "ensamplerie" like the *Confessio* is that it identifies that "siker weie" imaginatively and provisionally, in forms subject to correction.

CHAPTER THREE

CONTINGENT ORDERS: *LUST AND LORE*

Given his emphasis in the Prologue on the uncertainties of a world which, to human perception, seems dominated by fortune, Gower has chosen an especially apt subject for the body of the *Confessio*. At the outset of Book 1, he introduces images of the balance, the dice, and the wheel – figures which, in medieval literature, often link the deities of love with Fortune – to convey a sense of the injustice that he, or his exemplar Amans, has suffered. The woes of love are inescapable, should Love decide to inflict them, and "forto proven it is so," Gower points to his "own" recent experience, a "wonder hap" that was to him "bothe hard and fell, / Touchende of love and his fortune" (1.68–69). The work will describe this "wofull chance, / That men mowe take remembrance / Of that thei schall hierafter rede" (1.75–77). Thus, as Gower in the Prologue counsels readers to remember fortune, so he now will teach them by his own example:

> Wherof the world ensample fette
> Mai after this, whan I am go,
> Of thilke unsely jolif wo,
> Whos reule stant out of the weie,
> Nou glad and nou gladnesse aweie,
> And yet it may noght be withstonde
> For oght that men may understonde.   1.86–92

As the poet begins to recount his "fortune how that it ferde" (1.97), his initial meeting with Venus, his "querele" and his plea for grace, he also conveys the urgency of his need: a long "maladie" such as his "myhte make a wisman madd, / If that it scholde longe endure" (1.130–31). This is an apt warning for the wise reader, since the love that the poet has suffered "many a wys man hath put under" (P.75).

Although the wise person is quick to understand that "of his propre governance / Fortuneth al the worldes chance" (P.583–84), he is not so immune to fortune as, from the brief order of the Prologue, he might have supposed. Such a person can quickly fall to the status of Amans if Love chooses to vanquish him, for "love is maister wher he wile" (1.35). Nor does Gower encourage him to think that, once caught, he can moderate his love: in love "ther can noman him reule, / For loves lawe is out of reule" (1.17–18). Indeed,

> ther is noman
> In al this world so wys, that can

> Of love tempre the mesure.
> Bot as it falth in aventure.   1.21–24

Here, then, there is no necessary distinction between the wise person and fool: each might fall snare to passion and go "ther noman wole him bidde; / He stant so ferforth out of reule, / Ther is no wit that mai him reule" (6.1282–84).

With Love, as with Fortune, one gains no assurance in a right choice, because the god of love "yifth his graces undeserved" (1.51), and there "may no certeinete / Be set upon his jugement" (1.48–49).[1] One might suppose that ordering intention or knowing the meaning of choices would help a person to transcend fortune,

> Bot what schal fallen ate laste,
> The sothe can no wisdom caste,
> Bot as it falleth upon chance.   1.39–41

This idea undoubtedly forms a powerful piece of dissuasion against love, "a Sor" for which "may noman finde / The rihte salve" (1.32–33). From the outset Gower appears to concede the point that there are no remedies for such passion. What makes it worse, however, is that this love is natural, fixed by cosmic design:

> For yet was nevere such covine,
> That couthe ordeine a medicine
> To thing which god in lawe of kinde
> Hath set.   1.29–30

The formulaic "noman can," "noman mai," of this section of the Confessio does not bode well for Amans's "querele," but neither does it promise good for the wise reader. The best solution to the problem of love is to be warned off while there is time, but neither can that be thought a sure solution. The poem too often returns to the power of an irresistible love to provide a hope that wariness – or resistance – does much good: Love cannot be stopped "wher as evere him lest to sette" (1.37).

These lines from the outset of Book 1 seem to belie Gower's claim that the work, in its subject of created or "ennatured" love, constitutes a scaling down of the problem outlined in the earlier poems or in the Prologue. To be sure, the poet now admits that he "may noght strecche up to the hevene / [His] hand, ne setten al in evene / This world" (1.1–3). Rather than diffuse his poetic energies over a "querele" that rages in the world at large, he will focus those energies on a love-debate in an individual, an exemplary character. Such a subject, it would appear, can be more quickly grasped and more readily ordered. Unlike the love which "is fro the world departed" (P.169), the love that forms the subject of the

---

[1] On this blindness in both deities, see Pierre Bersuire, *Reductorium morale, liber XV: Ovidius moralizatus, cap. i: De formis figurisque deorum, Textus e codice Brux. Reg. 863–9 critice editus*, ed. J. Engels, Werkmateriaal-3 (Utrecht, 1966), pp. 24–25.

book is "noght so strange" (1.10). It is familiar to readers, and Gower will make it even more accessible by presenting it in a setting of "ese" and refined conversation: this confession is a recreation that can in some part "be take / As for to lawhe and forto pleye" (8.3056*–57*).

Nevertheless, Gower's new departure realizes a greater, not a lesser ambition than the one governing the Prologue. The love he will treat resists ordering:

> Naturatus amor nature legibus orbem
>   Subdit, et vnanimes concitat esse feras.   1.1.1–2

> Created love overcomes the world by the laws of nature,
> and incites everyone alike to be wild.

To this problem of an unregulated love that endures despite human efforts to control it, the poet can have no ready solution. The challenge with regard to love, as to "this worldes chance," is standing "upon a weer" without being confounded, enchanted, and ultimately destroyed by it.

Breaking the spell of chance or Love, Gower eventually argues, requires the intervention of divine agency, or grace; in that sense, the human task of reform hinges on a distinction that Thomas Aquinas had succinctly expressed in an earlier century:

> freely bestowed grace is ordained for the cooperation of one man with another so that he might be brought back to God. Now man cannot work towards this by moving someone internally, for this belongs to God alone, but only by teaching him or persuading him externally.[2]

What distinguishes the body of the *Confessio* is Gower's new instrument of external instruction and persuasion. Gower cannot alter "fortune" or even know it – these are God's prerogatives – but he now fully recognizes that reform itself depends on seeing the "uncertein" in one's structures of perception.

It is to the point that in the shrift Gower leaves behind his stance in the Prologue, where he was, in effect, a poetical "prechour" speaking in the common voice. The peculiar untruth of this voice that "mai noght lie" (P.124) is its detachment from a persona who experiences doubt and shares in human guilt, the fault that stands "plenerliche upon ous alle" (P.527). The common voice that describes the estates "at large" and presents an ideal of common profit does so at a level of abstraction that fails to model the careful self-appraisal most needed in a world "al miswent."

In this work, Gower wisely shifts to a strategy of effecting reform through a "tale" of confession, involving speakers engaged in serious "game," each working with the fortune of their perceptions to discover and express truths. When Genius, at the end of the confession, passes a verdict against the lover, Amans bitterly complains, as if the priest's action constitutes a breach of trust, "It is

---

[2] Thomas Aquinas, *Summa theologiae* 1a2ae, 111.4, trans. Cornelius Ernst, Blackfriars ed., 30:136–37.

riht esi to comaunde" (8.2159). Gower, in the represented confession, prevents his readers from issuing a like complaint: this portion of the work is notably tentative and free of commands, even in spite of the priest's efforts, from point to point, to issue normative statements.

As with all good rhetorics, Gower's begins in human psychology, with certain givens. His external instruction and persuasion are directed toward turning an already existent, familiar, and seemingly natural love into something better, into a love more adequately and profoundly *kinde*. His ambition is not to impose a rule of conduct or clearly defined justice on his readers, but to attract them to charitable love. Here he reverses the impetus of his earlier poems, where his rhetorical premise seems to be the medieval topos that a fear of penalty, not a love of good (*amor honesti*) draws the "perverse soul" to the good (*ad bonum*).[3] His new premise is suggested, by analogy, in the emperor Trajan's mode of ruling his people:

> Him thoghte it were a grettere ese
> With love here hertes to him drawe,
> Than with the drede of eny lawe.   7.3154–56

To transform an existent love, Gower must address the problem of habit or the *consuetudo* that makes a person reluctant to accept or desire change.[4] Delight has engraved on the memory of the "repentant" Amans all that it derives from the senses.[5] As he confesses to "misloke" – the first sin of the senses – in what for him is hardly an admission of a fault, the lover claims that the image of his lady has turned his heart to stone. Habit has imprinted, indeed fixed in memory the image living there.[6] This habit Amans calls love, but it is in a sense the opposite, a repeated dividing of the self such as we have witnessed in the world of the Prologue. In having Amans confess to what he does "ofte tyme," Gower pictures a character who is bound by habit, who resists change. The priest's task in relation to Amans, like the author's in relation to his readers, is to break habitual ways of thinking about experience, and to

---

[3] See Aegidius Romanus, *De differentia rhetoricae, ethicae et politicae*, ed. Gerardo Bruni, *New Scholasticism* 6 (1932): 9.

[4] See John G. Prendiville, S. J., "The Development of the Idea of Habit in the Thought of Saint Augustine," *Traditio* 28 (1972): 29–99.

[5] See Augustine, *De musica* 6.11.33: "[Carnal] delight strongly fixes in the memory what it brings from the slippery senses." Trans. Robert Catesby Taliaferro, FC 4 (Washington, D.C., 1947), p. 358; *PL* 32:1181.

[6] See Augustine, *Confessions* 10.30.41: "But, there still live in my memory, and I have spoken much about it, the images of such things which habit has imprinted therein." Trans. Vernon J. Bourke, FC 21 (Washington, D.C., 1953), p. 299; *Confessionum libri XIII*, ed. Martin Skutella (1934), rev. H. Juergens and W. Schaub (Stuttgart, 1969), p. 239 (hereafter Skutella); on the imprint of the beloved being so firmly impressed in memory that it will last forever, see Guillaume de Machaut, *Dit dou Lyon*, 207–11, in *Oeuvres de Guillaume de Machaut*, ed. Ernest Hoepffner, Société des anciens textes français (Paris, 1908–21), 2:166.

challenge modes of willful behavior. Such a task, as Augustine remarks, is rhetorical:

> Yet, because in the pursuit of the things which are rightly commended as useful and upright, unwise men generally follow their own feelings [*sensus*] and habits rather than the very marrow of truth – which indeed only a very exceptional mind beholds – it was necessary that they not only be taught to the extent of their ability, but also frequently and strongly aroused as to their emotions. To the portion of itself which would accomplish this . . . [reason] gave the name of rhetoric.[7]

Gower's end, it would seem, is not to arouse the emotions, but quite the reverse, to quieten them. Several times in the course of the *Confessio*, in promise or apology, he describes his style as plain, usually in reference to the goal of teaching. As he introduces the narrative of his "wonder hap," he thus promises "pleinly forto telle it oute" (1.72) and "teche it forth" (1.82); "Fro point to point I wol declare" (1.73), and again, "I / Woll wryte and schewe al openly" (1.83–84). This accommodation of style to a given function is consistent with Augustine's idea that a Christian orator, "concerning one and the same important thing . . . speaks in a subdued manner if he teaches, in a moderate manner if he is praising it, and in a grand manner if he is moving an adverse mind to conversion."[8]

There is, of course, good reason for the plain style to dominate Gower's poem. Amans, who cannot teach himself, expects to be taught, and the confessor meets that expectation by speaking so as to be understood. That, of course, is what plain means: "planum, proprie, facile ad intelligendum."[9] Gower's choice of style, nevertheless, does not neatly fit his larger concerns in the *Confessio*, for his end is not merely to teach, but to move adverse minds to conversion. How can he achieve that goal, or write of "subtle matir," or address complex moral issues with "rude" words and "pleyne," with calm simplification?

The point is that he does not: his is refined speech, pleasing especially to those who are familiar with gentle, courtly "conversacion." Gower, beyond striving for the clarity of the plain style, has sought to go a "middel weie" between "lust" and "lore," and even more, he has adapted that mixed procedure to his end of achieving conversion. In that task he does not introduce "colours" or "figures" designed to kindle "ardor of heart," but instead uses the sometimes confusing plainness of Genius's speech to test and finally reorder

---

[7] Augustine, *De ordine* 2.13.38, trans. Robert P. Russell, *Divine Providence and the Problem of Evil*, FC 5 (New York, 1948), pp. 315–16; *PL*, 32:1013.

[8] *De doctrina christiana* 4.19.38, trans. D. W. Robertson, Jr., *On Christian Doctrine* (New York, 1958), pp. 145–46; ed. William M. Green, 4.104, CSEL 80 (Vienna, 1963): 146.

[9] Alan of Lille, *Liber de distinctionibus dictionum theologicalium*, s. v. "planum," *PL* 210:902 (hereafter *Distinctiones*).

memory: his goal, even as he seems to write "openly," is to generate a commitment to something new by means of the deeper conflict in Genius's thought.

That conflict serves the poet's ultimate goal of conversion. To convert of course means to "turn" or "turn round," and it also carries senses of "to come back," "to change one's mind," "morally to repent."[10] In short, it means a transforming of habit. Such *conversio morum* or *metanoia*, often associated with penance, might extend from a change of direction to a complete break with the past, or a radical change of heart.[11] As I shall use the term, it refers not merely to an initial religious experience, a turning to God, but also to what Gerhart Ladner calls reform, the "free, intentional and ever perfectible, multiple, prolonged and ever repeated efforts by man to reassert and augment values pre-existent in the spiritual-material compound of the world."[12] For Christians, Ladner argues, an initial conversion "could never be more than a preparation. Christianity offered and demanded more: first of all spiritual regeneration, effected through baptism; secondly, lasting or repeated renewal or reform of the inner man as a continuation and a fulfillment of baptismal regeneration."[13] Ladner's definition usefully underscores the paradox that a breaking of habit, or a throwing off of the past, can be achieved only by recovering the past, and more precisely by a reforming of memory as that power "by which the mind is present to itself."[14]

Habit is not merely a resistance to change, but a resistance to counsel, to reperception. It consists in locking into a single mode of perceiving experience, a single *ordinatio*. It can even be exhibited in a certain mode of reading the *Confessio* which assumes that tales with morals appended are sufficient to produce wisdom. Gower knows, however, that wisdom is far too complex to be identified with a sum of extracted *moralitates*, all derived in like fashion from a series of exemplary stories. As he works to effect a conversion in readers, or the repeated reform that will make his readers wise, he also "converts" his sources in an artistic field, forcing a variety of reperceptions that give the human agent power and range, a capacity to deliberate and make intelligent choices in a world that "stant evere upon debat" (P.567).

---

[10] On the development of these various senses, see Y. M.-J. Congar, "The Idea of Conversion," *Thought*, 32 (1958): 5–20.

[11] See Louis Bouyer, *The Meaning of the Monastic Life* (London, 1955), passim; Henry Pinard de la Boullaye, "Conversion," *Dictionnaire de spiritualité*, fasc. 12 (Paris, 1949): 2224–65; E. R. Callahan, C. Williams, and G. F. Kirwin, "Conversion," *New Catholic Encyclopedia*, 4 (Washington, D.C., 1967): 286–92; see also Thomas Hibernicus, *Manipulus florum* or *Flores doctorum pene omnium tam Graecorum quam Latinorum* (Vienna, 1758), s. v. "conversio," pp. 167–70.

[12] Gerhart B. Ladner, *The Idea of Reform: Its Impact on Christian Thought and Action in the Age of the Fathers*, rev. ed. (New York, 1967), p. 35.

[13] Ibid., p. 50.

[14] Augustine, *De Trinitate* 14.11.14, trans. Stephen McKenna, *The Trinity*, FC 45 (Washington, D.C., 1963), p. 432; PL 42:1047; see also Thomas Aquinas, *In Aristotelis libros de sensu et sensata de memoria et reminiscentia commentarium*, lect. 1.308–09, ed. Raymund M. Spiazzi, 3rd ed. (Turin, 1973), p. 89.

It is to achieve that end that he takes a turn in his poetic career and embarks on writing his poetry in a new "Stile." The premise of this change is stated clearly in the Prologue:

> Bot for men sein, and soth it is,
> That who that al of wisdom writ
> It dulleth ofte a mannes wit
> To him that schal it aldai rede.   P.12–15

This statement provides the poet's rationale for using one style in the Prologue, the brevity of which may now be attributed to its being devoted entirely to wisdom, and another style in the long confession that follows:

> For thilke cause, if that ye rede,
> I wolde go the middel weie
> And wryte a bok betwen the tweie,
> Somwhat of lust, somwhat of lore,
> That of the lasse or of the more
> Som man mai lyke of that I wryte.   P.16–21

While Gower uses a mixed mode in order to please someone, he probably regards "Som man" as belonging to the class of wise readers whom he addresses elsewhere in the Prologue. The poet's statement, in other words, is more than a concession to readers who need delight because they cannot grasp the subtle arguments that the wise can comprehend.

The "middel weie" is, of course, a convention, and there is a sense in which Gower's promise holds out little to separate the *Confessio* from his earlier poetry. In all of his poems he is sensitive to Horace's dictum that the best poetry combines teaching and pleasure. He knows the truth implied in Augustine's question about the teacher, "Who would wish to hear him unless he could retain his listener with some sweetness of discourse?"[15] This *suavitas* is, according to some medieval witnesses, the distinctive feature of poetic utterance,[16] and it is, according to others, the source of its great rhetorical power.

---

[15] Augustine, *De doctrine christiana* 4.26.56, trans. Robertson, p. 163; ed. Green, 4.146, CSEL 80:164.

[16] This emerges, for example, in twelfth-century glosses on Cicero's *De inventione*. Cicero's statement that the function of rhetoric is "dicere apposite ad persuadendum" supplies the terms for distinguishing poetry or the *ars poetriae* from grammar, dialectic, and rhetoric. All four arts make a person skillful in speaking (*dicere*), but Cicero adds the term *apposite* to separate rhetoric from grammar and dialectic: "Et quia grammatici et dialectici dicunt, adeo adiunxit *apposite* ut per hoc removeat officum oratoris ab officio grammatici et dialectici qui non curant de ornatis verbis" (*Ars rethorice*, fol. 6va, MS Bodl. canon. class. lat. 201; quoted by Mary Dickey, "Some Commentaries on the *De inventione* and *Ad Herennium* of the Eleventh and Early Twelfth Centuries," *Medieval and Renaissance Studies*, 6 [1968]: 29). The poet shares with the rhetorician the term *apposite* – the use of ornate diction – and thus Cicero adds the term *ad persuadendum* precisely to distinguish their separate arts: "Apponit enim multa dum ornat verba, et quia poetae *apposite* loquuntur non *ad persuasionem*, ut velint fabulis suis credi sed ad

Roger Bacon respects that power, even describing the most effective rhetoric of all as "poetic" in honor of "veracious poets" who use this art "in swaying men to the honesty of virtues." For Bacon, pleasing is necessary for one who would move a person to do "the things that pertain to divine worship, civil laws, and virtues." Delight cannot be the exclusive or principal goal of the best poetry, however. Unlike "good poets, such as Horace and those like him," Bacon writes, "vain and gossipy poets, such as Ovid and his like, wish to delight without caring to be beneficial, and hence do injury to the honesty of morals."[17] Clearly Bacon is unfamiliar with, or unconvinced by, the considerable medieval effort to moralize Ovid. Even if we are inclined to dismiss his judgment for this reason, his distinction usefully identifies a feature of all of Gower's poetry. At every stage of his career, Gower is a "good poet," at the very least in always aspiring to, and so often achieving a *suavitas* of style that serves his doctrinal intent.

In what respect, then, does the *Confessio* promise to be a different kind of work? The terms "lust" and "lore" give us only limited help in arriving at an answer. One might wish to keep the terms "formally distinct" by identifying "lust" with Gower's "olde aproved stories," and "lore" with exposition,[18] or by assigning the former term to the delight, sometimes the truant delight of venerean love,[19] and the latter to orthodox Christian teaching. The poet never so precisely delimits his terms, however. While the richness of the work allows these and other readings, we shall do well to remember that Gower also claims to write "betwen the tweie." The effect of the poem depends less on its separable elements than on an interrelationship.

Among other things, the poem is a recreation that staves off the dullness that threatens the person who reads wisdom "aldai." The lover's confession indeed affords rest from the more "ernest" business of the Prologue, and even more, it subtly serves the end of the Prologue by using "game" to sharpen "mannes wit." As a courtly recreation, the work occasionally creates an impression that its author has lapsed into Bacon's class of "vain and gossipy poets." In one sense, its moral ambivalence may be seen to originate in the ambivalent concept of leisure and "idleness." On this point, Christine de Pisan later makes a useful distinction when she argues that the "prince and semelably all othir that be charged with grete and notable occupacions ought at some

---

delectationem, ad remotionem eorum addit persuasionem" (*In primis*, fol. 5va, MS. York Minster, XVI. M.7, quoted by Dickey, p. 29). The peculiar task of the poet, then, is to use colors *ad delectationem*, that is, to please.

[17] Roger Bacon, *Operis maioris pars septima seu moralis philosophia* 5.3.6–8, trans. Richard McKeon, Donald McCarthy, and Ernest L. Fortin, in *Medieval Political Philosophy: A Sourcebook*, ed. Ralph Lerner and Muhsin Mahdi (New York, 1963), pp. 381–83; ed. Eugenio Massa (Zurich, 1953), pp. 254–55.

[18] J. A. W. Bennett, *The Parlement of Foules: An Interpretation* (Oxford, 1957), p. 15.

[19] In the somewhat different terms of C. S. Lewis, "Delight, for a fourteenth-century poet, almost inevitably meant courtly love." *Allegory of Love: A Study in Medieval Tradition* (London, 1936), p. 198.

tyme ceasse of his labour and reste in ydillnesse." There are, she maintains, two kinds of idleness. The one causes all virtue to disappear, and it "maketh a man to inclyne to the lustes of his fleshe and sensuallite." If a person avoids this idleness, as Ovid advises in the *Remedia*, "the artes of the god [of love] be peryshed." The other, a moderate idleness, can be a "uertu," and it is at some time "necessarye for the recreacion of noble and excellent prynces," for by it, "the naturall uertues be refreshed."[20]

Gower's concern is mental relaxation, generated in a book that does not tidily separate kinds of leisure or "ydilnesse." The poet appears sometimes to encourage a necessary, recreative leisure, and sometimes to follow the Ovid who seems not to reprehend the idleness of love, but to encourage it: this issue, we shall discover, becomes pivotal in Book 4 of the poem. The power of this unsureness, as lodged in his fictive priest, is that it is ordered and, I think, intended and, paradoxically, sure: it is designed, in the end, to foster mental acuity in one who "schal [wisdom] aldai rede." Gower's "middel weie" in this larger sense adds a new sophistication to Horace's formula *prodesse et delectare*.

At the end of the Prologue, where Gower offers a case for recreation, not in the idiom of Aristotle's *eutrapelia* – the basis for Christine's defense of the rest from "grete laboure" to be found in "recreacion of some disporte"[21] – or in the idiom of courtly recreations inspired ultimately by Ovid. He does so in terms especially suited to the troubles he has just described. The world, he writes, needs a second Arion, one who, like the famed musician of Lesbos, has the capacity to unite a divided people in a particular way. Drawing lord and "comun" into accord, the first Arion "sette in love bothe tuo / And putte awey malencolie" (P.1068–69): that was a "lusti melodie," Gower argues, when every man laughed with another (P.1071–72).

In this example, the poet hints at the nature, tone, and intent of his own rhetoric in the *Confessio*. Choosing "game" as his means of "restauracioun," he avoids excoriation of an already contentious and "melancholic" world, a world "Full of ymaginacion / Of dredes and of wrathful thoghtes" (7.410–11). Like Arion before him, he will attempt to cure a psychological disease that he had diagnosed at the very end of the Prologue:

> wher that wisdom waxeth wod,
> And reson torneth into rage,
> So that mesure upon oultrage
> Hath set his world, it is to drede.   P.1078–81

Wisdom, already predicated of Gower's readers, is in this passage turned to a dire, yet possible, end. Rather than convert reason and wisdom to rage by one rhetoric, a rhetoric that might only increase rancor and hatred, recrimination, "malencolie," and the dread "Which stant at every mannes Dore" (P.1083), the poet will, by a rhetoric using play or game, strive to restore or nurture patience. The spleen, the seat of Malencolie, moves a person to laugh when it has been purged of uncleanness (7.473–74), and the *Confessio* itself reverses that process: it cures allopathically, that is, it "cleanses" by delight.

Inside the fiction, Genius must deal with a patient "oppressed / Of thoght" (3.49–50). This condition, well known to *infirmi*, *melancholici*, and *amantes*, centrally involves a profusion and confusion of fantasies deriving "ex passionibus naturae."[22] Fantasies, in a medieval sense, "sometimes . . . were of uncertain accuracy, sometimes not, which means that one could never be sure of them,"[23] and that is to some extent Amans's central problem. His fantasies are variable, uncertain and "out of reule"; he often suspects and suggests that they represent mere "wihssinge," but he cannot be sure even of that. They are his obsession, and, as in the melancholic whom Gower later describes, they cause him to "fret himselven al to noghtes" (7.412).

The problem of penetrating a mind so obsessed magnifies and makes exemplary the underlying problem of *consuetudo* or habit that Gower has set out to address. Readers of the *Confessio*, Gower intimates, are not immune to the dangers of fantasy, even though they are wise: their potential melancholy is also a species of "cruel Ire" that may well cause them to fall "out of conscience," oppose "pacience" (3.11–12), and "set this world unevene" (3.14). Gower has asserted that he cannot "setten al in evene / This world" (1.2–3), but that is the very task he assigns to Genius, on a much reduced scale, in the confession. That representation, despite the poet's disclaimer, serves to evince or restore wisdom, including patience, conscience, evenness of temper, in readers.

There is no question that Gower is skillful at introducing the problem of melancholy and obsessive passion; his success at solving it is less certain. According to David Benson, the poet proposes no remedies for this condition other than simple withdrawal; that, Benson argues, is Gower's final

> solution to the passion of Amans, the ostensible subject of the entire poem; all Genius's exempla never manage to teach Amans the proper kind of human loving, but instead he . . . simply walks away when he realizes he is too old for such emotions.[24]

Benson here raises a large question which, because it is centered on Amans, cannot be fully answered until we come to the end of the lover's story in Book 8. Here, however, we might consider how "withdrawal," more generally, enters into the poet's strategies for dealing with passion, fantasy, melancholy, and sickness.

Gower never identifies Amans's sickness as *amor heroicus*, but the symptoms

---

[22] Hugh Ripelin of Strassburg, *Compendium theologicae veritatis* 2.39, in *Alberti Magni opera omnia*, ed. A. Borgnet, (Paris, 1890–98), 34:66.

[23] John F. Benton, "Collaborative Approaches to Fantasy and Reality in the Literature of Champagne," in *Court and Poet*, ed. Burgess, pp. 43–57.

[24] C. David Benson, "Incest and Moral Poetry in Gower's *Confessio Amantis*," *ChauR*, 19 (1984): 107–08.

make such a diagnosis appropriate; certainly the medieval treatment of that illness is here germane. Those who suffer from *amor heroicus* or *heros* are, like Amans, oppressed by thoughts; theirs is an "intemperate love toward those to be possessed [sexually]," and if their "obsessive thoughts . . . are not removed, they necessarily fall into melancholy." If in another context, princes need a "lefful" idleness, a lover who suffers from *heros* or "falls into mania from the soul's labor," needs recreation, now as a cure. He may beneficially listen to music, for example, or to the conversation of friends, and if he does so "in gardens and meadows with flowing water, everything is altogether more delightful."[25]

Gower, in his role as a second Arion, makes use of these conventions in the setting, conversation, and poetical "Stile" of his work. It is also appropriate that he, like Boccaccio in the *Decameron*, should resort to story-telling as a cure for melancholy, for this is what medical treatises of the period prescribe; one example of this is provided by John Arderne:

> Also it spedeth þat a leche kunne talke of gode taleʒ and of honest that may make þe pacientes to laugh, as wele of the biblee as of other tragedieʒ; & any othir þingis of which it is noʒt to charge whileʒ þat þey make or induce a liʒt hert to þe pacient or þe sike man.[26]

Arderne's precept is effectively represented in Genius's story-telling. The priest seeks to induce a "liʒt hert," to remove an obsession, in the lover, and even his tales of "all-consuming passion," like Arderne's tragedies, can serve that purpose. In a larger context, of course, Amans himself, as a comically impassioned lover, is at the center of a story designed to "make þe pacientes to laugh." In both of these settings, the basic point is the same: one can lessen "malencolie" by a device of insinuation, by turning the mind from what it hates to what it loves,[27] in these cases from matters of contention to a "lusti melodie," the gentle conversation of a friend and *sapiens*, and well-told tales. Gower's readers and Amans are thus drawn to the "unlike" so that they might recover the like, or a truer self-perception.

The case of Arion hints at the poet's reason for addressing this problem of melancholy indirectly. Although it may appear that Gower withdraws from issues – that he fails to provide a cure for the madness and rage that threaten England, including the wise readers of the Prologue, or for the obsession that endangers Amans – it is precisely in randomly selected and often strangely

---

[25] The quotations are from *Liber de heros morbo*, ed. and trans. Mary Frances Wack, "The *Liber de heros morbo* of Johannes Afflacius and Its Implications for Medieval Love Conventions," *Speculum*, 62 (1987): 328–9. In *Viaticum* 1.20, Constantine the African includes "conversing with the wise" (*colloqui sapientibus*) as a cure (Wack, p. 331).

[26] John Arderne, *Treatises of Fistula in Ano*, ed. D'Arcy Power, EETS, os 139 (London, 1910), p. 8.

[27] Of insinuation, Cicero thus writes that "ab eo quod odit ad id quod diligit auditoris animus traducatur" (*De inventione* 1.17.24, Loeb, trans. H. M. Hubbell [London and Cambridge, Mass., 1960], p. 48).

revised stories, each adjusting perception and delighting, each obliquely generating or recovering likeness, that he suggests, indeed represents, his remedies for passion. His is not a facile retreat from or a denial of the "proper kind of human loving." The complete poem reveals a profound sensitivity to passion and also its cure, the means to displace that passion with a renewed capacity for love.

Against the creation of fantasies, Gower principally sets the literary form of the exemplum, an "imperfect induction" in which one does not advance "deliberately from several instances to a universal," but rather "leaps across by inference from one thing, introduced by way of example, to another."[28] To write an exemplum is to cast a likeness. Gower demonstrates one possible effect of this form, even inside tales of the Confessio, when he has a given exemplary character perceive a likeness and then be "converted" by it. Such occurs in the story of the idle Rosiphelee (4.1245–1446), a character who, seeing that she is "riht in the same cas" (4.1440) as an exemplar inside her tale, resolves to change her behavior "if I may" (4.1442).[29]

Life is never so simple for Amans or for Gower's readers. This story, as well as the others in the Confessio, surely have value, even in isolation: they can induce a light heart, and they can, on a specific moral point, prove that "every man is othres lore" (8.256). Their greater power lies, however, in the combination: the stories together, generating likeness upon likeness, work to the benefit of auditors by drawing them back to a more complex, less inflexibly understood, and truer self-perception than any single moralized tale can provide. The contingent and particular nature of "moral matir" requires that one know more than which "dedes" occur "ofte tyme."[30] It also requires that one advance beyond opinion based solely on proximate likenesses, or on the "like" most specifically identified through sense-impressions.

This is not a problem of the senses per se, for a reason John of Salisbury notes: "Since sensation gives birth to imagination, and these two to opinion, and opinion to prudence, which grows to the maturity of scientific knowledge, it is evident that sensation is the progenitor of science."[31] John goes so far as to

---

[28] John of Salisbury, The Metalogicon, 3.10, trans. Daniel D. McGarry (Berkeley and Los Angeles, 1962), p. 193; ed. Clemens C. I. Webb (Oxford, 1929), p. 156; see also Thomas Aquinas, In Aristotelis libros . . . posteriorum analyticorum expositio, lect. 1, ed. Raymund M. Spiazzi, 2d ed. (Turin, 1964), p. 147.

[29] For a fuller discussion of this narrative against the background of the exemplum as a genre, including its principle of likeness, see my article, "Rhetoric, John Gower, and the Late Medieval Exemplum," Medievalia et Humanistica, n.s. 8 (1977): 185–200.

[30] See Aegidius Romanus, De regimine principum, 1.1.1, pp. 3–4; Childs, pp. 192, 194, 196; Cicero, Tusculanae disputationes 2.2.5, quoted by John of Salisbury, Metalogicon 2.14, trans. McGarry, p. 106; ed. Webb, p. 87; Aegidius also comments on the rhetor's handling of moral subjects in De differentia rhetoricae, ethicae et politicae, p. 8, and Commentaria in rhetoricam Aristotelis (Venice, 1515, rpt. Frankfurt, 1968), fol. 2ra; see S. Robert, "Dialectic and Rhetoric: According to the First Latin Commentary on the Rhetoric of Aristotle," New Scholasticism 31 (1957): 484–98.

[31] John of Salisbury, Metalogicon, 4.12, trans. McGarry, p. 222; ed. Webb, p. 178.

argue that "wisdom itself [also] flows originally from the same fountainhead of the senses, with grace both preparing the way and providing assistance."[32] Only by an engagement of all its faculties can the mind advance through sense-perception and imagination, through likenesses confirming opinion, to wisdom.

This course is manifestly closed to the person trapped in the fantasies of melancholy, and that presents a great challenge to the poet. In the rhetorical settings of this work, Gower must remain sensitive to the kind of likeness the auditor wants, the kind by means of which he can learn, the kind the rhetor thinks appropriate, the kind he is capable of producing. To choose examples that fittingly address these variables, that serve the truth, but do so obliquely or by *insinuatio* is exceedingly difficult, especially in a work of so ambitious a scope as the *Confessio Amantis*, ambitious specifically because it sets out to reform those who by habit have fallen snare to passion, to unlikeness. The poet's immediate goal is to delight while he also strives to identify a proper "likeness"; his ultimate goal is to recover that likeness.

Gower hints at this larger problem in the revised Prologue, specifically when he directs the work to "Henri of Lancaster": his claim that "my wittes ben to smale / To tellen every man his tale" (P.81–82) is an expression of a topos, but it also restates what he implicitly affirmed a few lines earlier: no person has "wittes" great enough to know fortune, or the contingent particulars of individual experience: these can be known by God alone. This human limitation even extends to telling *any* man "his tale": while in the fullness of a fictive confession, one might suppose that Amans, assisted by his priest, will be able to tell his entire story, neither he nor the priest who supposedly understands him can do so, even at the last: the story of "John Gower" remains wrapped in enigma. And yet, for all that, the image recovered is sufficient to effect, indeed to represent a conversion.

[32] Ibid., 4.19, trans. McGarry, p. 231; ed. Webb, pp. 184–85.

CHAPTER FOUR

AMANS AND THE POET

The *Confessio* does not represent a "personal" confession: one cannot read it, as one might read Augustine's *Confessions*, hoping to find the evidence to piece together a life. Near the end of the work, to be sure, Venus counsels the lover, now identified as "John Gower," to return to the "bokes, as men telleth, / Whiche of long time thou has write" (8.2926–27), but this is part of an obvious literary strategy. In order to affirm a "truth" about love, the poet has claimed that "I am miselven on of tho, / Which to this Scole am underfonge" (1.62–63). Every confession recreates its subject, of course, but Gower's does so in a particular sense: his "John Gower" is a "wonder strange ymage" of himself. The writer obviously knows more than the earnest speaker who confesses, for example, that his brain is so "overtorned" with love

> That ofte, whanne I scholde pleie,
> It makth me drawe out of the weie
> In soulein place be miselve,
> As doth a labourer to delve,
> Which can no gentil mannes chere;
> Or elles as a lewed Frere,
> Whan he is put to his penance,
> Riht so lese I mi contienance.   6.133–40

With humor and wit, Gower can testify to Amans's melancholy, or can recapture his gladness, as when, in a famous passage,[1] he describes what the lover feels when he touches his mistress's hand:

> For whanne I mai hire hand beclippe,
> With such gladnesse I daunce and skippe,
> Me thenkth I touche noght the flor;
> The Ro, which renneth on the Mor,
> Is thanne noght so lyht as I.   4.2783–87

As the poet uses such analogies to present Amans at his morose and joyful extremes, he can hardly be thought to be presenting "himself." When he becomes most "expressive," we are kept at a distance by the detachment of one poetically crafting or recreating the vagaries of an amorous and foolish "imaginacioun."

---

[1] C. S. Lewis, *Allegory of Love*, p. 208.

Throughout the confession, as throughout his love experience, Amans is preoccupied with affecting a "gentil mannes chere." Indeed, he strives to fashion himself as a type, and the poet who creates him has made him a type, a pastiche of conventions taken largely from French court poets such as Machaut and Froissart; these writers also

> portray themselves as 'petis servans' of the God of Love, latterday lovers of a distinctly unheroic temper, who have to content themselves with winning trifling favours from their mistress by sending her little poems or doing her little services.[2]

But there are many differences between these French poems and the *Confessio*. What makes Machaut's *Voir-dit* a "true story" in the sense that Gower's poem apparently is not, is the struggle by its author to unravel, through the strict chronology of a narrative and "history," the complex interdependence of his roles as poet, narrator, lover, and clerk.[3] Gower's project seems a good deal simpler, for he concentrates on a single character, a lover who, as Burrow has argued, is largely kept to a single role, that aspect of character pertaining to love.[4]

The issue in the *Confessio*, to the extent that it is at all complex, seems only to center on the relationship between the lover and the poet or *auctor*. The marginal gloss at 1.59 simplifies even that relationship, for it would have us separate these figures:

> Hic quasi in persona aliorum, quos amor alligat, fingens se auctor esse Amantem, varias eorum passiones . . . scribere proponit.

> Here as it were in the person of other people, who are held fast by love, the author, feigning himself to be a lover, proposes to write of their various passions.[5]

This comment carries the weight of a tradition, centered in a question that Bonaventure applies to the author of Ecclesiastes. Asking why Solomon sometimes speaks as a carnal, foolish, and worldly person, Bonaventure explains that he speaks in this fashion not *in propria persona*, but *in persona aliorum*, and he does so in order to castigate, not to win approval for "those things which deserve to be attacked."[6] Against this background, the gloss in the *Confessio* supports Minnis's point that the commentator is "determined to prove that

---

[2] J. A. Burrow, "Portrayal," p. 6.

[3] See Kevin Brownlee, *Poetic Identity in Guillaume de Machaut* (Madison, Wisconsin, 1984), pp. 7–23, 94–156; Karl D. Uitti, "*Clerc* to *Poète*: The Relevance of the *Romance of the Rose* to Machaut's World," in *Machaut's World: Science and Art in the Fourteenth Century*, ed. Madeleine Pelner Cosman and Bruce Chandler, Annals of the New York Academy of Sciences, vol. 314 (New York, 1978): pp. 209–16.

[4] J. A. Burrow, *Ricardian Poetry: Chaucer, Gower, Langland, and the Gawain Poet* (London, 1971), p. 50.

[5] Trans. Minnis, *Authorship*, p. 189.

[6] Bonaventure, *Commentarius in Ecclesiasten*, prooemium, q. 3, rsp. 1, trans. Minnis

Gower . . . was a good *auctor*."[7] Earlier, in the *Vox Clamantis*, the poet had placed himself inside the vision of the Peasants' Uprising and there spoken *quasi in propria persona*.[8] That was an appropriate choice, given the character he assumed in the Latin narrative. When, in the *Confessio*, he speaks *quasi in persona aliorum*, he also makes an appropriate choice – at least to the commentator – presumably because a creditable author cannot simultaneously be a defensively impassioned or "carnal, foolish, and worldly" lover.

As suggestive as the marginal gloss is, however, the case for separating the author and the lover is not so clear when the Latin commentary is bracketed or cancelled – when it is perceived as "annexed" to the text, or when, as sometimes happens, it is omitted from a manuscript altogether. It is even less clear in MS Ashmole 35, a manuscript which lacks the Latin prose comments, but which, in their place, has English ones. The latter are not mere translations; they are usually shorter than the Latin comments, and often they do no more than gather phrases "found" in Gower's English text. The opening gloss on Book 1 is conspicuously longer than most, and it is germane in its perception of the relationship between Gower and Amans. After telling us that the *Confessio* is divided into eight parts, of which the first part "specifieþ of pride," the commentator continues:

> And also John Gower whiche was maker of þis boke made & deuysed it to be in maner of a confession þat þis said John Gower was confessid yn unto a priest whiche was called Genius whom Venus þe goddesse of loue sent unto þe said Gower to confesse hym þat he had trespast ayenst Venus & hir courte.[9]

By the time the commentator affirms that Gower "calleþ hym self a lover," he has committed himself: the "maker of þis boke," the "said Gower" confesses.

The author of the English gloss is not alone in identifying Gower and the lover at the beginning of the work. In two other manuscripts of the poem, when Venus initially asks the "penitent" who he is, the lover responds, "Iohn Gowere" (1.161).[10] Most manuscripts defer this naming until Book 8, but the exceptions point to the fact that there may have been reason for early readers, if not for Gower, to associate the writer with the lover even from the outset of the poem. Indeed, the "maker of þis boke" speaks in a single voice throughout the English text. There is no break in continuity, no distinction between the voices of the Prologue and Book 1, and within Book 1, between the utterances of the moralist who promises to change the form of his "writinge" and the speaker who promises to describe his recent (1.64) love-experience. In this

---

and Scott, in *Medieval Literary Theory*, p. 232; ed. S. *Bonaventurae opera omnia* (Quaracchi, 1882–1902), 6:7.

[7] See Minnis, *Authorship*, pp. 110–11, 189.

[8] *Vox Clamantis* 1. cap. 16, headnote (*Works*, 4:59).

[9] Oxford, Bodleian Library, MS Ashmole 35, fol. 4v.

[10] London, British Library, MS Egerton 1991, and Oxford, Bodleian Library, MS Bodley 294.

respect, Gower, for reasons of his own, refuses to make the lover a separate character.

This is not to say, however, that the English commentator is "right" in interjecting his statement, any more than are the two scribes, or, for that matter, the illuminator of MS Bodley 902, who at fol. 8r pictures the kneeling Amans as an old man and therefore, as Burrow remarks, gives away a surprise that Gower has chosen to save for the conclusion of the poem.[11] The problem in all these cases is impatience, an eagerness to complete what Gower is not yet prepared to finish in the English text. The lover will name himself, indeed discover himself, when the poet is ready to have him do so.

Such impatience, however, is also displayed by the Latin commentator when he separates Gower and Amans; he cancels a possible "poetic" identity before Gower has had the chance to explore and indeed affirm it at its appointed time. What complicates the judgment against this commentator, of course, is the likelihood that he is Gower himself. Putting aside the issue of scribes, writers of English glosses, and illuminators who may act independently to create another *Confessio*, Gower in his role as Latin commentator has himself rewritten the poem. His comments form a reading, certainly not a definitive reading, but one that merits consideration nonetheless.

Recent critics have found justification enough – beyond its function in a *compilatio* – for Gower's inclusion of this apparatus in the poem. Derek Pearsall has argued, rightly I think, that Gower "strove to establish his reputation . . . as a poet worthy to stand beside his classical forbears" even by means of his epigrams and marginal comments. The apparatus is designed to make the poem resemble "olde bokes," the works of the *auctores* that Gower consulted and, of course, profoundly respected. In Pearsall's words, "He . . . added Latin verse chapter-headings, prose summaries and glosses to his major English poem, as if to stabilise that poem within the Latin learned tradition as a self-conscious but not self-indulgent relaxation from more serious labours."[12]

Thus the marginal commentator, in the first entry of Book 1, provides an academic prologue to the work, doing what late medieval learned commentators so often did in introducing their subjects.[13] As he proceeds, he identifies sources of given passages, and he also quotes Latin *auctoritates* to illuminate ideas he perceives in the text, but which are not self-evidently there. What he reads about Fortune in the vicinity of P.567, for example, he expounds with a quotation from the *Consolation of Philosophy*: "Boicius. O quam dulcedo humane vite multa amaritudine aspersa est!" 'Boethius. O how the sweetness of human life is sprinkled with much bitterness.' By such means the commentator opens the work into a universe of other books, while he also, as Minnis argues,

---

[11] Burrow, "Portrayal," p. 12.
[12] Derek Pearsall, "The Gower Tradition," in *Gower's Confessio: Responses*, ed. Minnis, p. 182.
[13] For a valuable discussion of Gower's use of the devices of learned prologues, see Minnis, *Authorship*, pp. 177–182.

confirms the singleness of the author's purpose, the essential unity of his materials, and his own sympathy with the moral *intentio* of the poem.[14]

There is, however, a limitation to the commentator's perception. He is quick to grasp "truths" represented in the English text, and yet, while his comments often usefully point to important aspects of a narrative or an exposition, they often leave other aspects, equally important, out of account.[15] Surely he does what commentators are expected to do when he interpolates matter into the text, but by this procedure he sometimes creates the impression that he has read another work entirely. Set in what he remembers of a generic tale and what he remembers of Gower, he applies to that memory the moral truth which Genius has affirmed in the exposition introducing the tale, but which is sometimes not the only point of the tale actually told. If in his tellings, Genius sometimes displays too much imagination, the commentator in his readings displays too little. By affirming Gower's assumed "singleness" of purpose, he actually reveals more about his own single-minded reading: he is like the person who reads wisdom "aldai," a reader too earnestly wise. His insisting on one truth in this field of the particular and contingent, effectively seeking to compose a "digest" of wisdom, can be singularly unwise.

This wise reader need not be Gower the person, or Gower at all. He is, however, well-read enough to know that Gower, the author of books on "vertu moral," is himself too wise to fall snare to Love. That does not happen to a wise person, much less to a wise *auctor*. The commentator thus works to cancel what the English text affirms as an issue, if not as a reality: the plight of an *auctor* who, though presumably wise, is vulnerable to love.

By referring in his glosses to textual materials that suit a moralist-*auctor* and by excluding those that do not, the commentator joins in the larger fiction of the *Confessio*; his is a separate voice, and he also does exactly what Gower in the Prologue warns against: he divides the person – in this case the author – from himself. It is that kind of division, that exculpation, that brings on the troubled times that Gower laments. No person, not even the "wise man," is exempted from the charges levelled by the common voice. The lover, who is also "Gower," comes closer to seeing that truth than does the glossator, who creates a greater fiction by separating the *auctor* from the lover he feigns to be.

If we are inclined to heed his gloss, we shall be surprised at Amans's final meeting with Venus, when

> Sche axeth me what is mi name.
> 'Ma dame,' I seide, 'John Gower.'
> 'Now John,' quod sche, . . .   8.2320–22

---

14 Ibid., p. 187.
15 Charles Runacres is one of several critics who have commented on the inadequate moralizations in the glosses: "The Latin commentary always stresses the ethical import-ance of the material of the poem, and does not take into account the effects of the particulars of the *narraciones*. Its *moralitates* are thus all restrictive to some extent" ("Art and Ethics," p. 121).

Venus is having a game with Amans, but so too is Gower having a game with his readers: to deny the connection between lover and "Gower" is to join the reader of the margins, who strives so earnestly to preserve his memory of a Gower who no longer exists. The question for all characters, including the "wise man," is finding the play and the role-playing that best combine a double awareness of fortune or the indeterminate in human experience with a sense of an "ordered," stable, and yet continually remade self. The commentator is trapped by a remembrance of Gower as moral *auctor*, a role that Gower himself, for the purpose of this fiction, has revised.

The "value" of this misperception will become apparent when we look at examples later in this study: the glosses, precisely because they do not uniformly agree with the English text, encourage readers to reflect on the tale, to peruse it with greater care. In one sense, the words of the Latin glossator hurry readers along, allowing them to find immediately – *statim invenire* – the truths that they seek; in another sense, the words slow readers down, checking that very impatience which the commentator sometimes exemplifies and which, paradoxically, can form the greatest hindrance to achieving wisdom.

Gower has invented in this "persona" of himself a character who speaks as a clerk, and in that role he becomes a counterpart to the "clerc" in Machaut. But his invention of roles does not stop there, for the *Confessio* also includes a poet among its speakers. Amans does not present himself chiefly in this role, to be sure; he occasionally admits to writing poems for his mistress, but these references are occasional and incidental. Moreover, Gower presents no poem within his English poem until the confession draws to a close and he composes a poetical epistle to Venus. That instance is exceptional and therefore conspicuous, but it is not designed to remind us that its speaker is a poetical "maker."

A poet figure does appear in this work, however, in the maker of the Latin verses subdividing each book of the *Confessio* into its major sections or chapters. This writer, also a learned interpreter of the speeches in the English text, cannot be identified with the marginal commentator, and the differences in his *modus procedendi* reach far beyond his presenting his utterances in poetic form. His immediate purpose is to divide the text and give it an *ordinatio*, and in that sense he differs from the glossator, whose goal is not merely to "gather" principles from the text, but also to generate wise or learned matter. The glossator, who in his summaries also partitions the text, has the latitude to introduce his erudition wherever he thinks it relevant; his summaries can run down entire manuscript pages and sometimes fill bottom margins. In a sense, his role is "historical": he is tied to the particular, contingent speeches of the English text, and that sometimes leads to extensive commentary. The Latin poet, by contrast, can only introduce sections, and he must do so in very brief compass: he does not summarize material, but concisely and poetically presents and explores "philosophical" issues.

The marginal commentator, while he is tied to the literal statements of the text, does not participate in the world they describe. He always refers to Gower or the lover or any other figure in the third person; he does not present himself as a character in the confession or as Gower. The wiser Latin poet is conceptually oriented, and he is detached and objective in his perceptions; paradoxically, however, he is engaged directly in the making of the book and the confession. He thus refers to himself as the author of the work:

> Torpor, ebes sensus, scola parua labor minimusque
> Causant quo minimus ipse minora canam.   P.1.1–2

> Torpor, dullness of wit, little schooling, and minimal labor,
> cause me, least of poets, to sing lesser themes.

This author later identifies himself as the lover, again by the use of the first person:

> Me quibus ergo Venus, casus, laqueauit amantem,
> Orbis in exemplum scribere tendo palam.   1.2.7–8

> I strive to write openly, in an exemplum for the world, the
> misfortunes in which Venus has ensnared me, a lover.

A later epigram is also self-referential: "Hec michi confessor Genius primordia profert" 'Genius offers me these principles' (1.4.5), and

> Nunc tamen vt poterit semiviua loquela fateri,
> Verba per os timide conscia mentis agam.   1.4.7–8

> Now however, while my half-living tongue is able to
> confess, I shall fearfully force through my mouth the guilt-
> conscious words of my mind.

In this perspective, the Latin poet, the lover, and Gower are not expressly separated, but identified. The author of the Latin does not sustain the first person references for long, but the point has been made: whereas the glossator seeks to elevate Gower by separating him from the lover, the poet of the Latin refuses to do so. And in so humbling himself, he also raises Amans's stature, by his poetic figures giving to this unheroic character the assurance of being entered "Orbis in exemplum."

As with any other relationship of major speakers in the *Confessio*, however, this one is ambiguous. The Latin poet is not the lover, for he is more detached than is Amans from the story about to be recounted. In glossing the contents of sections, he reveals that he understands complexities in the English text; he conveys these, and orders them verbally, with a linguistic and conceptual wisdom wanting in both Amans and the reader on the margins. He is learned and urbane, and the conventions of his utterances are poetic, as when he catalogues the oxymora of love:

> Est amor egra salus, vexata quies, pius error,
> Bellica pax, vulnus dulce, suaue malum.   1.1.7–8

> Love is a sick health, a vexed quiet, a dutiful truancy, a warlike peace, a sweet wound, a pleasant evil.

He uses the metaphor of a military patrol to describe the function of an exemplum:

> Vt discant alii, docet experiencia facti,
>   Rebus in ambiguis que sit habenda via.
> Deuius ordo ducis temptata pericla sequentem
>   Instruit a tergo, ne simul ille cadat.   1.2.3–6

> So that others may learn, the experience of a deed teaches what path may be taken amidst uncertainties; the dangers having been tested, a company off the beaten track prepares the commander following from behind, lest he fall instantly.

In his poetic inventions, the writer of the epigrams reflects upon issues beneath the surface of the English text, and he comments wisely on features of the confession, including his own involvement in it.

Nonetheless, this speaker is also limited in his perspective. By definition, he is locked into the section he "contains" with his poetic observations. Unlike the "penitent" narrator, who recounts a past experience of confession, the Latin poet speaks in the present and does not know the future, beyond the section his verses introduce. While he thus anticipates the complex issues and enigmas raised by the interlocutors in the confession, he cannot always resolve them: sometimes his verses do not make sense until they are explicated by the dialogue that extends beyond the section the verses announce. He thus raises a doubt which only the poem as it unfolds can resolve:

> Confessus Genio si sit medicina salutis
>   Experiar morbis, quos tulit ipsa Venus.
> Lesa quidem ferro medicantur membra soluti,
>   Raro tamen medicum vulnus amoris habet.   1.3.1–4

> I shall know by experience whether having confessed to Genius may be health-giving medicine for the sicknesses Venus herself has brought. Limbs wounded by an unleashed sword heal, to be sure; nevertheless, the wound of love rarely has a physician.

The Latin poet poses questions, riddles, enigmas, or *demandes* to which the English text responds, but to which he himself can have no immediate answer: furthest from his awareness is the long reach of argument and the greatest riddle of all, the identity or the "center" of the person who is sometimes named – Amans, "John Gower," *auctor* – and sometimes, as in the case of the two Latin speakers, not.

The Latin poet and the prose summarizer do not acknowledge each other, of course; each only responds to the English text. Whereas in Machaut, such roles as performed by these speakers are presented and evaluated as aspects of a single person, in the *Confessio*, the lover, clerk, poet, and, we might also now observe, narrator, are separately tracked, each in his own domain. They develop views which are not brought together until the end of the work, in an affirmation of the Latin poet's assertion in the Prologue: "Statque nichil firmum preter amare deum" 'Nothing stands firm but the love of God' (P.5.6).

The Latin apparatus reminds us of the difficulty that inheres in the project of the *Confessio*: if the task is to have the speaker-narrator recover himself, to become "John Gower" once again, we cannot be sure, given the multiple personae introduced in the poem, that this character has a single "identity" at all. The Latin passages, though they cannot be treated exhaustively in this study, will help to illumine the problem of identity in the "Gower" figure who should concern us principally, the lover-narrator.

The narrator of the *Confessio* is and is not Amans: he recreates the lover inside the "wonder hap" that includes the experiences Amans confesses, the actual confession of those experiences, and the narrative of that confession. Presumably he is no longer the Amans of the first two time frames – either the lover or the confessional "penitent" – for he has undergone a conversion at the end of the shrift he will now recount. Yet, he does not describe or forewarn us of that ending before the event: in effect, he becomes the character of Amans confessing. And in that action, this speaker, like the other personae of Gower, implicitly raises questions about time and the stability, in time, of human character and perception.

Near the outset of his *Confessions*, Augustine explicitly asks questions about divine mysteries regarding contingency, time, eternity, and remembrance, but always with a clear sense of where the answers may be found. Given his confidence and hope, he can speak to God of a possible rejoicing in uncertainty: "What is it to me, if someone does not understand? Let him also rejoice and say: 'What is this?' Let him rejoice even so and desire to find Thee by not finding, rather than by finding not to find Thee."[16] Augustine sees a direction in this "not finding," this uncertainty; the questioning is a joyful questioning. The *Confessio* initially offers no such assurance.

Even in its formation of questions, Amans's confession is sometimes uncertain. The distant analogue for this troubled "narrator" is the persona Boethius in the *Consolation of Philosophy*, who, "confunded in foryetynge" of himself, has fallen into a stupefying "perturbacion" over his sorry chance. His mind, as Philosophy remarks, wanders in "foreyne dirknesses" (Bo 1, m. 2, 4), and he does not recognize the stately visitor who will eventually guide him to true consolation. A comparable situation occurs in Machaut's *Remede de Fortune*,[17] a work which, because it "translates" Boethian doctrine into the tale of a distraught lover, more closely resembles Gower's poem about Amans. Like

---

[16] Augustine, *Confessions*, 1.6.10, trans. Bourke, p. 11; ed. Skutella, p. 8.
[17] Ed. Ernest Hoepffner, *Oeuvres de Guillaume de Machaut* (Paris, 1908–2119), 2:1–157. See, for example, lines 872–96.

Gower's Amans, Machaut's main character, having judged Love to be like Fortune, protests that he has not been duly rewarded for his devotion and faithful love-service: indeed, Love gives him "tristece" in place of the "joieus guerredon" (1354–55) he thinks he deserves. Machaut's Amant will find his preceptor, Esperance, in a literary setting, a pleasance; he will be taught – perhaps only can be taught – this lesson in a fiction at one remove from the reality of his dread and admitted "misdeed" as an *amant couart*. Like the persona Boethius, Amant does not initially recognize his teacher; before she can offer her instruction, he must be wakened from a trance caused by his reflection on his extreme suffering (2094–96).

Gower's change of this setting, one common to a whole tradition of French "Court of Love" poems,[18] will affect the structure of argument running through the entire *Confessio*. The lover, out walking, finds a site for his complaint: "whanne I was the wode amiddes, / I fond a swote grene pleine" (1.112–13). This place, surrounded not by a high wall, but by a wood suggestive of the *selva oscura*, will provide only temporary and incomplete comfort: it obviously does not afford the "promise" of relief suggested by the formal garden of Deduit in the *Roman de la rose*, or of the Parc de Hedin (786) in the *Remede*. In this place, the lover, bemoaning his situation, faints several times, but finally awakens to conduct the "business" that will occasion the confession:

> I out of my peine awok,
> And caste up many a pitous lok
> Unto the hevene.   1.121–23

This "swote grene pleine," a place apart, provides the setting for a fiction unique in kind. Amans is fully awake when he casts his "lok" to the heavens, prays to Cupid and Venus, and sees them approach. He recognizes them, yet betrays no amazement at the dream-like wonder of their appearance. Cupid appears only briefly, and his single act before he departs, though definitive and wonderful, makes no sure impression on the narrator: "Bot natheles er he forth wente / A firy Dart me thoghte he hente / And threw it thurgh myn herte rote" (1.143–45). What occurs in dream in other, like works and is there invested with a dream-like importance consistent with the lengthy narrative it will inspire, is here reduced to the status of an apparently real, indeed quotidian, and, because of Amans's uncertainty (his "me thoghte"), not particularly over-whelming event. This, however, is Gower's own insight at work. The lover, though "awake," does not know he lives in a dream. Eventually Genius is called in, and Amans will then admit that he has lost his "wittes." Even so, it is a wonder that he does not seem particularly upset, or moved to "perturbacion," by this prospect of his own madness; his matter-of-fact statement is designed to show Genius how best to conduct his priestly business in the confessional.

[18] The structure of these poems, which is also relevant to the *Confessio*, has been described by Marc M. Pelen, "Machaut's Court of Love Narratives and Chaucer's *Book of the Duchess*," *Chaucer Review* 11 (1976): 128–55.

Whereas other, like works trace a steadying of perception and a maturation in the principal character, the *Confessio* does not seem to: in his fantasy, a waking dream, Amans shifts from persona to persona easily, but he does not thereby come to understand himself.

With ease, he slips into his role as a penitent, at Genius's word quickly falling to his knees and speaking "with full gret contricioun" (1.214). There is, of course, something comic in this penitent's "sad purpose to shryve him,"[19] since his grief is not "for his synne." It is such role-playing that leads to the eventual, rather than the immediate definition of the problem the confessional dialogue is supposed to resolve. The confession presumably appeals to the lover because it holds out promise of "spede" or profit in love; Amans, even in his self-doubt, thinks he can establish that he "merits" grace, and this influences his confident shifts from role to role, all in an effort to achieve a "gentil mannes chiere."

Gower saves the lover's greatest test and most important swoon for the very end of the work. Indeed, it takes a concluding shock – a chill, faint, and dream – for the lover to be turned around, effectively to see his "wo" as truly game, or to understand what Genius, at his best, has taught. With his love fantasy cooled, Amans can discriminate: he need not be concerned to put into practice the priest's counsel on love-service; conversion has meant a re-creation of his memory, "histoire," and identity. The case is very different in the *Remede*. Machaut's narrator, immediately after Esperance departs, sets out to record in order what this great teacher has spoken "De point en point" (2936). "John Gower," given his conversion, should no longer be content merely to "record" the teachings of Genius. His task is both more and less determinate: "with al myn hol entente / Uppon the point that y am schryve / I thenke bidde whil y live" (8.2968–70); given what the poet has told us about the change in "Gower," the revision of memory should be radical and the story of his applied "entente" should be an entirely new story.

Nevertheless, though in the real time of recounting the experience of the confession, the narrator has supposedly recovered his "wittes," been absolved of his sins, and inspired to reflect on the points of his shrift, he is not, as a narrator retelling the story from the start, expressly conscious of those events. He vividly presents his acts as a lover and blocks out the more recent "wonder" of his conversion; in short, he reenacts the process of confessing. Whereas Augustine writes his *Confessions* by interpreting the stages and events of his life from the perspective of a convert, Gower, in his role as narrator, does not.

That the poet does not reveal his newly found wisdom is perhaps stranger than the fact that in the fiction he is an *auctor* who has fallen prey to Love. Surely to re-enact a confession under a pretense that it has not yet occurred is a literary device. But it raises an important question concerning the remembering and forgetting of Gower's various personae: all are more or less limited to

---

[19] Chaucer, *ParsT* 128. Quotations from Chaucer are from the edition of Larry D. Benson et al., *The Riverside Chaucer*, 3d ed. (Boston, 1987).

issues of the moment, and that also sets a moral issue for the poem. The author in none of these roles can grasp an order in his past or a clear hope for his future: the re-enacted confession alone can lead him back to his past, an agedness that is his beginning. Gower refuses himself the luxury of knowing where he has been. Neither does he remember his conversion, nor, beyond his earliest statement about the power of Love, does he try to vindicate himself for falling from his status as an author of subjects of "vertu moral" to his status as a lover. In fact, he betrays absolutely no defensiveness at all. What is most remarkable is the ease with which he slips into one role and forgets others.

Amans's ease in forgetting his other "selves" is most prominently displayed near the end of the poem, when he suddenly learns that he is an old man. That discovery, given his other losses of his own history, perhaps should come as no surprise, and it is certainly appropriate to Amans as a type: no lover can judge himself too old, for that would be to concede his incapacity for love. Doubtless there remains the modern literary concern about Gower's "unfair tactics" in holding back this "vital" piece of information. For the moment we might note simply that the withheld explicit reference keeps the dialogue from slipping into repeated attack and defense on the question of whether Amans is too old to love. That is not Gower's major point in the *Confessio*, even at its end. Old age there forms a critical issue, but not exclusively in reference to Amans's limited "querele"; in the larger handling of this question, we shall find, there is sufficient power and warrant for Gower's decision.

The represented process of reform, including the discovery of *senectus*, will be a long and complex one, and surely the poem would have been a very different one had Gower set down his principles univocally in Book 1. As they stand, the early books present a legitimate moral ambiguity in Amans's quarrel. The narrator complains, in Book 1, that

> I was further fro my love
> Than Erthe is fro the hevene above
> As forto speke of eny spede.   1.105–07

This admission is rich in significance. It not only reveals Amans's frustration, but it affirms what he understands to be his true love. In using the simile of "Erthe" and "hevene," he might be doing what lovers are expected to do, humbling himself and ennobling the lady. More importantly, however, he also reveals his great distance from a state of love that is more properly his, the higher and certainly more profitable love that will fill his thoughts as the poem ends. There is little humility in the self-reference of the early speech. Gower, had he wished to pursue that question early, or even make its moral issue explicit, would have written a very different poem.

The value in his remaining inexplicit about so much until the end of the work will become increasingly apparent as we proceed. But we might glimpse that value by means of a contrast with a work of a very different kind, where the author initially speaks about himself, his old age, and his playing at love. In the opening passage of his *De amicitia christiana*, Peter of Blois defends his dual status as old man and lover:

> Someone will mock and reprehend me because I, an old man, play at love, I who am now in decline, having felt the tremor of death in my members. But should Michol ridicule the nakedness of David dancing, would that I might join him in his play and become more worthless in my eyes, even to the extent that I, with him, might escort the ark of the covenant into Zion. In truth, it would be a great thing for me if a few in the mass of all those who have been weakened and devoured by profane love and who, with eyes gouged out and hair shorn, labor at the mill with Samson, if they with the help of this little book might enter into the covenant of Jonathan with David, if in the sweetest love of Christ they might recover from sorrow and the tribulation of evil things.[20]

The play – the *ludus* – for both Peter of Blois and the David he presents is predicated on seeing oneself as common, vulgar before the greatness of God. As Pseudo-Vincent of Beauvais remarks, it is David's *ludus deuotionis* that Michol hates: "But Michol, seeing David dancing and playing, despised him, because the undevout always despise the devout and humble."[21] Gower, suffering a love that "myhte make a wisman madd" (1.130), obviously lacks David's humility and devotion; his game of proud, totally self-indulgent love is a *ludus insolentiae*: what others betray in their dancing, hunting, and fowling, he betrays in his "profane" love: he is one of those who "are so totally a slave to this pastime that they seem to think about or desire nothing else."[22] Indeed, it takes Amans eight books to realize that his "querele" is game, to discover the pride whereby he has resisted the truth and evaded the spiritual nakedness of confession. Eventually he is the object of Venus's derision, her "game" and "scorn." He then has no defense because he, unlike the aged Peter, has joined those who labor with Samson; precisely because he is *senex*, Venus's ridicule, unlike Michol's, is deserved.

By playing the fool in ways that Peter never intended, by debasing himself in his role as *auctor*, Gower can bring to fruition in a representation what Peter proposes as the goal of his own treatise. Peter of Blois is certain from the outset about what earthly love means. In his various roles, Gower is not. The witnesses to Amans's story, the lover, narrator, Latin commentator, poet, and of course Genius, all have opinions, but each of those opinions admits of uncertainty. These speakers are fallible, sometimes even bemused and "enchaunted" in their roles.

---

[20] Peter of Blois, *De amicitia christiana*, cap. 1, ed. E. De Boccard, *Un Traité de l'amour du XIIe siècle* (Paris, 1932), p. 106.
[21] *Speculum morale* 3.7.4, in Vincent of Beauvais, *Speculum quadruplex* (Douay, 1624; rpt. Graz, 1965), 3: col. 1361; Pierre Bersuire uses the same example to illustrate "ludus charitatis et innocentie," in *Dictionarium*, s. v. "ludere," 2: fol. 246v.
[22] Ibid., col. 1362.

But here we might see an inversion. It is by such role-playing that Gower – indeed every reader – comes to rediscover love. This, then, is how Gower sets the problem for his work. He recognizes, at the very least, that profane love is an enigma, and that people take sides in their perceptions of it. Some, in contrast to others like Peter, persist in seeing this love not merely as legitimate, but as gentle and good, and Gower does not reject that perception until he has fully explored its implications. The "maker of þis boke" thus refuses to follow wholeheartedly his commentator, who can be found to reject an assertion because it is not the truth, but the opinion of lovers. Gower allows profane and "gentil" love its claim; he introduces opinions through different aspects of "himself," as well as through a priest who partakes of both sides in this controversy. We shall now do well to consider this remarkable confessor: he is key to advancing through the comic enigmas of this work because inside the fiction he is in large part their source.

CHAPTER FIVE

GENIUS

Genius is, in Gower's handling, a richly allegorical figure. The poet never steps outside the fiction to identify this confessor, and that, to be sure, has prompted one recent critic to complain that if we are uncertain about his precise meaning, "it is not because [he] is concealed beneath a veil of allegory but rather because Gower does not offer enough information about [him]."[1] The latter point notwithstanding, Gower fully understands "veiling," how to achieve it, and most importantly, how to use it to enrich meaning. There may be good reason for the poet to preserve the enigma of Genius, even while he has him utter more speeches – and thereby potentially reveal more about himself – than any of his counterparts in ancient and medieval tradition. By not giving us a single, dominant, precise, or "correct" interpretation of this figure, Gower opens the character out into a very large field of possible significance; Genius potentially carries the weight of his entire ancestry, and our uncertainty about him allows, indeed encourages multiple and ultimately wiser responses to the poem.

Gower has assumed a considerable poetic burden in making Genius virtually the sole preceptor for Amans. While he thereby gains the prospect of a single sustained argument for the poem, he seemingly does so at the cost of a rich interplay of voices such as may be found, for example, in Jean de Meun's portion of the *Roman de la rose*, where the lover must sort through doctrines taught not only by Genius, but by others including Raison, Amis, Bel Acueil, Le Vielle, and Nature as well. The success of Gower's poem depends in large part on the character he assigns to Genius: the lover, narrator, Latin poet, and marginal commentator all add different perspectives to the poem, but centrally the confessor himself speaks in multiple voices and through them generates, but does not tidily resolve, conflicting opinions on key issues.

The project of Gower's fiction is to restore "John Gower" to his proper likeness. Superficially, the priest's task is more circumscribed: it is to hear a love-confession, not to free the lover from his bondage to the cruel "tirannie" of Love or to recreate him as himself. Nonetheless, while he performs that more limited function, he unknowingly prepares for what could be a greater success, should "John Gower," after the confession has ended, fulfill his resolve to reflect on the points of the shrift. Genius's ultimate contribution lies not

1 Michael Cherniss, *Boethian Apocalypse*, p. 112.

merely in his judgments, but in his provision of a storehouse of "ernest" matter which the converted lover can ponder meaningfully. It is to Gower's credit, in fact, that the priest's success should come late and only indirectly, in potentia. The power in the teaching lies not in the immediate rhetorical effect of any of the speeches, but in an imaginative range that allows the subject of Amans's condition, indeed of "malencolie" and passion generally, to be fully analyzed and evaluated, and, beyond the poem's unusual ending, more adequately resolved.

The confession involves more than merely formulaic shriving and teaching, and its richness depends in no small part on Gower's perceptive use of the literary tradition surrounding the figure of Genius.[2] The poet does not assign to this figure a precise ontological status. Genius is not identified, as he often was in tradition, as a spirit, angel, intermediate god, or daemon, but he shares certain functions with genii that had been so presented. Like the genius who, by tradition, was assigned to a person at birth, he is a guardian, protector, and mediator.[3] This last function is particular significant: what Genius gains through his priesthood, or as a mirror of "ensamplerie" between men and the "godhiede," he possessed as a divine power of "a middle nature" in Apuleius and others. Such genii, Apuleius writes, are "messengers between the inhabitants of earth and those of heaven," and "they carry from the one to the other, prayers and bounties, supplications and assistance, being a kind of interpreters and message carriers for both."[4] At best, Gower's Genius resembles certain genii of Bernardus Silvestris who are mediators "wholly bound to charity and the common good [quorum ita benivola, ita conmunis est servitus], for they report the needs of man to God, and return the gifts of God's kindness to men, and so seek to show at once obedience to heaven and diligence in the cause of man."[5]

---

[2] For useful discussions of this tradition, see Wetherbee, Platonism and Poetry in the Twelfth Century: The Literary Influence of the School of Chartres (Princeton, 1972), passim; Wetherbee, "The Theme of Imagination in Medieval Poetry and the Allegorical Figure of 'Genius'," Medievalia et Humanistica, n.s. 7 (1976): 45–64; Brian Stock, Myth and Science in the Twelfth Century: A Study of Bernard Silvester (Princeton, 1972), pp. 169–72; Jane Chance Nitzsche, The Genius Figure in Antiquity and the Middle Ages (New York, 1971). For interpretations of Gower's Genius, see especially George Economou, "The Character Genius in Alain de Lille, Jean de Meun, and John Gower," Chaucer Review 4 (1970): 203–10; Donald G. Schueler, "Gower's Characterization of Genius in the Confessio Amantis, Modern Language Quarterly 33 (1972): 240–56; Denise N. Baker, "The Priesthood of Genius: A Study of the Medieval Tradition," Speculum 50 (1976): 277–91.
[3] See Martianus Capella, The Marriage of Philology and Mercury, 2.152–54, trans. William Harris Stahl and Richard Johnson, with E. L. Burge, in Martianus Capella and the Seven Liberal Arts (New York, 1977), 2:51–52; ed. Adolf Dick, De nuptiis Philologiae et Mercurii (Stuttgart, 1969), p. 65.
[4] Apuleius, The God of Socrates 6.132–33, trans. anon., in The Works of Apuleius, (London, 1889), pp. 356–57; Liber de deo Socratis ed. Paul Thomas, in Apulei Platonici Madaurensis de philosophia libri (Leipzig, 1908), pp. 13–14.
[5] Bernardus Silvestris, Cosmographia 2.7, trans. Winthrop Wetherbee (New York and London, 1973), p. 107; ed. Peter Dronke, (Leiden, 1978), p. 135.

Gower's priest not only teaches service to the common profit, but in the conduct of the shrift displays such benevolence, deeply rooted in his nature as well as his idea of nature and the "godhiede."

Gower follows later writers in also making Genius a priest, but though this figure appears in a similar role in Alan of Lille's De plancu Naturae, and even as a confessor in Jean de Meun's portion of the Roman de la rose, Gower, in exploring aspects of Genius's function as priestly guardian of the individual soul and priestly confessor, does more to tie him to the roles of the daemon of earlier tradition. The richness of Apuleius' description of the guardian applies, in virtually all of its particulars, to what Gower later conveys through the activity of his fictive priest, even as it extends to the daemon's role as judge of the individual:

> He of whom I speak is entirely our guardian, our individual keeper, our watcher at home, our own proper regulator, a searcher into our inmost fibres, our constant observer, our inseparable witness, a reprover of our evil actions, an approver of our good ones.[6]

The two roles of protector and judge are so important in this tradition that they can be separated and each assigned to a different spirit or genius. Such is the case in the Secretum secretorum, a work which, in describing what "Aristotle" taught Alexander, will have some bearing on a later book of the Confessio:

> Witte thow, alexandre, that as Hermogenes seyth, that there byth two Spiritis abowte the; that oone is atte thy ryght hande that the kepyth, And that othyr in thy lyfte hande that the beholdyth. This Spyritte that al thy workys Seyth ande Parcewyth, yf thay be not good, he writyth ham and showyth ham to god that the makyd. This thynge ounly Sholde wythdrawe the, and make alle men enchu il workys.[7]

Again, the spirit who beholds is richly described by Apuleius, this time in an account of the "august" daemon whose role is to assist in passing judgment on an individual's conduct of life. This daemon, who "dwells in the most profound recesses of the mind, in the place of conscience," sees and "understands all things."[8]

From such testimony, it is not far to seek a possible relationship between Genius as confessor and Amans's own conscience. Critics have been quick to interpret Genius in this way, as mirroring some one thing in the lover's mind: he might stand for Love, "the master passion itself there speaking with a doubtful voice"; alternatively, he might stand for conscience, the lover's "inner voice – the voice, however, of his reason, not his love."[9] The priest does and

---

6   God of Socrates, 16.156, pp. 366–67; ed. Thomas, pp. 25–26.
7   The Gouernaunce of Prynces, or Pryvete of Pryveteis, trans. James Yonge, in Three Prose Versions of the Secretum Secretorum, ed. Robert Steele, EETS, es 74 (London, 1898), p. 143.
8   God of Socrates 16.155–56, p. 365; ed. Thomas, p. 25.
9   See C. S. Lewis, The Allegory of Love, p. 220; Baker, "Priesthood of Genius," p. 291.

does not represent something in the lover's mind, but to the extent that he does, I think he stands not for the one thing or the other, but for both. That, in fact, is his peculiar distinction, over against a tradition of late classical and medieval *genii*: he represents both conscience and the "master passion," specifically at the point where these are drawn into contact, or where body and soul meet in imagination.

Only potentially, then, does Genius resemble the traditional *genius* who represents the soul "perfect in virtue" or the "longing of the soul that is of good tendency." He is less like Apuleius' august *daemon*, who, freed of conjunction with a body, can understand all things, and more like the genius "after a certain manner, generated with man," the soul situated in a body.[10] The complexity of Gower's figure is that he represents body and mind drawn together, variously in harmony or conflict: what confuses his more august office is his devotion to corporeal nature, and specifically to the goddess Venus. This, of course, suits another side to his lineage, where he functions as a patron of generation.

In Bernard's cosmology, this function has a different significance in the celestial Genius – Pantomorphos, an intermediary between Urania and Natura – who "composes and assigns the forms of all creatures," and in the two sexual *genii* of physical things, who "fight unconquered against death with their life-giving weapons, renew our nature, and perpetuate our kind."[11] *Genii* of both orders, however, confer actual being, and in that office they are unlike Gower's priest, who performs their function figuratively, as a teacher.

Separated from the lover in the allegory, Genius is an "external" overseer. He must rely on Amans to follow Venus's bidding, to "telle it on and on" to him, her priest and "oghne Clerk."[12] Given the status of the historic *genius*, this point is worth remarking: he lacks the capacity of Apuleius' august *daemones*, for example, or of cosmic *genii* in Bernardus Silvestris, those whose "powers of vision are so subtle and penetrating that, plumbing the dark depths of the spirit, they perceive the hidden thoughts of the mind."[13] Gower's priest, instead, must work with external evidence. While his inference or guesswork might represent the arduous task of a self discovering itself in a psychomachia, it implies more. Genius depends on what the lover confesses as the material for judgment; he searches out thoughts, but neither is he conscience, nor does he dwell in conscience. Instead, as he tells Amans, he will describe the vices one by one "Wherof thou myht take evidence / To reule with thi conscience" (1.247–48).

Genius is therefore one who compiles and interprets evidence. This would be fairly straightforward if he simply mediated between Venus and the lover, or between God and the penitent. One cannot argue, one-sidedly, that he merely

---

[10] *God of Socrates* 15.150–51; 16.154, pp. 363–64; ed. Thomas, pp. 23, 24–25.
[11] Bernardus Silvestris, *Cosmographia* 2.3, 14, trans. Wetherbee, pp. 96, 126; ed. Dronke, pp. 125, 154.
[12] See *God of Socrates* 16.155–56, p. 365; ed. Thomas, p. 25.
[13] Bernardus Silvestris, *Cosmographia* 2.7, trans. Wetherbee, p. 107; ed. Dronke, p. 135.

advocates biological generation or that he mediates exclusively between Amans and Amans's idol, Venus, presumably the "godhiede" of fallen man. Even his remembrance of Venus is morally uncertain: he reads her character sometimes *in bono*, sometimes *in malo*, and she, neither *venus caelestis* nor *venus scelestis*, reflects the "doubt" in Genius's own "natural" world. Indeed, the priest advocates a *jus naturae* so rich that he does not always seem to comprehend its variable significance or the interdependence of the meanings that he himself introduces. Thus, in one sense, he represents the limited, carnal desire that rules Amans and, to a certain degree, Venus. He defends sensual nature or *kinde*, serves a Venus who fosters love "out of reule," condones Amans's affection, and urges him to persevere in his suit. In another sense, however, he champions reason or man's proper nature, attacks Venus, and strives to dissuade Amans from a passionate and ill-advised love.

Nor does Genius limit his advocacy to defending Venus and natural reason alternately. He is also a mediator between men and God, however much *in aenigmate*, and in that role he presumably explores what a person can, in the very best sense, become. He can extol marriage and *procreatio* within marriage, and in his spiritual office, he can even teach that

> Above alle othre under the Sky,
> Who that the vertus wolde peise
> Virginite is forto preise,
> Which, as thapocalips recordeth,
> To Crist in hevene best acordeth.   5.6386–90

In yet another dimension, then, Genius expounds Scripture, places his goddess among pagan idols, treats Amans's love as sinful, and hints at a Christian truth and a mysterious grace that will ultimately enable the lover, restored to his nature as "John Gower," to hope for a "joie" that is "endeles."

Gower's Genius is thus a composite of earlier *genii* and certain aspects of a Christian priest. Put simply, he pursues divergent causes, sometimes, as it seems, willy-nilly. All other *genii* in tradition are certain of their roles, even when in executing them they may, like Jean de Meun's figure, become buffoons. Gower's priest seems to have many different tasks, and to some extent he appears unsure in each of them.

The effect of Genius's divided loyalties is manifested in his literary creations. Figuratively, he "assigns" forms to creatures and, like Genius the scribe in Alan of Lille, endows images "with the life of their species."[14] Gower's priest mirrors "truths" as he generates types and confers "life" on them. These images in his mirror of "ensamplerie," however, are often distorted by the variable intent of their "author," as he moves among his multiple roles.

Indeed, Genius often seems to be a patron of too much. If in one sense, he monitors Amans's behavior, in another he represents a natural desire and

---

[14] Alan of Lille, *De planctu Naturae*, pr. 9, trans. James J. Sheridan, *The Plaint of Nature* (Toronto, 1980), p. 216; PL 210:479.

imagination that reach far beyond what Amans knows or feels; there often seem to be no checks to his power of invention. In tradition, his prototype in this regard may be found in a famous gloss by William of Conches on the Orpheus legend in *The Consolation of Philosophy*, describing a certain god called a *genius* – our natural desire – which is born and dies with us; no one can exist without it:

> Genius is natural concupiscence. But this natural concupiscence is well called 'Euridice,' or 'judgment of the good,' for whatever anyone judges to be good, whether rightly or wrongly, he desires.[15]

While William argues that this appetite goes against virtue and longs for its own pleasure, Gower never so describes his priest. Genius can eloquently defend either virtue or desire. What the passage from William more usefully points out is a character long on imagination, short on judgment. Genius represents a capacity to form images in the absence of their object, to seek out intention, even to estimate whether the imagined object will help or harm: in this last regard, however, the judgment is local, immediate, itself driven by an imagining of what merely seems, at the moment, to be good.

This has a profound bearing on Genius's role as mediator, as one who, on a verbal surface, connects things. He not only mediates between men and the "godhiede," but he mediates between the divergent values represented in each of these other mediations. He compiles these values and brings them into relationship, often into conflict, but does not consistently judge among them or reconcile their differences.

The advantage of Genius's ambiguous function is that he can begin with what Amans knows and feels: his assertion that a lover is compelled to love, or to follow "the lawe / Of thilke bore frele kinde" (1.772–73) is bound to be acceptable to Amans, a fair judgment of his condition. Out of such a premise, the dialogue might profitably proceed, since "everything receives what is above it only after the mode according to which it can receive it, not after the mode according to which the thing received exists."[16] In his "goodly chiere" and "softe and faire" speech, the priest reveals a nature that is kindly and genial, one responsive to the condition of his pupil. We might therefore expect him to proceed accordingly, at a pace suited to what his auditor can grasp at a given moment, changing his strategy as the doctrine becomes more complex, or as the lover's capacity to understand increases. In short, we might expect him to resemble the telescoping Philosophia in the *Consolation of Philosophy*, who modifies her argument, as well as her stature, to accommodate the increasing perception of her pupil. Genius, however, often seems to fall short in "under-

---

[15] Quoted by Edouard Jeauneau, "L'usage de la notion d'*integumentum* à travers les gloses de Guillaume de Conches," *AHDLMA* 32 (1957): 46; trans. in *The Literature of Medieval England*, ed. D. W. Robertson, Jr. (New York, 1970), p. 293; for discussion, see Baker, p. 286; Wetherbee, *Platonism*, p. 97; Nitzsche, pp. 63–64.

[16] *The Book of Causes* 9(10).99, trans. Dennis J. Brand, 2nd ed. (Milwaukee, 1984), p. 29.

standing and recollection," and he appears to lack the power to undertake the regulated changes of a *Philosophia*. He speaks on matters small and large, things known to fallen man, things beyond his vitiated perception, but he does not do so in a clear *ordinatio*.

We get the first indication of this in his opening speech. If he presents and his auditor receives only what the auditor is capable of grasping, it is because, as he admits, that is his only field of competence: "I with love am al withholde" (1.262), he concedes; "I ne conne bot a lyte / Of othre thinges that ben wise" (1.264–65). This is more than a rhetorical device: his admission reflects an ambivalence in his office and nature, as each had been defined by literary tradition.

Gower has exploited that ambivalence in a fashion unknown to his literary forbears. The priest is naturally drawn to questions raised in Amans's "querele," and he cannot address them as a priest because he is not used to speaking about moral questions; at the same time, because he is a priest, he cannot be entirely comfortable in his role of advocating venerean love or natural appetite. This is reflected in his tentative opening statement.[17] The priest has been "assigned hiere / Be Venus the godesse above" (1.234–35), but he must also touch on the cause of vice because his priestly office requires it (1.244–46). His end, however, is to conclude "For love, whos servant I am, / And why the cause is that I cam" (1.251–52). It belongs to his order "The vices forto telle arewe," but "next above alle othre" he will describe love's "propretes" after the "disposi-cioun / Of Venus, whos condicioun / I most folwe, as I am holde" (1.259–61). Nevertheless, though he knows little about other things – "Venus bokes" have taught him only about love – and though it is not his "comun us / To speke of vices and vertus" (1.267–68), he must, as a priest, organize the shrift so that Amans "ate leste . . . schalt hiere / The vices" (1.277–78), and this he promises to do by applying the vices to love so that Amans understands "what thei mene" (1.280).

While Genius here defers to his goddess as the reason for his appearance, he also reveals an unsure commitment to the duties she has assigned; on the other side, he wavers in his dedication to the tasks ordained by his "Presthode." Winthrop Wetherbee has concluded that in this speech Genius strives "to affirm the intrinsic importance of virtue in the face of Venus' dominating influence, and these lines define a kind of honorable compromise."[18] I do not think, however, that the matter is so neatly resolved: in these lines, the priest does not achieve a compromise, much less an honorable one. While on each side he states an obligation and commitment, the qualifier on the other makes him appear unsure in both. In that uncertainty, he cannot hold out much promise for the conduct or outcome of this shrift. Genius does not seem to

---

[17] See Winthrop Wetherbee, "Genius and Interpretation in the 'Confessio Amantis,' " in *Magister Regis: Studies in Honor of Robert Earl Kaske*, ed. Arthur Groos (New York, 1986), p. 243.
[18] Ibid.

know, when he begins, where he is going, where his invention and judgment will lead.

That unsureness about his direction and objective, even while he promises to conclude for love, is related to the question of who he is. This is not a new question in the history of ancient and medieval *genii*. Apuleius, through his own qualifiers, raises a series of questions about the *genius* who, in function, most resembles Gower's priest:

> You may call this demon in our language, according to my mode of interpretation, by the name of "Genius," whether quite correctly I am not altogether sure, but at all events, at any risk you may so call it; because, this God, who is the mind of every one, though immortal, is nevertheless, after a certain manner, generated with man.[19]

The question of whether Genius is "immortal" or "generated with man" Gower does not ask, but the poem raises the analogous issue by tying the priest's activity so closely to the character of Amans, figuratively a character with whom he is born, and with whom he dies. He lacks the stability of the *genius* who, in Bernard's *Cosmographia*, is assigned to the "new creation of man."[20] Potentially, he, like the lover, changes.

Is he then a creature of time, beset by the same contingency that Amans experiences, or does he know his entire argument before he states it, holding it in mind as in a kind of "eternal present"? There is a suggestion of a predetermined order of thought in his topics, of course. The lover asks the priest to proceed from point to point, and Genius promises to heed that request, discussing in order the "dedly vices sevene." This *ordinatio* is traditional, and it grounds the procedure a confessor must follow in relation to a penitent; as William of Bleys (1229) testifies, "he should more fully instruct him about the seven vices and their species, so that he might more easily call to mind in what species he has sinned."[21] Topics are aids to remembering: they will give Amans his bearings in recollecting his habitual behavior as a lover, and Genius his in garnering ideas and "ensamples" from old books. But they also provide a needed "foreknowledge": Genius's cautious and deliberate strategy of announcing his topics beforehand should make his teaching and shriving intelligible. Aegidius Romanus provides a brief justification for such a strategy when he introduces the divisions of *De regimine* with a statement, based upon Aristotle, that all teaching and learning require a pre-existent knowledge:

> hit is well fittyng to telle the order of thinges that schal be iseide to haue som forknowlech tharof. By forknoweleche the thinges that schal be iseid schal be the sonner vnderstonde. thanne it is to wetyng that it is oure entent to devyde this hole booke in þre partial bookes.[22]

19 *God of Socrates*, 15.150–51, pp. 363–64; ed. Thomas, p. 23.
20 Ibid.
21 *Concilia Magnae Britanniae et Hibemiae*, ed. David Wilkins (London, 1737), 1:624.
22 Aegidius Romanus, *De regimine principum* 1.1.2, pp. 4–5; Childs, p. 198).

Genius, while tentative in reconciling his offices, seems entirely in control of the project of the confession as he outlines its procedure. His insistence on absolute candor and plain speaking is obviously consistent with the traditional goals of a confessional exercise: the penitent must not "peinte" his condition, but "Tell pleinliche as it is befalle" (1.211), and the confessor too must speak plainly, for in the confessional he is obligated to teach as well as shrive:

> For what a man schal axe or sein
> Touchende of schrifte, it mot be plein,
> It nedeth noght to make it queinte,
> For trowthe hise wordes wol noght peinte:
> That I wole axe of the forthi,
> My Sone, it schal be so pleinly,
> That thou schalt knowe and understonde
> The pointz of schrifte how that thei stonde.   1.281–88

As the priest identifies his tasks as a teacher, he seems secure in what he knows.

In reality, while Genius is clear in speech, his thought is not consistently plain or easily understood. As a compiler of tales – in essence, one who organizes the past in its "histories," much as he orders the "remembrance" of the penitent in the confessional – he might be thought to have a vision that transcends occasion, to be concerned with philosophical *ordinatio* and coherence. But order is also for him contingent: as an "author" who augments, modifies, and transforms what he gathers, he overshoots his topics; as a compiler who gathers divergent opinions in a supposed *ordinatio*, he forgets his structures, for example, in so frequently introducing excursus which, if the history of critical responses to the poem constitutes meaningful testimony, have no bearing on his expressed topics. Even his topics contain an element of the contingent.

The general tidiness of the order of parts – the *forma tractatus* – of the *Confessio* has lulled critics into supposing that Gower never, or rarely, deviates from a pattern of assigning five species to each vice. The poet does follow such a number-pattern in his major French poem, but he does not "usually" do so in the *Confessio*, as J. A. W. Bennett has argued; certainly he does not abandon the pattern only with the last vice, as Rosemary Woolf has implied.[23] To Sloth, Avarice, Gluttony, and Lechery, he has assigned 7, 10 (or 12), 2, and 1 species respectively, and to each of these species he devotes a major section or chapter within the appropriate book. Something in the nature of the argument or the occasion has led Genius to depart from the tidiness critics expect of the maker of the *Confessio*.

More importantly, this order of topics does not necessarily mean an order of thinking or doctrine. Within his topics, Genius does not represent orthodox teaching consistently; his penchant to foster a desire for anything that he has judged to be good, whether rightly or wrongly, leads to an impression of undi-

---

23 Bennett, p. 419; Woolf, p. 223.

rected inventiveness. He is allowed to exercise his imagination to retrieve tales, images, forms from whatever sources come to mind and to construct whatever arguments seem to him appropriate within the broad topics of the "vices dedly." Even his stated goal – to conclude for love – is also really nothing more than a topic: Genius hints that this love is tied to his venerean office, but it could refer equally well to lechery, charity, or the *naturatus amor* with which the poet began.

That indeterminacy is related to the priest's devotion to the cause of *naturalis concupiscentia*, and such an attachment once again reminds us that he represents "generation" as well as "being":

> every substance that falls under eternity in certain of its dispositions and under time in certain other of its dispositions is simultaneously being [*ens*] and generation."[24]

Indeed, this figure, who derives his "being" from the "godhiede" and his priest-hood, has a being which also, as tradition claims, is *generatio* itself: contingency and temporality are his idiom, and he can even represent process without a clearly articulated end.

Genius has no firm grasp of the future. He cannot respond to the lover as Socrates' *genius* responds to Socrates when, in Apuleius' words, the latter "stood in need, not of counsel, but foreknowledge; in order that when he was vacillating through doubt, he might take a firm stand through being fore-warned."[25] Socrates' *daemon* can be relied upon for this prophetic power, in late medieval terms imagination, a faculty that forewarns as it discerns imagined objects as possibly helpful or harmful. Amans cannot so rely on his Genius. To a limited degree, of course, this priest applies a like faculty when he posits examples of what happens "ofte tyme," but at last he is subjected to a human rule, that "what schal fallen ate laste, / The sothe can no wisdom caste" (1.39–40). Genius is not present at Amans's initial meeting with Cupid and Venus, a meeting which in itself does not bode well for the lover's future. Almost immediately after his appearance, Cupid, "with yhen wrothe," turns his "chiere aweiward" (1.141), at his departure casting the "firy Dart" through the lover's "herte rote" (1.145). Venus offers Amans "no goodly chiere" (1.152), and when he asks for solace, "sche began to loure" (1.172). These gestures become even more ominous when Venus instructs the lover to confess to her priest, specifically as she declares, "how that it is / I wot miself" (1.191–92). The goddess holds the answer to the enigma of Amans's "querele," but she departs without revealing it and does not return until the end of the confession. Genius does not know what Venus knows, and certainly there is no lack of "goodly chiere" in him as he sets out to hear the confession. He betrays no sense of where this particular meeting tends.

In sum, Genius is defined chiefly not as an essence or "being," but as a

---

[24] *Book of Causes* 31(32).214, trans. Brand, p. 44.
[25] *God of Socrates*, 17.157, p. 367; ed. Thomas, p. 26.

process, a working through of his roles as a conveyor, a message carrier; he stands at a point, in the midst of things, where conflict, doubt, division occur and where issues are formed. One might argue that as an instrument of "external instruction and persuasion," he embodies a freely-bestowed, particular grace (*gratia gratis data*), a grace beyond the capacity of nature (*supra facultatem naturae*), by which he "cooperates" with Amans so that Amans "might be brought back to God."[26] Such grace might indeed secure his teaching, though the enigma remains and is now merely transferred to the source of grace, the identity of the "godhiede" who can bestow grace. Nevertheless, whatever god Genius serves, he still works, despite himself, to an ultimate good. It is a paradoxical strength of the *Confessio* that Genius acts beyond his capacity: we cannot know readily, without exercising our own *ingenium* and judgment, when he speaks the truth; we cannot trust him to tell us.

Thus we cannot anticipate what the priest will teach, or how he will order his teaching, on any particular point. This is especially true in the flow of his thought, in the *forma tractandi*, as he divides, defines, proves, refutes, and posits examples. If we cannot be totally secure in the topics, we can be less so in Genius's argument, where he deals in particulars, remembering and forgetting them as he moves from point to point. No character in the text or apparatus of this poem represents a stable center of meaning, but Genius seems least stable of all, and that unsureness will begin to appear in his treatment of the first subject of confession, as he sets out to gather evidence to help Amans "reule [his] conscience" on the question of the sins of the senses.

[26] Thomas Aquinas, *Summa theologiae* 1a2ae, 111.1, Blackfriars ed., 30:126–27.

CHAPTER SIX

SINS OF THE SENSES: THE ASP

It is entirely fitting that Genius should begin the confession with questions about the senses, since they

> be proprely the gates,
> Thurgh whiche as to the herte algates
> Comth alle thing unto the feire,
> Which may the mannes Soule empeire.   1.299–302

This assertion is, of course, a topos, and it is wholly consistent with the popular Augustinian teaching that delight in and consent to sin originate in suggestion, which "is made either through the memory or through the bodily senses."[1] Indeed, the question in this section of the *Confessio* turns ultimately on consent, as it does in Augustine's doctrine regarding stages in the process of sinning. To fix one's attention on a woman "with the aim and intention of lusting after her," the Father argues, "is not the same as to experience a sensation of carnal pleasure, but it is the giving of such full consent that the aroused desire for it is not repressed, but would be satisfied if opportunity presented itself."[2]

This is the very question raised by Amans's confession regarding sins of the senses. The lover has cast his eyes on the Gorgon Medusa, he tells us, and his heart has been changed to stone: "my lady therupon / Hath such a priente of love grave, / That I can noght miselve save" (1.554–56). Unlike Ulysses in relation to the Sirens, his "wit . . . hath lost his Stiere" (1.560); he does not repress his desire, but is "topulled" to the lady in his thought, "So that of reson leveth noght, / Wherof that I me mai defende" (1.566–67). To this confession, Genius responds with a perfunctory "My goode Sone, god thamende" (1.568), and well he might, given the implications of opening the confession with the subject of sense-perception.

The senses are the gates to the whole world of the amorous "querele" that Amans describes. At the outset, the priest cannot assume that Amans's love is sinful or wicked; he must at least entertain the possibility that it is, as Amans will claim, good, pure, and true. In effect, the Gregorian order of sins adopted

---

[1] Augustine, *De sermone Domini in monte* 1.12.34, trans. Denis J. Kavanagh, *Commentary on the Lord's Sermon on the Mount*, FC 11 (Washington, D.C., 1951), p. 53; PL 34:1246.
[2] Ibid.; PL 34:1246–47.

for this confession puts off that judgment of the love itself until the very end of the shrift. Nonetheless, the senses present an early dilemma for the confessor. Traditional *auctoritates*, including the passage from Augustine, exert some pressure on him to make a commitment, to render a judgment by which he will also defeat his purpose either as Venus's clerk or as a priest. Consent to carnal desire traditionally represents the most memorable example of "alle thing" that can injure "mannes Soule" through the senses. Literature *de amore venereo* repeatedly calls attention to the point: even Andreas Capellanus' playful opening to *De amore*, where he argues that the blind cannot love, is based on the more serious teaching on the dangers of sight. But one of the most telling cases where those dangers are shown to form a particular temptation to lechery or *luxuria* is presented in William Peraldus' very popular compilation, the *Summa vitiorum*. Peraldus does not begin the entire work by treating sins of the bodily senses, as does Genius; nor does he imply, though he could have, that all sins originate in sensation. His extended treatment of sense-perception occurs in his treatise on *luxuria*, specifically as he lists, chapter by chapter, the things that occasion the sin: in addition to such "causes" as idleness (*otium*) and the intemperate consumption of food and wine, Peraldus here explains the dangers occasioned by the senses of touch, hearing, and sight.[3] He argues that among the enticements of sight, for example, the appearance of women "is greatly to be feared."[4]

Genius initially avoids this issue of the causes of lechery. The danger in the eyes, he first notes, is that they permit spying, specifically

> In hindringe of an other wiht;
> And thus ful many a worthi knyht
> And many a lusti lady bothe
> Have be fulofte sythe wroth.   1.315–18

This utterance of Venus' clerk is certainly off the mark of the next point, a priestly *sentence* introduced as if in passing:

> And also for his oghne part
> Fulofte thilke firy Dart
> Of love, which that evere brenneth,
> Thurgh him into the herte renneth.   1.321–24

This promises a judgment, but the confessor never fully develops one in this section of the poem. He treats Amans's case gently; in his four "capsule" examples, *moralitates*, and verdicts, he avoids confrontation altogether.

Genius's first story concerns Acteon, who, in refusing to divert his gaze from the naked Diana, presumably advances from suggestion to delight and consent. But Genius does not make the connection. Nor does he analyze a psychology,

---

3 William Peraldus, *Summa virtutum ac vitiorum* (Mainz, 1618), vol. 2, tract. 3, pars 3, pp. 11–26.
4 Ibid., pp. 24–26.

to ask what one does with a perception, for example, to assess whether it has been, as it should be, subjected to rational judgment. His focus is suggestion itself, and his advice is simply that one not look too much: "For ofte, who that hiede toke, / Betre is to winke than to loke" (1.383–84). If, as John of Salisbury remarked, sensation is the progenitor of all knowledge, and if it is especially critical in learning and teaching *morale negotium* because this kind of knowledge depends so heavily upon sense-perceptible examples and *imagines*, one cannot reject the senses out of hand. Genius appears to know this a short time later, when, after his narrative about the Sirens, he urges the lover not to give things "credence / Bot if thou se more evidence" (1.533–34). In the treatise on blinking, however, he does not really teach his charge when to close his eyes. To be sure, he insists on the importance of deciding, among those images that pass through the gates of the senses, what represents "fol delit" (1.442), "vanite" (1.451), and "Sotie" (1.539), and what "to vertu is acordant" (1.455). Surely it is good moral advice to urge the lover to accept the latter and "torne . . . fro" (1.457) the former, but Genius never instructs Amans in judging which is which; rather, he assumes as he tells these first stories that his auditor is a moral agent who knows when delight is "fol delit," and so he casts his warning:

> For so wys man was nevere non,
> Bot if he wel his yhe kepe
> And take of fol delit no kepe,
> That he with lust nys ofte nome,
> Thurgh strengthe of love and overcome.   1.440–44

The first narrative, in its source, makes no such assumption about the "sureness" of human perception; Ovid does not judge Acteon's looking at the bathing Diana to be a crime (*scelus*), but instead attributes it to luck (*Fortunae crimen*).[5] There is, as Anthony Farnham notes, a "striking reversal" of this judgment in Gower's account, both in the marginal summary and the English version of the story, and Winthrop Wetherbee makes a like observation in his different interpretation of the tale.[6] As the marginal gloss states it (at 1.346), Acteon, looking upon Diana attentively, "oculos suos . . . nullatenus auertere volebat" 'did not wish to avert his eyes at all.' Genius, though he strives to make Acteon "a responsible moral agent,"[7] does not go as far as the glossator, for he does not identify what happens as an act of will: Acteon "his yhe awey ne swerveth / Fro hire, which was naked al / And sche was wonder wroth withal" (1.366–68). In the telling itself, the divine vengeance on this ill-fated man does not seem particularly deserved.

---

[5] Ovid *Metamorphoses* 3.141–42, trans. Frank Justus Miller, Loeb, 2d ed. (New York and London, 1921), 1:134.
[6] Farnham, "High Prosaic Seriousness," p. 166; Wetherbee, "Genius and Interpretation," pp. 248–50.
[7] Farnham, p. 166.

Ovid's tale speaks directly to Gower's perception of the problem of contingency, the "uncertein," even *Fortunae crimen*, in human affairs. The interpreters of this tale in the *Confessio* attempt to resolve that problem: the marginal glossator is quick to order experience by finding meaning in act and consequences, and so too, in this instance, is Genius in his moralization: the tale shows the effect on "A man to caste his yhe amis" (1.380), and the priest finds it sufficient to warn Amans to "do it noght" (1.382). In the telling, however, he has not made Acteon's deed a willed act, and his narrative is therefore closer to Ovid's than either the glossator or he, as a reader of his own story, perceives it to be. Fortune enters into one's perception, but Genius wants, even then, to respond with a consistent morality: the lesson is never to look or, at least, quickly to close one's eyes.

In all four narratives of this section, Genius stresses how difficult it is to come to a judgment about what one perceives. Not only in the first story, which focuses on Diana, "sche which was godesse" (1.369), but in the tales of the Gorgons, the enchanter who "wolde enchaunte" the asp, and the Sirens, he portrays victims either of poor luck or "sleyhte." Images can be presented to the "hertes wit" by enchanters, and it would appear that most people cannot know these agents of destruction until it is too late. Lacking the good fortune of a Perseus, who can kill the Gorgons because he has been given "wisdom and prouesse" by the gods (1.429), one must simply block the senses to enchantment, as the asp does in relation to the enchanter, or as Ulysses does in relation to the Sirens. The latter figures can identify "fol delit"; the priest has yet to teach his charge how to recognize it.

For much of this confession, in fact, the lover continues to resemble the "Schipmen" who, in seeking their paradise, "here rihte cours and weie / Foryete" (1.509–10). The voice of a woman, which Peraldus judged to be a possible cause of *luxuria*, does not seem to be a danger for Amans: his beloved is a good person who, alas, is not inclined to respond to his suit with a "goodli word" at all. Nonetheless, Amans later recalls that when he hears her sing, he imagines he is in Paradise, and such is the threat that Genius perceives in the Sirens:

> whan the Schipmen leie an Ere
> Unto the vois, in here avys
> Thei wene it be a Paradys.   1.500–02

Genius is here most concerned with a "reality" beneath appearance. The Sirens, of course, are monsters who sing "with so swete a stevene / Lik to the melodie of hevene" (1.493–94), but only to destroy. The focus of Genius's *narratio* is as much upon them as upon the shipmen who "wene it be a Paradys." Only much later in the confession does the real threat become manifest: it does not lie in what is perceived, or the seeming "melodie of hevene," but in the perception itself, including the imagination and recreation whereby the lover makes the song appear heavenly. Peraldus recognizes this problem when he writes about hearing amorous songs,[8] but Genius does not dwell on it here; instead he urges his charge to block the senses because there are in the world enchanters who enter these gates to destroy by "sleyhte."

The focus of these four tales is not on delight or consent, but on suggestion, and the question, here and subsequently, turns on whether "suggestion" is a persuasion or a compulsion. Augustine argues that it is the former, and because "persuasion is not compulsion," he contends that no one is forced to consent to carnal desire. Genius, it appears, sees suggestion as a compulsion: the danger thus lies in enchantment, and for him the asp exemplifies an ideal response to such a threat.

By laying one ear against the ground and covering the other with its tail, the asp "thurgh his Ere is noght deceived" (1.480). This "moralized" piece of natural history is variously refined in medieval sermons, collections of *distinctiones*, and encyclopedias. Brunetto Latini adds to the basic scriptural account another element, which Gower also adopts: the enchanter preys on the asp to win a precious stone embedded in its forehead. Brunetto does not moralize this feature of the serpent, and neither does Gower. Indeed, as Winthrop Wetherbee has remarked, Gower seems to do very little with the tale at all: he does not invite us "to read [the asp as exemplum] figurally, whether in *bono* or in *malo*. . . . Its status is wholly equivocal."[9] The point is not that the story lacks the potential for a gloss, but that it is open to multiple readings, and Genius rejects that wealth of significance.

Those readings, even by their absence, can tell us something about the ambivalent status of the principal speakers in the *Confessio*. In medieval tradition, the asp and the enchanter can each be read in *bono* and in *malo*. Genius would have us understand "aspis" in a good sense, and that is consistent with the poet's use of this same lore in the *Mirour* (15253–76), but the priest does not fully develop the point. Robert Holkot offers a typical reading: the serpent "that blocks its ears" represents the prudent man, and the enchanter represents "corrupt men, under the pretense of friendship enticing us to the vices of the world and the flesh." Robert thus enjoins us to cover our ears to "evil suggestions," lest those who delight us "should lure us to consent." In such a reading, of course, the prototype of the enchanter is the devil.[10]

Interpreters of the story can just as easily reverse the moral identities of the asp and enchanter, often by expanding terms found in Ps. 57:5–6: the "madness [of the wicked] is according to the likeness of a serpent: like the deaf asp that stoppeth her ears: Which will not hear the voice of the charmers; nor of the wizard that charmeth wisely." The serpent might now be understood as the person wise in the world, the reprobate, or the devil.[11] For Peter of Capua, Garner of St. Victor, and Nicholas of Lyra, the serpent represents the obstinate

---

[8] Peraldus, *Summa vitiorum*, pp. 24–26.
[9] Wetherbee, "Genius and Interpretation," p. 245.
[10] Robert Holkot, *In librum Sapientiae regis Salomonis praelectiones* CCXIII, lect. 74 (Basle, 1586), p. 263; see also Pierre Bersuire, *Dictionarium*, s. v. "auris," 1: fol. 136r.
[11] See *Angelus*, or *Allegoriae in universam sacram scripturam*, s. v. "serpens," *PL* 112:887.

man (*obstinatus*) who scorns hearing the *verbum Dei*, lest he be called back from his error; in the *Glossa ordinaria*, the enchanter (*incantator*) becomes by catechresis the wise man (*sapiens*), and for Hugh of St. Cher, he represents the preacher who draws those figured by the asp out of hiding and into the light of grace.[12]

The double valence of this story, though not introduced in Genius's moralization, is mirrored in the very relationship between the priest and his charge. Is Amans a just person being enticed by an evil *daemon*, or a proud, obstinate man being exhorted by a good priest? As the enchanter can be a wicked person or *diabolus*, a preacher or Christ, so also the figure of Genius can play different roles, counselling either good or, by suggestion, evil. In ancient and medieval tradition extending from the Book of Tobit through Bernard's *Cosmographia*, there are good and evil *genii*, to be sure, but they tend to be one thing or the other. Gower's confessor lacks the "divine" intensity of these austere *genii* or demons of tradition; he seems to partake of both worlds. In Bernard, evil *genii* enter "minds at rest, or concerned with their own thoughts, through the power of suggestion."[13] Gower's figure does that too – he works softly and gently by suggestion – but he is never entirely an evil charmer who lures Amans, a good man, from faith or grace.[14] He is, on the other hand, a priest, and yet, similarly, he is never entirely a preacher who seeks only to restore an obstinate lover to a forgotten *verbum Dei*.

The story of the asp, as Genius himself tells it, illustrates by analogy that difference in his character as a *genius*. Readings *in bono* and *in malo* of serpent and charmer disappear in the *narratio* and its simple, incomplete *moralitas*. Gower "centers" our attention on the telling, and as with the narrative, so with Genius: the poet provides no explicit readings of his persona; he "centers" him as narrator, even as judge, giving us little opportunity to make a definitive judgment *in bono* or *in malo*.

Indeed, Genius in his own character *represents* or personifies a common medieval procedure for reading texts. In a collection of *distinctiones* like Pierre Bersuire's, a given reading can quickly shift to its opposite: immediately after interpreting the *incantator* as the preacher, for example, Bersuire, using his customary phrase, "vel dic," writes, "Or say that the enchanter is the devil."[15] Such a procedure is familiar enough to students of medieval literature. For Ovid's tale of Jupiter and Callisto, a story Genius will retell later in the *Confes-*

---

12 Peter of Capua, *Rosa alphabetica seu Ars sermocinandi*, ad litt. 1, art. 67, in extracts printed by J. B. Pitra, *Spicilegium Solesmense sanctorum patrum scriptorumque ecclesiasticorum*, (Paris, 1852–58), 3:93; Garner of St. Victor, *Gregorianum* 3.31, PL 193:129–30; *Biblia sacra cum glossa ordinaria et postilla Nicolai Lyrani* (Antwerp, 1634), 3: col. 854; Hugh of St. Cher, *Opera omnia in universum Vetus et Novum Testamentum* (Cologne, 1621), 2: fol. 146v; see also Pierre Bersuire, *Reductorium morale, de rerum proprietatibus* 10.9, in *Opera omnia* (Cologne, 1730–31), 2:328.
13 Bernardus Silvestris, *Cosmographia* 2.7, trans. Wetherbee, p. 108; ed. Dronke, p. 136.
14 See Pierre Bersuire, *Reductorium morale, de rerum proprietatibus* 10.9, *Opera* 2:328–29.
15 Ibid.

sio, Bersuire has Jupiter signify *dei filius benedictus* in one reading, *hypocritas* in another.[16] We cannot anticipate what Genius will do with this particular tale: he may present either interpretation, both of them, or neither; indeed, he is additionally unpredictable because his frequently doubled terms are not usually taken from any single known source, or from a dominant exegetical tradition supporting a given text. Genius is a store of interpretations, a source of endlessly variable readings of books. Moreover, unlike the commentator Bersuire, he enacts the shifts from one kind of reading to another and never announces them.

This is bound to affect Amans's prospect as a learner: which counsel should the asp, or a man who would be good, seek and which avoid hearing?[17] The question is complicated by the gentle persuasions of this teacher: Gower never indicates that Genius's benevolence hides a deeper malice, but it is a problematic kindness nonetheless. He sometimes, but not always, encourages the

---

[16] See Pierre Bersuire, *Reductorium morale, liber XV: Ovidius moralizatus, cap. ii–xv, naar de Parijse druk van 1509*, transcribed by D. Van Nes, Werkmateriaal–2 (Utrecht, 1962), p. 52.

[17] An analogous problem arises with regard to the carbuncle, the stone that shines in dark places. If the carbuncle is cast into the fire, "it is yqueynt as it were among dede colis, and brenneþ if water is þrowe þeron" (Bartholomaeus Anglicus *De proprietatibus rerum* 16.25, trans. John Trevisa, *On the Properties of Things*, ed. M. C. Seymour et al. [Oxford, 1975], 2:839); see also Isidore, *Etymologiae* 4.6.16, 16.14.1; Marbode of Rennes, *De lapidibus* 23, ed. John M. Riddle, Sudhoffs Archiv: Zeitschrift für Wissenschaftsgeschichte, Beiheft 20 (Wiesbaden, 1977), pp. 61–62.

In this magical "history" of the carbuncle, there is a suggestion of the narrated history of Amans-"John Gower." Like the stone, "Gower" is thrown into the fire of his passion and is seemingly "yquent" by it; his later cold chill, like the water splashed on the stone, causes a dramatic change: he "revives from death," "flees the shadows of night," and, in accord with the gloss on the carbuncle, burns with renewed love. See Pseudo-Hugh of St. Victor, *De bestiis et aliis rebus* 4.3, PL 177:140.

For Pierre Bersuire, the carbuncle represents the perfect man: "Talis est vir perfectus, quia vere est igneus per ferventem charitatem, fulgidus per lucidam honestatem, & maxime talis debet esse praelatus. . . . Unde nulla nox, id est nulla ignorantia vel adversitas debet eum extinguere per peccatum" (*Reductorium morale, de rerum proprietatibus* 11.57, *Opera* 2:431–32). Bersuire's ideal is the *praelatus*, pre-eminent and exemplary in status: one can hardly credit Amans with possessing the light of wisdom and discretion or the splendor of good life and conversation by which "he might illumine efficaciously the night of others' adversity and ignorance," but that is the end – an end of authorship – to which he, and the "John Gower" who contains him, advance.

In another setting, Bersuire explicates the serpent who guards a precious stone lodged in its head as the just man who defends the *lapis preciosus* – Christ, faith, and grace – in his mind, knowing that in these things his life properly consists (*Dictionarium*, s. v., "serpens," 3: fol. 187r). The asp, in one of its meanings, signifies defense, and the stone can represent either the center of self-defense or what is defended. See Pseudo-Hugh, *De bestiis*, 4.3, PL 177:140. As with the asp and enchanter, however, so with the carbuncle in even greater degree: Gower gives us no secure interpretation of it; indeed, he provides no reading of it at all. The more important point is that if we suppose Genius to be an enchanter who seeks to win the carbuncle, we still do not know whether his intent thereby is to help or harm the asp.

lover to persist in his "natural" desire; he is neither entirely a *sapiens* nor entirely a fool, and this compounds Amans's difficulty. The lover must listen if he is going to amend his behavior. He will gain absolutely nothing by merely covering his ears, and yet, what he must listen to are the morally indeterminate suggestions of his priest.

Genius, the product of the poet's exercise as a *tumultuator*, "causes" debate by the very conflict in the doctrines he presents. Some of this may be attributed to his role as a compiler; he must yield to his authorities even when they disagree with each other. Genius is the product of another genre decision as well. The *Confessio* is a poem which, as it explores the problem of love, conforms to a tradition of "disputeisoun" extending back to antiquity, and specifically to the *disputatio in utramque partem* or "the method of arguing alternately on both sides of a question."[18] As a form of dialectic, such disputation is a method of arriving at a judgment of the relative worth of competing opinions.[19] It cannot achieve the certitude of apodictic discourse, but by means drawn from juridical practice, it can approach the truth through opinions; indeed, matters that admit of uncertainty are central to it:

> Anyone who is in possession of his senses will not posit something which either seems plausible to no one, or is apparent to everyone or [at least] to those whose judgment is sought. The latter sort of premise does not admit of any doubt, while no one would advance the former.[20]

The procedure of formulating questions, identifying points of controversy, and advancing to a judgment – a determination of which opinion better approximates (*aspirat*, aspires to or approaches) the truth – reduces elements of the irrational, subjective, and passionate by allowing the matched contestants fully to explore, debate, and resolve differences.[21]

Obviously this is not a procedure traditionally suited to a confessional, where the two speakers are not contestants, much less contestants equally matched. In confession, both speakers are guided by a single Truth, but only one of the two can legitimately claim "maistrye" in enunciating it. In this confession, nevertheless, there is "disputeisoun," and it is centered in the conflict of opinions voiced not merely by the paired speakers, but by each speaker separately, and especially by the confessor.

---

[18] For an important discussion of uses of this method by authors extending from Cicero to Andreas Capellanus and Boccaccio, see Wesley Trimpi, "The Quality of Fiction: The Rhetorical Transmission of Literary Theory," *Traditio* 30 (1974): 1–118, esp. 43–51.

[19] See John of Salisbury, *Metalogicon* 3.10, trans. McGarry, pp. 189–202; ed. Webb, pp. 153–64; Alessandro Giuliani, "L'Élément 'juridique' dans la logique médiévale," in *La Théorie de l'argumentation: perspectives et applications*, ed. Ch. Perelman (Louvain, 1963), p. 553.

[20] John of Salisbury, *Metalogicon*, 2.15, trans. McGarry, p. 109; ed. Webb, p. 89.

[21] Ibid., 2.14, trans. McGarry, pp. 106–07; ed. Webb, pp. 87–88; see also Giuliani, pp. 543–44.

The *Confessio* is not formally organized as a disputation, but proceeds by the representation of ideas in fictions. Undoubtedly, that feature of the work sometimes creates an impression of sophistry, but it is not Genius's "objective . . . to lose [an] adversary in a fog of delusions,"[22] though he sometimes appears to perpetrate falsehoods by defective principles or reasonings. The process of the poem is inventive, not sophistical. Both speakers are tale-tellers who seek to recover the past, and through it a "proper" likeness of and for Amans, one that restores a rightness of will, *rectitudo voluntatis*, and happiness. On the pattern of the body politic introduced in the Prologue, in which the prince is advised to regard counsel, to heed the "members" and their "trowthe allowe" (154), the poem gathers divergent counsel to the end of achieving a *determinatio* or decision, ultimately centered in the only place where meanings truly come together, that place "wher resteth love."

One can advance to that end, Gower shows, by generating and evaluating fictions. The inventive arts, according to Thomas Aquinas, are three: dialectic, rhetoric, and poetics. Each approaches the truth by inclining to one side of a contradiction, but their degree of certitude differs: dialectic generates belief (*fides*), rhetoric creates a suspicion, and poetics, by means of a representation, provides mere conjecture (*existimatio*).[23] All three of these arts will pertain to Gower's task as compiler, but he chiefly generates opinions in conflict with each other, not by expounding but by "representing" them. This is Genius's world of "suggestion": by the use of fictions introduced in multiple structures, opinions are brought into conflict and resolved poetically.

A virtue of the *modus procedendi* of such argument, whether in its ancient or medieval form, is that belief remains "suspended until the most probable solution [can] be identified."[24] This pertains directly to Gower's deferring judgment, even about Genius, and we would therefore do well to heed Wesley Trimpi's caution about the form, that we not succumb "to a didactic impatience to assert an explicit moral judgment"[25] before the occasion warrants it. Patience is especially necessary in reading a work such as the *Confessio* because its author, taking this form to its extreme, speaks alternately in *personae* of the wise man and the fool.

When Bonaventure analyzes the *modus procedendi* of Ecclesiastes, he is concerned to respond to an objection which in a later generation might be raised against Gower: "it is not known, when the writer speaks, whether he is saying this in his own person or in the character of someone else. So, one does not know what should be believed in this book and what should be rejected."[26] The

---

22 John of Salisbury, *Metalogicon*, 2.3, trans. McGarry, p. 79; ed. Webb, p. 65.
23 Thomas Aquinas, *Commentary on the Posterior Analytics of Aristotle*, trans. Larcher, p. 3; ed. Spiazzi, p. 148.
24 Trimpi, p. 47.
25 Ibid., p. 116.
26 Bonaventure, *Commentarius in Ecclesiasten*, prooemium, q. 3, obj. 2, trans. Minnis and Scott, *Medieval Literary Theory*, pp. 231–32; *S. Bonaventurae opera omnia* (Quaracchi, 1882–1902), 6:7.

marginal commentator of the *Confessio* tries to quiet such a concern by separating the *auctor* speaking in his own person from Amans. An even greater problem arises with regard to Genius, the teacher in the fiction, however, for we cannot be sure when he speaks for Gower. Bonaventure has a solution to a like problem in Ecclesiastes:

> The other (i.e., the rejected] side of a disputation [*disputatio*] cannot be known until the judgement [*sententia*] . . . is arrived at, for in the solution [*solutio*] it becomes known what is accepted and what is rejected. So, I submit that Ecclesiastes proceeds by using the method of disputation right up until the end of the book.

Only at that time, when the author offers a decision or verdict, condemning "all the opinions of the foolish, the carnally inclined, and the worldly," can we know that "everything which is in accord with this judgement he speaks in his own person." Bonaventure therefore concludes that this "book cannot be understood unless attention is paid to its totality."[27] Gower, like the author of Ecclesiastes, is concerned to defer the determination of "what is accepted," and to that end he keeps questions open as long as it is fruitful to do so.

One such question appears in the treatment of sins of the senses. This entire section, we might assume, is, like an "article" in a compilation or reference book, a totality having its own inner coherence. What now becomes relevant is its *ordinatio* and the poet's actual clustering of tales in it, since these might significantly shape a single, unified interpretation. The section does not so assuredly provide a self-contained meaning, however: the *ordinatio* of the larger confessional dialogue influences it, and even the grouping of stories within the section may not be Gower's own, but taken instead from some other compilation. It is indeed relevant to this case that Pierre Bersuire also links the accounts of the asp and the Sirens in his *distinctio* for *auris*, and that he, like Gower, uses these cases alone to elucidate the very problem that Genius has introduced. Pierre concludes his statement about the asp and begins one about the Sirens without a break: "We should be likened to the deaf asp that blocks its ears" and not to the "sailors who delight in the songs of Sirens and so sleep and dream and are devoured by the Sirens." Those "who do not close their ears to depraved suggestions, or Sirens' songs," Bersuire continues, "are so enchanted that they are compelled to sleep, that is, to consent to sin as if by necessity [*peccato consentire quasi necessario compelluntur*]."[28] Effectively, Bersuire sets a problem for Genius. Throughout the confession, the priest explores questions from both sides, and in the early books one of the basic questions he examines by "representation" involves this issue of persuasion and compulsion. It has been hinted at by Bersuire: whether persons – and now specifically, lovers – can "be compelled to consent to sin as if by necessity."

---

[27] Ibid., q. 3, rsp. 2.
[28] Bersuire, *Dictionarium*, s. v. "auris," 1: fol. 136r.

CHAPTER SEVEN

PRIDE, PASSION, AND *KINDE*

Under the distinction for *auris*, Genius does what Bersuire does – warn against
the dangers of hearing – but a meaning for this subject does not begin to
crystallize until, informally and over the course of the entire *Confessio*, the
priest creates other *distinctiones* that variously refine or modify what he presents
as "sure" opinion on this expressly stated topic. Of distinctions of this sort,
none is more important for the work as a whole than the one Genius generates
for the *jus naturae*. Through an array of meanings assigned to the law of nature,
the first books of the confession, while they formally concentrate on the vices
of pride, envy, and wrath, additionally explore the enchantment of sin or the
mechanism by which one consents to sin "quasi necessario." In Book 1, Genius
shows, in some of his cases, that pride originates in nature, but in others, that
nature sets the terms of strongest opposition to pride. This apparent conflict in
the *leges naturae* is developed over the whole book, and it is followed by other,
like conflicts developed over the course of the entire *Confessio*; what at first
appears to be a priestly ineptitude in using a major term now in one meaning,
now in another, turns out to be Gower's strategy for discovering, representing,
and fully exploring significant issues.

The priest's handling of the relationship between consent and the *leges
naturae* is embedded in a dialogue that mixes the amorous and "holy." In a
confession, one might expect to find *sancta conversatio*, or conversation directed "to expelling the sickness of temptation, arranging repose and soundness
of mind, and ordering the external senses chastely."[1] The words of such conversation will agree with the "internal disposition of the heart," much as – to
borrow an analogy from John Bromyard – the text of a book agrees with its
gloss.[2] The dialogue of the *Confessio*, however, is not so tidy. Its significant
elements of "amoureuse conversacion" convey a sense that the speakers do not
clearly understand their own intent or "disposition of heart": their glosses are
as variable and uncertain as their text. The problem for us is centering meaning
in the dialogue: at the literal level, a given tale can gloss a *moralitas* as easily as
a *moralitas* can gloss a tale, and these glosses, moreover, do not always agree
with their "text" or with each other. If, as I have suggested, the goal of the

---

[1]   Maurice of Provins, *Dictionarium Sacrae Scripturae Mauritii Hybernici* (Venice, 1603),
s. v., "conversatio," fol. 97v.
[2]   John Bromyard, *Summa praedicantium* (Antwerp, 1614), s. v. "conversatio," 2:157.

confession is to have Amans discover, indeed recreate an adequate likeness of himself, the difficulty for the reader, as for the lover, is finding where such an "intention" is served, or where, in the conversation, adequate meaning surfaces.

This question arises in the treatment of hypocrisy, the first species of pride. Genius opens the discussion with a statement about religious hypocrisy, and this sub-topic will influence his analysis of hypocrisy in love. The argument is further complicated by Genius's perspective on consent. What in a holy conversation might be construed as a reprehensible agreeing to sin "quasi necessario" is to the priest a matter of being compelled to sin by nature; the latter judgment is consistent with what lovers believe.

In the first of the priest's two tales regarding hypocrisy, Mundus, a supposedly "worthi knyht," wins Paulina by a scheme whereby, in collusion with two priests of Isis, he appears to her in the guise of the god Anubus. Paulina is a "worthi wyf," virtuous, chaste, innocent, and devout. In her wish to be "Fulfild of alle holinesse" (1.895), she falls victim to Mundus' trick, agreeing to meet the god "be hire housebondes leve" (1.857); her husband, also deceived, bids her to acquiesce "unto the goddes heste" (1.867). Soon after she falls victim to Mundus' "deceipte and flaterie" (1.676), she encounters him in his own person, and he cannot avoid boasting to her about the seduction. Paulina rushes home, offers an apostrophe to "derke ypocrisie" (1.956) and thanks the gods that she has "aperceived" it. Thus, almost as soon as Mundus wins "Of his desir the vein astat" (1.599), he loses it. He is later condemned by an imperial court, and his exile is apt punishment since it denies him the sight of what has enchanted him. But more immediately and more effectively, it is Paulina who provides Genius's greatest dissuasion from the sin: once deceived, she vows that "It schal nevere eft whil that I live" (1.963). Her piety and "gret holinesse," though they occasion Mundus' sin, also form the strongest argument against it.

The effect of the tale turns on casting Paulina in an entirely positive light. Presenting her as a humble, devout exemplar, Genius has left out the boasts of her counterparts in tradition: the Paulina of Josephus' *Antiquities* (18.3.4), the foolish Madonna Lisetta da Ca' Quirino of Boccaccio's *Decameron* (4.2), and the Olympias of Gower's later story of Nectanabus (6.1789–2366) all, to some degree, have an exaggerated sense of self-worth, and they easily succumb to the blandishment of a pretender-god or angel. The Paulina of Josephus brags to her friends about her meeting with the god Anubus, but the Paulina of Gower does not. Rather, the meeting with the god occasions in her a further expression of humility: "And sche began to bidde and preie / Upon the bare ground knelende, / And after that made hire offrende" (1.934–36).

Genius has sought by this one example to show that the hypocrite "schalt it afterward repent" (1.757). Nevertheless, just as important to the rhetorical effect of the narrative is the priest's excuse for Mundus; the knight consents to sin under compulsion. In opening his version of this story, the teller does not stress Paulina's ancestral rank and virtuous life, as does Josephus, but rather concentrates on her comeliness: she "was to every mannes sihte / Of al the Cite

the faireste" (1.766–67). This beauty is, in fact, the "cause" of Mundus' down-
fall, the excuse for his sin:

> It is and hath ben evere yit,
> That so strong is no mannes wit,
> Which thurgh beaute ne mai be drawe
> To love, and stonde under the lawe
> Of thilke bore frele kinde,
> Which makth the hertes yhen blinde,
> Wher no reson mai be comuned.   1.769–75

Genius finds his principle, it now appears, in a subject even more important
than hypocrisy; no man can resist beauty and, through beauty, love: "in this
wise stod fortuned / This tale, of which I wolde mene" (1.776–77). It is no
matter that this "worthi knyht" resorts to "sleyhte" when gifts and entreaties
fail: lovers can be expected to do whatever seems necessary to win the beloved.
Mundus, in short, cannot be held entirely accountable for an action to which
kinde has incited him.

The priest's effort to exculpate Mundus introduces into the tale a competing
lore and *moralitas*. Genius saves his strongest censure for the two priests: whereas the lover's action is excusable, theirs is not. It would appear, then, that the
narrative is ordered as an attack on religious hypocrisy, as well as a tribute to a
counterposed piety.

Both of these elements – the diverting of blame and the "religious" concern
– also appear in the next story, the tale of the Trojan Horse. This is a story of
"holinesse," "gret devocioun," "gret solempnite," and "gret reverence," focused
specifically on the pious Trojans' acceptance of the "noble Sacrifise" offered by
the Greeks. In the earlier tale the two priests assume a "contrefet simplesse" to
deceive a victim who is "al honeste / To godward after hire entente" (1.868–
69) and who "wiste of guile non" (1.890), and in this later tale the Greeks
overcome the Trojans through "contrefet Ipocrisie," a vice "feigned of simplesce." Genius now shifts the moral, however, and speaks on the "other half,"
arguing that "men scholde noght / To lihtly lieve al that thei hiere" (1.1062–
63). This second tale is less about religious hypocrisy than about credulity, and
Genius, by stressing the fault of the Trojans, further tempers his earlier judgment against Mundus: in retrospect, a portion of blame must be shifted to the
quickly believing Paulina.

The tales of hypocrisy thus raise a question about the true gloss or *moralitas*
for the section. One might even infer that this conversation supposedly organized to denounce religious hypocrisy actually exemplifies it. Genius urges
his charge not to make a woman believe something that is not "in thi bilieve"
(1.1216), and he does so on the grounds that

> love is deceived ofte;
> For feigned semblant is so softe,
> Unethes love may be war.   1.1219–21

The "feigned semblant" that injures Paulina has nothing to do with her "love" of Mundus, of course. The more serious problem, which Genius refuses to assess, is a falsehood that may inhere in the actual "belief" of venerean lovers.

The priest's language of exculpation is a form of religious hypocrisy that might, were this shrift in "ernest," threaten the whole exercise of confession. Genius has powerfully described the hypocritical "seculer" as a person who

> With *mea culpa*, which he seith,
> Upon his brest fullofte he leith
> His hond, and cast upward his yhe,
> As thogh he Cristes face syhe.   1.661–64

All the while, this person's heart "Goth in the worldes cause aboute, / How that he myhte his warisoun / Encresce" (1.670–72). This, in effect, is a portrait of Amans, a lover who frequently voices a *mea culpa* in confession, but who, throughout, indulges a fantasy of increasing his "warisoun" in "worldes cause." Thus, while the opening description of religious hypocrisy is part of a "cataloguing" of issues that we might expect to find in a *compilatio*, Gower here turns it back on the confessional dialogue itself, in effect as a gloss on its argument. Especially because it follows so closely on Genius's statement about his own priestly office and because it frames the lover's own confessional procedure, it becomes one source of meaning for the discussion that follows. Genius encourages hypocrisy even while he reprehends it.

The tale of Mundus, as it fits into this argument, provides the basis for a caveat against trying to define a "moral" Gower on the basis of isolated utterances of his fictitious priest. It is just such a conflation – indeed confusion – of the author and Genius that has led to a very curious recent judgment that Gower lacks the "moral scruples" that are supposed to be his distinction. In her provocative essay on "kindly" Gower and "moral" Chaucer, Rosemary Woolf has helped to break a tired habit of responding to Gower's work solely by a reflex based upon the famous epithet. By merely replacing one term with another, however, she unfortunately oversimplifies the case in the other direction. Woolf reads the tales exactly as her opponents often do, seeing, or wishing to see, in each of them the poet's univocal thought on a given subject: though that in itself might create frustration when, among the examples, Gower appears to contradict himself, it is central to Woolf's point: Gower is a "kindly" poet who strives to generate sympathy for sinful characters such as Mundus; at other times, when he does not, he betrays the fault in his kindness, an ultimate lack of critical acumen.

Rather than argue concerning a given story that "sensitive moral judgment has manifestly deserted Gower,"[3] we would do better to consider the poetic circumstances of his speeches. Woolf faults Gower for not being fully attuned to the variable meanings and relationships of his terms, charging him, for example, with "accidentally" debasing the notions of "love" and "kinde":

---

[3] Woolf, p. 230.

'Love' in the story of Mundus seems to be equivalent to 'kinde' in other contexts, and in some of these other contexts 'kinde' is apparently reduced to its most restrictive meaning of sexual instincts. This debasement is undoubtedly not intended but it represents a serious flaw in the poem.[4]

The danger in this judgment that something is "undoubtedly not intended," beyond the fact that Woolf provides absolutely no evidence to support it, is that it creates an unwarranted impression of the poet's intellectual slovenliness. With a basic knowledge of medieval academic discussions of the *jus naturae*, one does not have to course very far through the *Confessio* to discover that Gower was fully apprised of that tradition and knew the meanings of the concept as he introduced them. We shall do well to heed the advice of Peter Abelard and the generations of writers who follow him by paying closer attention to the range of meanings that medieval tradition assigned to important terms, as well as to the speaker and rhetorical context of given utterances. Indeed, it is to the point that Gower introduces the meanings of the *jus naturae* through Genius, a speaker whose field of "expertise" is, by medieval tradition, nature.[5]

To accept only one "moral" reading as legitimate and permissible for the terms of the *Confessio* is to close out much that enriches the poem and enriched the culture. Woolf does this – effectively locking into a single telling of a tale as the preferred, indeed acceptable one – when she faults Gower sometimes for trying to change too much in his sources, as when he revises Ovid's "intractable" story of Iphis and Anaxarete at a later point in the *Confessio*, and sometimes for changing too little, as when he refuses to revise the source of his tale of Mundus and Paulina:

> it is difficult for the reader to see why the passions that overcame Mundus should be so much more simply and gently described than those that moved Tarquin (cf. V.3998–4900). The explanation undoubtedly lies in the respective sources, but, though Vincent [of Beauvais] had referred to the *vis amoris* [in the tale of Mundus], Gower would have done better not to repeat him.[6]

The poet tells very different tales about Mundus and Tarquin simply because on these separate occasions he is pointing different "truths."

In the first instance, what Woolf calls the *vis amoris* might be identified with *kinde*, and of the various traditional senses of the *jus naturae*, none is more important in setting the premises of the *Confessio* than a meaning for it that

4 Ibid., p. 229.
5 In addition to the association of the priest with Nature in well-known medieval literary works, Genius is linked with nature etymologically. Drawing upon Hugutio's *Magna derivationes*, William Brito thus defines *ingenium*: "ingenium quasi intus genitum, scilicet a natura, ethimologia. Item hic genius dicitur 'deus nature'" (*Summa Britonis*, s. v. "ingenium," 1:340).
6 Woolf, p. 229.

here emerges; it is a meaning derived from the Roman jurist Ulpian and codified in the *Corpus iuris civilis*: "Natural law is what nature has taught all animals, for this law is proper not only to the human race, but to all living beings."[7] For Gower, natural law in this sense governs or affects every aspect of sentient life, including sexual desire.[8] It is, in medieval legal tradition, a natural instinct, or a *motus sensualitatis*, which in its first impulses is not subject to free will: "primi motus non sunt in nostra potestate."[9] With "legal" precedent, Genius can argue that a person has no choice but to submit to the power of "thilke bore frele kinde."[10] Later, however, in the very section of the poem where Tarquin's story is told, the confessor qualifies his earlier stance and treats natural instinct not as a compulsion, but as a mere persuasion: God gives man "reson forth withal, / Wherof that he nature schal / Upon the causes modefie" (7.5377–79).[11]

Reason should dissuade the "worthi" Mundus from consent, and the fact that Genius does not make this point in Book 1 sets a problem for his treatment of pride more generally. *Kinde*, in his argument, legitimizes Mundus's love: the issue then turns on the pride Mundus exercises in winning "loves spede," but

---

[7] *Institutiones* 1.2, ed. P. Krueger (Berlin, 1872), p. 3.

[8] Gower's opening epigram on *naturatus amor* and the *leges naturae* gives a first indication of this; see also the marginal gloss at 1.8, which uses terms reminiscent of Ulpian to describe the subject of the poem as that love "a quo non solum humanum genus, sed eciam cuncta animancia naturaliter subiciuntur." Portions of the argument that follows are adapted from my article, "Natural Law and Gower's *Confessio*," pp. 230–34.

[9] Azo, *Summa Institutionum* 1.2, ed. F. W. Maitland, *Select Papers from the Works of Bracton and Azo*, Selden Society, 8 (London, 1895), 32, 34.

[10] Cf. Guillaume de Lorris and Jean de Meun, *Le Roman de la rose*, 5733–36, 5745–54, ed. Félix Lecoy, Classiques français du moyen âge (Paris, 1970–1974), 1:176–77.

[11] This implies a refinement of Ulpian's definition of the *jus naturae*: Gower has advanced to a distinction, like one proposed by William of Auxerre, between natural, brute sensuality, which is not subject to free will, and human sensuality, which is set in motion voluntarily and can or should be governed and "modified" by rational judgment (William of Auxerre, *Summa aurea in quattuor libros sententiarum* [Paris, 1500–1501; rpt. Frankfurt am Main, 1964], fol. 131ra). Gower prefers the distinction between an *animalic* law of nature and reason to the distinction between a *rational* law of nature and sensuality, and in this he follows legal authorities who similarly choose as their principle Ulpian's definition; the emphasis among these writers falls upon reason modifying nature. See, for example, Accursius, *In Institutiones* 1.2 (Venice, 1499), fol. 3vb; *Summa Vindobonensis*, ed. J. B. Palmerius (Bonn, 1913–14), p. 6; *Summa Institutionum 'Iustiniani est in hoc opere*,' ed. Pierre Legendre (Frankfurt am Main, 1973), p. 27. For Gower, as for certain glossators, marriage is ordained not by the law of nature, but, once again, by reason modifying nature. See Johannes Faber, *In Institutiones commentarii* 1.2 (Lyon, 1557; rpt. Frankfurt am Main, 1969), 6v. W. Onclin gives other instances of this position in Accursius, Jacobus de Arena, and Albericus de Rosate ("Le Droit naturel selon les Romanistes des XIIe et XIIIe siècles, in *Miscellanea moralia in honorem Arthur Janssen* [Louvain, 1949], pp. 336–37). On the tendency of the civilians to accept Ulpian's definition and of the decretists to prefer those meanings where the law of nature is identified with reason, see the post-glossator Cinus of Pistoia, *In Digesti Veteris libros commentaria*, 1.1.9–12 (Frankfurt am Main, 1578), fol. 3v. For general background, see E. Cortese, *La norma giuridica* (Milan, 1962), pp. 37–96, 412–15, 438–39.

not on the love itself. That love, however, is itself a prideful, self-induced passion; in effect, though Genius does not here recognize it, *kinde* in his reading also legitimizes pride.

It is no wonder, then, that Amans is not immediately led to perceive his own deeply rooted sin. He is convinced that he is not a hypocrite, for he has absolutely no need to feign:

> So lowe cowthe I nevere bowe
> To feigne humilite withoute,
> That me ne leste betre loute
> With alle the thoghtes of myn herte.   1.718–21

Like the pious hypocrite, however, Amans engages in humble love-service to the sole end of winning profit in "worldes cause." By extension, he turns the psychology of reform upside-down, finding in the language of the confessional new devices for expressing, indeed justifying his passion.

Accordingly, he transforms the next species of pride, disobedience, into a virtue. He could "grucche" over his lady's "hevy chiere," he reports, but he dares not speak words "Wherof sche myhte be desplesed" (1.1387). Thus, he confesses, "thogh I make no semblant, / Min herte is al desobeissant" (1.1391–92). His lady bids him to be silent, that "I scholde hir noght oppose / In love" (1.1276–77), but he disobeys her: "Ayein hir will yit mot I bowe, / To seche if that I myhte have grace" (1.1284–85). In his perspective, however, this action constitutes a deeper obedience to Love, and in it "is no pride" (1.1305). Amans also refuses to obey his lady's command "To leven hire and chese a newe" (1.1311). She has argued

> if I the sothe knewe
> How ferr I stonde from hir grace,
> I scholde love in other place.   1.1312–14

It may well also be a claim of humble devotion that the lover, as he puts it, "moste hire loven til I deie" (1.1333). Once again his disobedience exemplifies a "higher" obedience.

Initially Genius seems to agree, telling the lover "That thou to loves heste obeie / Als ferr as thou it myht suffise" (1.1398–99). In the course of his next exemplum, regarding the "trouthe" of the knight Florent, however, he begins to show the willfulness in Amans's obedience. In its extreme form, this vice is represented in Murmur and Compleignte, figures who curse all fortune, "thogh thei have / Of love al that thei wolde crave" (1.1361–62). In their perspective, no situation is good, and choice is meaningless.

Genius's story of Florent is about choices, and in that regard it differs significantly from its well-known analogue, Chaucer's *Wife of Bath's Tale*. The "lusty bacheler" in the latter narrative is bound to the court that judges him, and once he meets the crone, he is never allowed to venture out of her sight. He has no choice but to learn from women what women most desire. There lies reason enough for his forced education in his crime, of course, a rape that is not represented in Chaucer's analogues; similarly, the two digressions – the "wrong" answers to the riddle (or the catalogue of women's other desires) and the bedroom lecture – are unique to Chaucer. These various elements contribute to a sense of necessary bondage: the "lusty bacheler" will not be free until he understands what he has done and must do. As a consequence, however, he almost becomes a non-character, a *passio* who must suffer his education, who is left virtually no choice, and who is allowed to complain only enough to render his conversion, or illumination, meaningful. The unusually masterful "clerk" who has organized his story makes it entirely certain that he will submit to a rhetoric that he will never again be allowed to forget.

Gower's story is very different. Like two of its analogues where Gawain is tested,[12] it shows a character who, in adversity, must exercise a freedom to make very difficult choices. Florent learns without a teacher – he is a character often left to himself – and because escape from his various captors is also possible, he can be seriously tested in his "trouthe" to moral principle. The poet relaxes the "controls" on Florent, but orders his freedom to elicit a comment on inflexible Inobedience, who "wol noght bowe er that he breke" (1.1248). Florent respects his oaths, and yet it is important to this tale that he be a character who also knows how to "caste his avantage" (1.1575).

When the crone gives him the choice "Or forto take hire to his wife / Or elles forto lese his life" (1.1573–74), Florent, on reflection, decides that her "lack" promises good: she is so old that "sche mai live bot a while" (1.1577), and he might even "put hire in an Ile, / Wher that noman hire scholde knowe, / Til sche with deth were overthrowe" (1.1578–80). Later, when he returns to her after being freed by his distant captors and sees her, the "lothlieste what" (1.1676), in a most consequential light, his heart nearly breaks "For sorwe that he may noght fle" (1.1701). But he will not be untrue; "for pure gentilesse" (1.1721) he places the vekke on his horse and leads her home to court.

Again, though Florent is never witless, he still has much to learn. A "gentil" opportunist, he takes her home "prively," and at court secretly tries to prettify her, only to find that "Tho was sche foulere on to se" (1.1759); finally he weds her "in the nyht" (1.1761). He undergoes his greatest test when, after the wedding, she "began to pleie and rage" (1.1764) and call upon him, her "worldes blisse" (1.1771), to respect the "strengthe of matrimoine (1.1777). This scene, unlike the comparable one in the *Wife of Bath's Tale*, takes place entirely in a chamber full of light, and central to it is a shock of visual dislocation. Florent stores one image of his new spouse in memory as, in bed, he turns on his other side to avoid looking at her. She insists that he turn back, however, and

---

12 *The Marriage of Sir Gawaine* and *The Weddynge of Sir Gawen and Dame Ragnell*, ed. Bartlett J. Whiting, in *Sources and Analogues of Chaucer's Canterbury Tales*, ed. W. F. Bryan and Germaine Dempster (Chicago, 1941), pp. 235–64; for a helpful comparison of these two versions with those of Gower and Chaucer, see Theodore Silverstein, "The Wife of Bath and the Rhetoric of Enchantment: or How to Make a Hero See in the Dark," *Modern Philology* 58 (1961): 153–73.

he, as if in a trance, "torneth him al sodeinly" (1.1801) to discover a woman "the faireste of visage" that he has ever seen. This double image relates directly to the crone's question – whether he will have her fair "on nyht" or "upon daies lyht." The alternatives, though simpler than those proposed by the Wife of Bath, form the greatest possible dilemma for Florent, for by either choice he will deny half the will that makes him the character he is. If he chooses her beautiful at night, he rejects his great desire for "worldes fame"; if he chooses her fair in daylight, he denies his amorous and "lusti" nature. For the first time in his career, he is totally "uncertein." In that very unsureness, however, he discovers the virtue of obedience or "buxomnesse."

Indeed, what saves Florent is his submission, the recognition that another must be "soverein" of his love. And there is magic here: in the virtue lies the power to dispel the enchantment cast on this maiden-crone.[13] Such magic suggests, by extension, the nature of Gower's "ensamples" in one of their most cogent forms. Inside certain stories the poet delineates the breaking of a spell or an enchantment, not merely of a character who has been transformed physically, as in this case, but of a character who has succumbed to enchantment morally. Gradually building by narrative means a counterforce to the "corage" of that character, Gower points the tale at the moment of greatest conflict. The resolution, once this encounter has occurred, takes place swiftly, and it involves for the auditor, if not for the character, an unexpected insight, the solution of a riddle, question, problem, or *demande*. The dispelling is, in a sense, the narrative assertion of a virtue, and it thereby constitutes not only a freeing from bondage, sometimes from passion, but a conversion.

When Florent grants to the crone-maiden his "hole vois," he submits totally: "what as evere that ye seie, / Riht as ye wole so wol I" (1.1830–31). It is key to Florent's humility not merely that he relinquish choice, but that he also cancel his willful setting of terms; he has learned to accept the truth that beneath a surface confidence,

> evere stant a man in doute,
> Fortune stant no while stille,
> So hath ther noman al his wille.   P.562–64

Florent has denied his distinction as a potential lover and knight of great renown; he has learned that his earlier sense of his own difference is a false distinction.

By so affirming the virtue, Genius also appears to deny Amans's claim to

---

[13] This motif can be seen in other works, such as Sir John Mandeville's *Travels*: in the comic story of Hippocrates' daughter, the spell that turns the maiden into a dragon can be broken only by the knight who will kiss her and live: when this knight is found, he will inherit her father's lands. Clearly, the kiss is a test of fortitude, ultimately of the competency to rule (*Mandeville's Travels*, cap. 4, ed. M. C. Seymour [Oxford, 1967], pp. 15–18). To Florent, the kiss the crone proffers on her wedding night, "As sche a lusti Lady were" (1.1773), is only the start of a process that leads to a far greater proof of his fortitude: an acceptance of his own limitation.

difference, his prerogative as a lover. The priest has given Amans what he requested, advice "So that I may myn herte reule / In loves cause after the reule" (1.1341–42), but not in the form he expected. The "reule" requires obedience not to "loves heste," but to the beloved:

> Forthi, my Sone, if thou do ryht,
> Thou schalt unto thi love obeie,
> And folwe *hir* will be alle weie.   (emphasis added)
>   1.1862–64

Amans has missed the point; because of this exemplum, he argues,

> I schal evermo therfore
> Hierafterward myn observance
> To love and to *his* obeissance
> The betre kepe.   (emphasis added)
>   1.1868–70

To obey Love is to serve oneself; to obey the beloved is not. The tale proves the "shift" of allegiance from the god Love to the beloved as a humbling of oneself. Amans has not heard the tale; nor does he understand the distinction. In his habitually excessive self-love – in his enchantment – he is like the asp *in malo*, an obstinate man who has covered his ears.

The tale of Florent, then, exposes the pride inherent in a self-isolating sense of difference. The proud exemplar can best be understood by negation: one guilty of *surquiderie* or presumption, the third species of the vice, for example,

> wol noght knowe
> The trowthe til it overthrowe.
> Upon his fortune and his grace
> Comth 'Hadde I wist' fulofte aplace
> For he doth al his thing be gesse,
> And voideth alle sikernesse.   1.1885–90

Such a person, who depends entirely upon his own "conseil" and "wit," is at last driven only by guesses, by fortune. This is not merely the problem of "everi man" not knowing the "certein." It is once again the problem of Amans, who, though he asks for mercy from his lady, denies the help – the cure – offered to him, and so he takes to an exercise in self-isolation:

> Thurgh hope that was noght certein,
> Mi wenynge hath be set in vein
> To triste in thing that halp me noght,
> Bot onliche of my oughne thoght.   1.1945–48

About his uncertain hope – his fantasy – he admits, "Ful many a time I wene it soth, / Bot finali no spied it doth" (1.1955–56).

Genius reflects on this confession in a series of three tales, of Capaneus, the Trump of Death, and Narcissus. The tale of Capaneus sets the definition of *surquiderie* as an ultimate denial of "godd, which alle grace sendeth" (1.1903). The second of these stories is especially poignant in relation to Amans, however, because the context for its argument is the courtly "pleie" and "conversacion" to which the lover aspires. It depicts a king of Hungary who rides

> Out of the Cite forto pleie,
> With lordes and with gret nobleie
> Of lusti folk that were yonge:
> Wher some pleide and some songe.   1.2031–34

In this setting, the king is approached by two pilgrims "of so gret age, / That lich unto a dreie ymage / Thei weren pale and fade hewed" (1.2041–43), and he, to the shock of his court, leaps down from his carriage and embraces them. The murmur, "desdeign," and complaint on every side over this action "So to abesse his realte" forms the question or "probleme" of the narrative. Key to it is perception shaped in the setting of a courtly recreation (1.2081–90); this forms a gloss on Amans's confession and, metaphorically, his love.

The king's brother is most offended that the king should have hurt his name by showing such "simplesce" to "povere wrecche." The king, however, then puts his brother to a test: he has a "dredful" trumpet blown before his gate, as a judgment that he "his deth deserveth," and this has the desired effect. The brother, his wife, and five children appear in "smok and scherte" before the king, seeking his pardon, and he, amidst their "wepinge," then explains his two actions. On the one hand, the brother is a fool to "gon despuiled" because of the mere sound of a trumpet, or to be "in doute / Of deth, which stant under the lawe / Of man," when "man it mai withdrawe" (1.2222–24). On the other hand, the brother should not marvel at the king's action toward the pilgrims, when, as the king remarks,

> I behield tofore my sihte
> In hem that were of so gret age
> Min oghne deth thurgh here ymage,
> Which god hath set be lawe of kynde,
> Wherof I mai no bote finde.   1.2228–32

What starts out as a statement of the king's difference, his action contrary to the expectation of his court, turns out to be an affirmation of likeness, specifically in what all people necessarily share "be weie of kinde." This self-abasement alone can provide "sikernesse."

Although the priest here asserts a "truth" more confidently, the only response he gets from Amans is a reminder that "I am amorous" (1.2258) and a request for an example "in loves cause." Amans, in short, wants to cross back, figuratively, into the pleasance of the story: he wants a safe literature and recreation. The next exemplum, the story of Narcissus, provides what he wants, but it also highlights his problem, for this Narcissus, even as he enacts a courtly ritual, isolates himself. The "natural" setting of the "pleie" in both stories quickly becomes unnatural, a setting in which one forgets or rejects one's *kinde*. Initially, Narcissus thinks no woman "worthi to his liche," but when he sees "his visage" in the well, he, unlike his Ovidian counterpart, thinks this an image of a nymph, then a woman. As Winthrop Wetherbee has perceptively noted, this folly also represents the "birth of love,"[14] and in that sense, it represents to the priest a good. Narcissus' desire does "noght wel betide," however, for as "He wepth, he crith, he axeth grace" (1.2338) of what he takes to be the woman in the well, he gets no grace,

> So that ayein a Roche of Ston,
> As he that knew non other red,
> He smot himself til he was ded.   1.2340–42

This unexpected end is followed by an unexpected visitation of nymphs, who, "For pure pite," bury Narcissus, presumably as a lover, not as a lover of self. The priest as narrator and moralist is torn in his interpretation: the tale suggests, ever so subtly, that Narcissus' fate is partially undeserved, partially warranted. And thus flowers spring out of the sepulchre, but they bloom in winter, "which is contraire / To kynde, and so was the folie / Which fell of his Surquiderie" (1.2356–58).

In this story, Genius betrays his divided loyalties: neither side to the narrative – the moral concerning *surquiderie*, the good of a love that is incipiently *kinde* – can fully engage his attention. Nor does he consistently do better with Amans's internal "querele." He does not get Amans to recognize that he is guilty of Narcissus' sin, that in setting "his pris most hyhe" through foolish imagination, he is just as "bejaped" as Narcissus is.

The other side to Genius's inability to draw the lover out of this passion, or to articulate fully the ambivalence in his own thought, is that his stories often do more than he, as a reader of his own tales, recognizes. The power to counteract the inordinate self-esteem of a Narcissus, like the power that generates it, lies in the *jus naturae*, and often the priest conveys this not in his *moralitates*, but in his story-telling. Often his stories identify the problem of pride, or the solution, or both together, better than Genius as moralist knows.

The tale of Albinus and Rosemund, an exemplum of boasting, explores a sickness in pride that is far more serious than Genius's applied moral might suggest. After Albinus, king of Lombardie, overcomes Gurmond, the "myhti kyng" of the Geptes, he marries Gurmond's daughter, Rosemund:

> And after that long time in reste
> With hire he duelte, and to the beste
> Thei love ech other wonder wel.   1.2487–89

It does not take us long to discover that something is profoundly wrong with this relationship. Genius understands the problem in terms of Venus' wheel:

---

14 Wetherbee, "Genius and Interpretation," p. 247.

> Bot sche which kepth the blinde whel,
> Venus, whan thei be most above,
> In al the hoteste of here love,
> Hire whiel sche torneth, and thei felle.   1.2490–93

Albinus, at a feast to show Rosemund the lords "That were obeissant to his heste," offers her wine in a Cuppe which, she later learns, is the polished and decorated skull of her father. An enraged Rosemund hides her anger at this "unkynde Pride," then by a ruse sleeps with Helmege, the lover of her maid Glodeside. Helmege, in "wylde loves rage," subsequently falls "al hol to hire assent," and joins the conspiracy to kill Albinus. Thus, Genius remarks, "And thus the whiel is al miswent, / The which fortune hath upon honde" (1.2624–65). The references to Venus' "whel" and Fortune's "whiel" hardly explain the grotesqueness of this action: nor can they explain the tale's final outcome, where the conspirators flee to the Duke of Ravenna, who, "whan he herde telle" what they did, poisons them. As the wheels cannot explain the motive of an Albinus, they cannot explain this final turn in the action, which seems only to divert our attention from the sin of boasting, the supposed focal point of the tale.

Genius's moralization, after this ending, seems to touch only on the surface features of the action:

> In armes he that wol travaile
> Or elles loves grace atteigne,
> His lose tunge he mot restreigne,
> Which berth of his honour the keie.   1.2658–61

Genius here speaks in another of his voices, one advocating courtly, refined behavior, and the lover finds "This scole is of a gentil lore" (1.2665). Nevertheless, the priest's application misses the deeper sickness in the participants in this action, where love means sexual dominance, a power to manipulate, control, and destroy. The priest traces the entire action back to Albinus' boast as the cause of all that follows. The marginal commentator similarly narrows the application (at 1.2501): "huius tocius infortunii sola superbie iactancia fomitem ministrabat" 'proudful boasting alone has provided the tinder of this entire misfortune.' The issue of the narrative runs much deeper than a mere lack of verbal restraint. No amount of surface sensitivity to politeness or honor would save the characters: a horrible, self-isolating and self-destructive pride transforms them. The priest does not explore this underlying cause of the "tragedy" explicitly. His narrative does that work, in ways that neither he, nor the marginal glossator, does in his application.

The lover is not responsive to the narrative, but instead persists in his assumption that he is uniquely "worthi." When Genius asks him whether he has boasted of "loves yifte," a "goodly word," "frendly chiere or tokne or lettre" (1.2423), Amans complains that he cannot even boast of a "Griet him wel" from his lady; his only claim to recognition is that Danger has nearly killed him. Yet, though he thinks he "nedeth . . . no repentance" on this count, his repeated complaint about unjust treatment is a boast: he deserves favor, the full attention of his beloved, because his love-service is different.

One of the tacit forms of dialectic in the *Confessio*, which takes on its fullest meaning only at the end, is a conflict between this lover's actual self-perception and a needed recognition of the law by which nature makes all living creatures "liche." That law has been expressed in one form in the tale of the Trump of Death: that narrative, and now others, will reveal a truth that Amans learns late, when he discovers that old age is upon him, that death is near. That is a point about the lover we can only know in retrospect, of course. At this moment in the confession, the point is a universal: "be lawe of kynde," all must die.

Mortality is also at issue in Genius's treatment of the fourth species of pride, vainglory. One guilty of this sin delights in the newfangled: "if that he myhte make / His body newe, he wolde take / A newe forme and leve his olde" (1.2691–93). It is very difficult not to see a mirroring of *Amans senex* in this portrait. The personified "veine gloire" makes himself "jolif," "evere freissh and gay,"

> And ek he can carolles make,
> Rondeal, balade, and virelai.
> And with al this, if that he may
> Of love gete him avantage,
> Anon he wext of his corage
> So overglad, that of his ende
> Him thenkth ther is no deth comende.   1.2709–14

To be sure, Amans can never fully place himself in the status of one who "thenkth his joie is endeles" (1.2717), but he strives to achieve that goal when he "his olde guise change" (1.2696) to gain distinction. Thus, even in this confession, he becomes the chameleon who "moste newe / His colour" (1.2700–01), specifically as he describes his activity as a love-poet and suitor:

> And also I have ofte assaied
> Rondeal, balade and virelai
> For hire on whom myn herte lai
> To make, and also forto peinte
> Caroles with my wordes qweinte,
> To sette my pourpos alofte.   1.2726–31

This confession, rare in its reference to writing poetry, is made most significant by the lady's astute perception of Amans's purpose. About his poetic endeavor,

> Sche saide it was noght for hir sake,
> And liste noght my songes hiere
> Ne witen what the wordes were.   1.2740–42

The lady here implicitly judges Amans's self-indulgent pride: he writes only for himself. Despite the potential contribution of this insight to a treatise on pride, Genius does not expound it; indeed, without even alluding to it, he acquits the lover of vainglory.

In the narrative that follows, however, he responds better to the manifest wish of the proud to be different. This is a story "noght of loves kinde" (1.2781), and often in such stories Genius is better able to perceive what really troubles Amans. The tale recounts Nebuchadnezzar's dream of himself as a "hihe tree" felled, with a root that

> schal no mannes herte bere,
> Bot every lust he schal forbere
> Of man, and lich an Oxe his mete
> Of gras he schal pourchace.   1.2841–44.

This tale "points" a recognition by this god-like king that he too must die. Nebuchadnezzar, however, lacks the imagination of the protagonist of the Trump of Death, who quickly perceives his own death in the "ymage" of the aged pilgrims. The Hungarian king, with the sensitivity and imaginative judgment that originate in humility, knows, as does a character in a later story, that he cannot "eschuie that fortune / Which kinde hath in hire lawe set" (2.3250–51). Nebuchadnezzar, on the other hand, thinks there is "no deth comende" (1.2714). Having considered himself a god, he must learn that he is a man, but he lacks the imagination to assimilate the dream, or the rational judgment to understand Daniel's interpretation. He can only recover his humanity at a most basic level of sense-perception, by seeing himself living for a time in "bestes forme." Inside this narrative, Genius thus tells Nebuchadnezzar's story three times, advancing through dream, interpretation, and enactment to what constitutes the king's painful, yet saving, discovery. In near despair, Nebuchadnezzar prays to "mihti godd," in whose "aspect ben alle liche" (1.3009–10), for mercy, and he also makes a promise:

> I woll make a covenant,
> That of my lif the remenant
> I schal it be thi grace amende.   1.3015–17

Thence, "in a twinklinge of a lok" (1.3033), Nebuchadnezzar's recovers his "mannes forme,"

> So that the Pride of veine gloire
> Evere afterward out of memoire
> He let it passe.   1.3037–39

Gower will write more about that divine power "that al has wroght, / And al myht bringe ayein to noght" (1.3005–06) later in the confession, and the doctrine will have an important bearing on the conversion of Amans. That conversion involves a slow process of recognition, a sudden revelation, and a passing "out of memoire" of sinful love. The shorter tale thus sets a pattern. The confession effectively, yet inexplicitly builds to a change, one that also occurs in the "twinklinge of a lok": the lover sees his limitations "be weie of kinde," and he thereby discovers humility.

The story of Nebuchadnezzar, like others in this compilation on pride, centrally includes the posing of an enigma, question, or riddle. The story of Florent, whose life stands "in jeupartie" until he correctly answers the question posed by his captors, the story of the Trump of Death, and the tale of the Babylonian king all turn on major characters being forced to respond to a life-threatening question; their response is a discovery that one can stand secure only in "humblesce." The final story of Book 1 analogously focuses on a life-endangering riddle whose answer "points" the participants to the virtue.

The tale of the Three Questions initially centers on a king who sets "gret pris" on his wits:

> Of depe ymaginaciouns
> And strange interpretaciouns,
> Problemes and demandes eke.
> His wisdom was to finde and seke;
> Wherof he wolde in sondri wise
> Opposen hem that weren wise.   1.3069–74

This king, who "the name / And of wisdom the hihe fame / Toward himself . . . wolde winne" (1.3087–89), is vexed by a knight who answers all his questions correctly, and he "began to studie and muse" to develop three questions to "confounde" this opponent: if the knight should fail in his answers, "he schal be ded / And lese hise goodes and his hed" (1.3115–16).

The knight, though he is confounded by the questions, finds solace in his fourteen-year-old daughter, Peronelle, who, in a remarkably effective speech about trust, wins her father's confidence and persuades him to let her be the respondent to the king's questions. Effectively, she converts her father to humility. Many think it "folie" that he should place "His lif upon so yong a wyht" (1.3236), but the king accepts the decision and lets Peronelle proceed.

To the first question – "What thing in his degre / Of al this world hath nede lest, / And yet men helpe it althermest?" (1.3100–02) – the maiden answers, "Erthe"; although man works hard to cultivate it, earth is "most nedeles" because

> every thing be weie of kynde
> Schal sterve, and Erthe it schal become;
> As it was out of Erthe nome,
> It schal to therthe torne ayein.   1.3262–65

This familiar medieval teaching is a key point in nurturing humility, and no proud exemplar in Book 1 has recognized it. To the second question – "What most is worth, / And of costage is lest put forth?" (1.3103–04) – the maid responds, "Humilite," and in proving the point, she gives the example of the Incarnation (1.3275–82). This virtue costs least to maintain, "For he desireth for the beste / To setten every man in reste" (1.3289–90). To the third question

– "Which is of most cost, / And lest is worth and goth to lost?" (1.3105–06) –
the maid, as we now anticipate, answers, "Pride": by it Lucifer fell from heaven
and Adam lost Paradise, and it causes all woe in "Midelerthe" (1.3305).

These wise responses make the king "inly glad" and thereby "his wraththe is
overgo": indeed, he tells the maid he would marry her if she were of the right
lineage; she, who is allowed to ask for a gift in its stead, a gift of "worldes good,"
requests an Earldom for her father. When that gift is conferred, of course, she
can point out that she is "An Erles dowhter," and thence the king can take
"hire to his wif."

Wetherbee has seen in this conclusion, and especially in the king's "very
human love," a response to the instances of pride exemplified in Book 1. The
difficulty with the tale, however, is centering its meaning. Humility is "softe
and faire," (1.3415), and in his application Genius focuses on humble speech:

> If eny thing stond in contraire,
> With humble speche it is redresced:
> Thus was this yonge Maiden blessed,
> The which I spak of now tofore,
> Hire fader lif sche gat therfore,
> And wan with al the kinges love.   1.3416–21

That the priest should stress "humble speche" seems to miss the much deeper,
theological root of the virtue. One might explain this in part by his devotion to
gentilesse, in an aspect of that virtue we shall consider later. In the narrative,
however, Genius more fully represents "humblesce" in relationships – of
daughter to father, subject to king, and, in prospect, wife to husband. Central
to the *moralitas* inherent in these three instances, of course, is the figure of
Peronelle, who excels in humility, and who saves others by persuading them to
enact the virtue. The king's love becomes most "human" and good because
Peronelle effectively breaks his pride in rank, a habit that has dulled his
imagination, making it impossible for him to perceive what Peronelle so quickly sees.

The author of the Latin epigram that heads this section is, as always, concerned with issues, and he seems to understand the moral and theological
richness of the narrative:

> Est virtus humilis, per quam deus altus ad yma
>   Se tulit et nostre viscera carnis habet.
> Sic humilis superest, et amor sibi subditur omnis,
>   Cuius habet nulla sorte superbus opem:
> Odit eum terra, celum deiecit et ipsum,
>   Sedibus inferni statque receptus ibi.   1.12.1–6

> Through the virtue of humility, the high God descended to
> a lowly status and took on the body of our flesh. So the
> humble person is exalted, and every love is set under her,
> whose wealth the proud person in no part possesses; the

earth hates him, heaven rejects him, and, having been received in hell, he remains fixed there.

Wetherbee sees in the first two lines of this Latin poem a doctrine that raises the argument of Book 1 to a new level, and indeed they do. Once again, the Latin poet perceives more than the wise marginal commentator does; the latter merely summarizes the questions and Peronelle's responses, without responding to the human experience of the tale or to the divine mysteries expressed through it. To be sure, the glossator touches on the problem introduced in the last two lines of the Latin poem: "Et tamen nullius valoris, ymmo tocius perdicionis, causam sua culpa ministrat" 'The fault of a proud man serves a cause of no worth, but, on the contrary, of total perdition.' Genius is more explicit about the fate of Pride when he recapitulates the tale, even rendering at its end the Latin "Odit eum terra": "In hevene he fell out of his stede, / And Paradis him was forbede, / The goode men in Erthe him hate" (1.3407–09). What the marginal commentator and Genius as interpreter miss, but Peronelle expresses and the Latin poet celebrates is the most significant act of humblesce, the Incarnation, in which the "hihe trinite" sent "His oghne Sone adoun" (1.3280).

Of these readers, then, the Latin poet appears to come closest to recovering the full sense of Peronelle's responses, even in celebrating the paradox of humility: "Sic humilis superest." None of the three, however, can match Peronelle herself in the understanding of *humblesce*. Indeed, what can be credited to Genius as teller, but not to the writer of the epigram, is a narrative sense of enacted humility. The Latin poet's play on words in itself forms a riddle, another "loose category," to which the narrative about this fourteen-year-old gives particular form and substance.

The tale raises a larger question in its own attention to the king's three-part riddle. One can pose riddles for various reasons, of course: sometimes, as in the story of Peronelle, or in the last story of the *Confessio*, the tale of Apollonius, one might pose a question to exclude, overcome, or destroy an opponent: the king does so in the story of the Three Questions; Antiochus does so in the last tale. But this mode can be introduced to just the opposite end: through the testing of wits, to "save" the participant by making her or him wise. This, we shall discover, is what will happen in the last tale, as Apollonius' daughter, a character like Peronelle, poses *demandes* to cure her mentally deranged father. Analogously, Gower has one persona – Amans – experientially present the matter, and another – the wise Latin poet – formalize it through his academic perception: participation in wisdom lies not merely in the formalizing, but in bringing the intellectual and affective experiences together, indeed making them one: that oneness, we shall find, constitutes wisdom. Underlying the union is the mystery of the Incarnation, an act that is most fully understood by the humble Peronelle at this point in Gower's recitation, but which takes on additional experiential or instantiated meaning as the confession nears its end.

Key to the progress to that end is Genius, who articulates the human dimension in Amans's story, often better than Amans himself: if the posing of a riddle is in a sense the casting of a spell, an enchantment, Genius strives to explicate the riddle – to disenchant – by responding out of common human experience, and specifically out of principles of natural law.

To this point, the priest has been working with two of these principles, that the human being cannot evade love or escape death: awareness of one's mortality, however, would appear to undercut pride and thereby the excuse and prerogative that lovers seem inevitably to find in their loving. This conflict is far from settled, and it can be resolved only as Genius, in other tales, refines our sense of what natural law means. He does not do this in an expressly formal manner. It is not uncommon for medieval writers of distinctions to follow a "rational" order in arranging the meanings of their chosen terms. Such a plan emerges, for example, in the *Epytoma sapientie* of Hieremias de Montagnone, a work (ca. 1300) that has some bearing on the subject of Gower's poem, specifically when it evolves, in one of its books, a distinction "de amore venereo."[15] For this treatment of venerean love, Hieremias gathers quotations from a few biblical sources and many more secular authors, including Aristotle, Terence, Ovid, Horace, Statius, Virgil, Seneca, Cicero, and Pseudo-Quintilian. The contents of the book are arranged in such a way that the quotations first praise this love, then build to an attack on it; the last author quoted is a "modern," Andreas Capellanus: "sexual indulgence is a thing which defeats us if we follow it, but is routed by us if we flee from it."[16]

Genius has yet to prove that one can flee from a "compulsion." If Hieremias's strategy for rejecting venerean love is to follow a more or less explicit order in arranging his quotations, the priest in Gower's fiction cannot be trusted to arrange his materials so clearly, in part because he is working with multiple *distinctiones* and *ordinationes*. Sinning "quasi necessario" is only one concern that he addresses by means of his tenets of natural law. Stories in Books 2 and 3 will introduce others.

---

15 Hieremias de Montagnone, *Epytoma sapientie* or *Compendium moralium notabilium*, pars 4, lib. 5 (Venice, 1505), fols. 109v–114r. On Gower's use of a rationally ordered *distinctio* to organize another of his major poems, see my article, "John Gower's Vox Clamantis and the Medieval Idea of Place," *Studies in Philology* 84 (1987): 134–58.
16 Ibid., fols. 109v, 114r; Andreas Capellanus, *De amore* 3.51, ed. and trans. P. G. Walsh, *On Love* (London, 1982), p. 303.

Chapter Eight

CONSTANCE AND THE ARGUMENT *AD MOTUM*

Genius's uses of conventional modes of the *forma tractandi* – definition, proof and refutation, division, and the positing of examples[1] – are chiefly tied to his topics of the "vices dedly." These topics, as divided and defined, obviously influence the selection and reforming of particulars for the tales Genius retells. Invariably, however, a choice about what to draw into a given narrative involves the contingent, since, as Aegidius Romanus points out, "moral dede fayleþ nouȝt complet þat is to saye fullich vnder tales";[2] no exemplary narrative can possibly represent the full complexity of a moral choice or action.[3] The same point might also be made the other way around: Genius's stories, even as recounted, do not always fit neatly into the moral topics designed to contain them, sometimes because the particulars of an original tale resist ordering, sometimes because Genius is not guided by his announced topic, but by some other, competing structure of thought, and sometimes because he shifts the argument on a given topic to a related, but not explicitly identified concern.

He follows this last course in his tale of Constance, a familiar medieval narrative here retold as an exemplum against detraction, a species of Envie. This moral ordering of the narrative makes it unique among its analogues. Genius's story has none of the rhetorical pomp of the better-known tale of Chaucer's "war and wys" Man of Law: it lacks the many apostrophes, prayers, Biblical allusions, crowd scenes, passionate speeches, rhetorical questions, and other devices used hyperbolically to bring tears for the heroine – for her woe and joy – and for the marvelous beneficence of God. The Man of Law impresses us with Custance's religious devotion, "humblesse," and "curteisye," as well as the goodness of a God who fortifies, protects, and repeatedly and wondrously

---

[1] J. B. Allen, *Ethical Poetic*, p. 68. As important as the *forma tractatus* is in providing a basis of knowledge, as well as a structure, for Gower's work, the *forma tractandi* is ultimately more important, for it is through this, as a manner of thought, that the moral argument of the poem is conducted. In various modes, it provides the imaginative opening on experience that Gower seeks for his readers. The list of five modes is by no means exhaustive. Minnis introduces other medieval possibilities in his discussion of the *forma tractandi* or, in alternative terms, the *modus tractandi, modus agendi,* or *modus procedendi,* in "Compilatio," p. 391 and n. 23; see also Minnis, "Authorial Role, pp. 41, 52–64.

[2] Childs, p. 192; "gesta moralia complete sub narratione non cadunt" (*De regimine principum* 1.1.1, p. 2).

[3] Runacres, p. 126.

saves her from extreme adversity. This story, grounded in analogies taken from Scripture, provides a memorial to God's acts of saving love; as an exercise in the "heigh style," it is designed to move the *affectus*, inspire religious awe, and nurture faith.

Genius's tale, by contrast, is plainly told, and that feature of the narrative has repeatedly attracted readers whose principal goal is to prove by the contrast something about Chaucer's singular verbal dexterity. Unfortunately, such comparisons rarely explore the suitability of style to narrative purpose. These versions of Constance's story are separated by a genre difference whose terms are effectively laid out in a passage late in the *Confessio*, where Gower describes the rhetorical procedures displayed on either side of the debate over Catiline's conspiracy. The issue there is "hou and in what wise / Men scholde don hem to juise" (7.1605–06). On the one side

> Cillenus ferst his tale tolde,
> To trouthe and as he was beholde,
> The comun profit forto save,
> He seide hou tresoun scholde have
> A cruel deth.   7.1607–11

Cato and "Cithero" take Silanus' side, but Julius Caesar

>   with wordes wise
> His tale tolde al otherwise,
> Er he which wolde her deth respite,
> And fondeth hou he mihte excite
> The jugges thurgh his eloquence
> Fro deth to torne the sentence
> And sette here hertes to pite.   7.1615–21

The distinction between the two rhetorical modes is then amplified:

> Thei spieken plein after the lawe,
> Bot he the wordes of his sawe
> Coloureth in an other weie
> Spekende.   7.1623–25

One may be tempted, in a modern idiom, to take sides in this distinction, to assume that there is something wrong in plain speech, something right in speech rhetorically charged: "the former is limited in appeal, the latter rouses its hearers in enthusiastic support of the speaker; the former [is] spoken against the reputation of a man in defeat, the latter in its favour."[4] Gower is more neutral. He is perfectly capable of emotional appeal when the occasion warrants it, but in the tale of Constance he prefers to take another course. Where-

---

[4] M. A. Manzalaoui, " 'Noght in the Registre of Venus': Gower's English Mirror for Princes," in *Medieval Studies for J. A. W. Bennett*, ed. P. L. Heyworth (Oxford, 1981), p. 182.

as the Man of Law, in his version of the story, strives to win the benevolence of his judges, Gower chooses not to set "hertes to pite," or to excite, but to speak "plein after the lawe" to the end of serving the "comun profit."

In presenting the two rhetorical styles, Gower finally argues that a speaker, in whatever mode he chooses, must set

> His Argument in such a forme,
> Which mai the pleine trouthe enforme
> And the soubtil cautele abate,
> Which every trewman schal debate.   7.1637–40

The Man of Law's version of Constance's story, on the one hand, does not seem subtle at all, and yet Chaucer raises a doubt about the telling through his revelations about the speaker elsewhere in the *Tales*: it is possible that the Man of Law, by a subtle trick, manipulates details in the story merely to serve his own rhetorical centeredness. Gower's tale, on the other hand, appears to inform the "pleine trouthe": though we also have good reason to doubt his teller, the story involves no "cautele" that would turn the issue into one centrally involving Genius himself. The subtlety of this version is lodged in the relationship between the narrative and its topic, the issue of detraction.

Amans is a detractor who, in using "false wordes" to turn "preisinge" and "worschipe" into blame (2.405–08), deludes himself. Motivated by a desire to triumph over the "yonge lusty route" of suitors who court his mistress, he convinces himself that his lady is an innocent beset by those who wish to deceive her: "And ech of hem his tale affaiteth, / Al to deceive an innocent" (2.464–65). Amans's self-assigned task is to protect his mistress from this "route":

> And evere I am adrad of guile,
> In aunter if with eny wyle
> Thei mihte hire innocence enchaunte.   2.479–81

In speaking against detractors, the lover acts for her good, but ironically, his own speech, as he colors "the wordes of his sawe," includes the deceit and enchantment he fears his lady is subjected to by others. It is also ironical that he should practice such blandishment, for he recognizes that the lady is a knowing person and not a mere innocent, and that she does not really need his protection:

> Sche lieveth noght al that sche hiereth,
> And thus fulofte hirself sche skiereth
> And is al war of 'hadde I wist.'   2.471–73

Clearly, the victim of Amans's enchantment is Amans himself, and this is all the more evident as he persists in creating an environment of distrust:

> So fayn I wolde that sche wiste
> How litel thei ben forto triste,

> And what thei wolde and what thei mente,
> So as thei be of double entente.   2.491–94

The final irony is that while Amans is preoccupied with winning the love of his lady, in his delusion about how to achieve the victory, he assures his isolation and rejection. He states his goal simply:

> For al this world I myhte noght
> To soffre an othre fully winne,
> Ther as I am yit to beginne.   2.510–12

By his detraction, he ensures that he will never begin: his intelligent and wary mistress cannot be won by enchantment.

Genius's argument is thus directed to a lover who wishes to enchant, protect, and thereby win an "innocent" beloved. His end in the tale of Constance is therefore not merely to indict detraction, but to celebrate a power that dispels its enchantment. Certain elements of this presentation also appear in the Man of Law's performance. The pilgrim's tale is of protected innocence; his end, however, is to enchant, though supposedly to good purpose. God guards Custance, and so too does the Man of Law protect her in his idiom of figured speech. As if to help Custance escape the pagan admiral's steward, for example, this teller prays for divine assistance: "Almyghty God, that saveth al man-kynde, / Have on Custance and on hir child som mynde" (*MLT* 907–08). While he magnifies the threat of the approaching villain "that hadde reneyed oure creance"(915) and the woe of this "wrecched" woman – "Hir child cride, and she cride pitously" (919) – he does so to stress great acts of saving intervention: "But blisful Marie heelp hire right anon" (920). After the steward drowns, the Man of Law explores the fuller implication of the scene through apostrophes – "O foule lust of luxurie, lo, thyn ende!" (925), including rhetorical questions: "O Golias, unmesurable of lengthe, / Hou myghte David make thee so maat" (934–35), and "Who yaf Judith corage or hardynesse / To sleen hym Olofernus in his tente" (939–40)? The teller thus creates around his central figure a ring of protective, talismanic texts, and by means of such narrative and rhetorical prompts, he draws his audience into that ring of protection.

In Gower's much simpler version of the incident, Constance is self-possessed. Seeing "ther was non other weie," she has the knight look out to sea to make sure they are alone, and by this ruse she gains time to pray:

> Sche preide god, and he hire herde,
> And sodeinliche he was out throwe
> And dreynt, and tho began to blowe
> A wynd menable fro the lond,
> And thus the myhti goddes hond
> Hire hath conveied and defended.   2.1120–25

Constance's being saved is not her own doing, of course, but the focus in Gower's narrative, nonetheless, is on her capacity to act: she is a wise and wary, a quick-witted and decisive person. Unlike the Custance of the Man of Law, she never cries "pitously" or thinks herself "wrecched," but displays a quiet confidence throughout.

This difference is apparent from the very outset of each narrative. Both figures are subjected to an arranged marriage. In the Man of Law's version, the merchants come to Rome and hear reports of her excellence. Having seen her, they return to Surrye, tell the Sultan, and he, to marry her, forsakes his pagan religion. In the marriage arrangement, the Man of Law sees the uncertain and forbidding, and Custance herself, though she accedes to the arrangement, is nonetheless deeply pained by what it implies: "Custance, that was with sorwe al overcome, / Ful pale arist, and dresseth hire to wende" (MLT 264–65). It is no wonder she weeps, the teller remarks, at being sent to a strange nation, subjected to one whose condition she does not know. Custance, in her self-perception a "wrecched child" and a wretched woman, is sent away, never to see her parents again. In her response to adversity, Custance frequently conveys a sense of "hadde I wist," and even more, of having been betrayed. Even at the end of the narrative, her reunion with Alla is clouded by "bitter peyne," a sense of his betrayal: "So was hir herte shet in hir distresse" (1056).

In Gower's tale, as based upon Trivet, Constance does not hold the visiting merchants in awe or fear: she conducts business with them and "worthili of hem sche boghte" (2.604). Indeed, she converts them, "So that baptesme thei receiven / And alle here false goddes weyven" (2.609–10). Ultimately, the wedding is arranged, Constance travels to Barbarie, and soon after her arrival attends the fatal banquet. In this presentation there are no narrative delays, few emotional appeals. The strangeness of the experience and the "unlikeness" of the Syrians initially make no difference to her. Genius conveys in her no mood of being wretched, no fear of the unknown. Undoubtedly, he shows that Constance is capable of feeling, as when, at the slaughter in Persia, she "Stod thanne, as who seith, ded for feere" (2.696), but Genius does not dwell on such scenes; he moves her – and his narrative – along. Quickly he has Constance put in her rudderless boat, and then shows her, with little narrative transition, arriving in Northumberlond. Constance is an agent, secure in herself and her faith. There is in her little tendency to the *passio*, the suffering, that so dominates the career of the Man of Law's Custance. Constance's security lies in her naturalness. Her eyes are always open, and her tale never betrays in her an attitude of "hadde I wiste." When, near the end of the narrative, she learns of Allee's presence in Rome, she swoons, but "For joie which fell in hire thoght" (2.1353).

The Man of Law's Custance, as Joseph Grennen has shown, is "the very embodiment of the virtue of *constantia*, a virtue she is given innumerable opportunities to demonstrate precisely because of the failure of human legal structures to protect her."[5] In that virtue, Custance is a "surrogate for *Justitia*

---

[5]   Joseph E. Grennen, "Chaucer's Man of Law and the Constancy of Justice," *Journal of English and Germanic Philology*, 84 (1985): 498.

herself," and the tale reveals, in the teller who celebrates her, a person who "can, when the circumstances of pilgrimage ignite his vision, glimpse the transcendent form of the Law behind the phenomena."[6] The Man of Law's style of enchantment, itself grounded in a legitimate affective theology, works to support that vision.

To be sure, this pilgrim betrays, in other activity described by Chaucer, a cynical "double entente" that cannot be equated with a wise *contemptus mundi*. He tends to make snap judgments: as all is a matter of "fee symple" to him, so he is bold in categorizing, quick to fit characters into classes of good and evil. He glimpses a divine Justice, perhaps, but his narrative is also built upon earth-bound excitement, surprise, violation of expectation, betrayal, and suspicion. As the Man of Law inspires a wariness of those whom "litel . . . ben forto triste," so we cannot trust him. He is inculpated in the "human legal structures" he criticizes, and his presence in the telling may distance the reader from the very faith and trust the story is designed to strengthen. The wonder of his story, however, is that its teaching is not thereby compromised; it may even be strengthened because the Man of Law is drawn into its fiction, proving its "truth" even by negation. His own case confirms that one can achieve security only in God, or in that divine justice that the tale imposes on experience.

Gower's tale is less vertical in orientation. Seeking to articulate a law present in human experience rather than one imposed upon it, his teller stresses the interaction and "entencion" of his characters. By drawing the action down to earth, even while he also remarks on God's needed intervention, Gower rehistoricizes the tale, in a special sense speaking "as the Cronique seith" (2.596). Unlike the Man of Law, who responds to human weakness by pointing to a transcendent justice, Genius, as befits his character, hopes to find a goodness and strength in *kinde*. His outlook is less cynical, more natural, perhaps more innocent; ultimately he celebrates a group of people drawn together in trust and "the wel meninge of love" (2.1599). A bond, openly realized as an inclination to trust others, unites the Romans and the converts, including the merchants of Barbarie, the Souldan, Elda and Hermyngheld, Allee and his kingdom. Surely, this natural love is validated by "Cristes feith," but the emphases, nevertheless, have here shifted from the supernatural, which in different senses dominates Trivet's and Chaucer's versions of the story, to the natural.

Centrally, this sense of the natural informs Genius's response to detraction. The plots of the envious, and especially of the mothers, clearly represent violations of *kinde*. The Sultaness, fearful that "myn astat schal so be lassed"

---

[6] Ibid., pp. 510–11, 514. The argument concerning Custance is supported by conventional medieval definitions of justice that Grennen draws from the *Dictionarium* of Albericus de Rosate (d. 1354): perhaps the most familiar and relevant of these is that "Iustitia est constans et perpetua voluntas ius suum unicuique tribuens" (s.v. "justicia").

(2.649), offers her enchantment, claiming to her son that marrying the Emperor's daughter will be "gret honour" and that taking a "newe feith" will serve his advancement: this sets up her most unnatural act, killing a son, rather than by the instinct of *kinde* sustaining and protecting him or advancing his interests. Domilde seems to be motivated similarly: she, like the Envie Genius describes, "forto be preferred / Hath conscience so differred" (2.3073–74). Incapable of natural love, she concerns herself entirely with her loss of status, preferment, advancement, possession. This does not explain the degree of her hatred of Constance, but Genius hints at that later when he describes Envie as the "werste vice of alle," having the "most malice" (2.3130–31); it can come only "out of helle" (2.3135). Domilde is, we might note, a "beste of helle" in the later judgment of Allee. While she falls outside nature in her ruse, in charging others with being unnatural – Constance is "faie," the child is a monster – she also, in a deeper sense, exemplifies this vice that "hath kinde put aweie" (2.3140).

Those who read Domilde's second message must set Constance adrift in her boat, and the horror they feel is described by an analogy in *kinde*:

> So gret a sorwe thei beginne,
> As thei here oghne Moder sihen
> Brent in a fyr before here yhen.   2.1046–48

Later Domilde is brought to judgment. Allee has a fire made "And bad men forto caste hire inne" (2.1287), and thus she is "brent tofore hire Sones yhe" (2.1293). This terrible justice of course represents an experience beyond nature, but the mother in Domilde is unrecognizable, and those who witness her death "Sein that the juggement is good" (2.1296).

The distinction of the morally righteous in this tale is that they know what to believe; as guided by *kinde*, they are not unduly susceptible to words of enchantment. Allee does not succumb to his mother's deceit, Elda does not give "ful credence" to the false knight's story, and, throughout, Constance in her quiet confidence loses none of her trust in human nature or her faith.

Genius needs no hyperbole to celebrate this kindness: as centered in the mutual attraction and union of characters who manifest "trewe hertes and . . . plein" (P.184), his subdued style is appropriate to that naturalness. Surely the Man of Law also knows what it means "to speke al playn" (*MLT* 219), especially in a judicial setting.[7] When the "privee conseil" of the Sultan argue over the proposed marriage, they see the "difficultee / Be wey of reson, for to speke al playn, / By cause that ther was swich diversitee / Bitwene hir bothe lawes" (*MLT* 218–21), the laws of Christ and Mohammed. While it is the case that the larger argument of the *Confessio* introduces an analogous difficulty in plain speaking because of the diversity of laws espoused by Genius, in this narrative of Constance, the priest most fittingly speaks "al playn": his style suits the *leges* he most wishes to inculcate.

---

[7]   See Grennen, p. 499, for a helpful quotation from Albericus, s.v. "De plano."

Given the rhetorical expansion of Chaucer's version of the story, one might expect it to be a longer tale than Gower's, but it is not. The two tales are almost identical in length, and Gower has made up the difference in the ending, where he roughly doubles the number of Chaucer's lines. Genius here develops the "natural" reunions in Rome, after Constance has been saved from the sea by the Senator Arcennus; these scenes do not contain the sort of spectacle that interests the Man of Law, but to Genius, they are critical. In the feasts and rituals of recognition, culminating in the union of the daughter Constance with her father, the priest once again celebrates the natural.

In that reunion especially, he sees wonder and, to a certain extent, the enchantment of the natural. Constance, "Upon a Mule whyt amblaunt," meets her father as he returns to Rome, and the father responds naturally, yet with sheer awe at the event: "For thogh his Moder were come / Fro deth to lyve out of the grave, / He mihte nomor wonder have" (2.1524–26). The tale thus begins and ends in *kinde*, in the natural bond of parent and child. Whereas the Man of Law in his narrative raises the prospect of "a father misusing his *potestas* over his daughter,"[8] Genius in his narrative does not. Neither teller, to be sure, goes so far as tradition permits, where, in one variant of this tale, the father exerts his power in the extreme, in an incestuous desire to wed the daughter. Genius, however, does not hint at the father's abuse of *potestas* in any respect whatsoever. His tale, in its ending, attends to a natural and ordered love of a father for his daughter and, even more, of a daughter for her father: this relationship forms the basis for a virtuous *amor naturalis proximi*.

In the represented action, all of the characters except Moris are eventually overcome by the "deth of kinde"; God, releasing Constance "fro this worldes faierie / Hath take hire into compaignie" (2.1593–94), and Moris is left to rule in "Cristes feith," the "cristeneste of alle" (2.1598). The wonder of this version of the story rests not on its tenets of faith alone, but on a love that includes the natural and excludes the unnatural. The isolated and rejected enchanters fade into insignificance, and the narrative fosters such responses as Allee's, for example, when he "loveth kindely" (2.1381) a child he does not yet know to be his son, while it also rejects the mothers who act against their children in murderous hatred and "bacbitinge." By the end of the narrative, the envious have been turned aside, and the good characters stand together: this involves a union of like, not only those related by blood, but all characters who are joined in nature and its virtues: "There is a law rooted in nature. . . . a certain innate force has implanted it, [and it finds expression in such things] as religion, duty, gratitude, revenge, reverence, and truthfulness."[9]

---

8 Grennen, p. 513.

9 Augustine, *De diversis quaestionibus octoginta tribus* 33.1, trans. David L. Mosher, *Eighty-Three Different Questions*, FC 70 (Washington, D.C., 1982), p. 58; ". . . religionem, pietatem, gratiam, vindicationem, observantiam, veritatem" (*PL* 40:20). This catalogue of "natural" virtues is derived from Cicero, *De inventione* 2.53.159–55.167, and it is repeated, for example, by Papias, *Vocabulista* (Venice, 1496; rpt. Turin, 1966), s.v. "ius," p. 168.

From this tale, Amans might certainly learn that he cannot hope to succeed with his "innocent" by means of detraction. Presumably, his fond desire and Constance's love grow out of common stock, and yet there is an obvious difference between them. Human kindness – restored by and grounded in "Cristes feith" – lifts a person above the affliction of Fortune; Constance undergoes great adversity, yet all the while, for her nature, she remains basically unaffected by it; in her naturalness, she is not susceptible to enchantment. A "quieter" exemplar than Custance, she faces misfortune with a perspective always reasonable, calm, and "honeste," and the very calmness of her love suggests, in the mirroring, that something is very basically wrong with Amans's expression of *kinde* and his perception of "trust" in his beloved: over his protestation of her knowingness, he simply does not trust her; indeed, he does not understand trust itself. Thus, maddened by his fortune, he enters a universe where he, enchanted, becomes an enchanter, one who freely colors "the wordes of his sawe."

The tale of Constance provides a useful example of Genius's procedure of displaying, even magnifying a virtue while he more explicitly presents his case against a particular vice. To be sure, the tale follows an expressed *distinctio*, the plan to present a normative array of vices,[10] and its formal sign-posts guide us only to its message about detraction. Genius is concerned entirely with the vice when he sets up the narrative, and the writer of the marginal Latin glosses follows in kind by "inventing" a tale that fits the initial definition and indictment of the vice in the English text. At 2.606, the commentator even accentuates the effect of such detraction on Constance, who "absque sui culpa dolorosa fata multipliciter passa est" 'abundantly suffered painful calamaties, without blame to herself.'

By this statement, however, the glossator gets farther away from the actual text, and effectively closer to the *Man of Law's Tale*. Genius as a teller is less interested in the dolorous fate suffered by a blameless Constance than in her virtue and ending, a love "ate laste set above" (2.1600). Once again, the author of the Latin epigrams seems to understand more than does the writer of the glosses. After describing *detraccio*, he concludes his opening statement with a telling comment:

> Set generosus amor linguam conseruat, vt eius
>   Verbum quod loquitur nulla sinistra gerat.   2.3.7–8
>
> But gentle love holds the tongue, so that the words it speaks
> convey nothing sinister.

This is, of course, to define the vice by contrast. But the story itself also represents the contrast and explores the concept of *generosus amor*. Genius not only shows the sad end of one who practices detraction, but impresses on

---

10 See Allen, *Ethical Poetic*, p. 142.

memory images of a good that heals division and makes an individual or community whole. *Generosus amor*, related to the "gentil love" and "gentilesse" later discussed in the English text, originates in a nature shared, in premises of the *jus naturae*, and it is thereby linked to the argument of other stories which, in similar fashion, do not neatly fit into Gower's announced topics. This love is made possible by a Nature who

> preferreth no degre
> As in the disposicioun
> Of bodili complexioun
> And ek of Soule resonable
> The povere child is bore als able
> To vertu as the kinges Sone.   2.3254–59

Nature unites the members of a species and enfranchises them through their very likeness; she encourages mutual protection, condemns acts of treachery, and promotes "felaschipe." Genius evolves a doctrine regarding nature through a *forma tractandi* distinct from that in which he explains the vices.

In the setting of explaining the vices, the poet generates for his stories a rhetoric that is "explicitly deductive": it is designed to "confirm and qualify the initial premises of the given plot by revealing their consequences in episode, speech, and character."[11] To follow a Ciceronian distinction, this represents one of two basic modes of proof used by the poet in the *Confessio*. It "aims directly at convincing (*ad fidem*)."[12] In presenting a story to prove what often happens to a given kind of sinner, Genius "begins with a stated proposition to be proved, establishes premises from which arguments in support of the proposition logically follow, and concludes when the proposition may be restated as a conclusion."[13] This, in essence, is the story also "told" by the Latin commentator.

The second mode of proof "devotes itself to exciting feeling (*ad motum*)."[14] In the tale of Constance, Genius uses this mode as well, but not in the sense in which the Man of Law can be said to use it. This method,

> withholding the proposition to be proved, discovers the premises necessary to produce it, confirms them, and finally supplies the proposition . . . which was initially withheld. . . . The unstated proposition is reached in such a way that at the time of its first explicit mention, it is already (emotionally) accepted as a conclusion.[15]

---

11 Trimpi, "Quality of Fiction," p. 54.
12 Cicero, *De partitione oratoria* 13.46, trans. Trimpi, p. 55.
13 Trimpi, *loc. cit.*
14 Cicero, *loc. cit.*
15 Trimpi, p. 56.

By an indirect method – effectively, an insinuation – the priest "discovers the premises necessary to prove" the withheld proposition, a statement concerning a nature shared and love "ate laste set above."

In this context, the plain style generates its own enchantment, one singularly unlike that perpetrated by Amans or, in another context, by the Man of Law. Whereas Amans hopes to disenchant his beloved innocent, only to re-enchant her, to get her to serve his fantasy, Genius disenchants and re-enchants in just the opposite way: his plain style cuts through detraction, but at the same time, it quietly and subtly builds a case in defense of the *jus naturae*. This larger argument is conducted over the whole of Book 2.

It is one of Gower's premises in the *Confessio* that every nature loves its own kind, and his strategy is to shift the gaze of his readers to what it loves, generating in them a surprise, delight, and pleasure in perceiving a "truth" as represented in their like. The large task he envisions for memory is to recover a "true" image of oneself, and he cannot foster that recovery if he limits his argument to treating an array of vices alone. At the same time, he has obviously chosen not to make the poem a book of virtues, and the reason lies partly in the *forma tractandi* directed *ad motum*. No doubt it is good to love chastely, but to know that truth and to live it are very different things. By an indirect method, an insinuation, he generates emotional appeals designed to attract readers to virtue and the "honeste" life. These appeals, not merely in Book 2, but in each of the first three books, are drawn to a conclusion in the "proposition" of the final narrative. Each of these three tales celebrates a virtue: the *forma tractatus* is such that the first truly explicit mention – and narrative proof – of the "unstated" proposition occurs in that final tale.

We have already considered one instance of this, the story of the Three Questions. Of the remaining two, the one that concludes Book 2 merits special consideration. It concerns

>   Charite,
>   Which is the Moder of Pite,
>   That makth a mannes herte tendre,
>   That it mai no malice engendre
>   In him that is enclin therto.   2.3173–77

Genius's exemplar of one whose heart is made "tendre" is the emperor Constantine. In the narrative, Constantine, suffering from leprosy, is forced to remain "in his chambre clos" until a convocation of great "clerkes" prescribe the horrible treatment of bathing him "in childes blod" (2.3206). Genius never reaches to the strictly emotional appeal of the kind generated by the Man of Law, but here he shows the effect of the edict to gather "yonge children" for the slaughter:

>   The Modres wepe in here degre,
>   And manye of hem aswoune falle,
>   The yonge babes criden alle.   2.3236–38

As if "abreide / Out of his slep" (2.3241–42) by this commotion, the emperor reflects on his status and his relationship to those he is about to sacrifice. The subject of that reflection is central to Genius's treatment of the *jus naturae* in the early books. Recognizing that divine "pourveance" has formed "every man in the balance / Of kinde . . . to be liche" (2.3244–45), Constantine

> tok a remembrance
> How he that made lawe of kinde
> Wolde every man to lawe binde,
> And bad a man, such as he wolde
> Toward himself, riht such he scholde
> Toward an other don also.   2.3274–79

This teaching is derived from the famous definition of the *jus naturae* in Gratian's *Decretum*.[16] Constantine, however, utters and then enacts this teaching "naturally" and not because he has read it, following Gratian's terms, "in lege et Evangelio."[17] Seeing the "grete mone" of the mothers and the woe of the children, he asks whether "so mochel mannes blod / [should] Be spilt for cause of him alone (2.3284–85). As a result,

> al his herte tendreth
> And such pite withinne engendreth,
> That him was levere forto chese
> His oghne bodi forto lese,
> Than se so gret a moerdre wroght
> Upon the blod which gulteth noght.   2.3289–94

In the *Legenda aurea*, Constantine rejects cruelty (*crudelitas*) in favor of *pietas* because he recognizes the latter as the source of the worthiness (*dignitas*) of the Roman people.[18] Whereas Gower fully develops a comparable distinction between "crualte" and "pite" in Book 7, here he is more concerned to expound the connection of the "herte tendre," "pite," charity, and "kinde" as the forces that make cruel "moerdre" unthinkable. What was only implicit in the tale of Constance – or emergent only in the actions and relationships of characters in that exemplum – now becomes explicit doctrine concerning the "lawe of kinde."

---

[16] "Jus naturae est quod in lege et Evangelio continetur quo quisque jubetur alii facere quod sibi vult fieri et prohibetur alii inferre quod sibi nolit fieri" (Gratian, *Concordia discordantium canonum*, ed. A. Friedberg, 2d ed. [Leipzig, 1879], 1. dist. 1); see also Alan of Lille, *Distinctiones*, s. v. "natura," *PL* 210:871; Peter Lombard, *In Epistolam ad Romanos*, *PL* 191:1345.

[17] Some writers explain such knowledge of the law as exhibited by Constantine on the basis of Rom. 2:14: "the Gentiles, who have not the law, do by nature those things that are of the law." See *Sententie Anselmi*, ed. F. Bliemetzrieder, *Anselms von Laon systematische Sentenzen* (Münster, 1919), p. 79; Hugh of St. Victor, *De sacramentis*, 1.11.7, *PL* 176:347–48.

[18] Jacobus de Voragine, "De sancto Silvestro," *Legenda aurea* 12.2, ed. Th. Graesse, 3d ed. (Breslau, 1890; rpt. Osnabrück, 1969), pp. 71–73.

The emperor, "overcome / With charite" (2.3301–02), releases the children; he "hath his oghne will forsake / In charite for goddes sake" (2.3323–24). There is medieval precedent for Gower presenting this virtue, as well as pity, as a manifestation of natural law; indeed, some authors go so far as to argue that "ius naturale nichil aliud est quam caritas."[19] Peter Abelard testifies that "the words of natural law are those that commend the love [charitatem] of God and neighbor"; Alan of Lille similarly advises hearers to "Ponder nature: she will teach you to love your neighbor as yourself."[20]

The linking of these biblical doctrines with the *ius naturae* is, however, controversial. Some writers, including Thomas Aquinas, argue that "charity is beyond the resources of nature, and therefore cannot be something natural, nor acquired by natural powers." It is "infused by the Holy Spirit" and therefore must be distinguished from "the love of God which is based on a sharing in natural goods, and [which] is to be found naturally in all things."[21] Gower knows the controversy even as he has Genius present one side of it in the tale of Constantine; indeed, he begins in this narrative other arguments *ad motum* that will later modify and refine the priest's present stance with regard to "charite" and "kinde."

God rewards the "worthi lord" Constantine for his response to the children by curing his leprosy, and that cleansing also involves a conversion and baptism. Guided by a vision, the emperor sends for Silvester and from him learns the basic tenets of the Christian faith. In a brief and clear, but also remarkably rich 42-line statement, Genius gives the substance of Silvester's preaching, effectively doing what Silvester himself has done:

> And thus Silvestre with his sawe
> The ground of al the newe lawe
> With gret devocion he precheth,
> Fro point to point and pleinly techeth.   2.3431–34

This doctrine recounts the promise of salvation. To save a mankind "forlore," the Son, sent by "hihe god" to earth, "bore was for mannes love" (2.3390), and "of his oghne chois / . . . tok his deth upon the crois" (2.3391–92). The statement, in its first half organized around phrases in traditional credal statements (e.g., the Apostles' Creed), builds to an account of Judgment or "thilke

---

[19] This is an observation by Simon de Bisignano, in a passage from his *Summa* printed by Odon Lottin, *Le droit naturel chez Saint Thomas d'Aquin et ses prédécesseurs*, 2d ed. (Bruges, 1931), p. 106.

[20] Peter Abelard, *Commentaria super S. Pauli Epistolam ad Romanos* 1.2, PL 178:814; Alan of Lille, *Summa de arte praedicatoria*, cap. 21, trans. Gillian R. Evans, *The Art of Preaching* (Kalamazoo, Michigan, 1981), p. 91; PL 210:154; see this passage also for many of the other topoi that form the basis for Constantine's moral awakening in Gower's narrative; the Biblical texts that ground this opinion are Tob. 4:16 and Matt. 7:12.

[21] Thomas Aquinas, *Summa theologiae* 2a2ae, 24.2, trans. R. J. Batten, Blackfriars ed., 34:38–39.

woful dai of drede" (2.3406); the later statement reinterprets Constantine's earlier thoughts about *kinde*, and more largely, this instruction in the "newe lawe" sets the premises for a later re-evaluation of both the *jus naturae* and charity. Here, as introduced in a narrative, however, it is fittingly presented briefly and plainly: Constantine has been moved by his sight of the children and their mothers, and he is prepared to respond quickly to Silvester's preaching: "With al his hole herte" he readily declares "That he is redi to the feith" (2.3443–44), and so he is baptized and cleansed (2.3461–64).

The "charite" represented in this tale, though it is identified as "the vertu sovereine" (3507), seems to be a *motus naturae*, essentially a natural benevolence.[22] By it Constantine is led to share his goods, but in his famous Donation to "holi cherche," he confuses things "temporal" and "spirital" (3491–92). The sharing is natural, but so too is the confusion, for, as Gower will show in Book 5, it originates in natural law itself, and specifically in the inheritance of the fall and a *natura lapsa*. For all that this tale articulates about a good in nature, just as important is what it does not explicitly develop.

Indeed, the tale of Constantine, while it concludes one argument *ad motum*, begins a number of others. Genius knows that man's distinction lies in reason or the "Soule resonable," and with that knowledge he builds an argument that follows a "psychological" order of modifying causes. Over the course of the work, he will gradually shift the basis of his argument from sentient to rational nature,[23] and he will judge the virtues associated with the "herte tendre" accordingly. In the early books, such virtues are shown to be based in part upon the *jus naturale* defined by Ulpian and explained by later writers such as the decretist Hugutio: by natural instinct, like rejoice in their like; they "nurture their offspring, desire peace, avoid injuries, and do the other things that must be done according to sensuality, that is, natural appetite."[24] Natural love begins in *cognatio* or a connection of blood, and it also extends outward, to other members of the same species. The tale of Constantine establishes the latter, while it also illustrates the former principle: the mothers weep for their "yonge babes," and the emperor shows "pite" toward both because they are, by nature, his "liche." The priest later refines this idea while he also expands what natural love means. One argument *ad motum* will establish the need for a love ordered by reason, and another, also hinted at in the tale of Constantine, will locate that love in a nature redeemed by the "verrai goddes Sone."

Genius's progress to a full defense of an elevated and reformed *jus naturae*, grounded in reason and the tenets of Christian faith, is related to, but also retarded by his exploration of other distinctions along the way. If books provide

---

[22] The identification of *caritas* with benevolence is a further point of controversy among the Schoolmen: see Thomas Aquinas, *Summa theologiae* 2a2ae, 27.2, Blackfriars ed., 34:164–167.

[23] See Thomas Aquinas, *Summa theologiae* 1a2ae, 71.2, trans. John Fearon, Blackfriars ed., 25:8–11.

[24] Hugutio, *Summa Decretum*, in the selection printed by Lottin, p. 109.

order, a means of becoming wise, a *compilatio* of material from various books might well introduce competing orders of discovery and knowledge. In the *Confessio*, the poet not only multiplies rather than reduces instances, but he orders instances in a variety of structures. That variety is necessary because any given structure is variable, tentative, and to some degree "uncertein" in what it contains and allows the mind to behold. Gower combines and thereby generates competing structures; one resulting conflict, also introduced in Books 2 and 3, centers on a problem in the "gentil" conversation of the confession itself.

CHAPTER NINE

ENVY, WRATH, AND COURTLINESS

Amans's confession that, despite his lady's wisdom, he has sought by detraction to protect her from the enchantment of his rivals, reveals a mind ensnared in self-delusion. His love is, by its native motion, fanciful – as the epigram opening Book 2 puts it, "Est amor ex proprio motu fantasticus" (2.1.9) – and Amans, even in the course of confessing, falls into greater and greater fantasy. He knows that he has no cause to suspect his beloved: no woman "Woll betre avise hire what sche doth" (2.57) or "Kepe hire honour ate alle tide" (2.59) than she. That, however, does not matter. What sickens him, and exacerbates his fantasy, is simply the lady's good cheer toward others. This is a typical condition, Genius astutely remarks, of a person who "is out of loves grace" (2.90).

Books 2 and 3 of the *Confessio* turn our attention to the lover's perception that his vices are little more than lapses in gracious behavior. In his Envie – his expression of sorrow over another's joy, or of joy over another's sorrow, for example – Amans betrays malice beneath a superficial grace, and additionally, he betrays the pettiness of one who more profoundly lacks grace; he is small-minded not only in his activities as a lover, but in his defense of those activities.

Amans thinks his behavior defensible because it extends only to his rivals: "of other alle" (2.71), he takes "bot litel heede" (2.74). Later, when confessing his "gladnesse" over the "hevinesse" of others, he makes much the same point: "Bot this which I you telle hiere / Is only for my lady diere" (2.249–50). He is guilty of detraction in "loves cause," but "otherwise of no mispeche, / Mi conscience forto seche, / I can noght of Envie finde" (2.545–47), and though, if it advances his cause, he will reveal "al that I hiere / . . . unto my ladi diere" (2.2053–54), yet he can argue, and "this wot wel the hevene king" (2.2058), that he has feigned no "semblant" to any "strange man" or lover who pursues a mistress other than "my ladi selve" (2.2064). One might wish to take these statements as further evidence that Gower, in the confession, speaks exclusively in the persona of a lover: as a type, that is all that there is to his character, and it is there alone that he must "seche" his conscience. The point, of course, is quite the opposite: he projects the image of a more generally and basically good person who is drawn to a type or role as Amans, and who, in that role, is forced to commit sins because, intolerably, he stands "out of loves grace."

The stories of Book 2 do not address the sickness of Amans's small-mindedness directly. Indeed, they sometimes appear to exacerbate it by implying that

the lover should worry most about the great sins. After he hears the story of
how Polyphemus, an acutely jealous and envious suitor, kills Acis because Acis
is preferred by Galatea, Amans makes a promise:

> It schal noght stonde with me so,
> To worchen eny felonie
> In love for no such Envie.   2.214–16

If the sin gets too big, the lover will avoid it: by implication, his envy is too
small to warrant more than a passing thought; the greater issue is the plight of
one whose deserts do not match his "grete love."

The tale of Acis and Galatea only begins to reveal what seems to be a miscue
in Genius's rhetoric, whereby he talks "over" the lover's situation. Most of the
tales compiled for this book concern cases larger than Amans's "querele." This
problem, however, extends beyond Book 2 to tale-telling throughout the *Confessio*. If an author's task is to "magnifie" cases, as Gower claims in the Prologue,
Genius does exactly that: he enlarges scale in the very instances he selects.

That impetus to increase scale also obtains in the construction of whole
books: Books 2 and 3 especially, in their series of cases, build to questions of
greater and greater moment. At the same time, the confession itself – the
linking dialogue – often seems restricted to minutiae: the lover is prepared to
respond confessionally only to questions about his courtliness of manner, his
deeds and peccadilloes as a "gentil" lover.

As Amans sets these terms of argument, he also narrows the jurisdiction for
deciding what he should and should not do. The rules that obtain in this
jurisdiction sometimes allow him to skirt questions about his sinful conduct,
tacitly even to legitimize that behavior. Amans's greatest wish concerning his
lady's other suitors, for example, is "That I al one scholde hem alle / Supplante,
and welde hire at mi wille" (2.2410–11). A certain "morality" of courtliness,
however, keeps him from asserting his will:

> that thing mai I noght fulfille,
> Bot if I scholde strengthe make;
> And that I dar noght undertake,
> Thogh I were as was Alisaundre,
> For therof mihte arise sklaundre;
> And certes that schal I do nevere.   2.2412–17

If there were a "seker weie" to win "So hihe a love" by means of supplantation,
he would pursue it. But he is a "good" man who obeys a rule of avoiding
scandal. Genius does not yet address the more basic trouble – Amans's fantasy
of wielding his will over the beloved – but focuses instead on "sklaundre" and
honorable conduct. The lover should avoid supplantation in order to keep his
"oghne honour" and "astat," and for the "worschipe of [his] name," he should
"Towardes othre do the same" (2.2443–44).

Genius's tales tell another story: they do not touch upon honor, but instead
reveal that supplanters often succeed: Agamemnon wins Brexeida from Achil-

les, Diomedes lures Criseida from Troilus, and Amphitrion, "With sleyhte of love" (2.2492), takes Almeene from Geta. This is hardly simple dissuasion from the sin, and the three cases underscore a larger complexity in moral experience than can be addressed by ordinary poetic justice. The priest must shape a negative response to these instances out of the lover's present ideas of "moral" rectitude.

The challenge is to identify a rightness that obtains in two separate jurisdictions or structures, in each of which the rules are formulated differently; in the one they are drawn from a language of received morality, and in the other they are taken from a language of courtesy, narrowly construed as pertaining only to *conversatio* or manners. The two things ought to be combined, of course: humility and "charite" are virtues that should also order the external behavior of a gentle lover. The link between these fields rests, for Genius, in natural law, but that connection, at this point of the confession, has not been formally stated.

In Genius's next case of supplantation, a false bachelor cheats his friend, the son and heir of the Roman emperor, supplants him in love, and becomes "Lord and Sire" of the Persians after wedding the beloved, the Sultan's daughter. The friend reveals the treachery, bids farewell to his "ladi swete," and, overcome with grief, dies. The ending of the story is ambiguous. The false knight is arrested in Persia, but cannot be punished there "Be cause that he was co-roned" (2.2771). That, curiously, is the point that stands out, not the fact that the traitor is finally taken to Rome, "Wher that Supplant hath his juise" (2.2781). This last line, which concludes the story, does not dispel a sense that Genius is less concerned with a narrow legal judgment than with a human response to the crime itself: the emphasis of this tale falls on the friend's grief over the false knight's perfidy. Retribution alone does not stabilize experience: also necessary is a "natural" response to the injury and its effect. Generating such responses is the end to which Book 2 seems written, as the concluding tale of Constantine suggests: because "as every man deserveth / The world yifth noght his yiftes hiere" (2.3268–69), it is all the more important that man should heed the *leges naturae*, showing a "herte tendre" to all, because they are, by nature, like. The *jus naturae*, in other words, allows for a broadening of legal and moral judgment. After telling the story of the false bachelor, Genius expands his field to supplantation in "holy cherche," and here he stresses divine retribution: death overthrows the supplanter Boniface VIII, and a like justice, exhibited in cases of highest authority, is applied to Joab for slaying Abner, and to Achitophel for conspiring against Absolon. But this progress into larger and larger fields culminates in the fullest celebration of the other side of this divine justice: to Constantine, "To him that wroghte charite" (2.3328), God is "charitous."

As Genius expands the discourse into this field of great causes, he does not expressly introduce the *jus naturae* as a term linking virtue and the apt behavior of a "gentil" lover. That connection becomes somewhat more apparent in Book 3. There, in fact, the refined behavior one wishes to see in a lover is lifted to a new prominence; like the law of nature, it becomes a virtue counterposed to wrath and comes to represent the other side to Amans's facile confession of trifles in Book 2. Ease or grace in manners here forms the basis for yet another *distinctio* in an argument which, book by book, is growing in complexity.

Key, opposed terms in the argument of Book 3 are provided by an insightful Latin poet in the opening distich:

> Omnibus in causis grauat Ira, set inter amantes,
>   Illa magis facili sorte grauamen agit:
> Est vbi vir discors leuiterque repugnat amori,
>   Sepe loco ludi fletus ad ora venit.   3.1.5–8

> In all cases anger oppresses, but among lovers it imposes its weight more easily; where a man is contrary and lightly opposes love, in place of play a wailing often comes to the mouth.

Grauat, facili, grauamen, leuiterque, ludi, fletus are terms that suggest that larger field of conflict in the *Confessio*, where the lightness, play, and recreative aspect of courtly discourse are set against melancholic gravity of a lover burdened by thought. In this passage, however, the Latin poet hints that these terms might cross psychologically: lightness may turn into gravity, and gravity may turn into perverse levity, easiness, and off-handedness of manner.

The initial concern of the book is melancholy itself, now perceived as the first species of wrath. Like the parent sin, melancholy is an enemy to patience: it "Wol as an angri beste loure, / And noman wot the cause why" (3.30–31). Amans is himself oppressed by a "Wrathe that I mai noght spede" (40), and in this state, he opposes all "gladschip" and game in others:

> I am so with miselven wroth,
> That how so that the game goth
> With othre men, I am noght glad;
> Bot I am wel the more unglad,
> For that is othre mennes game
> It torneth me to pure grame.   3.43–48

This impatience is manifested, more largely, in the lovers' quick changes of mood. On the one hand, when "al wakende" Amans dreams he meets the beloved and pleads with her for "som good ansuere" and she answers "nay withouten oth," he is left to reflect melancholically on his long service: "the more I with hir dele," he remarks, "myn happ and al myn hele / . . . is ay the leng the ferre" (3.69–71). On the other hand, if he should meet her and she chooses "To speke a goodli word" (3.99), all his "Anger overgoth":

> So glad I am of the presence
> Of hire, that I all offence
> Foryete, as though it were noght,
> So overgladed is my thoght.   3.103–06

As we might expect, this mood does not last, for if it then happens

> that sche miscaste hire yhe,
> Or that sche liste noght to loke,
> And I therof good hiede toke,
> Anon into my ferste astat
> I torne.   3.110–14

These mood changes perhaps constitute the major symptom of the lover's disease, a melancholy "Which groweth of the fantasie / Of love" (3.126–27), much as they appear to be the chief symptom of the sickness of the age, as that was lamented in the Prologue.

The mood swings reflect a deeper gravity. Amans's "gladschipe" is joyless; he cannot be glad, but only "overglad." Out of his inner sickness, he not only experiences fortune, as all people do, but succumbs to it. Indeed, it is only then that "happ" or fortune can occasion Ire, for the latter is a condition in which one is quickly "distraght be sodein chance" (3.7). The vice really originates in the condition of his faculties, as the lover himself knows: "all my wittes ben unsofte" (3.123). He suffers an oppressive "fantasie"; in his hardened wits, he lacks imagination, a capacity for play and true re-creation. While he is entirely serious, he is thoroughly off-handed in his behavior, and most manifestly in his confessing. A key to his restoration will be a softening, an ability to engage in "game," a recapturing of health-giving levity. This, as it pertains to the enlarged scale of argument and tale-telling we have considered briefly for Book 2, is a capacity to leave the pressing reality of the love "querele" and enter a fiction, to become engaged in issues which, while significant, seem distant from his case.

That conversion to "game" or "pleie" will depend upon building into the exercise an entirely new vocabulary, unexpectedly rich in its implications. The Gower who writes the Latin epigrams sees the need for such inventiveness before we do. Often he generates his "vocabulary" of interpretation by setting oppositions. In his own game, the Latin poet recreates the experience of the confession by using terms whose full meaning can only be gleaned from a very close reading of tales, and finally of the work in its entirety. In this book, for example, he likens anger to the Furies, since in both, "furor ad tempus nil pietatis habet" 'furor reserves no pity for the occasion.' (3.1.1–2). The conflict between *pietas* and *furor*, a rich literary topos deriving ultimately from such ancient poets as Virgil and Statius, sets an issue whose full relevance to the following narrative is not immediately self-evident from Genius's testimony, but which, in that very obliqueness, might give edge to the reader's critical faculty. Over the course of this and the remaining books, *pietas*, both the virtue of pity and the ancient ideal of piety, will be shown to originate in a soft or "gentil herte," effectively in a basic *lex naturae* to which the priest has already testified.

The Latin poet sets enigmas or riddles. Genius does not respond to these directly, of course, and yet he follows behind, setting his own enigmas in his game of gentle conversation. If there is a gravity in Amans's mood changes, so there is a levity in the priest's changes in his "ernest" doctrinal stance, even in his defense of *kinde* and courtliness. The issues Genius raises are often seriously provocative, no doubt: a case in point is the controversy caused by his first story in Book 3, a retelling of Ovid's tale of Canace and Macareus. But with a mood-swing, Genius follows this tragic story with others that are comic: both kinds of tale, fit into a moral field of recreative "pleie," might destabilize Amans's perspective, but obviously in a better sense than Amans's ire does: such unsureness might effectively provide a stay to passion.

Gower's version of the tale of Canace has attracted much attention because it appears to take a radical stance on the question of incest. The controversy centers on Gower's choice to excuse the incest of Canace and Machaire on the grounds that these siblings, in their love, merely "halt the lawes of nature" (3.157). Derek Pearsall perceives in the story "none of the stock responses of the narrow moralist, but a sober and compassionate meditation on the blind instinctual nature of sexual passion."[1] Such has been the prevalent opinion in Gower scholarship, and it certainly lends credence to Rosemary Woolf's epithet of the "kindly Gower." But this is not the only opinion of the tale. Among others, David Benson insists that Canace is "a 'wikke ensample' of one who loved sinfully." Gower, he claims, "does not invite our sympathy for the couple so much as our horror at the sin they have committed and the evil it produces."[2]

Melancholy, not incest, is the topic governing the tale. This condition, as represented in the person of the children's father, Eolus, leads to a crime far more heinous than the act of the children. Their love is a moral fault, a "vice" (3.388), and yet it is based on natural instinct. Eolus's passion is not: he is deliberately cruel, and in his vengeance, he betrays a malice unknown to Nature (see 3.386–87). Benson levels out this distinction, however, by suggesting that the children are at least as guilty as their father. Conceding that "the father's unrelenting cruelty toward daughter and grandson is certainly horrible," he nevertheless finds "some hint that his condemnation by Genius (and most modern critics) is excessive."[3] No such hint can be found in the narrative itself, however. The judgment against Genius's excess most basically misses Gower's distinction of sins.

In *De bono conjugali*, Augustine writes that "God wished to create all men from one, so that they might be held together in their society, not only by the similarity of race, but also by the bond of blood relationship [*cognationis*]."[4] When, many centuries after Augustine, Godfrey of St. Victor celebrates "natu-

---

[1] Derek Pearsall, "Gower's Narrative Art," *PMLA* 81 (1966): 481; see also Peter Fison, "The Poet in John Gower," *Essays in Criticism* 8 (1958): 20.
[2] Benson, "Incest in Gower's *Confessio*," pp. 102–03.
[3] Ibid, p. 104.
[4] Augustine, *De bono conjugali* 1.1, trans. Charles T. Wilcox, *The Good of Marriage*, in *Treatises on Marriage and Other Subjects*, FC 27 (Washington, D.C., 1955), p. 9; *PL* 40:373.

ralis amor proximi," or the natural love of neighbor, he finds it based upon a love for parents, or a love of sister for brother, brother for sister.[5] He is very careful to separate love of this order, however, from the "innaturalis siue inordinatus amor proximi" represented in incest.[6] Late in the *Confessio*, Gower makes another kind of distinction: for him incest may well be *inordinatus*, but it is not *innaturalis*. The problem in the relationship of Canace and Machaire, from that later perspective, is not that it is based upon sentient nature, but that it is restricted to that nature, to a sensual appetite for "what thing comth next to honde" (8.183). Nature "kepth hire lawes al at large" (3.174), but the human being is obligated to temper or "modifie" those laws by reason and, as derived from it, the "lawe positif."

Eolus is just as guilty of passion as are his children: he acts out of "wilde wode peine, / Whanne al his resoun was untame" (3.244–45). Driven by a "frenesie," however, he also betrays a passion that is at once *inordinatus* and *innaturalis*. The insensitivity to the problem of the children and their enchantment only calls attention to something missing in his character, to a deficiency of natural virtue: he is "unmerciable" (3.216); "no pite" tempers his "horrible crualte" (3.235–36); he lacks the "pacience" to restrain his wrath (3.242–43); and Canace "mihte for nothing pourchace" his grace (3.275–76).

We cannot expect Eolus, a stranger to love, to be "benigne and favorable" to it. But when he ignores Canace's plea – "Ha mercy! fader, thenk I am / Thi child, and of thi blod I cam" (3.225–26) – he rejects a basic good in nature, the good of *cognatio*. On this point, the Latin poet's opening epigram is most germane. Eolus in his furor "can no pite knowe" (3.317); nor can he recognize *pietas* in his daughter. He cannot respond justly to a corruption in nature because he does not know natural love of the first order, the bond that Canace displays from her side when, for example, she receives a message, in the form of a "naked swerd," from him: "Now that I wot my fadres wille, / That I schal in this wise spille, / I wole obeie me therto" (3.263–65). Eolus not only drives his daughter to suicide, but then also has her infant, still bloody and crying, abandoned in a "wilde place" where "som beste him mai devoure" (3.327); supposedly, this latter action will satisfy Eolus' offended sense of justice. The extraordinary power of this tale is that while it exposes a weakness in *kinde* itself, it also builds that perception into a dissuasion from melancholic wrath.

The poet's task of re-authoring this tale, or any other, is undoubtedly complicated by the pressure exerted on him by the particulars not only of the original, but of popular interpretations interposed between the original and the story Genius eventually tells. Gower undoubtedly knew the "medieval Ovid," and he was quite possibly familiar with the reading of the *Heroides* in which Canace was understood to represent "mad passion."[7] This reading, however,

---

5   Godfrey of St. Victor, *Microcosmus* 3.174, ed. Philippe Delhaye (Lille, 1951), pp. 193–94.
6   Ibid., 3.175, p. 194.
7   "Intentio eius est de triplici genere amoris, stulti, incesti, furiosi scribere. . . . furiosi

does not suit Gower's narrative, which focuses on the mad passion, "horrible crualte," and injustice of Eolus. The children do not suffer madness or "frenesie." To describe them, Genius uses the "softe and faire" language of his often repeated point that love is irresistible; they are "enchaunted"[8] by Nature, and so the judgment against them ought to be tempered accordingly:

> The reddour oghte be restreigned
> To him that mai no bet aweie,
> Whan he mot to nature obeie.   3.348–50

The controversy over this narrative indeed turns on whether lovers are entirely accountable for their love. Eolus implies that they are, and Genius claims that they are not. For a reader to choose either position as entirely right would, at this point of the confession, be premature, a reflection not necessarily of melancholic, but of intellectual impatience. Much as the entire Confessio, following Arion's song, is designed to counter wisdom that "waxeth wod" and reason that "torneth into rage" (P.1078–79), so this tale, in miniature a disputatio in utramque partem, is designed to nurture the patience to reflect carefully on moral questions; that is what Eolus refuses to do.

Such patience is critical for dealing with important features of the ordinatio of the poem in its entirety. Genius represents generatio, or a "motus ad formam." On a given subject he can utter different judgments at different times in the confession; he is continually reforming and refitting values to new contexts. In effect, critics of this tale have tended to replace generatio with ens as their model of interpretation: their premise is that the fictive priest, or the author speaking through him, can be trusted at any given moment to speak his final word on any given subject. He cannot, at least until he has issued a "conclusioun final" (8.2070). Thus, when he discusses incest in Book 8, he no longer displays the delicacy, compassion, and sympathy that he reveals in the narra-

habet exemplum per Canacem, quae Machareum fratrem suum dilexit" ("Accessus Ovidii Epistolarum [3]," ed. R. B. C. Huygens, Accessus ad Auctores [Leiden, 1970], pp. 31–32); see Minnis, "Academic Prologues," p. 347; in "John Gower, Sapiens in Ethics and Politics," Medium Aevum, 49 (1980): 213–214, Minnis uses the same accessus to show that Gower, in a tale of Book 4, follows the "medieval Ovid" in having Phyllis, rejected by a slothful Demephon, represent "foolish love." On Gower's knowledge of the Ovidian commentaries, see also Conrad Mainzer, "John Gower's Use of the Medieval Ovid in the Confessio Amantis," Medium Aevum, 41 (1972): 215–29.

8 Benson maintains that the Middle English enchauntment "usually carried a clearly sinister meaning" (pp. 103–04); nonetheless, moral blame for an enchantment is often transferred to an external agent, to an enchanter who beguiles the innocent: we have explored that above, in treating the sins of the senses; here, however, Nature's enchantment is not represented as sinister. More largely, we shall do well to remember that enchantment can sometimes be read in a good sense. When Pierre Bersuire glosses the figure of the Medea who restores Eson to youth, he introduces a reading in bono of incantatrix: by a "decoction" of contrition and penitence, the wise enchantress reforms man, and by the mediating influence of grace, restores him to his pristine condition (Dictionarium, s. v. "renovare," 3: fol. 146r).

tive of Canace. He attacks the vice, showing the worst kind of "tirannie and crualte" (P.49) in new exemplars such as Caligula, Lot, and Antiochus. Though his different tone and argument can be explained in part by the different content of these narratives, the stories themselves are presumably chosen because they accord with the topic in his expressed plan to show the "vices on and on." Incest is his principal confessional subject in Book 8. In Book 3, it is not.

A difficulty in the *forma tractatus* that obligates us to await the moment Gower chooses for judging a given "vice dedly," is that not all issues raised in a certain story can be settled there.[9] Canace's vice is thus subordinated to that of Eolus as an issue in Book 3. From the verdict against Eolus, moreover, we cannot assume that Genius will be concerned to condemn the "crualte" of unkind fathers in stories he tells later. In Book 8, he does render such a judgment against Antiochus, whose crime against his daughter is, significantly, incest. In Book 5, however, he does not expressly denounce Orchamus, another cruel father. This story concerns the maid Leucothoe, loved "out of mesure" by Phoebus and overcome by his "micherie." An enraged Venus reports the seduction – the "theft" – both to Phoebus' concubine and to Leucothoe's father, and he, not daring to express his anger to Phoebus, releases it by burying his daughter alive. Like Eolus, he "wol no pite have" (5.6773) as his daughter "deide anon in his presence" (5.6775), but Genius neither attacks nor condones Orchamus' action. The focal character is Phoebus, and the father's horrible act is merely presented as one of the effects of Phoebus's "micherie."

There is a good reason for such emphases. Gower not only judges according to *circumstantiae*, but presents cases rhetorically. To condemn every wrongful action in a given tale might be, in rhetorical effect, to condemn none of them. What complicates the question, however, is Genius himself. While we honor, as we must, the topics as the expressed starting points of Genius's argument, we must also be alert to the potential conflict in the structures of his perception. Even at its proper time, a verdict might possibly be compromised by the judge's own fluctuating opinion. Genius's topics are key starting-points for coming to judgment, but as we have seen in the exemplum of Canace, a judgment may be affected by tacit multiple perspectives: the attack on the vice of Eolus is framed by a Genius who also works out of sets of *distinctiones* independent of the sins: he is, by nature, responsive to a tenet that "What nature hath set in hire lawe, / Ther mai no mannes miht withdrawe" (3.355–56). The competing structures of perception will mean a certain disarray in the *ordinatio* of his argument.

Such a relaxation of the *ordinatio* is especially possible in gentle conversation, which in Book 3 becomes something more than the idiom of the confession. Genius breaks the spell of the tragedy of Canace when he next describes the "gret vengance" (3.359) visited on Tiresias because he, in his anger, "destourbed kinde" by smiting coupling snakes. Even then, this brief tale does not

<hr>

[9] See Henry Ansgar Kelly, *Love and Marriage in the Age of Chaucer* (Ithaca, N.Y., 1975), pp. 131–36.

provide sufficient warning for the priest's conclusion that "love hath evere his lust to pleie, / As he which wolde no lif grieve" (3.394–95). The latter part of this statement – "As he which wolde no lif grieve" – is consistent with the premises of natural law Genius has so far explored. Amans, in his entirely "ernest" love, now gives Genius the occasion to speak about the former part, the notion that "love hath evere lust to pleie." The lover is so overcome by his passion that, unless "that swete wif" amends it, "Mi glade daies ben despended" (3.410–12). Genius addresses the lover's disinclination "to pleie" not merely by teaching him the natural virtues, but by encouraging him to soften his behavior.

Courtliness is something Amans already knows. Whereas he admits, under the rubric of Cheste, that he chides himself, he protests that he is innocent of using "croked eloquence" (3.440) with his beloved. When he speaks to her about his "longe love" (3.525), he tells a "softe tale" (3.506) and speaks "most softe" (3.512). Genius merely reinforces this behavior: he counsels Amans "to be debonaire" (3.601), to cultivate "Fair speche" (3.604) and, when necessary, to hold his "tunge stille" (3.608). He recommends patience, illustrating its value in a comic tale about Socrates, who "spak evere softe and faire" with his "wickid wif." When Socrates refuses to respond to her verbal abuse – "he al softe / Sat stille and noght a word ansuerde" (3.674–75) – she empties a waterpot over his head, and then he speaks, calmly drawing an analogy between her conduct and winter, both of which bring wind and rain:

> And thanne he sette him nerr the fer,
> And as he mihte hise clothes dreide,
> That he nomore o word ne seide;
> Wherof he gat him somdel reste.   3.694–97

This tale, as delightful as it is, is one in a sequence of stories that seem to pale in moral significance next to the earnest exemplum of Canace. It is followed by another, for example, about a foolish Tiresias, who presumes to settle a dispute between Jupiter and Juno over whether "man or wif" is more amorous. The advice to hold one's tongue, while supported by this exemplum, is confirmed by yet another, the tale of Phoebus and Cornide. Chaucer's Manciple identifies a like moral in his version of the latter, but Genius's counsel and sequence of tales have an additional implied relevance to Amans: a lover who speaks "lest ful many time grace" (3.773). Indeed, from this range of examples it appears that the priest continues to separate his several concerns: he speaks narrowly about "softe and faire" behavior that might serve the lover directly, or broadly about moral issues that seem unrelated to his cause.

Perhaps there is good reason for sustaining this separation, for refusing to deal exclusively with the lover's particular case, which quickly degenerates into "fantasie." By interlocking tales touching on love with others that do not, Gower draws the lover, as well as his readers, closer to a stable moral vision of love and the "fortune of this worldes chance." Such a strategy is germane to the goals of confession, as well as *compilatio*: it is precisely an enlarging of perspective that Amans most needs, and most resists.

It is necessary to represent and transform Amans's perspective inside this persuasion, of course, and the shrift therefore includes cycles of separating and integrating structures whose principles are *kinde* and courtliness. Genius draws them together in treating Contek and Homicide, for example, where his statements about natural virtues – "pacience," "merci," "pite" – also form a response to Amans's complaint: his "hertes contek" (3.1132), his distress at fortune's estrangement (3.1137), his sense of wasted time (3.1141), his near despair (3.1144). Later, the priest again recognizes the lover's Contek when he urges "suffrance" to offset a "folhaste" such as that exemplified in Pyramus and Thisbe, reminding the lover that "He mai his grace abide longe, / Er he of love be received" (3.1616–17). Such "suffrance is the welle of Pes" (3.1672) and "hath evere be the beste / To wissen him that secheth reste" (3.1639–40). This patience involves much more than Socrates' silent endurance of his "wickid wif." Indeed, while patience is a "moral" subject in a series of tales in this book, it also forms a rhetorical end in the quest of wisdom. The shrift itself, by its very procedure, contains a response to Amans's sense of wasted time in modalities that nurture patience and encourage recreation.

This book, as the preceding ones, is organized so as to allow the lover to reflect on the most "ernest" matter at its conclusion. From the tale of Athemas and Demephon, where counsel, patience, and fair speech are set against vengeance, this portion of the work builds to Genius's first extended excursus on a subject independent of Amans's quarrel,[10] the question of war and just homicide. Arguing initially that "to socoure / The lawe and comun riht to winne, / A man mai sle withoute Sinne" (3.2230–32), the priest proceeds to defend peace vigorously: not only does the "lawe of charite" prohibit "dedly war" (3.2261–62), but also "nature it hath defended / And in hir lawe pes comended" (3.2263–64). Undoubtedly, the priest wishes to convey an impression that war is too frequently unjust – as when a "riche worthi king" will "cleyme proprete / In thing to which he hath no riht, / Bot onliche of his grete miht" (3.2326–28) – and also, beyond the wrong in the cause of "coveitise" or "worldes pride" (3.2470) that war violates the basic premise of the *jus naturae* he has been so concerned to expound:

> For every lif which reson can
> Oghth wel to knowe that a man
> Ne scholde thurgh no tirannie
> Lich to these othre bestes die,
> Til kinde wolde for him sende.   3.2473–77

It is inconceivable to the priest, when a beast will not prey on its like, that a

[10] On the relationship between this argument and Gower's own opinion, see R. F. Yeager, "*Pax Poetica*: On the Pacifism of Chaucer and Gower," *Studies in the Age of Chaucer* 9 (1987): 97–108.

man, who "kynde hath and resoun can," will "sle that is to him semblable" (3.2592, 2595).

This defense of peace culminates in a final tale, the story of Telaphus and Teucer, which celebrates not only Misericorde or mercy, the virtue that checks wrath, but a range of other natural virtues. Terms clustered and sometimes repeated in the narrative and Genius's conclusion recall the tenets of an argument that has run through these opening books: grace, pity, "socour," "gentilesse," mercy, "franchise," compassion, and patience all point to the *leges naturae* that might help cure the ills of the world and the lover; all manifest the law that like should rejoice in their like, and in that principle lies their interdependence, a basis for trust:

> Yit stant mi trust aboven alle,
> For the mercy which I now finde,
> That thou wolt after this be kinde.   3.2704–06

This speech brings to a close an argument that, in the three tales concluding each of the first three books, expresses features of a sentient *kinde* that supposedly counteract the "unnatural," malicious, and self-isolating vices of pride, envy, and wrath.

The limits of this natural law which focuses on sentient nature, the "herte tendre," and, more largely, the *affectus*, will be evident in the narratives of later books. Loving "naturally" is not invariably a good: as we have already seen, it does not always restrict, but often promotes self-regard. The priest has not formally recognized this; nor has he fully acknowledged that *kinde* alone is insufficient for man, that it cannot repair the damages of these early vices. He has yet to work through other *differentiae* or *distinctiones* to evolve an understanding that makes that apparent and thereby truly benefits his charge. As a step toward that goal, Book 4 will explore and tentatively resolve the conflict involving *kinde*, courtliness, and moral discernment by concentrating on *gentilesse*, one of the "natural" virtues catalogued in the tale of Telaphus and Teucer.

CHAPTER TEN

SLOTH AND *GENTILESSE*

In an excursus near the middle of Book 4, Gower argues that true *gentilesse* is based on virtue, and on nothing else that a person "can, / Ne which he hath, ne which he mai" (4.2276–77).[1] This is a popular medieval doctrine, of course, but for the poet it also represents a genuine topos, a device of poetic discovery that opens perception into other major issues of the confession. In all of the confessional books, Genius urges behavior that is genteel and refined; his dialogue with the lover on matters of courtesy provides a basic language of the confession, and after its own fashion, it also supports and confirms values that Gower shares with his courtly audience.

Gentle behavior may express different kinds of *gentilesse*, however, and it is not enough to applaud it without considering its origins and "entencion." On the one hand, such behavior may be based upon "vertu moral," or the *gentilesse* praised in the excursus. The "verrai gentil man" follows "resonable entencion" (4.2270), practices virtue, and manifests charity, "Which hath the vertus forto lede, / Of al that unto mannes dede / Belongeth" (4.2327–29). As a priest, Genius might well advocate such *gentilesse*, and it is not surprising that he should adapt it to his teaching and shriving of Amans.[2]

On the other hand, gentle behavior may be based upon the *gentilesse* that prevails in love's court and is championed by Venus, called the goddess not only of love, "worldes lust," and "plesance," but "ek of gentilesse" (5.1442–43). Near the end of the poem, the goddess identifies her court's distinction:

> For al onliche of gentil love
> Mi court stant alle courtz above
> And takth noght into retenue
> Bot thing which is to kinde due.　　　　　8.2345–48

Throughout the confession, being "gentil" always means to be courteous,

---

[1] For other uses of the topos, see, e. g., Boethius, *Consolation of Philosophy*, 3. pr. 6, m. 6; *Roman de la rose*, 6549–62, 18577–866, ed. Lecoy, 2:201, 3:58–67; Dante, *Convivio* 4.3, 10, 14, 15; Boccaccio, *Il Filostrato*, 7.94–99; Chaucer, *Gent*; *WBT* 1109–76; *ClT* 155–61; *ParsT* 460–68; Gower, *Mirour de l'Omme*, 12073–96, 17329–412, 23329–436. This chapter and the next one have been adapted from my article, "Aspects of *Gentilesse* in John Gower's *Confessio Amantis*, Books III–V," in *John Gower: Recent Readings*, ed. R. F. Yeager (Kalamazoo, Mich., 1989), pp. 225–73.
[2] See Chaucer, *ParsT* 460–68, for a definition of *gentilesse* consistent with this sense in the *Confessio*.

"debonaire" (3.601), and "soft in compaignie" (3.2734), and such behavior is wholly consistent with the lore of *kinde*. As Venus's own conduct reveals, however, nature itself does not provide a sufficient warrant against promiscuity or self-indulgence,[3] and that is the danger in the gentle love and *gentilesse* the goddess sponsors. Setting no limits on natural appetite or the work of the "gentil" affectus, she blurs the very distinction of being gentle. As Genius in his more priestly function notes, she puts all danger aside to advance her own carnal pleasure, commits incest with her lecherous son, lets every woman "take / What man hire liste, and noght forsake / To ben als comun as sche wolde" (5.1427–29), and teaches that women "scholde here bodi selle" (5.1431).[4] The *gentilesse* Venus prefers is not the virtuous busyness of the "verrai gentil man," but a form of sloth consistent with her own excessive regard for fleshly comfort and her desire "to live the soft life of barren ease."[5] As Venus's own clerk, Genius does not reject this *gentilesse*, but often appears to accept and defend it.

The conflict between these kinds of *gentilesse* comes to a head in a three-section subdivision of Book 4 devoted to an examination of idleness – the fifth species of sloth – and its remedies. The first section introduces the vice and one of its cures, love-busyness. The next two sections feature other remedies, and it is here that the author places his treatise on *gentilesse*. The one section treats "chivalerie" as well as "gentilesse," and the other explores invention, or the labor and study producing knowledge whereby "We be now tawht of that we kunne" (4.2390). Especially relevant to Gower's larger statement about *gentilesse* is a turn given to the contents of each of these sections by the rich medieval concept of *otium* or *otiositas*, in meanings ranging from "idleness" or "laziness," through "leisure," to "the fruit of leisure (i.e., authorship)."[6]

The third section celebrates the labor and study of ancient inventors who, through the full exercise of their natural ability or *ingenium*, discovered the arts and sciences:

> Here lyves thanne were longe,
> Here wittes grete, here mihtes stronge,
> Here hertes ful of besinesse.   4.2352–54

Such terms of praise are typical of late medieval encomia on the surpassing excellence of the ancients.[7] Following in that tradition, and specifically observ-

---

3   On "gentilesse" with a like meaning in various contexts in Chaucer, see Bernard S. Levy, "The Wife of Bath's *Queynte Fantasye*," *Chaucer Review* 4 (1969):106–22, and "*Gentilesse* in Chaucer's Clerk's and Merchant's Tales," *Chaucer Review* 11 (1977):306–18.

4   Cf. *Roman de la rose*, 13845–68, ed. Lecoy, 2:171–72.

5   Alan of Lille, *De planctu Naturae*, pr. 5, trans. James J. Sheridan (Toronto, 1980), p. 163; PL 210:459.

6   These meanings are taken from Alexander Souter, *A Glossary of Later Latin to 600 A. D.* (Oxford, 1949; rpt. 1964) s. v. *otiositas*, p. 281; quoted by Douglas Kelly, *Medieval Imagination: Rhetoric and the Poetry of Courtly Love* (Madison, Wis., 1978), p. 278 n. 53.

7   For like terms, see, for example, Richard de Bury, *Philobiblon* 9, text and trans. of E.

ing a convention in a didascalic literature I shall mention below, Genius describes the ingredients of learning or discovery: natural ability, busyness, commitment, discipline; also implied throughout is *otium*, the very leisure that allows one "to studie and muse, / As he which wolde noght refuse / The labour of hise wittes alle" (4.2385–87). In the context of the entire *Confessio*, this tribute to the inventiveness of the ancients is the first in a series of didascalic excursus culminating in Book 7, a book that actually organizes a program of study. In providing a catalogue of inventors and a context for invention, however, even this early section bears a likeness to chapters of a very important work in this tradition, the *Didascalicon* of Hugh of St. Victor. Hugh, after treating inventors,[8] describes the *ingenium*, discipline, and practice necessary for study, and then the condition necessary for discipline: "Quiet of life – whether interior, so that the mind is not distracted with illicit desires, or exterior, so that leisure [*otium*] and opportunity are provided for creditable [*honestis*] and useful [*utilibus*] studies – is in both senses important to discipline."[9]

The prospect of *otium* as leisure for disciplined study sets a point of reference for Genius's treatment of *gentilesse*. The value of such a freedom to learn will later become apparent to Amans; in effect, he will discover that "the love of truth makes one seek a holy leisure."[10] Now, however, he has other things on his mind, and when Genius encourages him to read a useful invention in "poesie," Ovid's *Remedia amoris*, his is an expected response: "It were an ydel peine / To lerne a thing which mai noght be" (4.2678–79). Amans has hardly achieved the quiet of life that will allow him to "studie and muse" or, at another level, enable him to clutch his beads *por reposer*, engage in contemplation, or "bidde and preie" (8.2961). Leisure will become meaningful and profitable – indeed, possible – only after he is released from the inner quarrel of his "gentil love."

As the last of these sections hints at a world beyond the *negotium* that vexes

C. Thomas, ed. Michael Maclagan (Oxford, 1970), pp. 98–101; on the consequences of shunning the ancients, see John of Salisbury, *Metalogicon* 1.3, ed. Webb, pp. 9–12; trans. McGarry, pp. 13–16.

[8] Hugh of St. Victor, *Didascalicon* 3.2, trans. Jerome Taylor (New York, 1961), pp. 83–86. Like Hugh, Gower catalogues advances made through study and manual labor: whatever the field of these inventors, theirs is an orderly and productive inquiry, providing a lore that endures: it "stant evere alyche greene" (4.2392). In the Latin verse headnote to this section, the English poet claims a special regard for mental labor and the teacher who transmits knowledge: "Set qui doctrine causa fert mente labores, / Preualet et merita perpetuata parat" (4.7.3–4). On the use of leisure to search for and discover the truth and to impart that knowledge to others, see Augustine: "In otio non iners vacatio delectare debet, sed aut inquisitio aut inventio veritatis, ut in ea quisque proficiat et quod invenerit ne alteri invideat" (*De civitate Dei* 19.19, ed. B. Dombart [Leipzig, 1905–09], 2:387–88).

[9] *Didascalicon*, 3.16, trans. Taylor, p. 99; ed. Charles Henry Buttimer (Ph.D. diss., Catholic University of America, 1939), p. 67.

[10] "Otium sanctum quaerit caritas veritatis" (Augustine, *De civitate Dei* 19.19, ed. Dombart, 2:388).

Amans, the first one places us squarely in that business and busyness: this is a world filled with distraction, where the confusion centers on a major ambiguity in the concept of *otium*. The subject is idleness – *ocium* in the Latin sidenotes – and especially a refusal to love. The cure, obviously, is love, but, as all Ovidian poets recognize, certain kinds of love exist because of idleness. Ovid's advice in the *Remedia* – "fugias otia" 'flee idleness', and "da uacuae menti, quo teneatur, opus" 'give the idle mind necessary work'[11] – might be the priest's own counsel, except that Genius really argues the contrary: making love the needed occupation, he essentially reverses Ovid's senses of idleness and work. Ovid's doctrine becomes a medieval topos: "Venus otia amat,"[12] the ancient poet writes, and Chaucer thus makes Ydelnesse the porter of her garden and principal abode (*KnT* 1940). His model for this figure, Oiseuse, the porter of the garden of Deduit in the *Roman de la rose*, has attracted a scholarly controversy that itself reflects the ambiguity of the Latin root. Some argue that Oiseuse represents a "genteel and courtly relaxation," a cultivated leisure that allows a gentle love to mature. Others, including John Fleming, maintain that she represents both idleness and *luxuria*.[13] This ambiguity in the concept provides one context for judging Genius's counsel.

In his own argument, the priest never expressly addresses the distinction between idleness and leisure or "relaxation." What makes his argument suspect, nonetheless, is the kind of busyness he champions. Medieval spiritual writers issue a warning:

> ydelnesse . . . is a synne þat doþ moche harm, as holy bookes tellen; for whan a man is ydele and þe deuel fyndeþ hym ydel, he him setteþ a-swiþe to werke, and makeþ hym . . . to desire foule harlotries, as lecheries, and þus lese his tyme and moche good þat he myȝt doo þat he myȝt wynne þer-þorw paradis.[14]

Genius seems to encourage work of this kind, and with it a loss of time and much good, when he justifies love as the means to preserve one's comforts: "Love is an occupacion, / Which forto kepe hise lustes save, / Scholde every gentil herte have" (4.1452–54). Even this statement is self-interested and idle, or at least it seems so to the writer of the marginal gloss (at 4.1454): the

11 Ovid, *Remedia amoris* 136, 150, ed. E. J. Kenney (Oxford, 1961), p. 210.
12 Ibid., 143, ed. Kenney, p. 210.
13 John V. Fleming, *The Roman de la Rose: A Study in Allegory and Iconography* (Princeton, 1969), pp. 72–81. See D. W. Robertson, Jr., *Preface to Chaucer: Studies in Medieval Perspectives* (Princeton, 1963), pp. 92–93. More recently, D. Kelly (*Medieval Imagination*, pp. 78–80) sees greater ambiguity in the figure of Oiseuse and raises questions about Fleming's specific interpretation. On the model of *otium-luxuria* in antiquity, see, for example, Jean-Marie André, *L'Otium dans la vie morale et intellectuelle romaine des origines à l'époque augustéenne*, Publications de la Faculté des Lettres et Sciences Humaines de Paris, Série "Recherches," vol. 30 (Paris, 1966), pp. 49–52.
14 *The Book of Vices and Virtues: A Fourteenth-Century English Translation of the Somme le Roi of Lorens d'Orléans*, ed. W. Nelson Francis, EETS, os 217 (London, 1942; rpt. 1968), p. 27.

doctrine "Non quia sic se habet veritas, set opinio Amantum" 'is not the truth, but the opinion of lovers.'[15] It may be "vilenie" to see "lecheries" or "foule harlotries" in the love Genius advocates – it is, after all, "gentil love" – and certainly the language of this judgment seems ill-suited to the genteel rhetoric adopted by Gower in the poem. Nevertheless, Genius's advice, though it befits the priest of a gentle Venus, remains questionable, and not merely in the context of an external spiritual tradition. In this very section, Genius attacks love according to "Cupides lawe" (4.1471) and offers his first defense of honest, chaste, or married love. The language of the external judgment aside, misguided or idle busyness remains a key moral issue in the *Confessio*, and in this section, it surfaces because of Genius's own apparent unsureness about the love he is advocating. In its ambiguities, the section exemplifies the trying work, for speakers and Gower's audience alike, of sorting through meanings in the *negotium* of the shrift.

The middle section of this "treatise" on idleness represents a state between the taxing business of the confession and the leisure that comes at its end. It promises to have practical value for Amans, since it will address the question of love-profit, and it also includes a modest confessional element: here too the lover "wol speke upon [his] schrifte" (4.1683). At the same time, it has other features that distinguish it from the sections that precede and follow it, separating it from the *negotium* of Amans's love-quarrel and from "studie" that is not, for the most part, directly related to that business.

Leisure or *otium* can be perceived as the goal of work: in antiquity, such a state of retirement or fulfillment permitted a devotion to cultural pursuits; in medieval monastic settings, it occasioned contemplation.[16] "Studie," in Genius's tribute to inventors, looks ahead to that state of leisure. The middle section of the treatise on idleness also involves leisure, but not as a goal. Its

---

[15] Opinion "est acceptio propositionis immediatae et non necessariae" (Vincent of Beauvais, *Speculum naturale* [Douay, 1624], col. 1937). It originates in sense-perception: "omnis opinio . . . habet principium a sensu" (Guillaume de Conches, *Glosae super Platonem*, ed. E. Jeauneau [Paris, 1965], p. 109). "The judgments of sensation and imagination are classed as 'opinion,'" but "sensation deceives the untutored, and cannot pronounce sure judgment" (John of Salisbury, *Metalogicon*, 4.11, trans. McGarry, pp. 220–21; ed. Webb, p. 177). "Imagination . . . possesses in itself nothing certain as a source of knowledge" (Hugh of St. Victor, *Didascalicon* 2.5, trans. Taylor, pp. 66–67; ed. Buttimer, p. 29). In the *Confessio* the distinction between opinion and truth will fit other perceptions of the self-interested lover, who, as we shall find below, depends on the unreliable judgments of sensation and imagination.

[16] See *Oxford Latin Dictionary*, ed. P. G. W. Glare (Oxford, 1982), s. v. *otium*, pp. 1277–78; Jean-Marie André, *L'Otium*, and, by the same author, *Recherches sur l'otium romain*, Annales Littéraires de l'Université de Basançon, vol. 52 (Paris, 1962); Jean Leclercq, *Otia monastica: Études sur la vocabulaire de la contemplation au moyen âge*, Studia Anselmiana, fasc. 51 (Rome, 1963); *The Love of Learning and the Desire for God: A Study of Monastic Culture*, trans. Catherine Misrahi (New York, 1960), pp. 84–85; Michael O'Laughlin, *The Garlands of Repose: The Literary Celebration of Civic and Retired Leisure* (Chicago, 1978), pp. 164–96; on *acedia* and leisure, Josef Pieper, *Leisure: The Basis of Culture*, trans. Alexander Dru (New York, 1952), pp. 48–58.

field, instead, is a leisure described by Glending Olson as the rest or relaxation that enables a person to return to work: it is a "re-creation, a re-constituting of one's normal . . . mental health."[17]

This part of Book 4 of the *Confessio* provides such recreation in a courtly or genteel setting. The topics of the section – chivalry, love, *gentilesse* – obviously belong to the court, and in treating them, Genius uses a specifically courtly mode of "argument." Next to the distracting "reality" of the confession proper, the section organizes experience as might a literary creation at one remove from real experience: as a gentle "tale," a refined and courtly "conversacion" fitted to a setting of "worschipe and ese," it offers an enabling rest.

Gower hints at the procedure of the section at another point in Book 4, when he has Amans describe some of the courtly recreations he might engage in, at the pleasure of his mistress:

> And whanne it falleth othergate,
> So that hire like noght to daunce,
> Bot on the Dees to caste chaunce
> Or axe of love som demande,
> Or elles that hir list comaunde
> To read and here of Troilus,
> Riht as sche wole or so or thus,
> I am al redi to consente.   4.2790–97

Asking "som demande" about love is the informing principle of Gower's treatment of chivalry and *gentilesse*, and it is so in a sense distinct from that of interrogation in a lover's confession. What I have earlier introduced as the mode of a *disputatio in utramque partem* becomes, in the context of late medieval courtly literature, the very popular activity of posing and responding to questions of love or *demandes d'amour*. The form orders love cases presented in Andreas Capellanus's *De amore* and in many later works.[18] Often such *demandes* are introduced in a quasi-legal setting, sometimes by two litigants of equal merit or with pleas of comparable worth, each seeking a favorable verdict. Such is the case in Machaut's *Jugement dou Roy de Behaingne*. The *demande* is also familiar to readers of Chaucer, who has several tellers of noble tales ask a

---

17 *Literature as Recreation in the Later Middle Ages* (Ithaca, N.Y., 1982), pp. 101–07; see also D. Kelly, pp. 78–80. On this point, Hieremias de Montagnone quotes Cicero (*De oratore* 1): "Ocium fructus est non contentio animi sed relaxatio" (*Epytoma sapientia* 4.4.8, fol. 106r).

18 For a late example of a work devoted exclusively to this activity, see *The 'Demaundes off Love': A Middle English Prose Version (1487) of the French Game 'Au roy qui ne ment'*, ed. W. L. Braekman (Brussels, 1982); for useful background, see John Stevens, *Music and Poetry in the Early Tudor Court* (Lincoln, Nebraska, 1961), pp. 154–67; Richard Firth Green, "The *Familia Regis* and the *Familia Cupidinis*," in *English Court Culture*, ed. Scattergood and Sherborne, pp. 87–108; Alfred Karnein, "*Amor est passio* – A Definition of Courtly Love," in *Court and Poet*, ed. Burgess, p. 215; John Benton, "Collaborative Approaches to Fantasy and Reality," in *Court and Poet*, pp. 46–47; and Wesley Trimpi, "Quality of Fiction," p. 115.

question pertaining to cases of individual characters: in the *Knight's Tale*, "Who hath the worse, Arcite or Palamoun?" (*KnT* 1347) or, of characters in the *Franklin's Tale*, "Which was the mooste fre, as thynketh yow?" (*FranT* 1622). In this tradition, the question is sometimes presented in the abstract – without reference to a particular case – and that will be so in Gower's usage and in a work I shall propose as having a special relevance to it. Whatever form the *demande* takes, however, it is introduced most frequently in a courtly setting to open conversation and especially "amoureuse conversacion": it organizes courtly leisure profitably, "en joieuse recreation."[19]

A useful model to guide our examination of Genius's procedure might be found in the *Trésor amoureux*, a *dit* tentatively attributed to Froissart. This poem ends with a series of *demandes*: both in the content of those questions and in the voices in the poem figuring opposed responses to them, the *Trésor* merits our attention. For our purposes, the focal characters are Love and Congnoissance. Late in the work, the latter seeks to win Love's favor for her charge, the poem's narrator, but Love refuses the request because the lover and Congnoissance each betrays a divided loyalty, the lover because of his devotion to Congnoissance, and Congnoissance because of her devotion to Reason; neither character, in other words, submits wholly to Love. This conflict is really a conflict of principle, of course, and Love and Congnoissance, to settle their differences, agree to ask readers for a verdict on seven questions involving the value and relative worth of love and arms, of conflicting means for securing high status or degree, and of biological nature or "blood" and nobility of character.[20] Effectively, the work ends with these questions, and thus the poem, itself a recreation, potentially effects another recreation – a conversation – in its courtly audience. Genius's excursus is designed to resolve these very issues; it is itself re-creative. Moreover, because its statements appear to contradict arguments the priest offers elsewhere in the confession, the excursus, together with the enveloping shrift, evolve *demandes* that help make the entire *Confessio* a recreation.

One of the distinctions of the *Confessio*, in fact, is that the opposed voices in its "debate" are Genius's own. Thus, in responding to the various *demandes* implied in the major question of this section – how a person "schal be take / The rathere unto loves grace" (4.2194–95) – Genius does what he often does elsewhere in the poem by arguing on both sides of an issue, speaking sometimes as a "clerk / Of love" (8.2053–54), sometimes as a priestly advocate of reason. Effectively, he thereby moves between stances represented by Love and Congnoissance in the *Trésor*. What distinguishes this section is its clear conceptual order and the resolution of its *demandes*. Genius finally arranges various kinds of gentle activity according to a hierarchy of worth.

---

[19] I have borrowed these terms from late medieval evidence quoted by Arthur Piaget, in "Un Manuscrit de la cour amoureuse de Charles VI," *Romania* 31 (1902): 601.
[20] *Trésor amoureux*, 3060–3104, ed. Auguste Scheler, *Oeuvres de Froissart: Poésies* (Brussels, 1870–72), 3:276–78. For a summary of the *Trésor*, see D. Kelly, pp. 114–20.

The courses to love's grace, the priest argues, are two: the worthiness of "manhode," or the prowess of those who "dar travaile" at arms, and the worthiness of "gentilesse." His opening topic is "Hou love and armes ben aqueinted" (4.2137). These subjects, as Froissart argued elsewhere, were the enduring themes of conversation in courtly society,[21] and Genius will later integrate them into his discussion of *gentilesse*. Here, in defending the honor of arms for a "worthi kniht," Genius more immediately answers several *demandes* also posed in the *Trésor*, one of which is especially important to Amans: in order to live always in delight – and with a true hope of earning reward – is it better to serve love faithfully or to pursue arms honorably?[22] Amans's own preference is clear: "What scholde I winne over the Se, / If I mi ladi loste at hom?" (4.1664–65), he asks, and then answers, "It were a schort beyete / To winne chaf and lese whete" (4.1709–10). Responding to Amans's pleasure – a desire to advance his own "delit" and "spede" – Genius tells many stories to prove that travail in arms can effect "decerte" in love. But when he also argues that "betre it were honour to winne / Than love" (4.1867–68),[23] he begins to set new priorities: "chivalerie" serves the common profit, and the love to which honor is preferable does not.

The excursus builds a case out of Amans's concern, but it advances to better senses of profit and "loves grace" than he can anticipate. In denying that "blood" and wealth can be the source of true *gentilesse*, the priest answers three more questions in the *Trésor*.[24] The priest rejects the notion that wealth is a source of *gentilesse* because, unlike virtue, it provides no "sikernesse" (4.2214–15, 2267–68). To be sure, he also remarks that a "povere vertue schal noght spiede" (4.2280) in love's court, and that the person rich and good is therefore "wel the more worth" (4.2287).[25] But this point he cancels at the next stage of

---

21 See F. S. Shears, *Froissart: Chronicler and Poet* (London, 1930), pp. 15–16.

22 *Trésor*, demande 2 (3070–74); see also *demande* 1 (3064–69).

23 It is beyond my present purpose to examine this segment of the excursus in detail, but it should be noted how, in relation to the enveloping shrift, it forms one of larger *demandes* of the *Confessio*. At the end of Book 3, Genius had attacked war both in "worldes" and in "Cristes" cause. In the "game" of the excursus in Book 4, however, the priest appears to reverse himself, and as he defends the travail of "men of Armes," the lover, taking the opposite side, introduces Genius's arguments from Book 3 to buttress his own refusal to travel and fight:

> I not what good ther mihte falle,
> So mochel blod thogh ther be schad.
> This finde I writen, hou Crist bad
> That noman other sholde sle.   4.1660–63

Although one might combine Genius's opposed stances in a single, consistent view – "chivalerie" ideally serves the cause of peace – the confessor does not attempt to reconcile them. Nonetheless, in this section he will indirectly support his earlier statement with a concluding tribute to charity. As I shall note, he reaches that conclusion by means of an argument independently generated in the excursus.

24 *Demandes* 3 (3075–80), 6 (3091–96), and 7 (3097–3104).

25 Contrast Gower's argument when treating *seignours* in the *Mirour de l'Omme*, 23329–436; see especially 23355–58:

argument, when he defends a love that yields a secure and truly gentle profit. "Honeste" love, he argues,

> in sondri weie
> Profiteth, for it doth aweie
> The vice, and as the bokes sein,
> It makth curteis of the vilein,
> And to the couard hardiesce
> It yifth.   4.2297–2302

In this progression, the excursus not only arranges goods hierarchically, but also works to interiorize "worthinesse." The good deemed superior in the first part of the argument – knighthood of arms "oghte ferst to be desired" (4.1881) – displaces the "sotie of love," but it is surpassed in the second part by a "genti-lesse" that might include chivalry, but is not limited to it. Love "honeste" is then deemed superior to external success in love's court. Because it inspires courtesy and "verrai prouesse" (4.2302) and thereby changes for the better those who submit to it, it helps redefine chivalry, and it also forms the substance of a response to another *demande* of the *Trésor*: whether a person can be born so elevated in virtue that he can serve both love and arms well.[26] In the tribute to "love honeste," Genius also rephrases his earlier assertion that the "gentil herte" must love "forto kepe hise lustes save," now in a more traditional, acceptable form: "love hath evere hise lustes grene / In gentil folk" (4.2309–10).[27] This answers the one remaining question in the *Trésor*, why Love works to better effect with one of his subjects than with a hundred others.[28]

In the final stage of his argument, Genius shows that honest love, praised in mere "bokes," is superseded by a love taught in "holi bokes wise": concerning it, and it alone, the priest claims to speak "After the vertu moral" (4.2321). Having answered such *demandes* as are presented in the *Trésor*, Genius now goes beyond them in this final encomium on love, identified in a marginal gloss as *amor caritatis*. With this shift, he moves into another sense of *gentilesse*, one espoused, for example, in late medieval handbooks of religious instruction: "For verrey nobleie comeþ of a gentel herte. For-soþe, þer is no gentel herte but to loue God; þer is no nobleye but to serue God . . . ne vilenye but þe contrarie þer-of."[29]

> Mais les richesces nepourqant
> Ne sont en soy digne a conquerre
> Le meindre que l'en porroit querre
> De les vertus, ne tant ne qant.

[26] *Demande* 4 (3081–86).
[27] The *topos* is perhaps most succinctly expressed in the opening lines of Guido Guinizelli's *Al cor gentil*: "Love returns always to a noble [*gentil*] heart / Like a bird to the green in the forest" (ed. and trans. Robert Edwards, *The Poetry of Guido Guinizelli* [New York, 1987], p. 21).
[28] *Demande* 5 (3087–90).
[29] *Book of Vices and Virtues*, p. 85. At this point in the work, Genius does not fully

The entire excursus, as it clearly unfolds to the praise of this supreme virtue, a virtue that transcends *gentilesse* in all forms that lack "sikernesse," becomes profitably reconstitutive, setting a standard for judging other behavior, especially "gentil" behavior, in the work. In reordering the idea of profit according to a model of true *gentilesse*, the excursus clears opacities of the confession proper. It offsets the great danger in *otium* as leisure – "not being occupied with profitable, serious activities"[30] – but it does so in a setting of "ese." In that courtly setting, in fact, it exemplifies a classical precept: "Leisure, which seems most contrary to industry and study, ought especially to be subjoined to them, not to the extent that virtue dies away, but to the extent that it is revived [*recreatur*]."[31] The *otium* of this section, though not a goal in itself, is in that particular sense re-creative.

As the concept of *gentilesse*, with various potential conflicts built into it, reveals central concerns of the poem, the placement of the excursus in the middle confessional book seems to have a special significance.[32] As fitted to Genius's double role, it might well occasion a shift in the focus of the entire confession away from Amans's love-quarrel to the more stable ground of virtue. The effect, though never so obviously the intent, of Genius's argument concerning *gentilesse* could be a new perception in Amans of a great good that he has manifestly loved too little.

The framing of that perception is not limited by forms of courtly fiction. This excursus, as it pertains to the entire *Confessio*, has a distant, yet suggestive analogue in the middle cantos of Dante's *Purgatorio*. On the cornice of sloth, in an episode Dante recounts in cantos 17 and 18, Virgil notes that "The love of good which comes short of its duty is here restored" (17.85–86):[33] as souls here

expound the concept of charity; nor does he distinguish its elements: love of God, love of one's neighbor. Traditionally "*amor proximi* is valuable only for God's sake, 'propter Deum'" (R. Freyhan, "The Evolution of the *Caritas* Figure in the Thirteenth and Fourteenth Centuries," *Journal of the Warburg and Courtauld Institutes* 11 [1948]: 68). The emphasis at most points of the confession falls on virtuous behavior in relation to one's neighbor; nevertheless, also evident, and especially at the end of the *Confessio*, is Gower's sense that such behavior must be founded upon, and ordered to, the love of God.

30 Siegfried Wenzel, *The Sin of Sloth: Acedia in Medieval Thought and Literature* (Chapel Hill, NC, 1967), p. 85.
31 Valerius Maximus, *Factorum et dictorum memorabilium libri novem* 8.8, ed. Carolus Kempf (Stuttgart, 1966), pp. 393–94.
32 Because *gentilesse* is equated with virtue generally, no single virtue or counterposed vice need be accorded necessary, privileged, or exclusive status in housing discussions of it. In the *Mirour de l'Omme*, Gower had used the concept to expound aspects of humility (12073–96) and chastity (17329–412); that he uses it here to "inform" busyness is unexceptionable; indeed, given the subject of this poem, as I have argued above, his decision is an especially fitting one; what I am also concerned with, in the present context, is the fact that in treating the concept in relation to sloth, Gower is able to place the discussion roughly at the mid-point of the confession.
33 This and subsequent quotations from the *Purgatorio* are from the translation of Charles S. Singleton, *The Divine Comedy: Purgatorio* (Princeton, 1973).

recover a love of good, so Virgil, seizing the moment of an enforced rest from a difficult ascent, instructs Dante in that love; and as Virgil on love, so Genius on *gentilesse*, each to his respective pupil.

Genius's excursus does more than present an ideal busyness to overcome what Virgil describes as the "lukewarm love" (17.130) of sloth. The implications in the pattern of idleness, recreation, and leisure reach far beyond the three sections of Book 4. Once "John Gower" is restored to himself in the final vision of the poem, he sets out "to take rest" (8.3142) and looks ahead to "thilke place / Wher resteth love" (8.3170–71); leisure, now a repose, occasions prayer and contemplation. A similarly comprehensive pattern obtains in the *Purgatorio*. In Canto 2, the pilgrim, his teacher, and gathered spirits, idly enthralled by Casella's singing of a *canzone* Dante himself had written, are wakened by Cato's interruptive "What stay is this?" (121). In the middle cantos, Virgil offers his re-creative instruction. And in Canto 27, the poet walks through the fire that purifies the lustful; he dreams of Leah and Rachel, who prefigure the virtuous or righteous busyness and contemplation he will experience in the Earthly Paradise and later;[34] and Virgil, in his final act, crowns and miters the pilgrim lord of himself, thus anticipating Dante's future repose. The point I wish to emphasize here is that in both texts, the middle episode "orders" the progress of the central figure from idleness to self-recovery and the *otium* or repose available only to the cleansed heart and rightly ordered will.

In that larger framework, Genius's stay in the "besinesse" of the confession to expound *gentilesse* may provide an especially enabling rest, re-creative in the enlarged sense of organizing the topics of confession and potentially the whole of the lover's experience. The principle of that larger program has a parallel in Virgil's teaching that love is the source of all human actions: "love must needs be the seed in you of every virtue and of every action deserving punishment." (17.103–05). By a distinction of loves, Virgil offers an explicit rationale or *sufficientia* for the sins,[35] a rationale that also serves to "map" purgatory. Genius does not attempt anything precisely like this in his excursus, and yet, implicit in his ideal of *gentilesse*, including especially the love that orders "al that unto mannes dede / Belongeth," is a drawing together of virtues that elsewhere in the confession form remedies for the sins.

I have already suggested that the remedies proposed during the course of the *Confessio* are based upon increasingly complex medieval notions of the *jus naturae* that include, but are not limited to, Genius's distinction between *kinde* and *reson*. That distinction is itself relevant to classifying virtues linked with *gentilesse* at various places in the confession. Associated with *kinde* and the

---

[34] For possible parallels with Oiseuse in the *Roman de la rose*, see Erich Köhler, "Lea, Matelda und Oiseuse." *Zeitschrift für romanische Philologie* 78 (1962): 464–69, and Fleming, pp. 77–78.

[35] See Siegfried Wenzel, "Dante's Rationale for the Seven Deadly Sins ('*Purgatorio*' XVII)," *Modern Language Review* 60 (1965): 529–33.

"gentil herte," on the one hand, are "frendlihede," pity, compassion, grace, mercy, and kindness.[36] Such virtues, growing out of a sensitivity to a shared humanity, offset what Virgil describes as the love of another's evil (113). Associated with *reson* and the "mesure" of *gentilesse*, on the other hand, are virtues such as chastity, discretion, sobriety, restraint: these check what Virgil calls love "in faulty measure" (126). Virtues of both kinds, displayed singly or in groups at various points of the confession, become remedies for the separate vices. Ultimately more important than their separate uses, or their being grouped into virtues of *kinde* and *reson*, however, is their integration. Charity, the supreme virtue in Genius's ideal *gentilesse*, unites *kinde* and *reson*, and as a love ordered by "resonable entencion" that allows a person to realize the fullest potential of his or her nature, it becomes the principle of all other virtues. As those virtues originate in it, of course, they also originate in true *gentilesse*.

Genius's excursus does more than merely open out into a universe of virtues: it implicitly draws the virtues into itself, specifically into its model of the gentle person who, in advancing to the rest and holy leisure that Amans himself will discover at the end of the *Confessio*, engages in a just and charitable "besinesse" in all things pertaining to "mannes dede." At the end of the excursus, Genius maintains, on the basis of scriptural precept, that love is a necessity (4.2325), and the effect of that point is to suggest, for the entire section, the Augustinian doctrine that "the necessity of love [*caritatis*] makes one undertake a righteous business."[37]

Given the strength of this ending, there is good reason to hope that the excursus will stabilize the confession by ordering the speakers' discursive and imaginative busyness. In fact, it does not. If the tribute to *gentilesse* is re-creative, offering an ideal that enables us to return to work with mental health restored, the "reality" of the confession seemingly works to cancel its value, making it appear the product of an idle leisure. The excursus seems too neat or tidy to account for the complexities of the lover's experience or the priest's confessional doctrine. Its failure to effect a lasting change in the perspective of either speaker may be attributed to a distinction of faculty psychologies. The priest and lover will continue to follow a "psychology" at odds with the one ordering the righteous busyness of the "verrai gentil man." Our immediate task, then, is to note the difference, to see how the psychology championed in the excursus is not the psychology advocated and practiced in the confession proper. It is to such exercises that Gower guides us through his strategies of *compilatio*, to the end of ensuring that the judgment of which "sentence" ought to be preferred is an informed judgment.

---

[36] The list of virtues that appears in Genius's brief tale of Telaphus and Teucer at the end of Book 3 (2639–2717) includes "gentilesce" as a single virtue in the series, whereas in the present excursus the priest says of "vertu" generally, "So mai that wel be gentilesse" (4.2267).

[37] "Negotium iustum suscipit necessitas caritatis" (*De civitate Dei* 19.19, ed. Dombart, 2:388).

CHAPTER ELEVEN

GENTLE INTENTION AND
THE USES OF IMAGINATION

In evolving his doctrines of *gentilesse*, Genius relies on topoi of medieval cognitive psychology which, for our purposes, are conveniently summarized by Dante's Virgil, again on the cornice of sloth. Once Virgil has established, in canto 17, that "Each one apprehends vaguely a good wherein the mind may find rest, and this it desires" (17.127–28), and that such a craving is love, he goes on, in canto 18, to describe the process of advancing toward that good: "Your faculty of apprehension draws an image from a real existence and displays it within you, so that it makes the mind turn to it; and if, thus turned, the mind inclines toward it, that inclination is love" (18.22–26). Of course, such a love must be evaluated, as Virgil warns when he remarks "how far the truth is hidden from the people who aver that every love is praiseworthy in itself, because perhaps matter appears always to be good: but not every imprint is good, although the wax be good" (18.34–39). For judging that imprint and making every will conform to a primal will, "there is innate in you the faculty that counsels and that ought to hold the threshold of assent. This is the principle wherefrom is derived the reason of desert in you, according as it garners and winnows good and evil loves" (18.61–66).

The complete process described by Virgil will emerge in the composite of Genius's exemplars of *gentilesse*, but in the excursus, the priest begins at the stage where good and evil loves are garnered and winnowed:

> after the condicion
> Of resonable entencion,
> The which out of the Soule groweth
> And the vertu from vice knoweth,
> Wherof a man the vice eschuieth,
> Withoute Slowthe and vertu suieth,
> That is a verrai gentil man.   4.2269–75

In this model, intention follows an ideal of willing, "a tending towards an object within the plan of reason."[1] Peter Abelard's treatment of intention in his *Ethics*[2] sheds some light on Gower's strategy in introducing this notion in

---

[1] Thomas Aquinas, *Summa theologiae* 1a2ae, 12.1, trans. Thomas Gilby, Blackfriars ed., 17:112–13.

[2] For relevant medieval background to Abelard's doctrine, see D. E. Luscombe, ed.

the excursus. Specifically, several of the analogies or instances Abelard uses to build the case that "an action does not bear anything good in itself" but "is good by reason of a good intention"[3] pertain directly to Genius's setting up his definition of the "verrai gentil man." The first is a simile of lineage or birth: a "man is said to be good by his own goodness, but when we speak of the son of the good man by this nothing good is indicated in him."[4] The second is the example of wealth. Genius, it will be recalled, remarks on the great value of wealth in love's court, where it makes a person "more worth." To Abelard, it is unthinkable that "a great amount of money . . . could contribute to merit or the increase of merit," or that it could "make anyone better and more worthy."[5] What is critical to him, once again, is good intention, and that would seem to be Genius's final point in the excursus as well, specifically as he separates riches from the *gentilesse* originating in "resonable entencion." The implications of that distinction are significant.

Gower is certainly not unique in working past the specious external signs or accidents of *gentilesse* to its substance, "vertu set in the corage" (4.2261), but he is unique in drawing the doctrine of intention into his definition of the concept. By this means he undoubtedly alerts us to false images of *gentilesse*, to the conventional ones of "hih lignage" and "richesse" especially. But he also forces us to recognize that even deeds and words that seem truly "gentil" are not always what they seem: the appearance of an honest love, for example, does not necessarily betoken an honest "entencion" or true gentility. Outside the excursus, that becomes manifest as Genius tests the *gentilesse* of characters not only by their external behavior, but by their internal acts of knowing and willing. Even then, however, the accuracy of judgment is not assured. Applying the standard of "entencion" remains extremely difficult, if not impossible, because, as Abelard noted, "men do not judge the hidden but the apparent."[6] The "psychology" Genius invents for characters in his fictions is, as we shall see, finally superficial: the priest still works with the apparent; Gower would have us remain sensitive to the hidden. If this effectively renders all judgments tentative, it also further points to Gower's end. What is finally most important to the poet in the exercise of judgment is not the testing of another, but the forming in oneself of a "resonable entencion." To that end, all that Genius records is significant.

Outside the section of the *Confessio* where he introduces this standard, Genius is especially interested in the stages of the knowing and willing process that precede consent or the formation of an intention. One of his topoi is the analogy used by Dante's Virgil of softened wax, a metaphor of the imagination

and trans., *Peter Abelard's Ethics* (Oxford, 1971), pp. xxxii–xxxv; Etienne Gilson, *The Spirit of Mediaeval Philosophy*, trans. A. H. C. Downes (New York, 1940), pp. 343–63.
3 Peter Abelard, *Ethics*, trans. Luscombe, pp. 52–53.
4 Ibid., pp. 46–47.
5 Ibid., pp. 48–49.
6 Ibid., pp. 40–41.

or heart impressed or imprinted[7] by images, or even by "virtue": thus Foryetel-
nesse "noght mai in his herte impresse / Of vertu which reson hath sett"
(4.542–43). Medieval poets, as J. D. Burnley has recently shown, also identify a
special power of imagination with the "gentil herte,"[8] for such a heart is
"neysshe" and therefore particularly susceptible to impressions. To soften the
heart or to make it "gentil," is, in a good sense, to make it particularly receptive
or sensitive to the good imprint, or to virtue. It is to such an end, in the larger
idiom of the period, that God "makeþ þe herte nesche . . . as wex tempered."[9]
Heightened sensitivity and perception associated with the heart also inclines
the "gentil" to love, of course, and this notion underlies Genius's assertion that
"love hath evere hise lustes grene / In gentil folk." The idle Rosiphelee presumably belongs to the "gentil nacion," for though initially no imagination "mihte
sette hire in the weie / Of loves occupacion" (4.1256–58), she is deeply affected by the images of a vision, and because of that experience, she changes
"al hire ferste entente / Withinne hire herte" (4.1444–45).

If a heart is truly "gentil," of course, it will be most deeply affected by a good
love. A tale about Ulysses near the outset of Book 4 reveals more fully how
such a love is ordered by "resonable entencion." In this exemplum, a much
revised version of a story in Ovid's *Heroides*, Penelope writes to Ulysses in Troy,
lamenting his slackness in returning to her. Genius's chief interest is the effect
of that letter. When it reaches Ulysses,

> he, which wisdom hath pourveied
> Of al that to reson belongeth
> With gentil herte it underfongeth.   4.204–06

Ulysses's imagination then identifies the goal of "resonable entencion": "love
his herte hath so thorghsesed / With pure ymaginacioun" (4.210–11) that he is
unable to "flitt his herte aside" (4.214) from Penelope's concern, and thus he
applies his whole "corage" to shaping his homeward journey. Genius does not
mention Ulysses' tardiness or wandering on the journey itself: once the war
ends, this hero makes "no delaiement" and hastens home, "Wher that he fond
tofore his yhe / His worthi wif in good astat" (4.228–29). Intent on magnifying
the virtue of his exemplar, Genius also foreshadows what he will later say about
"honeste love" and "gentilesse," for Ulysses represents in his journey to Penelope a response to the sloth that "hindreth many a cause honeste" (4.233).
This case makes clear how the "gentil herte," seized by imagination, is quickened to purposive, reasonable activity.

Elsewhere in Book 4, Genius represents in the imagination a power to
organize the busyness he has established as the chief antidote for sloth. Where-

---

[7] On the use of this figure by late medieval poets, see J. D. Burnley, *Chaucer's
Language and the Philosophers' Tradition*, Chaucer Studies 2 (Cambridge, 1979), pp.
102–104, 106.
[8] Ibid., pp. 151–65.
[9] *Book of Vices and Virtues*, p. 93.

as this faculty might quicken the heart to pursue a great and noble good, it might, when not ordered by reason, encourage promiscuity, at root fostering the opinion that "every love is praiseworthy in itself": this is the danger to the pliant, soft, or tender heart of "gentil folk," a reluctance to judge rationally whether the impression – the image – is good. The excursus on true *gentilesse* discourages such indulgence by providing a mechanism for garnering and winnowing. The other prospect for imagination, however, is a reality in the *Confessio*, and even Ulysses is not exempted from it.

The exemplum of that hero in the opening section of Book 4 is preceded by another story drawn from the *Heroides*, the tale of Dido's response to Aeneas's leaving Carthage. Unlike the story of Ulysses, which finally praises busyness, this tale is written exclusively to condemn sloth. Shortly after Aeneas departs for Italy, Dido writes a letter threatening suicide if he tarries in returning to her. With "thoghtes feinte / Towardes love and full of Slowthe" (4.118–19), however, Aeneas lets time pass, and Dido kills herself after she issues a final complaint: "Ha, who fond evere such a lak / Of Slowthe in eny worthi kniht?" (4.128–29). This story, like that of Ulysses, creates obvious problems for those who know it in other versions. To stress Aeneas' sloth, the priest gives little warrant for the trip to Italy, only hinting at a reason in an almost parenthetical "it scholde be." In Virgil's epic, of course, Aeneas displays "a lak / Of Slowthe" in a sense neither Dido nor her creator in the *Confessio* intends: he displays a virtuous busyness in obeying the gods' behest that he leave Dido for the sake of a great "cause honeste": to remain with Dido, or to return to her, in this frame of reference, would constitute *lachesce*. Given the emphasis in Gower's possible sources, however, Genius's opposed perspective is perhaps understandable: in the *Heroides* and relevant medieval versions of the story, the divine purpose in Aeneas' mission tends to be understated. Even more germane to the context of Amans's concern, of course, the omission makes the tale a better exemplum *in causa amoris*. The same might be said of changes in the second narrative. By having Penelope send the letter to Troy while Ulysses is still there, Genius effectively cancels the questions that even the Ovidian Penelope has about the reasons for Ulysses' delay. Her letter in Ovid has no clear destination. The war has ended, most of the Greek survivors have returned, but no one really knows the whereabouts of Ulysses, and Penelope is forced to give a copy of her letter to every sojourner in Ithaca who might later encounter him. Her uncertainty about what causes his delay, about where hard-heartedly (*ferreus*) he hides, and her fear that free to return, he wills to be absent,[10] make her complaint and appeal all the more poignant. Genius's tale is psychologically simpler, and had he stuck to its point throughout Book 4, centering imagination and *gentilesse* on the honest cause, this tale, like the first one, might have retained the power of its simplicity.

In the long reach of argument, however, Genius rarely does things simply.

---

[10] Ovid, *Heroides* 1.58, 80, ed. and trans. Grant Showerman, Loeb (London and Cambridge, Mass., 1914; rpt., 1963), pp. 14–17.

Later in Book 4 – in setting arms against a slothful ease – he finds occasion to
reverse the status of his two exemplars: Aeneas now becomes the positive,
Ulysses the negative figure. Aeneas, Dido's earlier testimony notwithstanding,
is a "worthi kniht" who wins Lavinia because he fights Turnus, thereby engaging in the travail expected of a person of his estate. Ulysses, on the other hand,
exemplifies deferred busyness once again, in this case before he joins the Greek
campaign: now, however, his eventual activity is called into question by virtue
of his "entencion." At home on Ithaca, he has "his herte fyred / Upon his wif"
(4.1882–83) and devises a trick to stay there – to avoid the war – so that he
might "welde his love at wille" (4.1828). Tricked in turn by his recruiters, he is
then taught a lesson in the "grete schame to a king" who

> wolt in a querele of trowthe
> Of armes thilke honour forsake,
> And duelle at hom for loves sake.   4.1864–66

Eventually, the chastened Ulysses, with "tamed . . . herte," joins the Greek
forces, leaving behind "al the sotie / Of love for chivalerie" (4.1887–88). The
context for these tales reveals that a busyness narrowly focused in amoris causa,
though obviously purposive, need not be reasonable or as worthy as a "vertu
moral" that opens out to a greater world, a social context.

Even more important, however, is the revision in Genius's opinion of these
figures, and especially of Ulysses. Certainly the Greek hero is not the exemplar
we might have initially thought: given the "sotie" of his love before the Trojan
War, we must now doubt his "resonable" intention in two directions, asking
whether he truly aspires to honor in battle, or is merely shamed into action,
and whether, on later receiving Penelope's letter, he truly seeks the honest love
of a worthy wife, or merely craves once again to indulge the foolish "lustes [he]
sette above" (4.1878) chivalry. His gentle heart, in other words, may be too
soft, too susceptible to impressions. Ulysses is quickly persuaded to join the
assault, then to return to Penelope: we are not much assured that he follows
the counsel of wisdom he is supposed to possess. And lest we think that Genius,
in these retrospective tellings, sees Ulysses changed for the better by his experience at Troy – that the first tale in this sequence does establish an ideal of the
better man – we need only look very briefly at Book 6, where the priest,
drawing on still other sources, reveals that his hero after the war does not
actually return to Penelope in all haste, as he had earlier claimed. No longer
impressed by "knihthod" or his "worthi wif," Ulysses pauses to dally with Circe
and Calypso, and while he avoids their "Art magique" and deception, "He tok
of hem so wel his part, / That he begat Circes with childe" (6.14560–61).
Ulysses knows what he is doing – "He kepte him sobre and made hem wilde"
(6.1462) – and yet, much as he has lost sight of the "cause honeste" imprinted
on his imagination and "gentil herte," he also soon forgets that he has begotten
a child on Circe (6.1614–16); for him, that lapse of memory will be fatal. These
tales together reveal that the gentle Ulysses attends only to what pleases him at

the moment. Quick to "flitt his herte aside," he clearly lacks the stability that virtue alone confers on the "verrai gentil man."

The exemplar of Ulysses, I shall later argue, has a special relevance to Genius, to the gentle make-up of his character, to his gentle busyness, and to the kind of activity he encourages in his charge. To Amans, however, Ulysses has less relevance, and the tales about him would appear to offer little solace, for, as the lover complains, "me was nevere assigned place / Where yit to geten eny grace" (4.271–72). In response to such complaints, Genius provides other tales of gentle love, better designed to console the lover and to inform his amorous busyness.

The exemplum of Pygmalion and the statue is one such tale. It begins in the strong imagination of Pygmalion, a "lusti man" who creates an image

> Wherof that he himself beguileth.
> For with a goodly lok sche smyleth,
> So that thurgh pure impression
> Of his ymaginacion
> With al the herte of his corage
> His love upon this faire ymage
> He sette.   4.387–93

Pygmalion's creation of the image and his busyness in asking grace, itself grounded upon an indefatigable hope, lead to "loves spede." In late medieval poetry, of course, Pygmalion is typically presented as an exemplar of idolatry, and yet at least one scholar has seen exceptions: whereas Jean de Meun uses the tale to represent "idolatrous love at once foolish and sensual," Machaut, in the Fonteinne amoureuse, uses it to display "faithful conjugal love," and Gower, it appears, follows in the tradition of Machaut: "Most examples of good love in Gower lead to marriage and offspring," and the English poet "extends the illustration [of good love] to Pygmalion,"[11] presumably because in this tale, that love is shown to lead to marriage and offspring.

Such an outcome, however, does not suddenly make the love "honeste" or good. By his prayers, Pygmalion "wan a lusti wif" (4.424) and she "obeissant was at his wille" (4.425). If the vivid account of Pygmalion's busyness prior to this event is not enough to disclose the nature and intent of his will, or to determine whether his intention is reasonable, we need only continue reading: because Pygmalion "dorste speke" his prayers, a happy Genius concludes, "his love he spedde, / And hadde al that he wolde abedde" (4.429–30). Thus the story ends, unless we wish to take its one remaining sentence, on the begetting of a knave child, as further proof of honesty, legitimizing all of Pygmalion's earlier labor as work in an honest cause.

The narrative of Pygmalion becomes a model to inform Amans's busyness. Amans never wavers in loyalty to his lady's image, and in that refusal to turn his heart aside, he, like Pygmalion, better exemplifies a truth embodied in

11 D. Kelly, pp. 234, 201.

Ulysses than does Ulysses himself. The outcome of his own tale is not assured, of course, but with Genius's support he will continue to follow Pygmalion, who profits because "he axeth grace" (4.410).

Through most of the confession, a hope nourished by imagination is all that sustains Amans; he has succumbed to the "gentil" counsel of will:

> Reson seith that I scholde leve
> To love, wher ther is no leve
> To spede, and will seith therayein
> That such an herte is to vilein,
> Which dar noght love, and til he spede,
> Let hope serve at such a nede.   3.1179–84

Hope never achieves the status for Amans that Esperance can have for the gentle lovers in the *dits* of French writers, including especially the poetry of Machaut. There, Douglas Kelly argues, hope enables a lover "to grow inwardly by [the lady's] example" and to be "content with less than might satisfy desire."[12] Love requires the beloved's *dous regard*, but, as hope replaces desire, the love becomes self-sufficient. The lover creates an Image, an idealized projection of the beloved, and that type supplants the individual as a perfection to be revered and imitated: the love no longer depends on the lady's *merci*, and the lover can thereby achieve a state of perfect contentment.[13] In the *Confessio*, it is true, Amans has formed an image of his lady's perfection, and because "Sche is the pure hed and welle / And Mirour and ensample of goode" (5.2604–05), he can readily express adoration. Until his conversion, however, he does not know contentment. Hope never displaces or sublimates desire; nor is it ever very secure. False and treacherous, it sets "the herte in jeupartie" (3.1173) with wishing and fantasy, and it never allows the lover to be satisfied with his lady's *dous regard*. Amans has given his beloved his whole heart, but she will not pay him back with a "goodli word . . . / Wherof min hope mihte arise, / Mi grete love to compense" (5.4503–05). Genius reminds him, however, of an earlier exchange involving the heart:

> Thou seist hou sche for o lokinge
> Thin hole herte fro the tok:
> Sche mai be such, that hire o lok
> Is worth thin herte manyfold.   5.4540–43

Driven by desire and obviously not content with "hire o lok," the lover does not understand that a return of favors is a matter not "Of duete, bot al of grace" (5.4555). Even more basically, he refuses to accept the truth he has learned from reason, that in his hope "ther is no feith" (3.1176).

---

12 Ibid., p. 136.
13 Ibid., pp. 130–37, 148–49; Brownlee, *Poetic Identity*, pp. 115, 125; for a key instance in Machaut's poetry of hope replacing desire, see the "Lay d'Esperance" in *Le Livre du Voir-dit*, 4106–4361, ed. Paulin Paris (Paris, 1875).

Amans's short-sighted desire underlies Book 4, whose project is to invent and foster hope by encouraging a frantic busyness, wishing, and fantasy. The lover is "so trewly amerous" (4.921) that he has diligently sought advice on how to conduct his suit; despite his enduring curiosity, however, he has "nevere herde . . . man recorde" what might avail to win love without fail. He is thus driven to his primary activity – pursuing his love – guided only by what is broadly expected of the gentle lover: "to serve is al his besynesse."[14] The activity Amans confesses – "I serve, I bowe, I loke, I loute" (4.1169) – is engagingly silly for its very busyness, but it always reflects an effort to be genteel and courtly. When, to entertain the beloved, he dances and carols, plays at dice, or reads about Troilus, that would seem to be enough to sublimate his love, allowing him, on the model of the ideal *amant* in Machaut, to realize "all his hope in the Image, the sight, and the *bel acueil* of his lady."[15] Throughout, however, he is frustrated by his failed attempts to satisfy his desire, and his "tristesce" is intensified by the knowledge that his entire, ambitious program of love-service is idle:

> Bot thogh my besinesse laste,
> Al is bot ydel ate laste,
> For whan theffect is ydelnesse,
> I not what thing is besinesse.   4.1757–60

This complaint even extends to imagination. When he makes a "collacioun" of his lady, "it doth [him] harm / Of pure ymaginacioun" (4.1142–43), for he always finds his "besi thoght / Is torned ydel into noght" (4.1150–52). For him, the lady's *bel acueil* in letting him serve her is insufficient encouragement: "sche ne wile / That I have eny cause of hope, / Noght also mochel as a drope" (5.4750–52).

Amans, however, is obdurate: a "gentil" and no "vilein," he follows the counsel of will in daring to love, but his tenacity and frustration together threaten to increase his impatience, bitterness, and "tristesce." Genius fittingly advises him to temper his "corage," but Amans already knows in his rational nature "That I myn herte scholde softe" (3.1164). To soften the heart, in this context, is to make it receptive to reason's counsel; it is to become debonaire or – to borrow words from Chaucer's Parson – "tretable to goodnesse" (*ParsT* 657). And where the lover cannot effect this end, we might expect the priest to assist him.

What occurs in the confessional sections of Book 4, however, is something quite different: Genius only encourages more wishing and fantasy. In the story of Iphis and Iante, for example, he builds an assurance that Cupid will take pity on a "grete love" (4.489) by making natural whatever in it "stant ayein" Nature's lore. Gower does not yet show us what this might mean to Amans, but the claim is likely to win the regard of a lover whom we shall later see as "olde

---

14 Chaucer, *Ven* 20.
15 D. Kelly, p. 136.

grisel" (8.2407). The priest encourages Amans to believe that a natural fulfillment of love is possible, no matter how remote, implausible, unnatural, or
ridiculous that love appears. To the end of nourishing that hope, he also
encourages a heightened activity that clearly lacks the ordering of a reasonable
intention: "pull up a besi herte," he tells the lover, "and let nothing asterte / Of
love fro thi besinesse" (4.723–25). Such advice can only increase the frustration Amans feels and succinctly identifies: "I seche that I mai noght finde"
(4.289).

The failure of the confession to do its work, however, is only partly explained by this kind of counsel. The poet explains more as he develops and
arranges the imaginative busyness of the confessor himself; in that process, he
will also generate a range of perspectives on *gentilesse* that will enrich the
concept and help to define it most meaningfully.

Genius's failure to garner and winnow types of busyness betrays a particular
kind of *ingenium*. He is inventive, but not an inventor who consistently uses his
"wittes alle." He relies chiefly on imagination, often in its worst form: a running about with vague mind, inspired merely by something seen or done a very
short time before.[16] Indeed, in exercising this faculty, Genius most resembles
the "gentil" Ulysses: quick to generate images, he is also quick to forget them,
to "flitt his herte aside." Topics fade as new attractions take their place, and in
the process "resonable entencion" gets lost. In putting Amans to work in
occupations that are sometimes idle, sometimes "leveful," the imaginatively
busy priest seems, like the personified Negligence, to set "of no vertu pris / Bot
as him liketh for the while" (4.907–909).

This is not to say, however, that the poet places no limits on the vagaries of
his confessor's imagination. Genius organizes much of his argument in these
middle confessional books around four images of what inspires or nurtures love
in the gentle man, and these exemplars or images of the beloved set boundaries
for his *evagatio mentis*. As certain of his arguments have made manifest, all is
not bad with Genius. In serving two masters, he is torn between conflicting
ideals of *gentilesse*, the one figured in his goddess, the other in "holi bokes
wise." Drawing on these conflicting sources, he impresses images on his pupil,
but, as Alan of Lille had earlier observed in his own figure of Genius,[17] he forms
those images sometimes with the right, sometimes with the left hand, and it is
obviously the priest's left-handed efforts that exacerbate Amans's inner strife.
In each of his two roles, Genius imagines a type and an antitype for the

---

[16] For like features, see the description of the bestial, as opposed to the rational,
imagination in Richard of St. Victor, *Benjamin minor* 16, PL 196:11. For useful medieval background on the relationship between imagination and *ingenium*, see Theodore
Silverstein, "The Fabulous Cosmogony of Bernardus Silvestris." *Modern Philology* 46
(1948): 98 n. 34; Wetherbee, "Theme of Imagination," pp. 46–51; Kathryn L. Lynch,
The High Medieval Dream Vision: Poetry, Philosophy, and Literary Form (Stanford, 1988),
pp. 34–42; on the relationship between *ingenium* and Gower's figure of Genius, see
Lynch, pp. 170–71.
[17] Alan of Lille, *De planctu Naturae*, pr. 9, trans. Sheridan, pp. 216–17; PL 210:480.

beloved: these images will order the intentions of the "gentil" lover. In Genius's perspective as a priest, the type is Amans's difficult and perplexing mistress; the antitype is Venus. In his perspective as a servant of Venus, the type is Pygmalion's "lusti wif," originally the statue; the antitype is Araxarathen, a figure introduced in the final tale of Book 4; we shall consider her presently. All of these figures are in one sense or another "gentil," but, as will be readily apparent, only one fully represents the ideal *gentilesse* defined in Genius's re-creative excursus.

The story of Iphis and Araxarathen is based upon a tale in Ovid's *Metamorphoses*. In the original, Anaxarete – a character Gower renames Araxarathen – spurns the advances of Iphis, and he, in despair, kills himself; Anaxarete is unable to avoid gazing at him on his bier, and while she looks on, as hard-hearted as she has been throughout, the gods turn her physically to stone. Genius transforms this tale significantly, and yet his ultimate exemplary purpose, like Ovid's, is to show the effect of the woman's hard-heartedness not only on another, but on herself. Genius makes Araxarathen the antitype of Pygmalion's "lusti wif," and the difference between these figures is readily apparent in their opposed careers. Whereas the "colde ymage" (4.422) of Pygmalion's statue literally softens, becoming warm in "fleissh and bon" (4.423), the "fleissh and bon" (4.3679) of Araxarathen turns cold and hardens, literally into the "figure of a Ston" (4.3680). As far as these women are concerned, however, the difference is cosmetic. Neither prospect can be particularly appealing, especially if we recall Genius's major point in the first tale: to the statue, all that being full of life can mean is that Pygmalion, at last, will have all that he "wolde abedde." The more important difference lies in the male perspective: the statue is "tretable" and therefore good; Araxarathen is not and therefore wicked. The one is "gentil," the other "vilein."

Nonetheless, Araxarathen's case is more complex than this contrast makes it appear, partly because Genius has so radically altered her character. In the original, Anaxarete is a Teucrian princess, but in character she is, in every respect, the contrary of gentle: *saeva, inmites, dura, ferrea, crudelis, impia, superba, ferox.*[18] In Genius's version, by contrast, Araxarathen is "a Maide of lou astat" (4.3521) who displays true gentility. Iphis also has a new status: though still "soubgit / To love" (4.3523–24), he is no longer a youth of humble origin, but Teucer's own son, "a potestat / Of worldes good" (4.3522–23). Through these changes, Genius obviously calls attention to the power of goodness and love over "degre," and by changing both figures, he draws out an even greater strength in the character of Araxarathen. As Iphis, by the privilege of status, might expect another to yield to the "fantasie" of his love, so Araxarathen, because of her status, might be expected to submit to the wishes of this "potestat." She does not, however, and she rejects him not because she has forgotten her place, or because she is proud or scornful, but because she is wholly devoted to virtue. In this version of the tale, Iphis

18 Ovid, *Metamorphoses* 14.698–761, ed. Miller, 2:350–55.

> excedeth the mesure
> Of reson, that himself assure
> He can noght.   4.3525–27

By a new pairing of terms – of Iphis's foolish love and Araxarathen's reason – Genius shifts the focus of the original, now turning Iphis into the principal negative exemplar:

> He was with love unwys constreigned,
> And sche with resoun was restreigned:
> The lustes of his herte he suieth,
> And sche for drede schame eschuieth
> And as sche scholde, tok good hiede
> To save and kepe hir wommanhiede.   4.3529–34

Iphis kills himself because the lady "wolt noght do [him] grace" (4.3585), but he has less cause for despair than does Ovid's Iphis because the woman acts not out of malice or cruelty, but out of virtue. Araxarathen refuses to yield to the kind of *gentilesse* that would force her to offer the "o word" to heal Iphis, thereby satisfying him with soft speech, proof of a "gentil herte," but also fostering in him a groundless hope and a false impression of her character.

Araxarathen also differs from the Ovidian character in another sense. Whereas Ovid's Anaxarete never really changes – she is turned to stone "quod fuit in duro iam pridem pectore" (14.758) – Araxarathen "softens" her behavior late in Genius's narrative. A tormented Iphis, just before he kills himself, blames his decision on her "herte hard" (4.3583), and she later confirms his judgment when she "takth upon hirself the gilt" (4.3610) for Iphis's suicide and seeks harsh judgment for what she has done: "For I ne dede no pite / To him, which for mi love is lore" (4.3628–29).[19] In her remorse, as "Sche wepth, sche crith, sche swouneth ofte" (4.3619), however, she proves that, far from being a "vilein" lacking in sensitivity, she is naturally gentle and perfectly capable of displaying *gentilesse*. Iphis does not give her much chance to reveal this side to her nature: nor is it Genius's wish to imagine it before it serves his exemplary purpose late in the narrative.

We may well ask, however, what that exemplary purpose is. It would seem that if the priest had wished merely to condemn hard-heartedness, the Ovidian figure would have served his purpose quite nicely. At the very least, Genius's revisions tighten the relationship between the exemplum and Amans's own "tale," for the now gentle Araxarathen displays in her actions the same paradox that Amans imagines in his own mistress, as when he complains, in Book 3:

> Ha, who sawh evere such a weie?
> Ha, who sawh evere such destresse?
> Withoute pite gentilesse,
> Withoute mercy wommanhede,

[19] On pity and the "gentil herte," see Burnley, pp. 156–59.

> That wol so quyte a man his mede
> Which evere hath be to love trewe.   3.1604–09

Both Amans and Iphis are bewildered by the lady's cruel response to their "trouthe," and both locate that cruelty in the figure of Daunger. Iphis thus complains that "Daunger shal to manye mo / Ensample be for everemo, / Whan thei my wofull deth recorde." (4.3589–91). Amans also sees in his beloved a potential for homicide. Should he die because Daunger keeps her from bestowing grace on him, the lover melodramatically argues, it would be a double pity. If

> I scholde in such a wise
> In rewardinge of my servise
> Be ded, me thenkth it were a rowthe.   3.1595–97

And if this happens, the mistress must be blamed, "Whan with o word sche mihte have heled / A man, and soffreth him so deie" (3.1602–03). These words are echoed in the story of Araxarathen: her effigy is presented "in ensample of tho wommen, / That soffren men to deie so" (4.3676–77).

The parallel between these stories is a curious one, however, for what Genius does with the shared topic of "tristesce." The "askinge of merci," Amans notes, is all that keeps him from despair (4.3497–99). Coming into this final narrative of Book 4, Amans has nourished a hope, modelled on the example of Pygmalion, that repeated pleas for grace will "deserve grace" (4.616). Very early in this last tale, however, Genius shows the effect of Iphis's pleas on the hard-hearted Araxarathen: "the more he preide, / The lasse love on him sche leide" (4.3527–28). Amans has made a like point about his own situation a short time before: "The more that I knele and preie, / With goode wordes and with softe, / The more I am refused ofte" (4.1748–50). The tale, rather than counteract despair, thereby seems by this precedent to encourage it.

Less superficially, however, the tale provides an exemplum against despair, and how it does so is significant for Gower's larger perception of *gentilesse*. The change in Araxarathen is created to support a certain kind of *gentilesse*: if at the outset of the tale she embodies a *gentilesse* of virtue, at the end, in her self-judgment and conversion, she is made to conform to a *gentilesse* of self-indulgent *kinde*. In this metamorphosis she has become the "soubgit" or victim of Genius's own "gentil" imagination, for the priest has her dismiss – indeed, not even consider – her virtue and original "resonable entencion," her justifiable modesty and caution in rejecting a foolish and sensual Iphis. What is worse, in making this flesh-and-blood character choose her status as a cold and lifeless "ymage" Genius effectively has her yield to the desires of such self-indulgent lovers as Iphis and Amans, assigning to herself an image of "vilenie" that they, as well as Genius, project in support of a certain kind of gentle love. Her reductive self-judgment thus legitimizes Genius's criticism of her in the epitaph he invents for the common tomb: "He [i.e., Iphis] was to neysshe and sche to hard" (4.3681). As we shall now observe, this statement, even while it cancels out aspects of Araxarathen's character manifested in the narrative, lends special support to Genius's rhetoric against a particular despair.

Tristesce is wrong chiefly because it represents a breach of decorum – a loss of will or "herte" – in the love of "gentil folk." The fact that Iphis has here been transformed into a "potestat," though it does not technically establish a further parallel with Amans's situation, does call attention to another, shared sense of privilege in these male figures. Both characters, in Genius's lesser vision of *gentilesse*, have right on their side: both enjoy the prerogative of "trewe" love. We have seen it in Amans's complaint in Book 3; Iphis also claims it in his final apostrophe, when he complains of the injustice in his dying: "I am ded for love and trouthe" (4.3587); even Araxarathen evidently comes to recognize this love-prerogative, and that is what her late display of a "gentil herte" may finally signify. In Genius's perspective she is a worthy person who makes a mistake, recognizes it, and regrets it profoundly: in coming to accept the privilege of love, Araxarathen thus "enacts" the lesson Genius is attempting to teach Amans. Iphis's sin, in Genius's perspective, is not the initial "wrong" of a foolish and sensual love, but effectively the opposite: it lies in being too "neysshe," in forsaking such love and his rights as a lover. As far as Amans is concerned, the special prominence given to Araxarathen at the site of the tomb – her image "as for miracle / Was set upon an hyh pinacle, / That alle men it mihte knowe" (4.3661–63) – serves to re-establish the prerogative of love: the focused picture of a female wrong and "vilenie" becomes the antidote for wanhope by consoling, vindicating, hardening the lover, making him even more "soubgit" to his tyrannical will, more inclined to decry the lady's injustice against one who is to "love trewe."

In such a setting of true but unrequited love, Iphis, Genius, and Amans all deal with paradox reductively: they simply fit the gentle woman to an image of "vilenie." The "verrai" gentle woman is not so "tretable," of course: she is not, like Pygmalion's "lusti wif," the mere product of wishing and fantasy; she will not succumb to a lover's desire merely because he claims "trouthe." With characters such as Iphis and Amans that very resistance can obviously cause "tristesce." Genius checks such an inclination to "desesperance" in his charge, however, by inventing a tale that includes the fantasy of a gentle woman admitting her want of pity, a villainy. Ultimately, the story of Araxarathen, like that of Pygmalion's quickened statue, serves an idolatrous love. The images of women in both stories nourish a foolish hope, a hope that "is noght trewe of that he seith" (3.1176).

As Amans moves between "tristesce" and hope, between the stances exemplified by Iphis and Pygmalion, he refashions his lady accordingly, fitting her variously to the types of gentle woman presented in these two tales: he transforms her sometimes into a character like Araxarathen, the cold "figure of a Ston," stonelike in her "herte hard"; sometimes into a character like Pygmalion's spouse, the "faire ymage" warm and "full of lif" (4.423), alive specifically to his "wihssinge."[20]

---

[20] We shall presently see an instance of the latter, as well as of the "excessive meditation" that produces it, in Amans's confession of sacrilege (5.7108–63).

But these are not the only ways in which Amans perceives his mistress. Her image becomes a "good imprint" when he recalls her from contexts other than her relationship to him. On such occasions, she is courteous, friendly, "soft in compaignie," and, as a true "gentil," she is also fittingly restrained. Reason and discretion order her kindness and "kinde," and thus, as Amans himself testifies:

> toward othre, as I mai se,
> Sche takth and yifth in such degre,
> That as be weie of frendlihiede
> Sche can so kepe hir wommanhiede,
> That every man spekth of hir wel.   5.4753–57

From what the lover says about his lady in contexts such as this, Genius forms another exemplar, this one not a single image, but a number of partial reflections of the lady's excellence. He uses these principally to explain and justify her seeming hardness – her want of pity – and also to rebuke Amans for lacking grace in implying that his mistress is sometimes less than "gentil." What emerges in the composite of these images is the lady's prudence and "mesure."[21] Following "resonable entencion," she retains a dignity wholly suited to her gentle nature. Thus she is not, like Genius's Araxarathen, too hard; it is rather the case that Amans's suit "to hire honour missit" (5.5213).

Even here Genius does not address complexity of character, or the delicate balance the lady achieves between potentially opposed sides of *gentilesse*, as in her "frendlihiede" and "wommanhiede," for example, and yet he forms this image with his right hand. Also with the right hand he forms an antitype in the Venus he serves. From the long excursus in Book 5 where he explores the "nyce fantasie" of pagan religions, Genius tries, but, thanks to Amans, fails to exclude his goddess, and to his shame, he must now reveal her character. Whereas Amans, in his Iphis state, sees his own beloved as too closely guarded by Danger, Genius now condemns the contrary in a Venus who

> alle danger putte aweie
> Of love, and fond to lust a weie;
> So that of hire in sondri place
> Diverse men felle into grace.   5.1389–90

Unlike Amans's wise mistress, Venus is preoccupied with fleshly comforts and desires. She is incapable of "mesure" or reason, and in her "gentil herte," the soft or "tender" affectus thereby run too quickly. Her "tenterhed or nessched of herte" is obviously not a mark of true gentility; it is, simply, a sloth wherein she "draweþ after þe likynges of [the] body."[22]

Especially in presenting these last two images, Genius reveals a capacity to

---

[21] For a useful discussion of "mesure" in late medieval literature, see Burnley, pp. 118–26.
[22] *Book of Vices and Virtues*, pp. 26–27. For a helpful schema of the branches of sloth represented in late medieval popular treatises, see Wenzel, *Sin of Sloth*, pp. 80–82.

make distinctions. But he does not seem to use those distinctions profitably; too infrequently does he project the type and antitype of "vertu moral," or the ideal of *gentilesse* he presents in Book 4. As a result, he seems incapable of freeing Amans from images of "gentil love" modelled in the tales of Pygmalion and Iphis. Neither kind of image – the "lusti wif," the woman of "herte hard" – will make Amans into a "verrai gentil man," of course; nor will either ever allow him to understand true *gentilesse*.

The four exemplars of *gentilesse* we have just considered are not drawn to resolution in a single perspective in the *Confessio*, and the reason lies in the gentle imagination or the *ingenium* of Gower's two major characters. The issue here is a poetics of *gentilesse*: by that I do not mean merely a poetry with *gentilesse* as subject, but *gentilesse* as implying different kinds of imagination out of which poems, loves, and deeds are invented and come to have meaning. If I might follow a metaphoric distinction made by John of Salisbury, Amans's *ingenium* is the type that creeps or "is mired down to earth, and cannot rise."[23] To the extent that his gaze is fixed on images inspired by a venerean *gentilesse*, he "can make no progress." Genius's *ingenium* is the type that flies: lacking stability, it reaches to both kinds of *gentilesse*, but settles in neither. This also, as we have seen, is a form of sloth. At extremes of creeping and flitting about, these two speakers cannot stand and climb, or make evident progress to wisdom. What the poem appears to lack in its major characters, then, is a third type of *ingenium*, one "that goes to neither extreme [and walks]"; one that enacts a righteous or truly gentle busyness; one, in short, that follows a "resonable entencion."

Despite the speakers' tendency to get lost in the maze of their own gentle language, however, Gower uses many devices to keep the work advancing steadily toward the wisdom he has promised to his readers. These include *recreationes* such as the excursus of Book 4, entire sections of the work that are in some respect detached from the business of the confession and the leisure or state of fulfillment towards which the entire poem moves. Another is the *gentilesse*, including the "grace," of Amans's beloved: her gift is a gift of resistance, of remaining a "reality" beyond the fiction of the confession, a person who in her complexity remains inaccessible to the fragmenting imagination: she will not conform to the partial images priest and lover generate. That complexity, which the speakers can only hint at in their partial reflections, is attributable to her being a truly gentle person: throughout, she is an illusive, yet enduring reminder of the *gentilesse* and good intention that Amans, in his own person, lacks.

Also at work in moving the argument to wisdom, but paradoxically and on another level entirely, is Genius's own unstable *ingenium*. His divided loyalties and attention destabilize his doctrine of love and *gentilesse*, to be sure; he cannot by example or precept give Amans even a superficial "sikernesse." In

---

[23] John of Salisbury, *Metalogicon* 1.11, trans. McGarry, p. 35; ed. Webb, p. 29. Wetherbee introduces this distinction in "Theme of Imagination," pp. 46–47.

that apparent ineptitude, however, he sustains the lover's attention – the language of Venus is an imperative in this confession – while he also prepares him for the greatest, most consequential profit. Surely Genius cannot be trusted to be wholly committed to arguments he presents on either side of an issue. He is, in effect, a personified *demande*. In the double perspective of a *demande*, or of this Genius, the excursus on *gentilesse* might be seen as the product of idle leisure or of "ernest," and the enveloping shrift as the product of "game" or just business. Given Genius's centrality to the poem, however, that very doubleness makes the whole of the *Confessio* a "joieuse recreation." The work teaches a fruitful leisure, both as a courtly poem and a compilation, by not allowing us to close the "conversacion," quickly to accept solutions, however right they are, to problems we do not yet fully understand. This is a critical principle of the literary form of the *demande*, and it becomes a critical principle of the *Confessio*. By design, the work checks a human tendency to make easy, premature, unwise, and falsely secure judgments in a world where "evere stant a man in doute" (P.562).

The premise underlying this "game" is a doctrine whose import neither Amans, nor the priest who utters it, can comprehend:

> love moste ben awaited:
>
> . . .
> Thou might noght of thiself been able
> To winne love or make it stable,
> All thogh thou mihtest love achieve.   4.263, 267–69

The ellipses in this quotation cover another promise of "decerte" for busyness. Genius is always quick to offer such advice because, like Chaucer's "fader of gentilesse," he "loved besinesse, / Ayeinst the vyce of slouthe, in honestee" (*Gent* 1, 10–11). Genius is even busier than this exemplar, however, for in him all of Chaucer's terms become protean, variable in content, and that means increased activity, specifically as in word and deed the priest busily combines, mixes, reverses senses of idle and "leveful bisynesse." By that very means, however, Gower builds into this "amoureuse conversacion" a potential of invention or discovery, of a re-created intention. Indeed, as busyness, leisure, and idleness change in valence in the course of the work, "gentil" busyness comes to mean "Som newe thing" (P.51*), and Amans is being prepared to discover it with his "wittes alle." That "besinesse" is what he awaits, and ultimately it will come to him in the form of a gift, a love taught in "holy bokes wise" that will make him gentle and give him rest, but a rest far greater than the *otium* that has occasioned his "gentil love" and made him a superficially "gentil man." Book 5 of the poem, as it refines the concept of profit, will point him to that goal in yet another way.

CHAPTER TWELVE

AVARICE: THE THREE "LIEVEST" THINGS AND IDOLATRY

In its opening epigram, Book 5 reintroduces the subject of natural law – "Obstat auaricia nature legibus" 'Avarice obstructs the laws of nature' – and this subject is now re-examined in an historical perspective, effectively in a new structure of conversion. Shortly after Creation, Genius asserts, "al was set to the comune" (5.5), but then avarice, or the press for "worldes good," caused war, "Which alle love leide aside / And of comun his propre made" (5.14–15). In presenting this history, Gower draws upon the literary topos of the Golden Age,[1] but he also relies on legal authors who treat issues of property according to principles of the *jus naturae*. The poet understands an original "state of nature" to refer to nature *ante peccatum* – that time, in Chaucer's words, "er that synne began, whan natureel lawe was in his right poynt in paradys" (*ParsT* 920). In essence, the impulse to make the common proper is a product of nature *post peccatum*.[2] This historical distinction, as it is developed over the course of Book 5, will bear on our perception of Amans and his notions of "gentil" behavior, natural love, and profit. The book will reveal, most basically, a defect in the *jus naturae*, a law that has been tainted by the lapsed nature it is supposed to correct. Because of that corruption, Gower argues, the species cannot hope naturally to recover its original condition, or "thastat of Innocence" and Paradise.

Early in this book, the marginal commentator reminds us that "Auaricia . . . omnium malorum radix dicitur." As the root of all evils or "harmes" (*ParsT* 738), avarice represents the antithesis to charity, the love "Which hath the vertus forto lede" (4.2327). Gower's distinction is traditional: whereas "sin springs from the desire for transient goods" and the love of riches that enable one to acquire those goods, virtue "derives from the desire for the changeless good; thus, charity, the love of God, is described . . . as the root of all virtues."[3]

---

[1] *Roman de la rose*, 9491–95, ed. Lecoy, 2:39; see also *Consolation of Philosophy*, 2. m.5; Chaucer, *The Former Age*. Portions of the present chapter have been adapted from my article, "Natural Law and Gower's *Confessio*," pp. 237–40.

[2] See, for example, Ambrose, *De officiis* 1.28.132, PL 16:62; Isidore, *Etymologiae* 5:4; Gratian, 1. dist. 8, pt. 1, C. 1; Johannes Teutonicus, *Glossa ordinaria*, ed. Lottin, p. 23; John of la Rochelle's contribution to the *Summa fratris Alexandri* 248 (Quaracchi, 1948), 4.2: 350.

[3] Thomas Aquinas, *Summa theologiae* 1a2ae, 84.1, trans. T. C. O'Brien, Blackfriars ed., 26:62–63.

For Gower, avarice is indeed a *cupiditas* that includes more than an inordinate love of "gold, of catel or of lond" (5.25); it is a misdirected or excessive love "for any sort of temporal good," and becomes, most basically, "the propensity of corrupt nature to crave transient goods inordinately."[4] It is related as a cause to the other vices, but from them it also draws a purported "strength." As a propensity of corrupt nature, it represents more than a natural desire that simply exceeds measure; it quickly turns into a twisted love that sets no limits to its "tirannie" and malice.

Given the magnitude and complexity of this problem, it should come as no surprise that Gower devotes much attention to it. Book 5 is 2–3 times longer than any other "confessional" book in the poem; it introduces 12 species of Avarice in 10 formal divisions; its excursus on the world's religion is the longest "digression" inside any book treating a specific vice. The poet also conveys a sense of the multifaceted nature of the sin through his *forma tractatus*, the division of the book into its formal sections. Whereas in the *Mirour* he had introduced 13 species of avarice, he there distributed these over only 5 major sections:

Confessio	*Mirour*
1. Avarice	1. Covoitise
2. (Goddes That Ben Believed)	a. Chalenge
3. *Covoitise*	b. Soubtilite
4. Falswitnesse and Perjurie	c. Perjurie
5. *Usure*	d. Tricherie
6. *Skarsnesse*	e. Ingratitude
7. Unkindeschipe	2. Ravyne
8. *Ravine*	a. Robberie
9. Robberie	b. Larcine
10. (Virginite)	c. Sacrilege
11. Stelthe and Mecherie	3. Usure
12. Sacrilegge	4. Simonie
13. Prodegalite (and Liberalite)	5. Escharcete

In the *Confessio*, all species of Avarice are elevated to the same level of importance. The book, for its length, and the sin, for the number of its species and the extent of the permutations made possible by this new mode of division, effectively dominate the poem.

While the poet divides Book 5 into 13 sections, however, he also finds another mechanism for ordering his discussion, and this will help make its contents more accessible. This schema is introduced in the opening narrative, the story of Midas's special gift of touch. Gower takes this tale from Ovid, but following a medieval precedent, he transforms it into an instrument for exploring major topoi regarding avarice, topics he will then use to order other discussions in the book. In the telling, for example, Genius likens the vice to the

---

4 Ibid., 60–63.

sickness of dropsy, wherein "The more ydropesie drinketh, / The more him thursteth" (5.253–54). This figure, which also appears in the Midas narrative in the *Ovide moralisé* and in medieval treatises on avarice, here opens out into other references: it is related to the pain of unsatisfied thirst and hunger, described in the next narrative of Tantalus, and to the long discussion of thirst in Book 6.[5] That topos is related to another – "Avarus vir similis est inferno," or "So is he lych unto the helle" (5.29) – showing that the desire of the *avarus* can never be satisfied.[6] Avarice

> Is as the helle wonderfull;
> For it mai neveremor be full,
> That what as evere comth therinne,
> Awey ne may it nevere winne.   5.349–52

Gower is concerned not merely to collect these figures, but to make them interdependent. In the *Mirour*, he had proceeded differently. There also, in the lines dealing with *Avarice par especial* (7585–7704), he had identified avarice with the pit of hell (7585–96), dropsy (7603) or fever (7651), and the torment of Tantalus (7621–22). It is his practice in the French poem, however, to use each stanza break as an invitation to introduce a new figure or analogy to characterize the subject. The images are strung together without an expressed logic to connect them, and each one simply occasions a separate insight into the sin. The effect, at another level entirely, is a clear impression of *compilatio*, a gathering, even a random gathering of discrete figures.

On the surface, the *Confessio* appears equally "compiled" in its presentation of exempla, images, similes, and maxims. At a deeper level, however, these figures are drawn into a sustained argument. The tale of Midas, as it introduces certain topics of Book 5 and amplifies others, loses some of its power as an independent narrative; at the same time, however, it enriches and is enriched by the poet's fuller statement regarding avarice. Ovid's simpler tale effectively "points" a warning against the love of gold. Gower's version does more. It refers us back, for example, to the opening lines of the book: it draws out of Midas's final warning to his people – the "encress / Of gold" causes "the breche of pes" (5.331–32) – a lament over a lost mythic past, "er gold was smite / In Coign,"

---

[5]   On the analogy of dropsy as introduced in the *Confessio* and other relevant texts, see Richard Newhauser, "The Love of Money as Deadly Sin and Deadly Disease," in *Zusammenhänge, Einflüsse, Wirkungen: Kongressakten zum ersten Symposium des Mediävistenverbandes in Tübingen, 1984*, ed. Joerg O. Fichte, Karl Heinz Göller, and Bernhard Schimmelpfennig (Berlin, 1986): 320–26. In the *Mirour*, Gower similarly relates avarice to *mal d'idropesie* (7603) and makes Tantalus (7622), for his insatiable thirst and hunger, a key exemplar of the sin. Alan of Lille uses Tantalus to exemplify avarice, a vice he compares to dropsy, in *De planctu Naturae*, m. 7, trans. Sheridan, pp. 181–82.
[6]   See Alan of Lille, *Summa de arte praedicatoria*, cap. 6, PL 210:125; for other medieval uses of these topoi, see, for example, Thomas Hibernicus, *Manipulus florum* or *Flores doctorum pene omnium tam Graecorum quam Latinorum* (Vienna, 1758), s. v. "avaritia," pp. 68, 73.

when "Ther was welnyh noman untrewe" (5.334–36). Remarking that "the florin / Was moder ferst of malengin" (5.343–44), Genius echoes the opening argument regarding the lost Golden Age, and this repeated emphasis is key, as it happens, not only to the book in its entirety, but also to the whole poem: it will tie Nebuchadnezzar's vision of the statue, as described in the Prologue, to Gower's ending for the work.

More immediately, Genius "finds" another topic of like importance in the story, though it is certainly not in the original. Before Midas decides what "worldes good" (5.179) he wants Bacchus to give him, he considers three things which "Ben lievest unto mannes kinde" (5.186): delight or *joie bodily*, profit, and *worschipe*. Eventually Midas will succumb to a desire for the profit of "worldes good," of course, but before he does, he has a moment of insight in which he sees the limitation in all three things. Delight cannot endure; it "schal passen in myn age" (5.191). Riches provide no "sikernesse" (5.205), and lordship is vain: all men share "o weie, / Whan thei be bore and whan thei deie" (5.201–02).

Perhaps Gower lists these goods to show, in Midas's fall, that wealth offers the greatest temptation. Midas rejects the three "lievest" things, only to turn around and ask for "worldes good," and his warrant is that such goods will enable him to do anything he wants. The desire for wealth thus becomes the root of all evils, and Midas's action forms a gloss, or an exemplum, on the earlier marginal gloss.[7]

But the tale does even more. The "dearest" things form the three temptations, "the three delights which soften the human heart to vice and lead it to the sleep of death." They are "the three related disturbances of the empassioned seat of desire," "all of them . . . examples of the perversion of love."[8] Lordship, "worldes good," and delight are obviously *temporalia* and also gifts of Fortune: worship, or "the excellence conferred by praise or honour" promises completeness; profit promises self-sufficiency; and delight promises "a third condition essential to happiness," pleasure itself.[9]

Avarice, in Gower's perspective, involves not one, but all three of these temptations, and as the tale of Midas frames a judgment against them, it also provides an "academic" gloss on Amans's confession to a love which, by meta-

---

[7] Thomas Aquinas so interprets the "sentence" of St. Paul that provides the basis of Gower's marginal gloss ("Auaricia, que omnium malorum radix dicitur"): the Apostle "is clearly speaking in the text against those who, *because they seek to become rich, fall into temptation and the snare of the devil.*" Aquinas argues that "money helps a man to obtain all manner of temporal goods" and commit all manner of evil. *Summa theologiae* 1a2ae, 84.1, Blackfriars ed., 26:60–63.

[8] Honorius of Autun, *Speculum ecclesie*, PL 172:856, trans. and discussed by D. W. Robertson, Jr., *Preface to Chaucer*, p. 144; Newhauser, pp. 325, 318; in his article, Newhauser also notes and discusses this presentation of the temptations in Gower's tale.

[9] *Summa theologiae* 1a2ae, 84.4, Blackfriars ed., 26:74–75.

phoric extension, is avaricious, and which is motivated by an interest in profit, delight, and worship.

For the lover, profit most obviously means "joie bodily," and in that respect he provides no major exception to the exemplars in the stories Genius recounts in this book. Occasionally the tales of love in Book 5 reveal a character like a Jason or the king's steward who uses a relationship for the sake of material gain; often, however, as in the treatment of robbery, "micherie," and ravine, the "possession" is sexual. Genius begins to explore the relationship between carnal pleasure and avarice at the outset of the book, immediately after he pictures the *avarus* or miser who hoards his money, keeping it locked in a coffer except at those moments

> whanne him list to have a syhte
> Of gold, hou that it schyneth brihte,
> That he ther on mai loke and muse.   5.35–37

When the priest asks the "amerous" penitent if he fares "of love so," Amans responds that he sees a likeness between this avaricious man and himself, but literalist that he is, he also notes an important difference: he has never gained "full possession of love" (5.64), even though there is no lack of avarice in his will:

> If I that swete lusti wif
> Mihte ones welden at my wille,
> For evere I wolde hire holde stille.   5.76–78

In this fantasy, the comically-presented lover even imagines his own complete lack of restraint in satisfying the "lustes" of his will:

> If I hire hadde, I wolde hire kepe,
> And yit no friday wolde I faste,
> Thogh I hire kepte and hielde faste.   5.80–82

In a sense, of course, Amans does not suffer the miser's love of money, and that is because he seeks a greater fortune: gold would not make him "so riche / As sche, that is so inly good" (5.88–89). One might suppose that he would therefore find a gladness – indeed a gladness superior to that of the *avarus* inspecting his gold – in being allowed to "loke and muse" upon his beloved. Such activity is not enough for him, however; the miser has, in this regard, attained the greater fortune:

> Bot, fader, I you herde seie
> Hou thaverous hath yit som weie,
> Wherof he mai be glad; for he
> Mai whanne him list his tresor se,
> And grope and fiele it al aboute,
> Bot I fulofte am schet theroute,
> Ther as my worthi tresor is.   5.99–105

The priest has said no such thing. This is Amans's invention, and while it surely captures the essence of what a miser might do, it also hints at Amans's less than "gentil" desire. If the lover is not to be exculpated, however, neither is Genius: he excuses the lover because the love of a woman differs from the love of money: the former "to kinde acordeth" (5.119); the latter – literal avarice – does not.

The point that Genius appears to have missed, of course, is that his charge imagines the beloved as "worldes good," an object to be possessed and "hielde faste." Whereas Genius condemns the miser because he "is unto his good a thral, / And as soubgit thus serveth he, / Wher that he scholde maister be" (5.54–56), he vindicates and encourages Amans's love-service: that service, at a level unexplored by the priest, feeds the lover's aspiration that "he scholde maister be." Profit for Amans is tied not only to "joie bodily," but to "worschipe," or the lordship that might enable him to control his "swete lusti wif" at will.

This is related to worship in another sense. Pygmalion worships and strives to exert "maistrye" over his creation, and Amans, after his own fashion, does likewise. This worship is, of course, self-worship or idolatry, and it is so presented in Book 5 as the poet further develops his argument regarding avarice and the three "lievest" things.

Amans describes his idolatry late in this book, though the sin he is supposedly confessing at the time is sacrilege. He admits that he lacks "holinesse" (5.7162) whenever he sees his beloved, but that lack is most noteworthy in church, where he pretends to be devout, largely in the hope of effecting a miracle his "ladi herte forto chaunge" (5.7123). His real devotion there emerges as an ogling that might be deemed "excessive meditation":[10] "al mi contemplacion," he boasts, "Is only set on hire ymage" (5.7126, 7128). When he leads her to the offering, the image warms, and he experiences the miracle he has long desired:

> Whan I beclippe hire on the wast,
> Yit ate leste I stele a tast,
> And otherwhile 'grant mercy'
> Sche seith, and so winne I therby
> A lusti touch, a good word eke.   5.7143–47

"Such Sacrilege" is innocent, he claims, and it "I holde a grace" (5.7156). In his greater fantasy, the confident Amans now believes he "mihte gete assignement / Wher forto spede in other place" (5.7154–55).

Although in this devotion Amans never matches the action he imagines of the *avarus*, he discovers a tactile "delit" when his mistress complies with his fantasy. It does not matter that her compliance is also his invention, that the

---

10 Concerning "nimia cogitatione rerum visibilium" and its effects, see Augustine, *De Trinitate* 11.4.7, *PL* 42:989; Andreas Capellanus, *De amore*, 1.1, ed. Walsh, p. 32.

touch – a gentle embrace – is entirely his doing, and that her "good word" is really a plea, even a rejection. To Amans, her action is entirely "a grace," a promise that he can hold her fast.

The moral Genius finds Amans's desire faulty, but does not dwell on it: "Thi will, mi Sone, is forto blame, / The remenant is bot a game" (5.7183–84). He is less interested in Amans's humorously idolatrous passion or his wish "forto spede in other place" than in the place where the initial meeting has occurred: "The cherche serveth for the bede, / The chambre is of an other speche" (5.7189–90). The surface interest in "sacrilege," then exemplified in the tale of Paris and Helen, is to him more critical than Amans's more serious failing.

This is especially curious because idolatry is a major subject of Genius's long excursus on the world's religions, also presented in this book. Writing more largely about the excursus, Gower's editor has complained that "there is no more reason why this should come in here than anywhere else,"[11] but its warrant lies in its focus on idol-worship and the Pauline teaching that "avaritia est idolorum servitus."[12] The presence of this doctrine in a treatise on avarice should not surprise us. It appears also in the *Mirour* – "Ce dist l'apostre, q'avarice / Est des ydoles le service" (7609–10) – and more generally, it forms a theme of medieval sermons against the sin: "If the preacher wishes to incline the hearts of his listeners against covetousness and greed, let him take the theme of his sermon from that authority which declares avarice to be the service of idols."[13]

The excursus forms a gloss on a common medieval division of history into periods of natural law, written law, and grace.[14] In the first period, natural law formed a remedy for the sin "that Adam wroghte" (5.1739), but was itself corrupted. The written law was given to repair natural law,[15] and the second period thus begins with Moses, to whom God "yaf the lawe." This period ends, as the third begins, with the "baptesme of the newe lawe, / Of which Crist lord is and felawe" (5.1779–80). All three ages are relevant to the argument of the *Confessio*, but the first, as it manifests the effects of natural or fleshly concupiscence in the idolatry of the earliest religions, provides a structure for assessing Amans's condition.

The "worschipe of ydolatrie" is based "upon the fantasie" (5.1587–88) of those who "couthen noght the trouthe finde" (5.1590). Its repeated "forsfai-

11 Macaulay's note for 5.729 ff. (*Works*, 2:515).
12 See Eph. 5.5: "avarus, quod est idolorum servitus"; the quotation in the text is from Alan of Lille, *Liber sententiarum ac dictorum memorabilium* 37, PL 210:250; cf. Gal. 5:19, Col. 3:5.
13 Alan of Lille, *The Art of Preaching*, cap. 6, trans. Evans, p. 38; PL 210:123; see also *ParsT* 747–51.
14 Hugh of St. Victor, *De sacramentis* 1.8.11, trans. Roy J. Deferrari, *On the Sacraments of the Christian Faith* (Cambridge, Mass., 1951), p. 149; PL 176:312; see also Anselm, *Sententie diuine pagine* 5, and *Sententie Anselmi*, ed. Bliemetzrieder, pp. 35, 78–79.
15 *Ysagoge in theologiam* 2, in *Écrits théologiques de l'école d'Abelard*, ed. Artur Landgraf (Louvain, 1934), p. 132; see also *Summa sententiarum* 4.2, PL 176:120; Thomas Hibernicus, *Manipulus florum*, s. v. "natura," p. 366.

ture" is taking the honor "Which due is to the creatour" and giving it to creatures (5.777–80): thereby, the idolater, like the *avarus*, serves "as soubgit" where "he scholde maister be." In the earliest history, the Chaldeans, Egyptians, and Greeks worship planets, "sondri constellacion," zodiacal signs, and the elements; they venerate "diverse bestes" (5.791) and sacrifice to human gods, particularly "suche as weren full of vice" (5.841). The history is not limited to the "forsfaiture" of these religions, however. After the Flood, the people God chooses "for himselve" (5.1599) also lapse into idol-worship: they "the hihe god ne knewe, / Bot maden othre goddes newe" (5.1621–22). Indeed, the entire period before Abraham "fond out the rihte weie" (5.1629) passes in a confusion over goods, which are small, which great, which are proper, which common. All is "torned to likinge / After the fleissh" (5.1616–17) as, in these cases, idolaters worship, appropriate, and become "soubgit" to created things.

The instances here recounted provide an important lesson for Gower's contemporaries, who live at a time, as Genius remarks, when avarice has become the chief vice.[16] The poet draws the history largely from *Barlaam and Ioasaph*,[17] a text which, after it censures the religious practices of the Chaldeans, Greeks, Egyptians, and Jews, praises the Christians for so admirably upholding the true religion. On this point, however, Genius tells another tale. While he agrees that "Ther is a feith aboven alle" (5.1734), he sees no stay in the practice of idolatry after the birth of Christ: even at the present time, he witnesses a "world fulfild of Mist," where "noman seth the rihte weie" (5.1866–67). Such, in other words, is the enduring legacy of the *tempus naturalis legis* and of "men of the natural law," who, in Hugh of St. Victor's terms, "direct their lives by natural reason alone, or rather walk according to the concupiscence in which they were born." They are "openly evil," whereas "men of the written law [are] fictitiously good, men of grace truly good."[18] Genius sees, in his modern exemplars, few men of grace: driven by their corrupted nature, most are either openly evil or fictitiously good. Specifically, he notes in the Church a pervasive serving of "the fleisshes wille" (5.1940) in desires for "vein honour" (5.1920), pleasure, and wealth. This appears, at last, as a quickness to the "worldes Avarice," now likened to sacrifice "openly ayein the feith / Unto thidoles yove and granted" (5.1954–55).

From the excursus, Amans claims to have learned something, for after it he issues a promise: "evere whil I live / I schal the betre hede yive / Unto miself by many weie" (5.1961–63). What then might he have learned? Idolaters exalt images and "to hem knele, / Which is here oghne handes werk" (5.1504–05). Their idolatry, even as an excessive love of creatures, is directed toward fashioned or projected images that foster an illusion of possession: the loved

---

[16] 5.7610. See Lester K. Little, "Pride Goes Before Avarice: Social Change and the Vices in Latin Christendom," *American Historical Review* 76 (1971): 16–49.

[17] *Barlaam and Ioasaph* 27, trans. G. R. Woodward and H. Mattingly, Loeb (London, 1967): 396–425.

[18] Hugh of St. Victor, *On the Sacraments*, 1.8.11, trans. Deferrari, p. 149.

object turns into something like the *avarus'* gold. The process of imagination leading to such an end is an *opus carnis* (Gal. 5:19) based upon a "likinge / After the fleissh," and it includes an aspiration not only to carnal delight and profit, but to an attendant "worschipe." Amans does not recognize this, however, in the later confession of his delight in church, when the image of his lady comes to life, or when the lady herself appears to yield, "as soubgit," to his wishing and fantasy.

Despite the lover's promise to heed himself "by many weie," he only heeds what promotes his own "maistrye." His is a form of "passive" idolatry embodied, according to the late medieval *Rosarium theologie*, in "euery proude man" who "aspireþ . . . þat he be noght subiecte to his aboue, þat is propre to God."[19] Genius himself hints at another dimension of this in his account of the origins of idolatry: Cirophanes, grieving for his dead son, has a memorial or "faire ymage of his semblance" set in the marketplace and decrees that those who would please the father "scholden it obeie" (5.1534, 1539). Genius does not elaborate on this tale, but Robert Holkot, also recounting it, does: "As Aristotle says in the *Poetics*, man naturally delights in his own representation."[20] The father's worship of his son's image, however, betrays an excessive self-love. The literal connection between parentage and idolatrous worship in this example may be extended analogically to Amans's own case: the lover is the creator of images, and thence of himself through those images; like the foolish Cirophanes, he takes more than a natural delight in his own representation.

Amans has therefore not learned as much from the excursus on idolatry as he claims, but neither does his teacher seem to understand fully what he has taught. The problem is analogous to the one we have observed in Book 4. Surely this digression, like the excursus on *gentilesse* in Book 4, grounds an accepted opinion. On the basis of it, one might expect Genius to assess more candidly what Amans confesses late in this book, especially because the priest has in the excursus distanced himself from Venus: she is an exemplary idol. Once again, however, Genius appears to miss the very point of his own doctrine after he breaks out of his excursory mode: he cannot be wholly excluded from the misty world of idols and idol-worship that he has just indicted.

This is not to say, however, that we can entirely dismiss his teaching. Gower has him sort through an extraordinarily complex and varied mass of material in dealing with avarice, and the priest more often than not makes sense of it. He occasionally seems to recognize the "mist" in Amans's perception, that blurring of a distinction between the image he worships and reality. He also speaks incisively about others who love idols – in particular, the "worldes good" of money, success, and power – and who, in hoarding, coveting, or wasting those goods, become "thral" to them. They are in that sense fools, but they are no

---

[19] *The Middle English Translation of the Rosarium theologie*, ed. Christina von Nolcken, Middle English Texts, 10 (Heidelberg, 1979), p. 96.
[20] Robert Holkot, *In librum Sapientiae*, lect. 164, p. 540; see also John Ridewall, *Fulgentius metaforalis*, ed. Hans Liebeschütz (Leipzig, 1926), pp. 65–71.

less dangerous for that. Genius, as we shall now discover, shows considerable insight into their threat to society; we must now also consider whether he understands the depth of evil he portrays in his narratives of avarice, or whether he grasps the difficulty of finding adequate remedies for the sin.

CHAPTER THIRTEEN

JUSTICE AND THE REMEDIES FOR AVARICE

Avarice variously manifests the self-love of a corrupted nature. The personified Usure sets his love "al toward himselve / And to non other" (5.4404–05); Skarsnesse sees little "good in helpinge of an other, / Noght though it were his oghne brother" (5.4695–96); and Unkindeschipe "can no good dede aquite" (5.5487) and is a friend "toward himself al one" (5.5493). The will of Covoitise "schal stonde in stede of riht" (5.2022), and by him others are "destruid fulofte" (5.2023). There is no natural protection against him; "no lawe mai rescowe / Fro him that wol no riht allowe" (5.2019–20). The *avarus* disregards all human legal structures; he is impervious to correction because he accepts no society. The only sure redress against him originates in the "grete god alofte" (5.2024).

Gower uses several Ovidian tales of the gods to underscore the point that the avaricious, hardened against the "riht," are often unaware of their crime. Jupiter "robs" the maid Calistona of her virginity; after she suffers the rape, she, not Jupiter, suffers a horrible justice. Rejected by Diana, her goddess, and changed into a bear by a jealous, "wroth and hastif" Juno, she retains, in her new form, a maternal love that "kinde hath set under his lawe" (5.6323). In that natural love lies the potential for the greatest injustice: years later, on seeing her hunter-son, she is so overcome that, "Toward him [she] cam, and tok non hiede / Of that he bar a bowe bent" (5.6327–29). Before the son can shoot his arrow at this approaching "beste wylde," however, Jupiter intervenes. In a very brief, indeed perfunctory conclusion, Genius observes,

> Jupiter, which wolde schylde
> The Moder and the Sone also,
> Ordeineth for hem bothe so,
> That thei for evere were save.   5.6334–37

This ending, both for Jupiter's easy self-vindication and for the teller's precipitate effort to disengage himself from the narrative, trivializes the crime and the guilt: justice has not been served.

A like effect is created in a second tale, in which Leucothoe, victimized by the "stelthe" of Phoebus, also suffers more than a rape. Venus reports this "micherie" to Phoebus's concubine, Clymene, who in turns tells Leucothoe's father, and he, as we have already remarked, thinks he can achieve justice by burying his daughter alive. Whatever hint there may be in Ovid of Leucothoe's guilt – she "accepted the god's embraces without complaint" – is dropped in Genius's account. Ovid also mitigates the judgment against Phoebus by noting the god's bitter grief, his futile attempt to revive the girl. Genius, by contrast, has Phoebus act tardily, and mostly out of self-regard: "for the reverence / Of that sche hadde be his love" (5.6776–77), he causes her to spring "up out of the molde / Into a flour" (5.6779–80), a flower that fittingly reaches to the sun, to Phoebus himself. Once again – now even in the metamorphosis itself – the crime is trivialized. Genius passes no verdict against the father or against the supporting cast of judges, including his own goddess. Neither does he judge Phoebus nor prove that the god has reason to regret his crime. "And thus whan love is evele wonne, / Fulofte it comth to repentaile" (5.6782–83), he argues, but whatever repentance is manifested in Ovid's tale, this version has displayed absolutely no "repentaile."

What is worse, the tale is given a context – before it an attack on "stelthe" and after it a tale about Hercules – that makes a serious judgment against Phoebus and his crime difficult and, at best, short-lived. We are not prepared for the tale of Leucothoe by the priest's generic treatment of *stelthe* and *micherie*; instead, the dialogue builds to the priest's description of a "game" of stealing kisses and Amans's confession of a fantasy in which he magically and stealthily enters his lady's chamber, "forto se / If eny grace wolde falle" (5.6678–79). The familiar tale of Hercules and Faunus that follows the story of Leucothoe recounts a game of dress-up in which Hercules and Iole exchange clothing, and Faunus, in the dark, picks the wrong bedfellow. Gower has made this a funnier story than the "amusing tale" in his source, Ovid's *Fasti*. Genius's moral is suited, by its unintended irony, to the spirit of the tale, and it leaves far behind the events in Leucothoe's life:

> Mi Sone, be thou war withal
> To seche suche mecheries,
> Bot if thou have the betre aspies,
> In aunter if the so betyde
> As Faunus dede thilke tyde,
> Wherof thou miht be schamed so.   5.6937–41

It is perhaps the greatest irony that between the tales of Calistona and Leucothoe Genius offers a tribute to virginity. This excursus supposedly provides a "moral" justification for Juno's rage against an "unchaste" Calistona, but it thereby gives confused signals about the point of the narrative, the crime of Jupiter's "robberie." By his choices as a compiler, Genius also creates a peculiar setting for the next narrative. In the statement about virginity, Genius argues that

> If maidenhod be take aweie
> Withoute lawes ordinance,
> It mai noght failen of vengance.   5.6430–32

The champion of virginity, in the tale Genius uses to prove this, is Phoebus: the

god sends a "comun pestilence" in judgment against the Greeks for Agamemnon's rape of Criseide, the daughter of one of Phoebus's priests. The tale of
Leucothoe that follows not only compromises the justice of Phoebus, but also,
and more seriously, undercuts Genius's claim of certain vengeance against
unlawfully taking a "maidenhod."

These tales, while they focus on crimes of the gods, also address the larger
problem of avarice. The person guilty of this sin is, of course, *unkinde*: "he
nomore than the fend / Unto non other man is frend" (5.5491–92), and while
he serves himself, he cannot be brought to understand himself. Unaffected by a
"riht" – even a natural "riht" – that protects others, he is not seriously drawn to
"repentaile" by seeing the effects of his crime.

In another of Genius's Ovidian tales, Jason, after Medea has killed his two
sons and Creusa, might guess that he has done something wrong. But the priest
does not show him guessing: he assigns only one line – the last line – of this
very long tale to the effect of Medea's act on this false man: "And he was left in
gret destresse" (5.4222). The reader might sense in this the power of Gowerian
understatement, but Genius's auditor is not moved by it to reflect on "what
sorwe it doth / To swere an oth which is noght soth" (5.4223–24). Amans's
chief worry, after the telling of this story, is how the fleece got to Colchis in the
first place.

The sorrow Gower's reader is responsive to is Medea's, and herein lies
another feature of many of the stories about avarice. The exemplar of the sin
often takes advantage of an innocent, using strength and "tricherie" against a
character powerless either to withstand the assault or later, to retaliate. Medea,
however, has the strength to punish, and Gower is concerned to examine how
her attempt to administer justice or cause "repentaile" affects her. Unlike
Chaucer in the *Legend of Good Women*, Gower does not suppress everything
bad in Medea: he does not skirt the issue of her own "tricherie" and injustice,
specifically in the attack on Jason that destroys others and only less certainly
affects Jason himself. Nor does he suppress everything good in Medea by
stressing, as did Ovid in Hipsipyle's letter to Jason (*Heroides* 6), her barbarity:
in that letter, Medea is presented as a "barbarian witch" and "barbarian whore"
(19, 81) who has won Jason by enchantment (97–98), and who is capable of
every crime (128, 138).[1] Closer to Gower's perspective is the view generated in
Ovid's *Heroides* 12, the letter of Medea to Jason: now it is Medea who is the
victim, swayed by Jason's beauty and sweet but deceitful speech (12); once she
sees him, she is lost (33); now he is the foreigner, "an alien and a thief" to
whom she, in her "virgin innocence," falls plunder (111). Medea is the person
acted upon, enchanted. For Jason's sake, she renounces much and yields to "the
coercion of evil" (193, 132); because of what he does, her heart turns cold ("in
toto pectore frigus erat" 142).

---

[1] For quotations from *Heroides* 6 and 12 in this chapter, I have used the translation of
Florence Verducci, *Ovid's Toyshop of the Heart: Epistulae Heroidum* (Princeton, 1985),
pp. 34–55.

The early picture of Medea in this version forms the basis for Chaucer's defense of a Medea who embodies "trouthe" and "kyndenesse" (LGW F 1664). Gower does not disagree, at least to start with, but he eventually shows a Medea transformed by her passion and, as supporting it, her sorcery: initially a maiden of "tendre herte," she is changed by bitter experience into a character godlike in her capacity to injure. Initially, she is modest, even shy before the Jason she hopes to marry: "sche with simple chiere and meke, / Whan sche him sih, wax al aschamed" (5.3480–81). Later, when Jason returns with the fleece, Medea "wolde have kist him wonder fayn, / Bot schame tornede hire agayn" (5.3789–90). Though she is shamefast in outer behavior, however, she is so overcome by love that "al hir world on him sche sette" (5.3637). The strength of this love, moreover, is intensified by a magic that can transform her, "As thogh sche were oute of hir mynde / And torned in an other kynde" (5.4083–84). In her magical science, indeed, Medea "was, as who seith, a goddesse" (5.4107), and late in the narrative, she resembles an avenging goddess, intent on punishing the "untrewe."

The vengeance of Medea – like that of other exemplars introduced in Book 5 – embodies a paradoxical justice: as Genius shows here, indeed repeatedly in this book, an act of retribution against the untrue, though it is based on an instinct for justice, can really represent another kind of untruth, a false sense of a person's due, of the punishment a given crime "merits." Medea's action is obviously unjust to Creusa and to Jason's sons, and, moreover, it has no certain effect on Jason himself. What is worse, it does not even satisfy Medea's own need; in her perspective, her vengeance, despite its enormity, has not closed the case, for "she pleigneth upon love" (5.4220) even after she ascends to Pallas's court.

In Genius's tale, Medea is an unsettling character. If Jason is the instrumental cause of what she does, she is ultimately accountable for her actions: passions merely hidden in the tender-hearted and shamefast innocent are finally released; these are her passions. The problem of this tale is a common one in the Confessio: it lies in the conflict in the structures of perception Genius "intends" and actually creates. He wants this story to illustrate "perjurie" in love, as that is represented in Jason. But to argue this case, he would have done better to follow Heroides 12, or Chaucer's version in the Legend, or the Roman de la rose, where Jason is presented as an "evil trickster" and "false, disloyal thief."[2] In the story the priest actually tells, however, Jason is not alone in using a calculating "tricherie." Medea is also treacherous in serving her passions, both her love and her need for vengeance. If Jason exemplifies a form of "covoitise" in his actions, she displays a form of avarice proper, or "streit holdinge," in hers.

In a sense Medea is the more frightening exemplar: in this maid of "tendre herte," an unleashed need and will to control, "holde," and dominate, yoked

---

2 *Roman de la rose*, 13225–26, trans. Charles Dahlberg, *The Romance of the Rose* (Princeton, 1971), p. 229; ed. Lecoy, 2:152.

with her special, quasi-divine power, causes the death of other innocents. Ultimately the tale shows how easily a victim of evil – no matter how simple and meek of cheer she may seem – can lose control of that power latent in the species for the unkindest crimes.

In the *Confessio*, such a release of passion is not uniquely exemplified by Medea. A like phenomenon occurs later in Book 5, in the tale of Tereus. This story also reveals that the sin of Avarice is effectively too "large" to be accommodated to the genre of the exemplum, if the purpose of that form is the simple "pointing" of a moral. The story lacks a simple "poetic" justice to assure or console us; instead, it shows in the desire for retribution a "covoitise" that can never be satisfied.

Tereus is a covetous man who draws others into the vortex of his passion. The effect of this tale depends in part on the picture of Tereus attacking a trusting and innocent Philomene; this episode presents a gradual transformation of Tereus into a frenzied "tirant raviner," until, with Philomene in his power, "in a rage on hire he ran, / Riht as a wolf which takth his preie" (5.5632–33). As horrifying as this episode is, however, the effect of the tale, in even greater part, rests on Philomene's failure to achieve just satisfaction against Tereus. She joins with her sister to wreak vengeance, but in planning and executing that justice, they too are transformed.

Progne is a woman "gentil and kinde" who, when she discovers the truth, "makth a vou it schal be wroke" (5.5816): she kills her child, butchers him, and serves him, spiced and cooked, to the father. This is in the *donnée*, but whereas Ovid, before this killing, has the mother vacillate in her love for Itys, her hatred for Tereus, Genius shows her, "mad / Of wo" (5.5891–92), immediately transformed, one who, "Withoute insihte of moderhede / Foryat pite and loste drede" (5.5893–94). Once Tereus, "ayein kinde," devours his own flesh and blood, the sisters together place Itys' head on the table to prove what they, and Tereus, have done: the world, Progne proclaims, will "evere" sing and read about Tereus' shameful tyranny. In one sense, as Macaulay argues, Philomene is removed from this act of vengeance: she is not directly mentioned during the planning; nor does she, as in Ovid, throw the bloody head of Itys at Tereus. Instead, she joins her sister in a ritualized and macabre procession:

> This Philomene tok the hed
> Betwen tuo disshes, and al wrothe
> Tho comen forth the Sostres bothe,
> And setten it upon the bord.   5910–13

This act, which certainly does not excuse Philomene, is formalized and more clearly calculated than is the impulsive act of Philomela in the *Metamorphoses*, but that makes it more horrifying: the sisters' "cruel joy" in revenge is in its calmness more sinister.

The sisters are saved from Tereus' retaliation by the gods' intervention: all three characters are transformed into birds. Genius's story does not end with the act of metamorphosis, however, and in its continuation the narrative reaches to yet another *moralitas*. It is not Gower's intent merely to make Philomene a "good woman" and expose Tereus as another "crewel man." Had it been, he, like Chaucer, might have ended his legend with the reunion of the sisters in the castle prison: the rest, Chaucer has written, "is no charge for to telle, / For this is al and som" (*LGW* F 2383–84). Chaucer's ending has had its champions: Rosemary Woolf cites it as an example of this poet's "moral good taste." He "adopts the clever strategy of lapsing into a kind of mumbling reluctance to tell [the story] and indeed stops short." The "morally horrific" was beyond Chaucer's range, "but he knew it, and . . . evaded the issue;" on the other hand, "Gower, unaware of the morally perilous nature of his material, stolidly and weakly completed the story."[3]

On closer scrutiny, however, Chaucer's telling of this story is a school-boyish exercise in *ethopeiae* next to Gower's effort to plumb the moral depths of what sin and vengeance do to transform their agents. Gower goes beyond Chaucer, even beyond Ovid in reflecting on the moral significance of such metamorphoses. It is one of Gower's best tales, as Macaulay says, but not because Gower has become more delicate, less shocking than Ovid. In a profoundly moral sense, it shocks more than Ovid's version by using the metamorphoses to reveal the horrible effects – in sin, suffering, and vengeance – of irrecoverable loss.

In his revision generally, Gower makes more prominent the sisters' thoughts and speeches on retribution. These characters passionately seek justice – a vengeance based upon keeping strict accounts – but they never achieve it, and in the end their passion hurts them more than it hurts Tereus. This becomes apparent after the metamorphoses, when the three characters in their bird-activity "interpret" the justice enacted before they were transformed. Tereus' case is distressingly simple. He has been changed into a lapwing, "the brid falseste of alle" (5.6047). As a man he is unresponsive to what *he* has done – he shows no awareness but that his will is "riht" – and similarly in his bird-form he does not recall his crime: in a sense, this makes the crime all the more horrible. In Ovid's version of the tale, Tereus before the metamorphosis is not quite so indifferent: he experiences a twisted form of "repentaile" as he tries to disengorge the meal he has just swallowed. Genius does not even credit Tereus with that: we see only his rage while alive, his foraging, without memory, after the metamorphosis. If we are inclined to see justice in the fact that Tereus is now "from his oghne kinde stranged" (5.6040) because in life he became so "unkinde" and "untrewe," we might note that either Tereus does not know it, or to him it does not matter.

Even in life the sisters are, like Tereus, dehumanized, but their change is obviously more tragic. It is in one sense caused by Tereus's evil; in their passion for justice, they descend to his evil and are drawn into his "ravine." What is worse, after their metamorphosis, the women, unlike Tereus, remember. They are estranged from their "kinde," but they must know and suffer it, each in her own way.

3   Woolf, "Kindly Gower," pp. 233–34.

Progne as a swallow "chitreth out in hir langage / What falshod is in mariage" (5.6011–12). She becomes a tale-bearer who, in betraying her own obsession with Tereus the "Spousebreche," renders a justice that overreaches its case; it is entirely negative, divisive, injurious in its effect on others:

> Among the folk sche comth to house,
> To do thes wyves understonde
> The falshod of hire housebonde.
> That thei of hem be war.   5.6018–21

Philomene is private: in her retreat, she pathetically embodies the oxymora of love: her plaint – "O why ne were I yit a maide?" (5.5979) is mixed with "gret joie and merthe" that "Schal noman se my chekes rede" (5.5988). In "loves maladie" she thus "seith love is a wofull blisse / . . . / A lusti fievere, a wounde softe" (5.5993–95). This is surely no celebration. Both birds are, in the vestiges of their humanity, "unkinde." They retreat from society and "ben toward the men so lothe, / That thei ne wole of pure schame / Unto no mannes hand be tame" (5.6025–27). This remains in their mind, we are told, because they found a "man unkinde": that man has rendered them "unkinde."

At the end of the tale, Genius would have Amans focus on the figure of Tereus; he cautions the lover that if he gets his pleasure in love by ravine, "it mai thee falle thus, / As it befell of Tereus" (5.6050). The power of his telling, however, rests upon his treatment of the sisters, who are not merely violated, but ensnared in Tereus' evil.

Like many other tales in Book 5, this one fails to present a clearly defined antidote to avarice. In Book 2, natural generosity, trust, "charite," and friendship seem adequate to the task of overcoming Envie. Constantine can be persuaded to eschew Crualte and follow Pite and charity; he has retained the good of kinde. In Book 5, however, kindness is proven to be wanting in the "gredi wille" not only of the avaricious, but of those who seek justice against the avaricious. Now the priest, however unknowingly, demonstrates that a mythic prelapsarian innocence – restored in various fictions – cannot survive in a world of vitiated nature. The ultimate consequence of supposing it possible, as in the case of the sister birds, is "pure schame," a retreat from all society. That is the effect, but obviously it is no answer.

One might hope to see a good in shame: it could represent a knowledge and rational judgment of one's own guilt. Just as easily, however, it could represent a hiding of lost innocence, a further strategy of "streit holdinge," of retaining "lordschipe" and control; its danger is that it becomes unkind, a deliberate, calculating, and entirely destructive response to societas, masking an ignorance of one's own lapsed nature. So much is implied in Progne's tale-bearing: in her "schame," she sets out to protect the innocent, possibly the "enchanted" innocent; in another sense, however, she seeks to gain "maistrye," to destroy the marriage of others by singing the guilt and "falshod" of all husbands. Like the "helle" of avarice, such vengeance "mai neveremor be full" (5.350).

Book 5 pictures a world without love, a world whose inhabitants have replaced a God who infuses grace into nature with idols that merely affirm the self, leaving no power to offset the willful "tricherie" of sin. This concern, most clearly presented in the excursus, is focused in one sense on idolatry, and in another on the inheritance of the Fall: "man born of carnal desire [sets] up himself as the object of his own desire; . . . he loves himself in the first place, and then all the rest for pure self-love."[4] In the confessional portions of Book 5, Genius proposes cures for avarice, but none is equal to the task of dealing with this problem of lapsed nature, a condition from which man "ne mihte himself arise" (5.1745). The excursus finds the only possible cure in God's sacrifice and presents it in a traditional language that is especially apt in a discussion of Avarice. Christ's act of largess, by which he bought "The Sinne which that Adam wroghte" (5.1739), paid "thilke rancoun," (5.1755), and took "on himself the forsfaiture" (5.1764), restores the promise of "hevene mede" (5.1792).[5] In this brief outline of central Christian doctrine, and specifically regarding Christ's payment of a ransom for the "caitif" heirs of Adam, Genius would seem to have discovered the remedy he has sought. Grace, the excursus suggests, is pivotal. Eventually we shall see that the book, especially in the opening, excursory, and closing arguments taken together, will locate that grace "historically," showing how it might enter the "tydes" of the species and of Amans in particular.

At first it appears, however, that the key response to the dilemma of sin, presented in an excursus, is not readily available to speakers in the confessional dialogue, or to Genius in his tales or *moralitates*. To be sure, there is a legitimacy in the "grace" Genius proposes to offset avarice at the end of Book 5: this is the virtue of Largess, which stands between the excesses of "streit holdinge" on the one hand, and wasteful spending or Prodigalite on the other. The priest has elsewhere praised gracious, "fre," and generous behavior, and now he commends as the "siker weie" a like principle that "Betre is to yive than to take" (5.7725). True largess is a generosity ordered by reason, and Genius's advice to "hold largesce in his mesure" (5.357) is unexceptionable. It is a premise shared with Chaucer's Parson, who describes the gentle person as liberal, "that is to seyn, large by mesure, for thilke that passeth mesure is folie and synne" (*ParsT* 464). This virtue, presumably modelled on the "fre largesse" of Nature herself, should provide a strong check to the prodigality exemplified in Venus and her court. It has that kind of power in *De planctu Naturae*. When Alan of Lille sets Largitas against *Venus scelestis* near the end of that work, he has Nature express her own special affinity with the virtue:

> O Maiden, by whose outstanding architectonic skill, the mind of man
> is destined to be a palace of virtues: through this mind man attains the
> rewards of favouring grace, through it the long-dead days of the Golden

---

4   Gilson, *Spirit of Mediaeval Philosophy*, p. 270.
5   Cf. Mark 10:42–45.

Age come again to life, through it men bind themselves together by the bond of heart-felt love.[6]

As powerful as Largitas can be in this setting, however, Gower tells another tale and stresses another point in his confessional dialogue: the stories in Book 5 of the *Confessio* repeatedly demonstrate that the days of the Golden Age are indeed long-dead. While the virtue, in Gower's perspective, might point us toward every goal Alan's Nature sets for it, achieving or sustaining such a virtue in a fallen world, where "alle love [is] leide aside" (5.14) or where "largesce is Avarice" (5.1958) may prove impossible.

Gower's genial priest is not fully attuned to this problem, though in Book 5 he has uttered the entire doctrine explaining it. The mist in his perception is the idol of *kinde* and venerean *gentilesse*, for often it blinds him to the most serious depravity of the vices he expounds. A particularly telling example of this is his account of jealousy. A person jealous in love, like one "averous / Of gold" (5.597–98), is merely a fool. When the loathly, jealous, and "malgracious" Vulcan exposes Venus's infidelity, for example, he only earns scorn for his misgovernance (5.693). Genius has found another, happier way to deal with suspicion:

> Yit scholde he noght apointe his herte
> With Jelousie of that is wroght,
> Bot feigne, as thogh he wiste it noght.   5.708–10

In this statement, Gower adds another level of humor to the ironical "not to know is the best" that opens the same tale in Ovid's *Ars amatoria*.[7] Genius is interested not merely in a prudent strategy for dealing with a wife's deceptions, but in a device to avoid jealousy. One escapes this sin, he suggests, by not thinking about its cause. Feigning represents shamefast, paradoxically "honeste" behavior in the much-restricted setting of venerean *gentilesse*, where the safe and admirable course is always to *display* a seemly and genial nature: that is to define a good "entencion." All would be happy, he suggests, if Vulcan had been gracious instead of "malgracious."

Genius in this book poses worthy arguments when he uses the rules of nature to expose the follies and dangers of avarice, and the "mesure" of reason to expose prodigality. What he fails to address, in its own complexity, is the issue of self-love. Neither nature nor reason is sufficient to address "worschipe," or the vanity of control and "streit holdinge": nature may teach only a superficial grace, and reason may make one only clever enough to keep up appearances. One deludes oneself in order to avoid "sklaundre," a loss "of al the comun grace," and public "schame." Vulcan lacks grace, of course, but politeness would get him no closer to understanding Venus or himself.

---

[6] Alan of Lille, *De planctu Naturae*, pr. 9, trans. Sheridan, p. 213; PL 210:478.
[7] Ovid, *The Art of Love*, 2.555, 561–98, trans. Rolfe Humphries (Bloomington, Indiana, 1957), p. 147.

The good that Vulcan lacks – generous, outgoing, "fre," and gracious behavior – can itself be prodigal, merely a means of serving oneself: "if thou wolt
pourchace / To be beloved, thou most use / Largesce" (5.402–04), Genius
argues, and again, "if thou wolt grace have, / Be gracious and do largesse"
(5.408–09). Genius, in his dependence on a venerean *gentilesse*, even in a book
in which he has denounced his goddess, leads him to connect grace, desert,
self-interested profit, and "worschipe"; his point appears to be that one can
merit grace.[8] That connection might even underlie his statement of accepted
truths, as at the end of Book 5:

> For that thing is appourtenant
> To trouthe and causeth to be fre
> After the reule of charite,
> Which first beginneth of himselve.   5.7740–43

On this occasion, the "reule of charite" becomes a caution not to overspend
because it hurts one's prospects. This only confirms in the lover what he has
already betrayed, a concern over a return on his investment. He has given his
lady a "grete love" (5.4505), but she has not repaid him with the smallest favor
or grace, the slightest "worschipe." The more urgent problem, a "generous"
Amans contends, is the lady's: "I preie to god such grace hir sende / That sche
be time it mot amende" (5.4531–32). Amans's repeated concern over whether
his love will "spede" or "spill" is a concern for the world and the goods of
Fortune. His desire for self-gratification, for "delit" and "spede," becomes a
quest of "timely" worship and control, a means to "save his life," but by that
quest he becomes a thral to goods, and thereby to "aventure."

At the end of the book, Amans insists that he is not guilty of "prodigalite" in
the sense of setting his "love in sondri place," but he fears he has been prodigal
in another sense: in wasting his time in an unreciprocated suit. The problem of
a self turned back on itself still remains; this is a matter of casting false images
of the self, of being a self dispersed and scattered. It is a problem of mind, and
specifically a memory that has wasted time in a sense that Amans does not yet
understand. On his own, the sinner cannot find his center, a place of rest: this
is the condition of "mannes Soule," long exiled (5.1783–84); it is the condition
of those who crucified Christ, those who, driven "out of goddes grace," are
dispersed "in alle londes out" (5.1726–29).

Book 5, as it begins with and draws us back to images of a Golden Age and
"Paradis," sets the course to that lost center as a passage through time. It
reorders issues of the *Confessio* in relation to Fortune, the "uncertein," and
temporality itself. Without understanding the full implications of what he
seeks, Amans expresses the urgency of recovering grace "in time," in both
senses of that phrase.

Amans's beloved exhibits a natural grace: not merely a physical beauty and

8   On the issue, more generally, see Burnley, p. 168.

gentle demeanor, not merely a gracious manner, but a native goodness.[9] In that virtue, she might even be said to reflect a divine gift, a grace that "orders all things sweetly," even a "radiance of the soul" that attracts "holy love."[10] This image is mediated, of course, by a lover who does not know "holy love," and in his perception, the lady's acts of favor[11] do not measure up to his desert or "grete love," loyalty, and service. She, like Fortune, appears to withhold grace capriciously; indeed, her grace is transformed to mean mere "happ" or luck. Amans does not invent that relationship, of course; "grace" in Middle English can mean fortune or a stroke of fortune.[12] And that meaning is consistent with Genius's counsel regarding the lover's uncertain future, when he urges him to hope, to expect grace in time, indeed to await what must be the grace of time.

Amans cannot know "what chance schal betyde" (4.1779) or when "love his grace wol [him] sende" (4.3504), but he is told to be patient: "Mi sone, bot abyd thin ende, / Per cas al mai to goode wende" (5.4565–66). Genius encourages the lover to think that his "time com noght yit" (5.5214) and to assume that

> Per cas the revolucion
> Of hevene and [his] condicion
> Ne be noght yit of on acord.   4.1783–85

Late in Book 5, Genius is still reluctant to discourage Amans, and his strongest proof is still grounded in fortune and "aventure":

> Of time which thou hast despended,
> It mai with grace ben amended.
> For thing which mai be worth the cost
> Per chaunce is nouther wast ne lost;
> For what thing stant on aventure,
> That can no worldes creature
> Telle in certein hou it schal wende,
> Til he therof mai sen an ende.   5.7813–20

Such a mixing of terms, whereby Genius inspires the lover to put his trust in Fortune, time, the "happ of love" (5.707), Love's grace, and the "constellacion," centers on the link between grace and fortune. Thus following a seasonal model, he poses a possible sudden turn in Amans's fortune: although summer "is with Wynter wast and bare," he argues,

> Al is recovered in a throwe;
> The colde wyndes overblowe,
> And stille be the scharpe shoures,

---

[9] See *Middle English Dictionary*, ed. Hans Kurath, Sherman M. Kuhn, Robert E. Lewis et al. (Ann Arbor, 1952–), G.3, s. v. "grace," 5a, 5b.
[10] Wisd. 7:1; *Glossa Lombardi*, PL 191:936; discussed by Thomas Aquinas, *Summa theologiae* 1a2ae, 110.2, Blackfriars ed., 30:112–15.
[11] See *Middle English Dictionary*, G.3, s. v. "grace," 4.
[12] Ibid., "grace," 3b.

And soudeinliche ayein his floures
The Somer hapneth and is riche:
And so per cas thi graces liche,
Mi Sone, thogh thou be nou povere
Of love, yit thou miht recovere.   5.7827–34

It does not appear to be the priest's intent to fit this argument to a rhetoric of conversion. Curiously, however, such statements, whatever his intent, will ultimately contribute to a reperception of grace: his is a rhetoric of "goode entente" both because it identifies the problem of "hap" or chance so central to Gower's thinking, and because it uses a language that can be transvaluated, shifted ultimately to a universe of theological significance, wherein the soul might be blessed with "a grace which shall first heal its wounds and then turn it towards its true object."[13]

The poetic power of this conclusion to Book 5 is buttressed by the priest's handling of the topics of nature, "ende," fortune, and grace elsewhere in the poem, and especially as the work draws to its own conclusion. Fallen man "of necessity loves first of all himself, and only by gradual steps rises to the love of God."[14] The order of argument in the *Confessio* hints at those gradual steps; they appear, for example, in Genius's extension of the argument regarding grace and fortune into Book 6. Even later in the work, the poet reorders the perception of this statement describing the passage of the seasons. The very style that keeps us from seeing "in certein" how Amans's case "schal wende" is ordered by the lover's own unsureness about his "aventure," his nature, and his ending. The priest here describes a natural cycle, and the lover, late in the poem, will compare his life to the passing of the seasons. Obviously the cycle will not repeat itself in his physical nature: summer will not come again suddenly; it will not recur at all. At a higher level, however, the lover's "graces" will be restored: he will recover a love unlike the one that now binds him to his uncertainty, an unsureness caused by his desire for the three "lievest thinges."

This change requires a reordering of memory and remembered time. As we approach the end of the poem, we might remark that it works through an issue earlier set in Augustine's famous discussion of time in the *Confessions*. In the singing of a psalm, the Father notes, memory is "lengthened out by a shortening of the function of expectation – until the whole of expectation is used up, when the completely finished act has passed over into memory." This holds true for a longer action: "for the whole life of a man," indeed for the entire history of mankind.[15] What is true of the confession is also true of Amans's entire "life," as it approaches its ending, and fittingly, to the extent that Amans is a type, an Everyman, it is also true of humanity, "the parts of which are all the lives of men." What is especially significant is how time is understood as an extension of the mind, an extension which Augustine finally confesses has

13 Gilson, *Spirit of Mediaeval Philosophy*, pp. 282–83.
14 Ibid., p. 281.
15 Augustine, *Confessions* 11.28.38, trans. Bourke, p. 362; ed. Skutella, pp. 291–92.

been a "distraction and dispersal" in his own particular history. The Father prays

> that I may be gathered in from the days of old and follow the One. Forgetting what is behind, not straining outward to things which will come and pass away, but straining forward to what is before, not according to distraction, but with mental concentration, I press on toward the prize of my heavenly calling.[16]

In this antecedent to Gower's very different confessional work, Augustine sets important terms for what will happen to Gower's penitent, who eventually, and in figure, is gathered up and no longer distracted. Book 5 concludes with a treatment of an avarice of time, a seeking to hold, acquire, or waste time. Amans is indeed a lover who scatters time, though not in the sense he imagines. Eventually, time will be redeemed when he comes to his conversion, a moment when he recovers an intention to stretch forward to what is before. The lover's task is clearly not finished in Book 5. In the excursus on religion, Genius has warned him about a necessary condition for salvation and happiness:

> So stant the feith upon believe,
> Withoute which mai non achieve
> To gete him Paradis ayein.   5.1785–87

In the next book, the lover is still uttering a very different kind of praise than that of Augustine's confession. Amans finds "Paradis" in the sight of his beloved and a "blisse of hevene" in his lady's voice. This scattering of sense-perception, imagination, and understanding will eventually be resolved in a confession reminiscent of the ending of Augustine's prayer: "I have disintegrated into periods of time, of whose order I am ignorant," the Father confesses, "and my thoughts are rent asunder by tumultuous diversities – until such time as I shall flow together into Thee, purged and melted . . . by the fire of Thy love."[17]

Gower allows his Genius to pose the terms of this double sense of conversion – an expected turn in the "happ of love," a surprising conversion of soul – but does not let him bridge the one idiom and the other. The effect of this priestly ambivalence is noteworthy: whatever Genius's intended design, he clearly does not attempt to cancel Amans's love in these books: his teaching, as idle as it sometimes appears, is designed by Gower to organize and redirect that love, even while the thoughts compiled in that teaching seem to reflect "tumultuous diversities." Terms such as time, fortune, grace, and love open out, then come back into focus, and gain in force as the work progresses. They also form one of the thematic centers of Book 6, whose announced subject is Gule or gluttony.

---

[16] Ibid., 11.29.39, trans. Bourke, p. 363; ed. Skutella, p. 292. For a useful discussion of this passage, see Robert Jordan, "Time and Contingency in St. Augustine," in *Augustine: A Collection of Critical Essays*, ed. R. A. Markus, (Garden City, N.Y., 1972), pp. 260–62.

[17] *Confessions*, 11.29.39, trans. Bourke, p. 364; ed. Skutella, p. 292.

Chapter Fourteen

GLUTTONY, CONSOLATION, AND
THE REGION OF UNLIKENESS

In Book 6, Genius promises to limit his discussion to two species of gluttony. Although the book, the shortest in the *Confessio*, lacks the range of the discussion of Avarice, its treatment of gluttony remains an exceedingly rich one, partly because of the variety of source materials compiled in it. The credit for this or any other gathering inside the work may not be entirely Gower's own, to be sure, for as Judson Boyce Allen has proven through the case of Langland, a late medieval poet could borrow materials "already batched" or combined in one of his sources.[1] Such borrowing, however, might itself inspire new invention or discovery. An unexpected and suggestive instance of it possibly occurs in Gower's own procedure in Book 6 of the *Confessio*.

Several elements in Gower's treatise on gluttony are also collected in Nicholas de Gorran's *Distinctiones*, in the form of brief statements under the heading not of *gula*, as we might expect, but of *consolatio*.[2] Nicholas turns figures later used by Gower to an apparently different use. He alludes to the person suffering from dropsy: "ydropicus in potu superfluo consolatur." He presents the figure of the two tuns (*dolia*, Gower's *duale*), the one holding a bitter drink, the other sweet. He refers to the biblical story of Dives and Lazarus; he does not mention Gower's tale of Bacchus in the desert, but does capture one of its themes by alluding to Isa. 52:9: "Rejoice, and give praise together, O ye deserts of Jerusalem: for the Lord hath comforted his people: he hath redeemed Jerusalem." Nicholas includes many similar biblical references, such as Ruth 2:31: "I have found grace in thy eyes, my lord, who has comforted me." Although these statements are not reproduced verbatim by Genius, allusions to God's grace and comfort form a substructure in both treatises, and in each they complement the author's use of Boethius, something we might expect in a *distinctio* on consolation, but not necessarily in a book on gluttony. Basic to understanding both texts is the contrast that Nicholas develops between the solace to be found in

---

[1] Judson Boyce Allen, "Langland's Reading and Writing: *Detractor* and the Pardon Passus," *Speculum* 59 (1984): 344; see also John A. Alford, "The Role of Quotations in *Piers Plowman*," *Speculum* 52 (1977): 80–99.

[2] Nicholas de Gorran, *Distinctiones*, Oxford, Bodleian Library, MS Bodley 427, fols. 21v–22v; I have also consulted Cambridge University Library, MS Gg.1.33, fols. 29v–30v.

Fortune's goods, as in "deliciis" (Gower's *delices* or, in his Latin, *deliciis*), and the spiritual consolation to be found in the "caritas incarnationis."

Ultimately, the two authors go their separate ways, even after they converge on the same material: Nicholas alludes to David comforting Berthsabee after the death of their child (2 Kings 12:24): Gower alludes to David "adoted" and drunk with love at first seeing Berthsabee: "The knihtli David him ne mihte / Rescoue, that he with the sihte / Of Bersabee ne was bestad" (6.95–97). The subjects the authors share can be turned to support either topic as their principle. In the story of Dives and Lazarus, Nicholas sees the false *consolatio* of riches, but Gower sees the excessive love of "bodily delices," and in this, the English poet follows another tradition of *distinctiones* on *gula*. Alan of Lille thus introduces the story in his model sermon on gluttony: "In life [Dives] feasted splendidly. After death he thirsted for a drop of water."[3] The latter text is additionally relevant because of its allusion to thirst, a basic motif in this book of the *Confessio*, as it is in Nicholas' *distinctio*. This is not to say, however, that Gower simply transfers such elements as may be found in the texts of Alan or Nicholas into a context narrowly focused on gluttony. It is rather the case in this book, as in others, that Gower interweaves lines of argument involving multiple topics.

Gluttony is, as Genius remarks, the "grete Senne original." It is the fate of a species that has separated itself from God that it follows its fleshly desires. The *opus carnis*, the work of the flesh to which the species is heir, can please but never satisfy, and this want of satisfaction Gower represents as a thirst, specifically as it is drawn into relationship with "dronkeschipe," but more largely as it represents the desire that engages the "derke" and "nyce fantasie" of the idolater.[4] The poet is aware, as he explores this image, that it has multiple meanings, including the opposed ones Alan introduces in his distinction for *sitire*, literally "to thirst." The term "means *to desire*, and so the Lord says, *Whosoever drinketh of this water, shall thirst again*, that is, out of carnal pleasure." But the term also "means *to burn with charity*, and thus the Psalmist writes, *For thee my soul hath thirsted*."[5]

The prevalent sense of the term in Book 6 of the *Confessio* is the first of these, a carnal desire that can never be quenched. Amans's condition, like that of the *avarus* described earlier, is "dropsical":

> As I am drunke of that I drinke,
> So am I ek for falte of drinke;
> Of which I finde no reles.   6.285–87

The more Amans's "herte" drinks, the more it wants to drink, and thus his "thurst schal nevere ben aqueint" (6.265).

---

3 Alan of Lille, *Art of Preaching*, cap. 4, trans. Evans, p. 33; *PL* 210:120.
4 In Alan of Lille's terms, gluttony, like *auaricia*, is "one of the daughters of idolatry" (ibid.), and in this book Gower will also explore that relationship.
5 Alan of Lille, *Distinctiones*, s. v., "sitire," *PL* 210:947.

Added to this dropsical condition is another, familiar to readers of Boethius and Chaucer; a person drinking this kind of drink, Genius argues,

> wot noght whider
> To go, the weies ben so slider,
> In which he mai per cas so falle,
> That he schal breke his wittes alle.   6.377–80

The lover obviously seeks a union with his beloved as the most desirable, indeed the sovereign "good," but because of his "love drinke," he has assumed a status developed in Chaucer's analogy:

> A dronke man woot wel he hath an hous,
> But he noot which the righte wey is thider,
> And to a dronke man the wey is slider.
> And certes, in this world so faren we;
> We seken faste after felicitee,
> But we goon wrong ful often, trewely.   KnT 1262–67

Boethius had attributed this condition of going wrong to a "dyrkyd memorie" (Bo 3. pr. 2.82–88). Genius, who has already spoken of the exile of "mannes Soule" from its true home, now talks about the drunkard's loss of reason:

> alle hise wittes he foryet,
> The which is to him such a let,
> That he wot nevere what he doth,
> Ne which is fals, ne which is soth.   6.39–42

Whereas, for Boethius, man is "semblable to God" and "a devyne beest be meryte of his resoun,"[6] so for Genius, the drunkard "that reson understod / So soudeinliche is woxe wod, / Or elles lich the dede man" (6.49–51). The fact that "The cuppe is al that evere him pleseth" (6.63) is merely a symptom of a more serious madness and death-likeness. As the drunkard loses reason and "the vertus, / Wherof reson him scholde clothe" (6.548–49), so in him "Wisdom hath lost the rihte weie, / That he no maner vice dredeth" (6.555–57).

From the outset of the confession, Amans knows that he has lost his "wittes," but he does not recognize his love-sickness as a sin. Now he admits that his brain is sometimes so overturned by *lovedrunke* "That I foryete al that I can / And stonde lich a mased man" (6.131–32), and yet, this is still no sin, but a simple, uncontrollable passion. He suffers it when his beloved is not present; then "alle lustes fro me strangen" (6.158) so that others swear "it am noght I" (6.160). When she appears, on the other hand, "I mai wel, if I schal, / Bothe singe and daunce and lepe aboute, / And holde forth the lusti route" (6.186–88). In a powerful sequence, the lover then recounts how, at the sight of her, he

---

6   Bo 2. pr. 5.128–29, 134–35.

falls into a trance-like rapture, "Riht as me thoghte that I syhe / Of Paradis the moste joie" (6.206–07); he is overcome with a "gret desir, / The which is hotere than the fyr," and it "Al soudeinliche upon me renneth / That al mi thoght withinne brenneth" (6.209–12); he feels transported – "I not where I am become" (6.214) – and experiences a "thoght so swete in mi corage," presumably of union with the beloved, that he feels "As thogh I were at myn above" (6.221). As long as he can sustain these thoughts, "Me thenketh as thogh I were aslepe / And that I were in goddes barm" (5.226–27).

Clearly, the language of this metaphor, while used to describe a carnal love, might just as easily describe the progress of thirst when it means *fervere charitate* or to yearn for God and seek one's rest in Him. Amans, in introducing radically different levels of experience in the terms of his analogy, unwittingly hints at a possible course for his love, wherein it might be "translated" into a desire for God, perfected and fulfilled in charity.

In actuality, of course, such a conversion is not yet available to him. He sees only a single possible release from his love-drunkenness:

> Bot if I myhte natheles
> Of such a drinke as I coveite,
> So as me liste, have o receite,
> I scholde assobre and fare wel.
> Bot so fortune upon hire whiel
> On hih me deigneth noght to sette,
> For everemore I finde a lette.   6.288–04

Amans thinks that getting what he covets in "o receite" will cure his dropsical love, making him sober and happy, but such a "receite," effected solely by a turn of Fortune, will at best yield a short-lived satisfaction.

The lover's claim wins from Genius another rich, and typically ambiguous doctrine, this one regarding the relationship between sobriety and fortune. The priest uses a Boethian topos to introduce his story of Jupiter's two tuns:

> For the fortune of every chance
> After the goddes pourveance
> To man it groweth from above,
> So that the sped of every love
> Is schape there, er it befalle.   6.325–29

Jupiter has in his cellar

> Tuo tonnes fulle of love drinke,
> That maken many an herte sinke
> And many an herte also to flete
> Or of the soure or of the swete.   6.333–36

Gower's immediate source for the image of Jupiter's casks is perhaps, as Macaulay points out, the *Roman de la rose*, specifically Reason's discourse on Fortune: from Jupiter's casks Fortune "draws absinthe and sweetened wine in cups, to make sops for everybody."[7] Genius has delimited this image: the tuns contain "love drinke," and Cupid, not Fortune, "is boteler of bothe" (6.345). Once again the priest stresses the "chance" of love: although "the sped of every love" is shaped before it occurs, Cupid makes "men drunke al upon chaunce" (6.363), and thus some "Drinke undeserved of the beste" (6.358).

This argument regarding Cupid can be pointed in either of two directions. For Genius as Venus's clerk, cupidinous love is a good, and "relese" depends on a special grace or favor, on the lover getting what he covets. For Genius as a Christian priest, that same love is a "fated" concupiscence derived, after the "grete Senne original," from a corrupted nature; release requires a different kind of grace or favor, a "remission of sin."[8] In one of his structures of perception, Genius appears to understand grace in the latter sense, and with it the Pauline teaching that we "hold fast our confession" and go "with confidence to the throne of grace" (Heb. 4:14–16). He implies this much when he points to the source of the lover's amendment. Amans's drink will remain bitter "til god the sende / Such grace that thou miht amende" (6.389–90).

The means to achieve this release, or to quench this thirst, lies in prayer, as the tale of Bacchus in this book reveals. Genius urges the lover to "bidde and preie"

> That thou the lusti welle atteigne
> Thi wofull thurstes to restreigne
> Of love, and taste the swetnesse.   6.393–95

Bacchus and his "compainie," returning from a military campaign in the Orient, are nearly destroyed by "bodiliche thurst" in the Libyan desert. Bacchus prays to Jupiter:

> Behold, mi fader, and tak hiede
> This wofull thurst that we ben inne
> To staunche, and grante ous forto winne,
> And sauf unto the contre fare,
> Wher that oure lusti loves are
> Waitende upon oure hom cominge.   6.420–25

Bacchus's prayer is answered: "grace he gradde and grace he hadde" (6.445), for a wether guides him to life-giving water, a "welle freissh and cler" from which every man can "drinke his fille." This story, celebrating a "grete grace" manifested through the "wether," has rich spiritual overtones: the well of living water, as Robert Yeager has shown, hints at numerous passages in Scripture, including especially John 4:13–14, where Jesus makes an important distinction as he teaches the Samaritan woman:[9]

---

[7] *Roman de la rose*, 6791–94, trans. Dahlberg, p. 131; ed. Lecoy, 1:208.
[8] Alan of Lille, *Distinctiones*, s. v. "gratia," *PL* 210:805–06.
[9] Robert F. Yeager, "John Gower and the Uses of Allusion," *Res Publica Litterarum* 7 (1984): 201–13.

Jesus answered, and said to her: Whosoever drinketh of this water, shall thirst again; but he that shall drink of the water that I will give him, shall not thirst for ever: But the water that I will give him, shall become in him a fountain of water, springing up into life everlasting.

This is one of the scriptural passages, we recall, that grounded Alan of Lille's distinction concerning thirsts of carnal desire and charity. In the tale of Bacchus, Genius possibly gives to a literal or "bodiliche" thirst a spiritual meaning. The story concludes as a grateful Bacchus builds a temple to Jupiter on this spot, where it "evere" stands "To thursti men in remembrance" (6.439). This recalls a temple – the Church – that serves another kind of homecoming, namely of the soul returning from exile to a place where a most pleasant "love" is waiting.

Like Nicholas de Gorran, Gower knows the difference between true and false consolation. The nature of the language of this confession is such, however, that the thirst of charity – ultimately a thirst for the grace of "eternal life or of virtue"[10] – is sometimes confused with the thirst of carnal delight, and that confusion rests specifically on the fact that the two thirsts are described by a shared terminology.

Genius advises the lover to "prei erli and late" (6.451) in order to quench his thirst, but this advice, set in the *moralitas* for the tale of Bacchus, is rendered dubious by another reference to the blind butler. The lover must trust to chance, to a god who cannot see:

> if it mihte so betyde,
> That he upon the blinde side
> Per cas the swete tonne arauhte,
> Than schalt thou have a lusti drauhte
> And waxe of lovedrunke sobre.   6.455–59

By so framing the tale of Bacchus, the priest would appear to undercut its message: the "lusti drauhte" that will make the lover "sobre" is a fulfilled carnal desire. The "spede" of such love occurs "per cas," and grace once again becomes mere fortune.

Genius's argument here carries residual premises from some of his earlier statements. He has already argued that the lover might "deserve grace" (4.616) only by asking for it, but his proof was drawn from the case of Pygmalion, whose prayer Venus "of hire grace herde" (4.419). In that same setting, the priest had encouraged the lover to be persistent, since

> fortune suieth
> Fulofte and yifth hire happi chance
> To him which makth continuance
> To preie love and to beseche.   4.366–69

---

10 Alan of Lille, *Distinctiones*, s. v. "gratia," PL 210:805–06.

In the context of Book 6, however, such a devotion to "fortune," "happi chance," and the blind butler god manifests the unsure prayer of the "dronke man" who finds the path "slider." Even in its dialogue, Book 6 itself becomes "slider," manifesting Chaucer's "We witen nat what thing we preyen heere" (*KnT* 1260).

Such confusion extends to the tales and *moralitates* Genius introduces after his tribute to prayer. He offers a brief summary of the tale of Tristan and Bele Ysolde to warn the lover to avoid potions. He tells the story of Ipotacie (or the marriage of Pirithous) to show the evil of drink at wedding parties: the guests, who happen to be Centaurs, are not only rude in "compaignye," but they abduct the bride; the point to note is that drink ruins "mannes grace" (6.533). Things get worse in the next narrative, as Galba and Vitellus, drunken tyrants of Spain, are shown to be even more violent than the Centaurs:

> Ther was no wif ne maiden there,
> What so thei were, or faire or foule,
> Whom thei ne token to defoule.   6.572–74

This sequence of stories illustrates the effects of a more literal *dronkeschipe*, no doubt, and it reflects a compiler's impulse to gather material to fit an announced *ordinatio*. At the same time, the priest, driven to include much in his role as a compiler, appears to give major issues, also gleaned from his sources, cursory attention. Often he comes back to emphasize surface graces, using his sources as a fund of strategies to ensure Amans's good fortune in a relationship where willy-nilly his love may "spede" or "spill" (5.4560). As a *compilator*, Genius often appears to be driven as much by Fortune in his domain as Amans is driven by Fortune in his. His problem, in such a setting, is finding stories that really teach and truly console.

What the lover wants is lodged in the external, temporal world of "foreyne and subgit thynges" (*Bo* 2. pr. 5.124–36). He cannot reject his *dronkeschipe* "be no weie," he argues, because "It stant noght upon my fortune" (6.604–05), and Genius, given his own ambivalence, cannot disabuse him of this notion. Cupid might give Amans a "lusti draught" of the sweet wine that can make him sober, or satisfy him carnally. Genius, having said this, then offers a curious piece of advice: "And thus I rede thou assobre / Thin herte in hope of such a grace" (6.460–61). The statement is paradoxical. To "assobre" the heart would seem to mean a rejection of carnal thirst; it would mean a restoration to one's proper nature, and that, in its turn, would render moot the "hope of such a grace," or the favor of a satisfied fleshly desire. This is an occasion on which Genius, in his double role, clearly "points" a contradiction.

Another confusion in the statement is perhaps more significant, for it gets at a paradox basic to the entire confession. Genius appears to suggest that one needs grace to turn sober, but must also turn sober in order to receive (or hope to receive) grace. This is an issue to which medieval *auctores* were especially sensitive: whether one can prepare for grace without the external assistance of grace. To this question, Thomas Aquinas's response is familiar: the preparation of the will for good cannot take place without the gift of grace, without "the gratuitous assistance of God moving the soul within, or inspiring a good purpose." To prepare oneself for grace is a conversion, a "turning to God," but the righteous are turned to God only by God's having turned them.[11]

The "turning" of the lover is not certain until the end of the poem, and Genius's role in that particular conversion, as an instrument of grace, is minimal. In effect, however, the work represents two sorts of preparation for what Aquinas describes as a "glory that is not yet possessed."[12] Aquinas notes that preparation can be instantaneous, as it was for Paul on the road to Damascus: thus God sometimes moves a man suddenly to the good, and that person receives grace all at once. Sometimes, however, preparation proceeds gradually. Ultimately, "it makes no difference whether someone reaches the state of complete preparation in a moment or gradually."[13] The conversion of the lover at the end of the confession has to many readers seemed too sudden, but it fits another kind of preparation that has been occurring throughout, a preparation that Genius, seemingly by ignorance, caprice, or negligence, has slowed down: even this retardation turns out to be a grace: at the instantaneous preparation, it gives the lover a field of knowledge to reassess. Despite the lover's recalcitrance and the priest's own slowness, the process of getting ready for conversion is a converting; it is *generatio* or a "motus ad formam."[14]

The preparation occurs even in the midst of false consolation. Genius looks for stories that can direct, even reform the lover, and thereby provide apt consolation. In Book 6, Amans confesses to having looked for such tales as well: he is a reader of fictions that might provide solace for his own "real" suffering and misfortune. He has taken special pleasure in the

> redinge of romance
> Of Ydoine and of Amadas,
> That whilom weren in mi cas,
> And eke of othre many a score.   6.878–81

This reading provides refreshment because, "for the while yit it eseth / And somdel of myn herte appeseth." (6.893–94). It is, once again, an exercise in discovering likeness; the lover looks for those who "weren in mi cas."

This isolated, past activity of reading captures, at another level of reality, what the lover's confession is about. The stories Genius tells depend for their rhetorical effect on the lover's ability to discover likeness in them; so also, Amans himself, in recovering his past love through confession, creates a likeness of himself, an invented persona that he reconfirms by his reading of

[11] *Summa theologiae* 1a2ae, 109.6, Blackfriars ed., 30:88–91.
[12] Ibid., 112.2, pp. 148–49.
[13] Ibid., pp. 150–51.
[14] For a helpful discussion of the relationship of generation, grace, and conversion in Aquinas and as applied specifically to Dante, see Charles Singleton, *Journey to Beatrice*, Dante Studies 2 (Baltimore, 1958; rpt. 1977), pp. 44–54.

fiction.[15] Reading, hearing, and telling "tales" are acts of inventing "resemblance," and to the extent that they succeed in doing so, they are all consolatory.

There lurks beneath such activity, however, a question of what the discovered likeness is fit for. Amans reads romances as a "restauratif," but they are more than mere "game" or rest from labor. Through reading, as through hearing and telling, Amans rewrites his love, feeds his "fantasie," and reconstitutes his memory. He remarks about his romances that

> with the lust of here histoire
> Somtime I drawe into memoire
> Hou sorwe mai noght evere laste;
> And so comth hope in ate laste.   6.885–88

These words provide a foil to those of Machaut's lover-narrator in the *Remede de Fortune*, who, after Esperance has left the Parc de Hedin, promises faithfully to inscribe her words in memory. Esperance has never appeared to Amans: instead, he creates *esperance* by a process of selectively reading his histories of lovers. This act ultimately constitutes a remaking of his own history, and it forms the basis for a whole sequence of remakings.

Amans's "redinge" predates the confession, and it reorders – and fictionalizes – a more distant past, specifically by generating hope. The confession, in its turn, reforms the "redinge" and its implications. And finally, once the confession ends, the lover will presumably refashion the reading and the confession of reading, giving a new form to these various histories out of his new, and radically different, perspective.

In Machaut, the "istoire" of Esperance is designed to negate the effects of Fortune: it has the power to comfort lovers, just as, within the history, Esperance has claimed that power: "I succour them; I comfort them against Desire, who attacks them" (2156–58). In Gower, the solace of history has just the opposite effect on Amans as reader: reading about those who "were in mi cas" makes the lover even more dependent on "aventure" and the temporal grace that merely heightens his unstable desire and *tristesce*.

While the lover struggles to find likenesses to console him, the poet evolves a perspective on such consolation and on Fortune that goes beyond what he may have seen in the *Consolation* or any *dit amoreus*. The consolation of "resemblance," for the poet, bears a connection to the plight of sin and vitiated nature, both inherited from Adam in the longer reach of history and memory, and to the larger question of re-creation. Book 6 extends the problem implied in Book 5, where Adam's original sin was described as "the cause in special / Of mannes worschipe ate laste" (5.1768–69); that sin was a *felix culpa* because God, in his might, remade man so that "in his degre" he "Stant more worth"

---

[15] For alternatives to Amans's use of likenesses gleaned from fictions, see my article, "Rhetoric," pp. 185–200.

(5.1776–77). God reconciles the soul to Him and thus draws man back to himself, to self-possession, true "worschipe" and likeness.

In its lapsed nature, the soul, figured in the wandering of a "soubgit" or exiled people, no longer resembles God, and thus no longer resembles itself, *unde anima dissimilis Deo, unde dissimilis et sibi.*[16] Gluttony, like avarice, causes the loss of self, a forgetting and ultimately a restless wandering, drawing ever farther away from the repose to be found in God. Gower, cognizant of a rich tradition of responses to this question of unlikeness, ultimately seeks stability, a center, in God. As Book 6 proceeds, he shows how far the lover has wandered from himself: when Amans casts a likeness, he effectively makes a self unlike himself. He steps into a *regione dissimilitudinis*, the land of unlikeness which Augustine described in a famous passage: "Shining Thy light upon me so strongly, Thou didst strike down my feeble gaze, and I trembled with love and with awe. I discovered that I was far from Thee in the area of unlikeness."[17]

Gower enlarges the scale of his poem by allusions to the tradition of the land of unlikeness and the related issue of *nosce teipsum*, but he carries this learning lightly.[18] What begins as a Boethian statement regarding self-knowledge and consolation expands to a theological statement that implies much in this larger tradition. Amans does not know that his "swote grene pleine" is in one sense a figure of a land wherein the "likeness to God has been forfeited."[19] There he

[16] Bernard of Clairvaux, *In Canticum canticorum* 82.5; quoted and discussed by Gilson, *Spirit of Mediaeval Philosophy*, pp. 295–96. "So it is that the soul is unlike God and consequently unlike itself as well." Trans. Irene Edmonds, *On the Song of Songs IV*, Cistercian Fathers Series, 40 (Kalamazoo, Mich., 1980), p. 176.

[17] Augustine, *Confessions*, 7.10.16, trans. Bourke, p. 181; ed. Skutella, p. 141. This and other, later uses of the image are presented by Pierre Courcelle in "Répertoire des textes relatifs à la 'région de dissemblance' jusqu'au XIVe siècle," *AHDLMA* 24 (1957): 24–33; see also "Tradition neo-platonicienne et traditions chrétiennes de la 'région de dissemblance' (Platon, *Politique*, 273d)," *loc. cit.*, 5–23; idem, "Témoins nouveaux de la 'région de la dissemblance,' " *Bibliothèque de l'École des Chartres* 118 (1960): 20–36; Etienne Gilson, "Regio dissimilitudinis de Platon à Saint Bernard," *Mediaeval Studies* 9 (1947): 103–30; Gervais Dumeige, "Dissemblance," *Dictionnaire de spiritualité*, fasc. 3 (Paris, 1957): 1330–46; Robert Javelet, *Image et ressemblance au douzième siècle de Saint Anselme à Alain de Lille* (Paris, 1967), 1:266–85.

[18] On the theme of *nosce teipsum*, see Pierre Courcelle, " 'Nosce teipsum' du bas-empire au haut moyen âge: l'heritage profane et les developpements chrétiens," *Il Passagio dall' Antichita al Medioevo in Occidente*, Settimane di Studio del Centro Italiano sull' Alto Medioevo, 9 (Spoleto, 1962): 263–95; Gilson, *Spirit of Mediaeval Philosophy*, pp. 209–28; L. de Bazelaire, "Connaissance de soi," *Dictionnaire de spiritualité*, fasc. 13 (Paris, 1950): 1511–43; Robert Javelet, *Image et ressemblance*, 1:368–71; E. Bertola, "Il Socratismo Christiano nel XII secolo," *Rivista di Filosofia Neo-Scholastica* 51 (1959): 252–64."

[19] Bernard of Clairvaux, *In Canticum canticorum* 36.4.5, trans. Kilian Walsh, *On the Song of Songs II*, Cistercian Fathers Series, 7 (Kalamazoo, Mich., 1976), p. 178; see William of St. Thierry, *De natura et dignitate amoris* 11.34, PL 184:401: "Videbat quippe Dominus quantum ad hominem omnia confusa, omnia turbata; nihil stare in loco suo, nihil procedere ordine sui. Videbat hominem abisse in regionem dissimilitudinis tam longe, ut per se nec sciret nec posset redire."

cannot find the "rihte weie," or even recognize, as he later does, that he is lost; it is only at the end of the work, as he returns from exile and once again possesses himself, that he can, in more than a literal sense, report that "Homward a softe pas y wente" (8.2967). As long as he re-creates himself out of the likeness he finds in romances – a likeness that merely serves his hope and desire – he will not break free of his false paradise, a place of "tribulation and inquietude."[20]

A literary analogue to Amans's exile and homecoming occurs in the dream-within-the-dream of Passus XI of *Piers Plowman*, in which a "rauysshed" Will is brought by Fortune "into þe lond of longynge [and] loue" (11.7), a land which, as Joseph Wittig has convincingly argued, is the *regio dissimilitudinis*.[21] There Fortune has Will look "in a Mirour þat hiȝte middelerþe" where he might see "wondres," know what he covets, and win those things "paraunter" (11.9–11). An attendant of Fortune, *Concupiscencia carnis*, then adds her enticement, reminding Will that he is young, that he has "yeres ynowe / For to lyue longe and ladies to louye" (11.18–19). Having encountered all three temptations, however, Will is called back to himself by Elde:

> 'Man,' quod he, 'if I mete wiþ þe, by Marie of heuene!
> Thow shalt fynde Fortune þee faille at þi mooste nede.'
> 11.28–29

While Gower does not use these personified figures, he introduces the same elements in his account of Amans: the lover has been tempted by Fortune and the three "lievest" things, and as we shall discover, old age alone can call him back from carnal desire and its attendant delusion of youth.

The paradigm for the tale retold by these poets is the parable of the prodigal son, who travels to a distant land, *in regionem longinquam* (Luke 15:14), lives luxuriously, and wastes the substance given to him by his father – by "ratione, memoria, et ingenio," as the gloss of Hugh of St. Cher puts it. Like the last books of Gower's poem, Hugh's gloss focuses on nature dissipated, *luxuria*, and the land of unlikeness – Gower's pleasance or "swote grene pleine" – as a region of idolatry: "the gentile stock departed into a distant land, that is, separated itself from God, turned to idols, and worshipped the work of its hands."[22]

Amans, not knowing himself even while he prefers himself, must suffer a shock of self-recognition before he can leave his own region of unlikeness; this is a grace "by means of which the image of God in the soul, deformed through sin, is again reformed."[23] For the greater part of the confession, he is not himself and does not know himself; surely he lacks the calm self-assurance reflected, for

---

[20] Pseudo-Bede, *In Psalmorum librum exegesis*, 45.2, PL 93:725.
[21] Joseph S. Wittig, " 'Piers Plowman' B, Passus IX–XII: Elements in the Design of the Inward Journey," *Traditio* 28 (1972): 222; Langland quotations in this paragraph are from *Piers Plowman: The B Version*, ed. George Kane and E. Talbot Donaldson, rev. ed. (London and Berkeley, California, 1988), pp. 437–38.
[22] *Biblia sacra*, 6: fol. 224r.
[23] Bersuire, *Dictionarium*, s. v. "gratia," 2: fol. 98r.

example, in St. Paul's famous "Gratia Dei sum id quod sum" (1 Cor. 15:10). At no point during this confession can Amans claim that he is what he is by God's grace. When he fears that others who see him love-drunk might think that "it am noght I" (5.160), the "I" he thinks he has lost is gracious behavior. The lady – his source of grace – is absent, and all he then sees in himself is forgotten manners: he has simply become poor company. Even in its silences, this poem speaks to the troubled depths of Amans's nature.

Amans's loss of his "wittes" in a false paradise is a featured subject of his confession of Delicacie, a yearning for whatever food extends the "lustes" of appetite beyond what is required for sustenance. Delicacie seeks variety and ever new delight, and metaphorically the person delicate in love, though he has the "beste wif of al the lond, / Or the faireste love of alle" (6.668–69), rejects what is known for the distant and as yet untested pleasure. Amans hardly seems guilty of this sin, and yet he suffers love-delicacy in a different form, as a lover who, though "his ladi make him chiere," will find no relief until he has the "surplus" or "al his appetit" (6.686).

It is common enough for a lover to want more than his lady's good cheer, and this desire need not be a vice, of course. The *amant* in Froissart's *Paradis d'Amour* reveals a gentler wish:[24] not content with his lady's "bonne chiere" (1531), he wants her to accept him as her "loyal servant" (1536), and she readily accedes because his desire is entirely consistent with *courtoisie*. Things never seem so simple for Amans's beloved, or for Gower's lover. Amans does not really know what he wants, and what confounds him is a deficient memory, an imperfect gleaning of likenesses. We might expect him to remember, throughout the shrift, his "joie" at the "grant mercy" he won from his beloved in church. A short time before he recounts that episode, however, he complains that "Noght als so moche as 'grant mercy' / Hir list to seie, of which I mihte / Som of mi grete peine allyhte" (5.4518–20). His is a topically inventive mind: he recalls only what his topics allow him to remember. The more serious problem, however, lies in his present failure to connect topics or instances. The denials, lapses, and reversals betray the condition of a person dominated by Fortune, of one who too quickly forgets: under these circumstances, it is natural for him to complain bitterly, despite his other recent testimony to the contrary, that the lady does not feed his heart "with o goodly lok" (6.715).

Amans builds his complaint on sense-perceptible examples that he imperfectly remembers, and this is the plight of one delicate in love: while he depends on the senses, he also suffers a loss of the "wittes," memory, and reason that can order perceptions meaningfully. Momentary refreshment provides his only contentment. He claims that three "smale lustes" (6.737) – sight, hearing, and thought – sustain him, giving him a "restauratif" and "recreacioun." In this confession, however, he admits that his thought is idle: mixed with "fantasie" and "desir" and filled with "woldes" and wishes, it can provide no final com-

---

[24] The following terms are quoted from Jean Froissart, *Le Paradis d'Amour*, ed. Peter F. Dembowski (Geneva, 1986).

fort. "Real" consolation is to be found in sense-perception. In the physical beauty of his beloved, all that his eye "seth is full of grace" (6.776), and his "Yhe" persuades him that "he hath ful sufficance / Of liflode and of sustinance / As to his part for everemo" (6.797–99). The experience of the "Ere" offers another delight. The lady's words especially are full of truth and faith, and when "sche carole upon a song," Amans confesses, "I am fro miself so ledd, / As thogh I were in paradis" (6.870–71). He has entered the region of unlikeness.

The lover's re-entering paradise, faith and works aside, recalls the very opening of Book 6 and the priest's description of gluttony:

> The grete Senne original,
> Which every man in general
> Upon his berthe hath envenymed,
> In Paradis it was mystymed:
> Whan Adam of thilke Appel bot,
> His swete morscel was to hot,
> Which dedly made the mankinde.   6.1–7

Gower here relies on a topos – "Consider, man, how through gluttony, Adam lost paradise"[25] – but in Book 6 he inverts that image in his figure of Amans. By his gluttony, the lover thinks he has regained paradise. The futility of Amans's effort to recreate paradise out of transitory, earth-bound pleasure suggests the pattern that has emerged in his feeding his "Ere" upon romances; he has shortened his memory of himself.

Confession is designed to lengthen memory, to restore the hope of redemption. Ordering time is a repeated topic in the last confessional books, particularly as the priest traces histories back to their origin, ultimately in "Paradis," and one might think that Amans, by being placed in this long reach of history, might thence begin to restructure the meaning of his love-experience. At present his desire lacks a history, and most especially a place in the central history of redemption. By a distraction and a forgetting, a *distentio animi*, Amans has become scattered in time and memory.

---

[25] Alan of Lille, *Art of Preaching*, cap. 4, trans. Evans, p. 33; *PL* 210:121.

CHAPTER FIFTEEN

CURIOSITY: "SORCERIE" AND NECTANABUS

The last two major topics of this book, Delicacie and Sorcerie, are like the first one in attending to sense-knowledge and the consolation of the senses, but Genius in these later sections also introduces a danger related to carnal desire, a sense-knowledge turned into "lust of the eyes." Especially with Sorcerie, the desire for "bodely delices" is combined with an unchecked desire for knowledge, an idle *curiositas*. Such curiosity is a fit subject for this confession, since, in medieval tradition, Venus is associated with that vice, and with fleshly curiosity especially: not only in such works as Alan's *De planctu Naturae*, but in the central *Ovide moralisé*, she is pictured as "intent and curious to find every carnal pleasure."[1] Curiosity is often associated with sloth, but we shall also find sufficient warrant for Genius's picturing it in his exemplars of gluttony, and most pointedly in sorcerers. The last major tale of this book is linked with the whole of Book 7 not merely because each centers on a teacher of Alexander, on Nectanabus and Aristotle respectively, but because these teachers manifest the difference between curiosity and *studiositas* or a "controlled devotion to learning."[2] By looking at the first of these terms here, we shall be better prepared to understand the point of Aristotle's lore in Book 7.

Sense-perception, as we have already noted, is the progenitor of all knowledge, and it is a critical faculty to the responses Genius seeks for his narratives. His version of the story of Dives and Lazarus, one of his two tales regarding Delicacie, is changed little from its Biblical source, and yet in the application the priest modifies a basic teaching in the original when he encourages Amans to recreate the tale in sense-perceptible terms. At a key point in the tale, Dives asks Abraham to send Lazarus to warn Dives' brothers about the pains of hell that await them: in "pure fere" of a man arising from the dead, Dives argues,

[1] *Ovide moralisé*, 11.2430–31, ed. C. de Boer (Amsterdam, 1915–38), 3:176. In this passage Venus represents the "vie voluptueuse," and she is contrasted with Pallas, who represents the "vie contemplative." Pallas is also "curieuse et pensive," but

> D'une chose tant solement:
> Ceste a tout son entendement
> En Dieu cognoistre, en Dieu orer,
> En Dieu servir, en Dieu loer.   11.2450–52

For additional discussion of this vice, see my article, "Grammar, Manhood, and Tears: The Curiosity of Chaucer's Monk," *Modern Philology* 76 (1978): 1–17.

[2] Thomas Aquinas, *Summa theologiae* 2a2ae, 166.2, trans. Thomas Gilby, Blackfriars ed., 44:196–97.

the brothers "scholden wel be war" (6.1099). Abraham refuses the request, arguing that the brothers, who have failed to obey those who "alday preche," will not suddenly heed a dead man who appears "in dede." For Genius, however, the use of the senses or, in this case, the imagination, is critical to grasping the proof:

> If thou, mi Sone, canst *descryve*
> This tale, as Crist himself it tolde,
> Thou schalt have cause to *beholde*,
> To *se* so gret an *evidence*,
> Wherof the soth *experience*
> *Hath schewed openliche at ʒe*,
> That bodili delicacie
> Of him which yeveth non almesse
> Schal after falle in gret destresse.
> And that was *sene* . . .   (emphases added)
>   6.1110–19

Here Genius obviously directs the use of the senses to wisdom. But the importance he assigns to sense-perception poses a special danger in a treatise on Delicacie. Amans seeks "restauracion" in bodily "delices"; by his dominant attention to proximate and momentary delight – identified through sense-perception and imagination – he effectively cancels history, order, and meaning in his experience. An analogous danger exists in curiosity.

In a second tale regarding Delicacie, Nero is shown to crave exotic "delices," now including a knowledge perversely sought, generated, and applied. Nero sets out to investigate his own delicacy, specifically "for glotonie / Of bodili Delicacie, / To knowe his stomak hou it ferde" (6.1161–63). In a "wonder soubtil" plan, he picks three men like himself, and has them "pleie, / And ete and drinke als wel as he" (6.1170–71); after getting the first to ride, the second to sleep, and the third to walk "faire and softe," he calls all three together and kills and eviscerates them to discover which of their three stomachs worked best: thus Nero writes his future by digestive precedent, by creating a likeness in stomachs. This inquiry allows him to increase his delicacy, to pursue it with "non abstinence" (6.1212). And thus he subjugates reason, "delicate" in its quest of strange things, to appetite.

The tale of Nero is not contained by its literal topic, but points back to the first species of gluttony and ahead to Sorcerie: Nero takes his "draught" where he will and is "drunke in al his wit" (6.1222); as one "delicat, / To knowe" (6.1184–85), he anticipates the major failing of curiosity that Genius next perceives in the practice of Sorcerie.

Sorcerie, another legacy of self-worship, is aptly chosen as a species of gluttony, for by medieval precedent it is one of the sins of the mouth.[3] Its

---

[3] R. F. Yeager, "Aspects of Gluttony in Chaucer and Gower," *Studies in Philology* 81 (1984): 45.

premise has already been exemplified in Nero's rejection of God: "Ayeins the pointz of the believe, / He tempteth hevene and erthe and helle" (6.1258–59). A sorcerer commits such "blasphemye," Friar Lorens remarks, "for couetise to wynne þerwiþ."[4] It is that point, including the effects of such "couetise," that we might now usefully explore.

Genius's concern is the lover who "Magique . . . useth forto winne / His love, and spareth for no Sinne" (6.1333–34). In place of belief – "Ther is no god . . . / Of whom that he takth eny hiede" (6.1278–79) – he cultivates a range of magical arts, and Genius takes great pains to catalogue them, even to interject a defense of those "craftes, as I finde, / A man mai do be weie of kinde, / Be so it be to good entente" (6.1303–05).[5] But the defense of magic used "to good entente" is brief compared to the catalogue of practices in Nigromance that follows: this densely packed treatise earns a fit comment from Amans, who with good reason cannot understand what he is supposed to confess: "I wot noght o word what ye mene" (6.1363).

This, however, does not stop the lover from a confession that reintroduces Lorens's terms:

> I wol noght seie, if that I couthe,
> That I nolde in mi lusti youthe
> Benethe in helle and ek above
> To winne with mi ladi love
> Don al that evere that I mihte;
> For therof have I non insihte
> Wher afterward that I become,
> To that I wonne and overcome
> Hire love, which I most coveite.   6.1365–73

Following this admission, the emphasis in Genius's treatise falls upon the type of lover who practices magic "for couetise," specifically to satisfy his carnal desire.

Such is the case with Ulysses. This "worthi knyht and king" is also a clerk who, for example, knows rhetoric, magic, astronomy, philosophy, dream theory ("the slepi dremes"), navigation, and surgery. Most importantly, he seems by his knowledge to have mastered Fortune: "he thurgh wisdom that he schapeth / Ful many a gret peril ascapeth" (6.1419–20), and with that wisdom, he appears to get everything he wants:

> Thus hath Uluxes what he wolde,
> His wif was such as sche be scholde,

---

[4] Book of Vices and Virtues, p. 67; quoted by Yeager, p. 49.
[5] Included in the series of such crafts is geomancy, and this defense is perhaps intended to ameliorate the attack, since geomancy is the topic of the lone book we know Richard II commissioned: this "geomancie libellum," the Liber judiciorum, is preserved in London, British Library, MS Royal 12 C v, and Oxford, Bodleian Library, MS Bodley 581.

> His poeple was to him sougit,
> Him lacketh nothing of delit.   6.1505–08

His story takes a Boethian turn, however, in proving that "noman," not even the wisest of men, knows "what schall befalle" (6.1512). Man has knowledge

> Save of himself of alle thing;
> His oghne chance noman knoweth,
> Bot as fortune it on him throweth.   6.1568–70

That unsureness is compounded in one who "goth ther noman wole him bidde" (6.1282). For those who choose to live outside the plan of providence and redemption, science or knowledge lacks order, and that adversely influences remembrance. Thus, for all that Ulysses knows, he easily forgets. This appears to be Gower's point about these interrelated species of gluttony, all in a sense drawn into the pattern of *delicacie*: idle curiosity, the desire for the distant and strange, induces forgetfulness of the profoundest sort. Ulysses's knowledge lacks an *ordinatio*, or a field of topics to organize remembrance, and that is because he is driven by *sensualitas*, by a desire for immediate gratification of his "lustes." He is a character who has lost his history.

At first glance, the final exemplar of sorcery, Nectanabus, appears to be the wiser man, at least because he can "sih tofor the dede" (6.1798). Fleeing Egypt to evade enemies who will most certainly overpower him, he arrives in Macedon and there, when he first sees the queen, Olympias, he is entranced by her beauty:

> He couthe noght withdrawe his lok
> To se noght elles in the field,
> Bot stod and only hire behield.   6.1858–60

The curious Olympias, on this "feste of hir nativite," is similarly fascinated by Nectanabus, who is "unlich alle othre there" (6.1862): "The queene on him hire yhe caste, / And knew that he was strange anon" (6.1864–65). She sends for him, strangely to discover why he stares at her "Withoute blenchinge of his chere" (6.1867). This is enough to enact the seduction in which he will appear to her as the god "Amos of Lubie."

This opening scene manifests a curiosity: Nectanabus's "inspection of a woman leads to lechery,"[6] and Olympias's own curiosity leads to an identical end for herself. That, however, is not the extent of the issue. The wanton Nectanabus increases fleshly delight by creating exotic settings for achieving his pleasure.[7] The fleshly curiosity not only of Nectanabus, but of both characters, is fully presented in the sweep of the entire narrative; it includes that lust of the eyes which, in Bede's terms, extends "to the learning of magical arts" and

---

[6]   Thomas Aquinas, *Summa theologiae* 2a2ae, 167.2, Blackfriars ed., 44:206–09.
[7]   "Hec est anima, que studio curiositatis seducta uadit uidere cogitationes carnales et eas amplectitur" (MS Troyes 1251, fol. 128r; quoted by Courcelle, "Répertoire," p. 28).

"watching spectacles"; these are spectacles which, to borrow John Chrysostom's terms, make watchers "adulterous and shameless."[8]

Through his magical bedtime transformations, Nectanabus "putte him out of mannes like" (6.2062), becoming a dragon, then a wether, "And soudeinly, er sche was war, / As he which alle guile can, / His forme he torneth into man" (6.2078–80). The story is filled with spectacles, in scenes involving Olympias, and later Philip, for Nectanabus also puts on a show for the king, "rampende" into the hall in the "lothly forme" of a dragon, then changing into an eagle so magnificent that when, on its perch, it shakes itself, "al the halle quok, / As it a terremote were; / Thei seiden alle, god was there" (2206–08). Indeed, the narrative throughout is a spectacle. As the "king hath grete mervaile" at this performance for his benefit, the queen is amazed at the spectacle designed for her, and both are additionally moved by the spectacular dreams created by Nectanabus for each of them, so that the auditor experiences like wonder in hearing the tale as a whole. That, at first, appears to be a problem in the telling: by providing an abundance of gratuitously exotic detail, Genius not only represents, but would seem to nurture *delicacie*. Nevertheless, there is another power in this narrative: through its spectacle it shows very pointedly what that delicacy or, more largely, curiosity means and thereby offers the strongest dissuasion against it.

Olympias is not exempt from Gower's attack. To be sure, she seems a better character than the exhibitionist Olimpias of Thomas of Kent's *Romanz de tute chevalerie*. Peter Beidler has argued that Gower made her into a shamefast, mild, and innocent character in order to shift "the focus of moral censure to Nectanabus" and to reinforce the parallel with the story of the Annunciation: in that parallel a "promiscuous" Olympias "would have been unthinkable."[9]

Nevertheless, in a period replete with such "Annunciation" stories, the parallel is never lost, even when Mary's counterpart is more wanton than Thomas's Olimpias; the likeness is recognizable even in comic inversions such as Boccaccio's tale of the laughably foolish Madonna Lisetta (*Decameron* 4.2). Indeed, the point about Gower's story, as Patrick Gallacher more correctly notes, is that it represents a "false Annunciation."[10] The queen is not a blameless victim of Nectanabus' evil. She is unstable not because she is lascivious, or even, more positively, because "withoute guile" she "Supposeth trouthe al that sche hiereth" (6.2284–85). She is unstable because of her own *delicacie* or love

---

[8] Bede, *In Primam Epistolam S. Joannis* 2.16, PL 93:92; John Chrysostom, *Homiliae in Matthaeum* 6, *Patrologia graeca*, ed. J. P. Migne (Paris, 1857–66), 57:72; quoted by Thomas Aquinas, *Summa theologiae* 2a2ae, 167.2, Blackfriars ed., 44:206–09.

[9] Peter Beidler, "Diabolical Treachery in the Tale of Nectanabus," ed. Peter Beidler, *John Gower's Literary Transformations in the Confessio Amantis: Original Articles and Translations* (Washington, D.C., 1982), pp. 86–88. See Thomas of Kent, *La Romanz de tute chevalerie*, in *Alexandre le Grand dans la littérature française du moyen âge*, ed. Paul Meyer (Paris, 1886; rpt. Geneva, 1970), 1:177–235.

[10] Patrick J. Gallacher, *Love, the Word, and Mercury: A Reading of John Gower's Confessio Amantis* (Albuquerque, N.M., 1975), p. 41.

of the distant and strange. This feature of her character begins to appear in her initial meeting with Nectanabus. Over the course of the narrative, it becomes even more apparent that she enjoys watching spectacles and listening to speeches feigned with "wordes wise" as much as Nectanabus enjoys producing them. This in the end is a form of self-praise: the love of spectacle is consistent with Olympias' easy consent to the appearance of the god, after she learns that her child will be feared by all "erthli kinges" and even called "god of erthe" (6.1940). If she wins such "gret worschipe," she promises, she will make Nectanabus rich. Hers is hardly a humble, restrained, or modest submission to a god's will.

Both characters, then, are intrigued by the strange and the unknown; neither moderates an eagerness for new knowledge and the power such knowledge might bring. No doubt, Nectanabus seeks "to learn from an illicit source"[11] to the more immediate end of gaining carnal pleasure:

> He wolde into the helle seche
> The devel himselve to beseche,
> If that he wiste forto spede
> To gete of love his lusti mede.   6.1351–54

That, however, is not his only end: in taking to the "dieules craft" (6.2345), he also strives to gain "pouer" and "maistrie" (6.2341) over creatures. His "guile and Sorcerie" (6.1951), in other words, manifest his ambition to be godlike. Thus, as it is important to Olympias that her son should become a "god of erthe," so it is equally important to Nectanabus to create an impression that in himself a "god was there." This goal of the *curiosus* is aptly described by Augustine:

> Some there be who, forsaking virtue and ignoring what God is . . . , fancy they are doing something great when they strain inquisitively to explore the whole mass of this body we call the world. So great is the pride thus engendered one would think they dwelt in the heavens about which they argue.[12]

This very knowledge leaves Nectanabus ignorant about himself:

> The sterres suche as he acompteth,
> And seith what ech of hem amonteth,
> As thogh he knewe of alle thing;
> Bot yit hath he no knowleching
> What schal unto himself befalle.   6.2293–97

This quality of character makes Nectanabus' shape-shifting early in the narrative especially significant: the exercise in which he draws himself "out of

---

11 Thomas Aquinas, *Summa theologiae* 2a2ae, 167.1, Blackfriars ed., 44:202–03.
12 Augustine, *De moribus ecclesiae* 21, PL 32:1327; quoted by Thomas Aquinas, *Summa theologiae* 2a2ae, 167.1, Blackfriars ed., 44:202–03.

mannes like" and, after various transformations, his "forme he torneth into man" is a mockery of re-creation. It is, for Nectanabus, a kind of game-playing: we are led to note the most unremarkable of the changes – his becoming "himself," a man – as possible only because this magician knows "alle guile." The point is, of course, that he is never himself; he is truly no one thing, but a series of unconnected roles. This tale not only deals with "worldes chance," but with a human agent who changes his appearance at will, indeed who assumes that he can have "al his wille" (P.564): in the end, however, he is "formed" and driven entirely by chance.

The ending of Nectanabus' story is remarkable for several reasons. When asked by Alexander how he will die, the enchanter responds that his "oghne Sone" will slay him. Alexander, to prove "this olde dotard lieth," shoves him over the wall and proclaims, "Thou knewe alle othre mennes chance / And of thiself hast ignorance" (6.2313–14). Ironically, as Alexander quickly discovers, Nectanabus does know himself, or at least knows his "chance." Perhaps this ending should not surprise us, for it is like the ending in the *Historia de preliis*. The real surprise lies in Nectanabus' revelation of "What schal unto himself befalle," for it represents an unknowing response to the knowledge he possesses: he appears to have absolutely no interest in his end.

Olympias' response to the "merveile" of Nectanabus is similarly dulled. When the queen learns the truth, she

> stod abayssht as for the while
> Of his magique and al the guile.
> Sche thoghte hou that sche was deceived,
> That sche hath of a man conceived,
> And wende a god it hadde be.
> Bot natheles in such degre,
> So as sche mihte hire honour save,
> Sche schop the body was begrave.   6.2329–36

What is notable here is how quickly Olympias comes out of shock to repair her life and save her honor. Strangely, the "wonder" of this entire experience has no profound effect on her. She, in other words, is like the Nectanabus who does not seem particularly anxious when he announces his fate: it is as if both characters see their "other" life as another story for another role, another person.

What each major character, but most obviously Nectanabus, fails to address is the loss of the person in the roles played. The wonder of shape-shifting in this tale is that it compounds "mishap," whereby "for o mis an other mys / Was yolde, and so fulofte it is" (6.2359–60): the exercise to win "maistrie" and power is destined to ensure their loss. This exposure of the knowledge and power which debilitate rather than enable is another of Gower's responses to the question of will raised in the Prologue: the curse of Nectanabus, paradoxically, is that he never stands "in doute."

This false Annunciation, by inverting the story told in the excursus on religion in Book 5, displays the worst exile of "mannes soule," an exile in which there can be no hope of recovering the self, God, or "paradis." The characters, in a *regio dissimilitudinis*, create and revere "unlike" images, or false images of the self: rather than lead them to a recovery of paradise, the sins of *delicacie*, *sorcerie*, and curiosity – all creators of unlikeness – only distance these image-makers from the nature they have lost. And such image-making completes the story of idolatry initiated in the tale of Pygmalion. Now we see, and the final, brief story of Zoroaster confirms it, that "An ende proveth every thing" (6.2383).

At the close of Book 6, the lover asks Genius to describe Alexander's education, and he makes the request in terms reminiscent of his earlier statement about seeking "ese" and "restauracion" in the reading of romance:

> if I herde of thinges strange,
> Yit for a time it scholde change
> Mi peine, and lisse me somdiel.   6.2417–19

The "tale" Genius will now recount, however, is not a mere diversion serving the lover's *delicacie* and curiosity. Even as it introduces "thinges strange," it represents a controlled "devotion to learning." In effect, the epitome of Alexander's education, in a new language, re-creates the "verrai" gentle man, the person who is properly himself.

CHAPTER SIXTEEN

THE FORM OF ARISTOTLE'S LORE

That Gower should devote a book to "thinges strange" perhaps does not trouble readers as much as it once did, for, as M. A. Manzalaoui has remarked, "we have become less prone today to dismiss as otiose the frequent departures in medieval narrative or expository structure from the straight and narrow path of post-Renaissance linearity,"[1] As a compiler Gower draws into his poem whatever he thinks might usefully expand its frames of reference, and the very otherness of his various excursus serves to break intellectual and imaginative habit, moving readers to see something new or reperceive something they presumably already know. What used to puzzle critics – that this book has no direct bearing on the lover's complaint, or on the "dedly vices" so far confessed – turns out to be a source of power in Gower's invention and *compilatio*. Other excursus in the poem are doubtless easier to understand: they are invented out of and drawn back to topics of the books in which they appear; they thereby enlarge perception of the meanings of the various sins. The power of Book 7, an excursus in its entirety, is that it refers back and begins to draw together *distinctiones* that have been emerging in the confession as a whole.

J. A. Burrow has suggested that this extra book may "be meant to point beyond the 'temporal state' represented in the other seven."[2] In certain respects, Book 7 is indeed an "atemporal" book. It forms a pause in the sequence of dialogue, in the *negotium* of the shrift; in a single sustained speech, Genius rarely touches on Amans's particular cause and focuses instead on cosmic design and an ideal "policie." In effect, Gower allows time to stop as he creates a composite model of king and wise man, and at the end he celebrates virtues through which the "Soule diere" might glimpse the wonder of its creation:

> lich to god it hath a forme,
> Thurgh which figure and which liknesse
> The Soule hath many an hyh noblesse
> Appropred to his oghne kinde.   7.496–99

Despite this noble subject, Book 7 is less "poetical" than the other parts of the *Confessio*, and in that respect, it resembles the final "myrie tale" of the

---

[1] M. A. Manzalaoui, "Registre," p. 159.
[2] J. A. Burrow, *Ricardian Poetry*, p. 60.

Canterbury Tales.[3] The Parson's warning – "Thou getest fable noon ytoold for me" (*ParsP* 31) – might be extended to Gower's book, and so too might the Parson's promise "To knytte up al this feeste and make an ende" (*ParsP* 47), as it looks ahead to "the temporal state [being] closed by eternity."[4] These points of contact suggest likeness, and yet there are features of Gower's book that tie it more closely to Boethius' *Consolation*, specifically to that section which Philosophia introduces apologetically: "But although the noryssynges of dite of musyk deliteth the, thou most suffren and forberen a litel of thilke delit, whil that I weve to the resouns yknyt by ordre" (*Bo* 4, pr. 6, 36–39). Book 7, whose reasons are also "yknyt by ordre," frames values that will form the basis for a final judgment of the lover and his *causa*. That judgment is the point. One full book of the *Confessio* follows the outline of Alexander's education: in both the *Confessio* and Boethius' work, a carefully articulated "reule" will now be applied to the main character, who, in each fiction, is linked with the author himself. Closure thus comes not with the exposition of a system of thought or belief, but with the end of that character's story.

Gower does not cast us adrift in Book 7, but uses it as an occasion to reset his terms of judgment. Between Books 1–6 and Book 8 of the *Confessio*, the premises of argument change: in the leisure of Book 7, Genius comes to celebrate "free eleccion," and after it, he no longer holds to the premise that man has absolutely no control over his love-destiny: Genius's new supposition is a refinement of the natural law that the human being shares with the beasts; he henceforth insists upon a freedom that is unique to man and "Appropred to his oghne kinde."

That insistence emerges gradually in the epitome or "outline" of Alexander's education. Nowhere is Genius's task of gathering so manifest as in presenting this curriculum: his is an office of sorting that Hugh of St. Victor urges on medieval readers of texts:

> . . . just as aptitude [*ingenium*] investigates and discovers through analysis, so memory retains through gathering [*colligendo*]. . . . Now "gathering" is reducing to a brief and compendious outline things which have been written or discussed at some length. . . . Now every exposition has some principle upon which the entire truth of the matter and the force of its thought rest, and to this principle everything else is traced back. To look for and consider this principle is to "gather."[5]

The principle Genius has "gathered" from this education of Alexander is suggested by a Cambridge University Library manuscript of the *Confessio* which, in its layout, contains page headings that announce the subject not by book number (e.g., Liber I, Liber II) – as is the practice in most manuscripts – but by

3   See Russell A. Peck, *Kingship and Common Profit in Gower's Confessio Amantis* (Carbondale, Ill., 1978), p. 142.
4   Burrow, *Ricardian Poetry*, p. 60.
5   Hugh of St. Victor, *Didascalicon*, 3.11, trans. Taylor, pp. 93–94; ed. Buttimer, pp. 60–61.

topic (e.g., Superbia, Ira, Accidia, Luxuria). For Book 7, the "truth of the matter" is gathered in the heading *Sapientia*.[6] Genius prepares us for such an inference when he introduces the program he will outline in the book:

> wisdom is at every throwe
> Above alle other thing to knowe
> In loves cause and elleswhere.   7.15–17

Of course, this statement cannot convey "the force of thought" of Book 7 without further refinement and distinction. Often enough we have had occasion to be wary of Genius's enthusiasms, and here we might take pause at his boast to Amans that he too is an eager learner: "to knowe more / Als wel as thou me longeth sore" (6.2429–30). The education itself might nurture such enthusiasm; quite possibly it molded the medieval Alexander into what he became by reputation, an avid learner.[7] More largely, of course, the "sore" longing to know is natural, as medieval writers who had read Aristotle recognized; knowledge is "the natural perfection of man."[8]

It is, however, a perfection only if it is organized and fit to an "entencion." Without such an intention, Genius would have no reason to choose or not to choose "astronomie" as a principal or featured subject of this curriculum. When he makes choices of this kind, we therefore must ask whether he does so by design – and especially in the hope of gathering the "truth of the matter" – or by caprice.

As a medieval reader "restates" by headings, so too does the confessor as he subdivides each of three branches of knowledge – Theorique, Rethorique, and Practique – into three disciplines, and further subdivides Mathematique into the arts of the quadrivium:

Theorique:	Theologie
	Phisique
	Mathematique
	Arsmetique
	Musique
	Geometrie
	Astronomie
Rethorique:	Rethorique
	Gramaire
	Logique
Practique:	Etique
	Iconomique
	Policie

[6] Cambridge University Library, MS Mm.2.21, fol. 137v.
[7] "Quantum auiditatem inquirendi habuerunt principes antiquitus circa sapientiam, patet specialiter de Alexandro Magno" (Robert Holkot, *In librum Sapientiae*, lect. 75, p. 266).
[8] Ibid., lect. 110, p. 370.

This classification is derived chiefly from Brunetto Latini's *Tresor*, but with some important differences. Whereas Brunetto subdivides Theorique and Practique similarly, he makes his third branch of knowledge Logique and its subdivisions dialectic, demonstration, and sophistic; additionally, he combines the arts of the trivium, including logic, with the mechanical arts in a role of supporting Practique.[9] Not only is Gower's choice of disciplines different; so too are his emphases. He "devotes 1,487 lines to the seven Liberal Arts, but concentrates 1.315 of those lines upon the single mathematical art of 'Astronomie.' He uses only 1,5179 lines to define and explain 'Theorique' and 'Rethorique,' but spends 3,712 lines exemplifying 'Policie' after setting forth brief definitions of the other elements in 'Practique.' "[10] Why then does the poet, after cursorily describing the three sciences of Theorique, dwell on the knowledge of "erthli" or bodily things and of the "hevene" that so strongly influences them? Why does he introduce the verbal arts second, and why does he single out Rethorique for special emphasis? Why, in expounding Practique, does he select five "political" virtues as the basis of all moral discipline?

There is little in Gower's account, and nothing in Brunetto's, to explain these decisions. The poet has promised to present the "forme of Aristotles lore," but neither the *Tresor* nor any other medieval work boasting an Aristotelian lineage supplies a definitive paradigm for the curriculum Genius here presents.[11] Brunetto himself, after devoting three early chapters of the *Tresor* to expounding "philosophie et . . . ses partes," puts aside that conceptual model to follow another in organizing his own treatise.[12] Gower does likewise: despite the structure to which he testifies at the outset of each division of this book, he departs from it to stress certain subjects as especially critical to the education: this is the effect of his "gathering," of finding a principle upon which the truth of the matter rests. It is not the case that here we have an "atemporal" book that willy-nilly, out of a randomly selected structure, attends to "truths" that transcend contingent particulars. Truths are sought because the contingents – ultimately the particulars of the lover's case – need an *ordinatio* that has not yet been supplied.

At the very least, wisdom means useful knowledge; "wisdom, hou that evere it stonde, / To him that can it understonde / Doth gret profit in sondri wise"

9   James J. Murphy compares in detail the arrangement of disciplines in Book 7 of the *Confessio* and in the *Tresor*, in "John Gower's *Confessio Amantis* and the First Discussion of Rhetoric in the English Language," *Philological Quarterly* 41 (1962): 401–11.

10 Ibid., p. 403.

11 Gower's use of sources in Book 7 has been well described in the scholarship. In addition to Murphy, see Macaulay, 3:521–22; George L. Hamilton, "Some Sources of the Seventh Book of Gower's *Confessio Amantis*," *Modern Philology* 9 (1911–12): 323–46; Allan Gilbert, "Notes on the Influence of the *Secretum secretorum*," *Speculum* 2 (1928): 84–93; John H. Fisher, *Gower: Moral Philosopher*, p. 198.

12 Brunetto presents his plan for the *Tresor* in 1.1.1–4, pp. 17–18; he divides philosophy into its parts in 1.2–4. About this disparity between plan and conceptual model, Murphy expresses misgivings, in "First Discussion," p. 409.

(6.2421–23). As is suggested by the phrase "hou that evere it stonde," Genius can assign a wisdom to any branch of learning: astronomy, for example, "is the science / Of wisdom . . . / Which makth a man have knowlechinge / Of Sterres in the firmament" (7.670–73), and ethics, for its part, teaches wisdom regarding "the reule of [the] persone" (7.1665). Genius will never expressly argue, as writers who followed Augustine often did, that "there are not many wisdoms, but only one Wisdom which makes man wise, and this Wisdom is God."[13] In the latter paradigm, the sciences of the physical universe are ordered to *sapientia*, a knowledge of divine things and specifically of the Creator.[14] Accordingly, Hugh of St. Victor sees the goal of philosophy as "a knowledge of the highest good, which is situated in the one Creator of all things."[15] The sciences that explain temporal things can be valued if they serve this end or, in Augustine's terms, nourish a "wholesome faith."[16]

Gower certainly understands this course: his major French work teaches "viam qua peccator transgressus ad sui creatoris agnicionem redire debet" 'the way by which the sinner who has transgressed ought to return to a knowledge of his creator.'[17] But this course is formulated differently when he introduces the sciences in Book 7 of the *Confessio*: what the separate works share is a reciprocal relationship of discovering oneself and discovering divine perfection – "Noverim me, noverim Te"[18] – but in Book 7, such discovery is uniquely concentrated on analogies of rulership.

The poet's emphasis in Book 7 is practical: Genius orders the teaching of "Aristotle" not to a knowledge of divine things, to Theorique and "speculatio veritatis," but to action, Practique, and an ethical *policie*. Philosophie in this book is based on another premise, also a medieval topos: it is ordered to ethics, "non ad speculandum, sed ad opus."[19] Alexander's education thus mirrors a structure written into the rest of the *Confessio*: speculation exists to confirm, express, or advance what is essentially a moral argument bearing directly on Amans's "querele." Whereas the lover looks ahead to the treatise as a diversion

---

[13] Jerome Taylor, in his edition of Hugh of St. Victor, *Didascalicon*, p. 14; see Augustine, *De libero arbitrio* 2.9–10, 12–13, PL 32:1253–63.

[14] On the popular Augustinian distinction between *sapientia* and *scientia*, see *De Trinitate* 12.15.25, PL 42:1012. See also *De libero arbitrio* 2.16.43, PL 32:1264; for a later formulation, see Honorius of Autun, *De animae exsilio et patria*, cap. 1, PL 172: 1243.

[15] *Epitome Dindimi in philosophiam* 1, in *Hugonis de Sancto Victore opera propaedeutica*, ed. Roger Baron (Notre Dame, 1966), p. 190.

[16] Augustine, *The Trinity*, 14.1.3, trans. McKenna, p. 413.

[17] Macaulay, 3:479.

[18] For medieval background, see G. Verbeke, "Introductory Conference: Peter Abelard and the Concept of Subjectivity," in *Peter Abelard: Proceedings of the International Conference, Louvain, May 10–12, 1971*, ed. E. M. Buytaert (Louvain, 1974), pp. 1–11.

[19] Dante, "Epistole XIII," 40–41, in *Le Opere di Dante: Testo Critico della Societa Dantesca Italiana*, ed. M. Barbi et al., 2d ed. (Florence, 1960), p. 406; see also Robert Kilwardby: "Omnis philosophia ad moralem ethicam ordinatur" (*De ortu scientiarum*, cap. 64, ed. Albert G. Judy, Auctores Britannici Medii Aevi, vol. 4 [Toronto, 1976], p. 222).

to ease his pain – essentially to allow him to forget – Genius looks upon it as contributing to this different end:

> Al ben thei noght to me comune,
> The scoles of Philosophie,
> Yit thenke I forto specefie,
> In boke as it is comprehended,
> Wherof thou mihtest ben amended.   6.2432–36

Genius has other medieval precedent for defining wisdom itself in practical terms. Robert Holkot asserts that "truly the end and perfection of wisdom is to make man capable of ruling himself and others virtuously."[20] Not merely in the sections devoted to Etique and Policie, but throughout the book, Genius celebrates the perfection especially of ruling oneself. His sustained argument, as applied to a king, articulates a doctrine briefly stated in the Secretum secretorum and repeated elsewhere, as in the popular Parvi flores: "in a king the highest wisdom is to rule himself."[21]

Book 7 is designed chiefly to explain and nurture this capacity to rule. While it is a book about wisdom and, in the long section devoted to Policie, virtue, its issue, centrally, is power – the potestas, dominion, or majesty of rulership – and the ordering of that power by means of wisdom and virtue.[22] The book teaches a doctrine of governance and obedience based upon premises of a God "whos mageste / Alle othre thinges schal governe" (7.102–03) and of creatures whose role lies most fundamentally in serving and obeying God:

> The god, to whom that al honour
> Belongeth, he is creatour,

---

[20] Robert Holkot, In librum Sapientiae, lect. 74, p. 261. See also lect. 75, p. 264.

[21] Secretum secretorum cap. 10, ed. Robert Steele, Opera hactenus inedita Rogeri Baconi, fasc. 5 (Oxford, 1920), p. 48; Parvi flores 19.5, ed. Jacqueline Hamesse, Les Auctoritates Aristotelis: Un florilège médiéval, étude historique et édition critique, Philosophes médiévaux, 17 (Louvain, 1974), p. 271; on the critical importance of "maistrie" or "seignourie" over oneself, and over the penchant to seek lordship "by force and wylle," see Jacobus de Cessolis, Liber de ludo scaccorum, tract. 1, cap. 3, trans. William Caxton (ca. 1483; rpt. London, 1976), unfoliated.

[22] On this relationship, see also Vincent of Beauvais: "Sicut igitur princeps ceteros excellit potestate sic etiam excellere sapiencia debet et bonitate maximeque ut ista duo potestatem eius moderentur et reprimant et in opus virtutis flectant" (De morali principis institutione, cap. 10 [Rostock, ca. 1476], unfoliated). In the same chapter, Vincent further develops the relationship between these qualities in the ideal prince – his exemplar is David – and the three Persons of the Trinity. The text of this work has been recently edited by Robert J. Schneider, The De morali principis institutione of Vincent de Beauvais: Introduction and Critical Edition, Ph. D. diss., University of Notre Dame, 1965 (not seen). The trinitarian model is useful in identifying principal terms that also emerge in Gower's treatise: as Book 7 concerns rulership, so its argument develops the topos (Prov. 8:15) that by wisdom kings reign; for additional background, see Helinand of Froidmont, De bono regimine principis, PL 212:736; Pierre Bersuire, Dictionarium, s. v. "regere," 3: fol. 142v.

And othre ben hise creatures:
The god commandeth the natures
That thei to him obeien alle. 7.105–09

This focus has several important implications. In Book 7, the poet situates man in a hierarchy of creatures, but without exploring the likenesses that tie creatures of different orders together. Although man combines "certain attributes of the lower orders of creation and of the angels,"[23] Gower does not develop that idea or examine the analogies between the macrocosm and microcosm in this book, as he had done in the Prologue of the work.[24] He now focuses on man, not as he "comuneth with other bestes," not as he "comuneth and is partyner with angels," but as he "is somwhat in hymself."[25] Presenting what is "lich" man in the created universe (P.949–53) might have served another end: from such things, as signs, the poet could have traced an intellectual ascent to divine Wisdom.[26] His greater concern in this book, however, is to place man in a field of causes, influences, and powers that necessarily affect his moral choices. Out of that field a uniquely human capacity will emerge, and that is the power conferred when God "the Soule al only made / Himselven forto serve and glade" (7.513–14).

In a very particular sense, the field of Book 7 is political life and "worldlych dedes." Aegidius Romanus remarks that those given "to worldlych dedes bien ofte destourbed in many thinges for diuers doynges þat fallen and feleth of passions of the flesche," whereas those given to contemplation "bien somdel withdrawe from suche passyons." Life in the "flesch and nou3t by the flesch," Aegidius argues, "is more angels doyng þan manys doyng,"[27] and the concern of political life in its quest of "polletic felicite" is to manage passions of the "flesche."

For Gower, the often troublesome union of body and soul is entirely distinctive to man, making him unlike the "bestes" and the "holy angels," the creatures that he, in his respective natures, most resembles. Like Aegidius, the poet knows that "Out of his flessh a man to live" is more "Lich to an Angel manyfold, / Than to the lif of mannes kinde" (5.6395*, 6398*–6399*). In Book

---

[23] Elizabeth Porter, "Gower's Ethical Microcosm and Political Macrocosm," in *Gower's Confessio: Responses*, ed. Minnis, p. 137.

[24] P.949–52. See Gregory the Great, *Homiliae in Evangelia* 29.2, PL 76:1214; Alan of Lille, *Distinctiones*, s. v. "homo," PL 210:755. For a discussion of these and other related passages, see Rudolf Allers, "Microcosmus from Anaximandros to Paracelsus," *Traditio* 2 (1944): 321–22, 345–46.

[25] Aegidius Romanus *De regimine principum*, ed. Childs, p. 216.

[26] Thus, one might structure an education that considers macrocosm and microcosm to account for how one comes to know God and oneself. Such is the case, for example, in Bonaventure: one returns to the exemplary principles and thus to a knowledge of God through shadows, vestiges, and images of divine Wisdom in the created universe. For relevant bibliography, see Richard McKeon, *Thought Action and Passion* (Chicago, 1954), pp. 125–26 and notes.

[27] Childs, pp. 218, 220; *De regimine principum* 1.1.4, p. 12.

7, he is concerned specifically with the "lif of mannes kinde." Whereas "many an hyh noblesse" (7.498) belongs to the soul, and the soul aspires "upward to the hevene" (505), the body draws the human being downward:

> So schul thei nevere stonde in evene,
> Bot if the fleissh be overcome
> And that the Soule have holi nome
> The governance, and that is selde,
> Whil that the fleissh him mai bewelde.   7.506–10

This is a political issue, a question of power, governance and obedience, "tirannie," submission, and rebellion.

Later in the poem, Gower argues that if man misrules his kingdom, "He lest himself," and "what man that in special / Hath noght himself, he hath noght elles" (8.2115, 2118–19). A king's self-governance is a "lordschipe" or dominance that is nothing other than self-possession, as Aegidius also remarks: a "man hath nou3t hymself 3if his appetite desire is contrary to resoun."[28] To be united in oneself means to be at "reste," ultimately to be at peace with God, and so for Gower, as for others, the high "noblesse" of the soul is to "serve and glade" God: "vera nobilitas sola est voluntatem dei facere."[29] The treatise of Book 7 evolves a model of that unity in oneself and with God: it celebrates human capacity, lordship, "maistrye" in one sense as displayed in an ideal king, and in another sense as mirrored in anyone who returns to the self from a *regio dissimilitudinis*.

THEORIQUE

In virtually all medieval books on governance, the power or capacity to rule is seen to come from God. The root doctrine for Gower and others is scriptural: "there is no power but from God: and those that are, are ordained of God" (Rom. 13:1).[30] God is the "ferste cause" (7.86) upon whom all creatures depend absolutely, and from whom comes their every capacity: "Withouten him, what so befalle, / Her myht is non" (7.110–11).[31] Genius begins his discussion of Theorique with *theologie*, the study of the Creator from whom "every creature /

---

28 Childs, p. 210; *De regimine* 1.1.3, p. 9.
29 John of Wales, *Communiloquium*, pars 3, dist. 3, cap. 2 (Strasbourg, 1518), fol. 62v.
30 For the formula "omnis potestas a Domino Deo est," see, for example, *Oculus pastoralis pascens officia* 1.1, ed. Dora Franceschi, Memorie dell' Accademia delle Scienze di Torino, 4th ser., no. 11 (Turin, 1966), p. 23; John of Viterbo, *Liber de regimine civitatum*, cap. 4, ed. Caietano Salvemini, Bibliotheca Iuridica Medii Aevi, 3 (Bologna, 1901), p. 219; John of Salisbury, *Policraticus siue De nugis curialium et vestigiis philosophorum* 4.1, ed. Clemens C.I. Webb (Oxford, 1909), 1:236.
31 For this idea of dependence – that "every creature, no matter how low in the hierarchy of being, proclaims itself to be immediately *ab alio*" – in Matthew of Aquasparta and others, see Zachary Hayes, *The General Doctrine of Creation in the Thirteenth Century, with Special Emphasis on Matthew of Aquasparta* (Munich, 1964), pp. 72–73.

Hath his beinge and his nature" (7.89–90). This is the principle, as well as end, of the education outlined in Gower's treatise.

It is, nonetheless, only briefly stated. In Theorique more broadly, Gower's particular concern is the creature, and specifically the relationship between man and the great forces of the natural universe that so profoundly affect him. That focus is reflected in Gower's choice of disciplines and emphases: natural history, which receives extended treatment in Brunetto's compilation, is omitted entirely, for example, and the priest concentrates instead on sciences such as Astronomie: without the latter, "All othre science is in vein / Toward the scole of erthli thinges" (7.628–29).

Beginning with the elements, upon which "The creatour hath set and leid / The kinde and the complexion / Of alle mennes nacion" (7.382–84), Genius notes what the elemental order of the universe contributes to the human constitution, in what organ each of the four complexions has its "propre hous" (7.457), how these organs are "Servantz" to the heart as to a "chief lord above" (7.469), and "To whom reson in special / Is yove as for the governance" (7.488–89). Expounding the relationship of body to Soule, and noting that "to reson the Soul serveth," Genius distinguishes man from "bestes," which only "serve unto here oghne kinde." After discussing the Mappemounde with its divisions of Asia, Africa, Europe, Genius looks upward to Orbis, an element "Above the foure," and then "upward fro the mone" (7.195) to the subject of Astronomie, showing how the planets, the signs of the zodiac, and the stars bear special influence over geographical place, the human complexions, time, and other bodily or "erthli" things.

In this discussion of the external determinants of human conduct, Genius relies on the testimony of scientists who maintain that all things "upon this Erthe" are governed by the planets; Fortune or the "chances of the world also" depend upon "constellacion" (7.636–42). He will take this case to its conclusion:

> yit the lawe original,
> Which he hath set in the natures,
> Mot worchen in the creatures,
> That therof mai be non obstacle,
> Bot if it stonde upon miracle
> Thurgh preiere of som holy man.   7.658–63

Although the lover has sought from Genius, a "holy man," a prayer on his behalf, the priest does not here allow for "miracle," but insists instead on identifying a nature within which man must discover his freedom and power. Liberation will come to the good and wise person – through the power of words and of reason, shaped by the next major branches of knowledge – but only after a full recognition of the "lawe original" that Amans has forgotten. This is a difficult lesson for the lover to learn, especially in an excursus where he hopes to take his ease.

Genius, in attending to the natural influence of the stars on man as a physical creature, at first glance only seems to reinforce what Amans has argued, that he is driven by a natural love to do what he does. Now that coercion seems all the more destinal because of powers in the external, physical world that also influence him. Of the "nacion / Of lovers" governed by the "constellacion" of Venus, Genius assures Amans, "I trowe thou be on" (7.776). That may be construed as a good, for "of this Planete / The moste part is softe and swete" (7.781–82): the person born under it

> schal desire joie and merthe,
> Gentil, courteis and debonaire,
> To speke his wordes softe and faire,
> Such schal he be be weie of kinde.   7.784–87

Amans has diligently sought to follow his "natural" inclination and practice these "virtues," even to the point of making his observance during Gemini's "propre Monthe" of May,

> Whanne every brid upon his lay
> Among the griene leves singeth,
> And love of his pointure stingeth
> After the lawes of nature
> The youthe of every creature.   7.1046–50

Youth is still not at issue for Amans. He thinks he has done everything right in following a "lawe / Ther mai no maner man withdrawe" (7.793–94), and yet his desert has been entirely wrong. There seems to be no escaping his sad destiny.

Seen correctly, this impulse, even should it exist "be weie of kinde," is not entirely destinal. Later in this epitome Genius will defend the opinion of the "clerkes of divinite" who argue that a man, because of his soul, is not bound by his corporeal nature or by stellar influence:[32] "if men weren goode and wise / And plesant unto the godhede, / Thei scholden noght the sterres drede" (7.652–54). The timing of that reversal in Genius's opinion is especially appropriate to the order of Amans's confession. The seventh vice, chosen by Amans even though he denies the choice, more than any other confuses his perception of himself. For Amans to be free enough to affirm his best nature, he must see the fallacy of his own ideas of a "natural" determinism.

The treatise on Theorique reveals that all things in the cosmos are interdependent, and that revelation has a serious implication for what man might regard as his freedom, or his power or capacity to "be" himself. The *jus naturae* now becomes a natural justice manifested "in the concord of all things; Plato treats such natural justice in the *Timaeus*: one element cannot exist without another."[33] On this premise, the creature is not only bound and ruled by its own

---

[32] See, for example, Dante, *Purgatorio*, 16.67–83.
[33] William of Auxerre, *Summa aurea* (Lottin, pp. 33–34); for a like opinion in Roland of Cremona and Hugh of St. Cher, see also Lottin, pp. 115–16.

nature, but also dependent on and restricted by what surrounds it.[34] From the place set for the human being in a predetermined order there can be no escape, and in that place there can be no absolute freedom.

Gower thus constructs his treatise on Theorique to show precisely where the human being is not free: true liberty – or "free eleccion" – can exist only if one understands the limits within which it must, of necessity, exist. The soul "must deliver itself from [sense] illusions in order to recognize itself for neither more nor less than it really is."[35] Book 7, in providing this *scientia uera*,[36] thus forms a gloss on the career of Nectanabus, who in his false science, attempts to become, or to express freely his capacity to become, all things.[37] In that activity, he is trapped in illusions, loses himself, and falls to a far greater ignorance and bondage.

Book 7, rather than giving the human being a license to move about the cosmos, even in figure, shows the precise place and boundaries that have been set for human activity. It is man's task, Hugh of St. Victor writes, "to know himself, not to be ignorant of his foundation and order and obligation, whether above himself or in himself or under himself, to understand of what nature he was made and how he should proceed, what to do, what similarly to avoid."[38] That is precisely what Gower begins to teach in the epitome of Theorique. In the next section of the book, he will refine his statement about the limits set for man and begin to identify the source of his freedom.

RETHORIQUE

Gower's treatise on Rethorique is problematic for its very brevity. The poet writes so little *about* rhetoric, in fact, that James J. Murphy has been led to conclude that he "had no very clear idea of what he meant by the term. . . . He does not know the technical vocabulary of the discipline"; nor does he know the work of ancient rhetors; he never defines the " 'eloquence' for which

---

[34] The assumptions underlying Gower's sense of universal harmony are topoi quite variously formulated in writers such as Boethius, *Consolation*, 3, pr. 11; John of Salisbury, *Metalogicon* 1.1, ed. Webb, p. 6; trans. McGarry, p. 10; Chalcidius, *Timaeus a Calcidio translatus commentarioque instructus*, ed. J. H. Waszink, Corpus Platonicum Medii Aevi: Plato Latinus IV, 2d ed. (London, 1975), p. 206.

[35] Etienne Gilson, *Spirit of Mediaeval Philosophy*, p. 215.

[36] For a relevant discussion of the topics of Solomon's "true science" – in essence, the topics of Gower's treatment of Theorique – and the difference between true science and the falsehood of magicians, see Robert Holkot, *In librum Sapientiae*, lect. 99 (numbered 109 in the Basle edition), p. 335.

[37] For a sense in which the mind legitimately "is said to *be* all things," see Hugh of St. Victor, *Didascalicon* 1.1, trans. Taylor, p. 46; ed. Buttimer, p. 5; on magic as a response to a sense of being deprived of one's freedom by the design of the universe, see Allers, pp. 322–23.

[38] Hugh of St. Victor, *De sacramentis* 1.6.15, trans. Roy J. Deferrari, pp. 103–04; *PL* 176:272.

'Rethorique' makes rules"; and when he links rhetoric with disputation, Murphy remarks, "he seems to mean that it rules every use of words."[39]

These criticisms are, however, beside the point: Gower need not catalogue tropes or list ancient rhetors if neither serves his purpose in this section of the poem, and that purpose is certainly not to prove his technical knowledge of rhetoric. In the mere 133 lines he devotes to the subject, he seeks instead to identify the relationship between words – the "matter" of the trivium – and the content of the other divisions of "philosophie," to the end of showing the special power or "vertu" of language.

As in each of the other divisions of Book 7, Genius here first identifies the relevant disciplines. Grammar attends to questions of "congruite" (7.1531), logic to questions of "trouthe" and "falshode" (7.1533), and both serve rhetoric, "the science / Appropred to the reverence / Of wordes that ben resonable" (7.1523–25). Rhetoric is, more largely, a science that develops verbal *potestas*, or a skill at affecting others by means of words. For that reason alone, Gower is justified in making it the architectonic art of the trivium, specifically in an education focusing on the relationship of rulers, counsellors, and "subgetes." To those who rule, whether over the self or others, words are a source of the capacity or strength to govern: in the regiment of princes, rhetoric does in fact order all uses of language.

Genius sees the power of words in relation to *kinde* and *reson*. The first relationship, introduced in the poet's Latin epigram for the section (7.5.3–4), is explained in the English text:

> In Ston and gras vertu ther is,
> Bot yit the bokes tellen this,
> That word above alle erthli thinges
> Is vertuous in his doinges,
> Wher so it be to evele or goode.   7.1545–49

Man, by his unique faculty of speech, seen "Of kinde with non other beste" (7.1515), gains control over other "erthli thinges," including other men. The one extended instance Genius here records – those speeches concerning Catiline – illustrates the point, but so too does Genius's catalogue of the "conversions" effected by language. This latter statement takes up about a third of the treatise (7.1545–1587), and its purpose is to display not only a magnitude, but a diversity of power: "The word under the coupe of hevene / Set every thing or odde or evene" (7.1579–80):

> Word hath beguiled many a man;
> With word the wilde beste is daunted,
> With word the Serpent is enchaunted,

---

[39] Murphy, "Gower's *Confessio* and the First Discussion of Rhetoric," p. 408. Brunetto places disputation in dialectic: "dyaletique . . . ensegne tencier, contendre, et desputer, les uns contres les autres, et faire questions et defenses" (*Tresor*, 1.5.2, ed. Carmody, p. 22).

> Of word among the men of Armes
> Ben woundes heeled with the charmes,
> Wher lacketh other medicine.
> Word hath under his discipline
> Of Sorcerie the karactes.   7.1564–71

There is moral danger, of course, in this linguistic power, and Genius is not content to rest his case on potency alone. Words reflect choice, ultimately the power of the speaker's will: they can just as easily disguise as disclose intention, and they can be used for good or evil. The priest is thus concerned to give this power a moral determinacy, to make rhetoric a "moral" science. It is finally not enough for a man to possess language; in using it, he must

> be the more honeste,
> To whom god yaf so gret a yifte,
> And loke wel that he ne schifte
> Hise wordes to no wicked us.   7.1516–19

An ethical Practique thus delimits the use of language, making it a "techer of vertus." And this leads us back to the priest's opening definition, that rhetoric is "Appropred to the reverence / Of wordes that ben resonable." In an ascent up a scale of power, Genius advances from *kinde* to words to *reson*, at each stage coming closer to the source of human weal: language more than *kinde*, and *reson* more than mere words allow man to "serve and glade" God. Rhetoric takes man closer to the center of his freedom precisely because it involves that kind of choice: it is a choice finally ordered by Practique.

The tale of Nectanabus again reveals why Practique, or science that focuses on the *disposition* of man's free election, is, for Gower, so critical. As a magician, Nectanabus displays a mastery over things in the physical universe and the "scole of erthli thinges"; as the seducer of Olympias, he also reveals a mastery with words. What Nectanabus's "knowing" lacks – indeed what makes him an unusual and yet suitable exemplar of gluttony in the preceding book – is moral discipline: his failure to understand Practique, which inculcates an "honeste" use of reason, keeps him from achieving true security, power, and freedom: as he falsifies his "physics" and twists his rhetoric to "wiked us," he becomes the victim of his vast knowledge. The ordering of such knowledge is the task of the next major division of this education, Practique.

CHAPTER SEVENTEEN

PRACTIQUE

In the ordering of this model curriculum, Genius evolves hierarchies of power that ascend not only through the three genera of knowledge, but through their species as well. Under Theorique, the astronomer knows that in his subject lies the chief power "be weie of kinde" to affect earthly things, and under Rethorique, the orator knows that in his subject lies the chief power of the word, to persuade, move, transform. So also, under Practique, the student of Policie knows that in his subject, the king, is lodged the fullest capacity to rule others, especially to the degree that such power is combined with virtue:

> For as a king in special
> Above all othre is principal
> Of his pouer, so scholde he be
> Most vertuous in his degre.   7.1745–48

Gower's treatise on Policie attends exclusively to kingly virtues, and in that respect it differs from most books written *de regimine principum*. He has done his work with the other sciences when he turns to *policie*, and he does not expressly consider politics as a "master art" served by other arts such as military strategy, economics, and rhetoric.[1] Nor is he particularly interested, in this treatise, in the day-to-day practicalities of ruling. While he depends for certain aspects of his discussion upon Brunetto and the author of the *Secretum secretorum*, Gower differs from both in limiting the virtues or "pointz" that constitute *policie* to five, and in also developing each of these points, some at great length, through exemplary narratives. For this section, by far the longest in the book, the poet has compiled material according to a new *ordinatio*, and it will be our immediate task to understand that new structure of perception and conversion.

Gower's choice of five particular virtues – truth, largess, justice, pity, and chastity – has puzzled readers. Allan Gilbert thought the series "would probably have been derived from some treatise rather than devised by the poet himself," but he took the inquiry no further.[2] More recently, scholars have given up seeking a source, and have instead sought to justify this virtue or that as providing a thematic center not merely for the treatise, but for the *Confessio* as

[1] See Aristotle, *Nicomachean Ethics* 1094a27; Brunetto Latini, *Tresor*, 2.3.1, ed. Carmody, p. 176.
[2] Gilbert, pp. 85–86; see also Manzalaoui, "Registre," pp. 169–70.

a whole. Patrick Gallacher has found that center in Trouthe, "the principal moral excellence," and John Hurt Fisher has found it in Justice.[3]

In the virtues treatise itself, however, Gower offers no license to cast out four of the virtues for the sake of a fifth. Even the proportion of attention Gower devotes to each point might warn us against singling out either Truth or Justice as his "real" subject:

Truth	(1711–1984)	=	273 lines
Largess	(1985–2694)	=	709 lines
Justice	(2695–3102)	=	407 lines
Pity	(3103–4214)	=	1111 lines
Chastity	(4215–5389)	=	1174 lines

This is not to say that we can, merely on the basis of line count, assign authorial privilege to any one virtue: it is a principle of this treatise, on the contrary, that no one virtue can exist fully without the complement of the other four.

These virtues enable a ruler to secure and uphold a lordship or "maistrye" greater than the illusory might bestowed by Fortune. When medieval writers assert that every power comes from God, they often do so to remind princes of the limits of earthly majesty: "Consider the greater power set above you," Alan of Lille remarks, "which will judge you in [the Day of] Judgment."[4] The danger lies in false majesty, and John of Salisbury casts the problem in familiar Boethian terms:

> The most dangerous situation, in my opinion, that men of eminence have to face lies in the fact that the enticements of fawning fortune blind their eyes to truth. . . . Who [is] more contemptible than he who scorns a knowledge of himself, who lavishly wastes upon life and squanders to his own disgrace time which has been sparingly meted out for life's needs?[5]

These Boethian tenets provide a basis for Gower's judgment of the effects of fortune on the king who has forgotten himself; they also provide a link between Gower's regal exemplars and Amans, who not only scorns a knowledge of himself, but also, as a *senex*, squanders time at the worst possible time. A king, in being "set aboven alle" on Fortune's wheel, might seem to have experienced all that Amans wants, a turn in the wheel, an ascent to the majesty of good fortune. But as the *de casibus* tradition abundantly testifies, of course, the danger of a fall from the "grace" of Fortune is proportionate to the increase in lordship: "Fortune gladly hath sette hys eyen on hem that ben in

3 Gallacher, pp. 102–03, 149; Fisher, pp. 200–03.
4 Alan of Lille, *Art of Preaching*, cap. 42, trans. Evans, p. 154; PL 210:188.
5 *Policraticus*, 1.1, trans. Joseph B. Pike, (Minneapolis, 1938), pp. 11–12; ed. Webb, 1:18.

hye degree, and on the soueraynes yet more." She only smiles at "the meschief of poure peple," but "she lawgheth wyth ful mouth, and smyteth her paulmes to gydre, whan she seeth grete lordes falle in to meschyef."[6] A king must fortify himself accordingly, avoiding especially the foolish self-indulgence that John of Salisbury finds so lamentable in men of eminence.

Gower has found that strength in the five virtues or "pointz." A king has a special capacity to serve others well, even becoming "godlike" in his power, because "on the whiel / Fortune hath set [him] aboven alle" (7.3173–74). Blessed with power (*civilis potentia*), wealth, honors or office, fame, and bodily pleasure,[7] he might rule worthily, provided he transvaluates each of these gifts of Fortune into a virtue.

It is not exceptional for an author writing *de regimine principum* to warn against the five gifts. Aegidius Romanus does so in five early chapters of his treatise, for example, arguing "That it semeþ nouȝt a kyng [or a kynges mageste] to sette his felicite" in any of them.[8] Gower takes this argument a step further. Each of his five points displaces a gift – Truth-power, Largess-fame, Justice-wealth, Pity-office, Chastity-sensual pleasure – and together they provide the surest foundation for ruling oneself and others.

THE POINTS OF POLICIE

Genius's first virtue, Trouthe, checks Fortune's gift of civil power. This virtue is principal, as Gallacher notes, for without it "ther is no myht / . . . in no degre" (7.1968–69), but about it Genius chooses to tell only one tale, a story concerning three trusted wise men who are asked by King Darius to decide which is most powerful, a king, wine, or woman. Arpaghes argues that "the strengthe of kinges / Is myhtiest of alle thinges" (7.1825–86) because the king has power over man, the "moste noble creature" (7.1830). Manachaz argues that wine is more powerful because it "fulofte takth aweie / The reson fro the mannes herte" (7.1852–53). Finally, Zorobabel argues that woman is the "myhtieste," for a man in love will obey a woman, "wher he wole or non" (7.1879). To exemplify this point, Zorobabel recounts a comic tale about the courtesan Apemen, who

---

6 Alain Chartier, *The Curial Made by Maystere Alain Charretier*, trans. William Caxton, ed. Frederick J. Furnival, EETS, es 54 (London, 1888), p. 6.
7 On these five goods, see Boethius, *The Consolation of Philosophy*, 3, pr. 2; these are discussed at length in 2, pr. and m. 5–7; 3, pr. and m. 2–9.
8 Aegidius Romanus, *De regimine* 1.1.6–10, pp. 17–33; Aegidius recapitulates these points in Chapter 11 (p. 36), where he also considers another good included in Aristotle, but not in Boethius: "That it semeþ nouȝt þe kynges maieste to sette his felicite in bodyliche strengþe noþer in feyrnesse noþer in virtues of þe body" (Childs, p. 190). It is not unusual to find these various goods of Fortune discussed in other medieval political treatises, See for example, Thomas Aquinas, *On Kingship, to the King of Cyprus*, 1.7–8, trans. Gerald B. Phelan, rev. I. Th. Eschmann (Toronto, 1949), pp. 30–38. Aquinas argues that a king should look to God alone for his reward: no earthly good is perfect, and we cannot hope to find happiness – or the end of our desires – in honor, glory, pleasure, or riches; only God can still our desires.

does with the tyrant Cyrus "what evere hir liketh" (7.1895); the devotion of this subjected "king" merely provokes "game," a sheer wantonness in Apemen's exercise of power:

> And be the chyn and be the cheke
> Sche luggeth him riht as hir liste,
> That nou sche japeth, nou sche kiste.   7.1892–94

This inverted tribute to the power of woman, though it also speaks tellingly about the folly of Cyrus, hardly supports Zorobabel's following statement, that woman is man's "solas" and "worldes joie," a source of his "knihthode," "worldes fame," and "honour" (7.1900–07). But the advisor has not finished. In a second tale – this one not included in 3 Esdras, Gower's principal source – Zorobabel readjusts our perception of woman's strength and at the same time modulates his argument to celebrate something stronger than a king, wine, or woman: "trouthe above hem alle / Is myhtiest" (7.1955–56). This tale-within-the-tale concerns "goode and kinde" Alceste, who "proves" the virtue of Trouthe by her self-sacrifice:

> next after the god above
> The trouthe of wommen and the love,
> In whom that alle grace is founde,
> Is myhtiest upon this grounde.   7.1945–48

Thus, without entirely cancelling his initial point – that woman is "strengest" – Zorobabel represents in Alceste a virtue that surpasses other strengths: truth abides, and in it there can be no injustice (3 Esd. 4:36). Just as Alceste – secure even in her choice to die – restores her dead husband to life, so a stable truth frees the person oppressed by adverse fortune:

> It mai wel soffre for a throwe,
> Bot ate laste it schal be knowe.
> The proverbe is, who that is trewe,
> Him schal his while nevere rewe.   7.1959–62

Trouthe, which "Mai for nothing ben overcome" (7.1958), thus transcends fortunal power and "maistrye." The virtue, celebrated late in this discussion, easily displaces the other "strengths," and Genius, in showing its power, effectively transvaluates the idea of might.

Largesse, the second point, represents a mean between greed and Prodigalite, but Gower here concentrates on its power to offset Prodigalite and its attendant Flaterie. Most of the very many tales Genius recounts under the heading of Largesse present the virtue as specifically opposed to false praise, a second gift of Fortune. Largess upholds a truer renown and "noblesse" and best "serveth to the worldes fame / In worschipe of a kinges name" (7.1987–88). The last 545 lines (7.2149–2694) of the section, over three-quarters of the whole, form a response to the question of why a king "shewith out his goodes immoderatly or inordinatly to vnworthy."[9] As the prodigal king encourages flatterers, of course, he also flatters himself. To correct this kind of misperception, the Romans invented a custom whereby an emperor, returning triumphant from battle, was joined in his carriage by a "Ribald" offering sage advice:

> For al this pompe and al this pride
> Let no justice gon aside,
> Bot know thiself, what so befalle.
> For men sen ofte time falle
> Thing which men wende siker stonde.   7.2387–91

The wise fool thus reminds the emperor of a precarious Fortune, of the fact that "The whiel per chance an other day / Mai torne, and thou myht overthrowe" (7.2394–95).

Gower frames the advice to "know thiself" in stories that precede and follow this one. In the first, two friends, Diogenes and Aristippus, return from school in Athens to pursue different careers. Diogenes chooses to "duelle / At hom," "to take his reste" and "To studie in his Philosophie" (7.2239–40, 2243, 2245). Aristippus leaves philosophy and "to richesse himself uplefte" (7.2264). Entering the court he finds what he most desires, the "worldes pompe" and the "ese / Of vein honour and worldes good" (7.2254–55), and he wins these things by flattery. The tale ends abruptly at the reunion of the friends, when Diogenes remarks that flattery "is gretly descordant / Unto the Scoles of Athene." (7.2314–15). That teaching, which presumably includes the doctrine to "know thiself," is carried to its conclusion in the third tale of the sequence, concerning a custom wherein masons of the emperor, at his coronation, ask his instructions concerning the making of his sepulchre: "Tho was ther flaterie non / The worthi princes to bejape" (7.2432–33). The worthy prince who cultivates largess comes to understand himself and his subjects: discerning the truth, he does not spend what is not his to win what is not his:

> A king after the reule is holde
> To modifie and to adresce
> Hise yiftes upon such largesce
> That he mesure noght excede.   7.2152–55

The third virtue, Justice, shifts the focus to matters of common profit. A king who would possess this virtue must "himself ferst justefie / Towardes god in his degre" (7.2730–31); once he has set his own deeds in moral order, he might, "of his justice / So sette in evene the balance / Towardes othre in governance" (7.2740–42). Justice overcomes a desire for "lucre," the "lawe of covoitise," or false wealth, a third gift of Fortune. Gaius Fabricius, in refusing a bribe, thus "kepte his liberte / To do justice and equite" (7.2816–17). To serve the common "riht," "lawe," and profit is to remain free, to achieve and sustain a

---

[9] "The 'Ashmole' Version: The Secrete of Secretes," ed. M. A. Manzalaoui, *Secretum Secretorum: Nine English Versions*, vol. 1, EETS, os 276 (Oxford, 1977), p. 33.

sufficiency that wealth promises, but fails to provide. In a series of lawgivers, including Lycurgus especially, Genius exemplifies most fully such "forthringe of comun profit" (7.2957).

By itself, this third virtue can make a rule precarious: "Justice which doth equite / Is dredfull, for he noman spareth" (7.3130–31), and it must therefore be complemented by Pite. The latter virtue opposes a fourth gift of Fortune, unsure, false honor, exhibited especially in those who, in a presumption of the rights of office, exercise not justice, but "dredfull" cruelty. Genius exemplifies the latter trait in a sequence of tales concerning Leontius, Siculus, Dionysius, Lichaon, and Spertachus, all tyrants blinded to their precarious position on Fortune's wheel. Against their felonies, "God is himself the champion" (7.3252): although cruelty "mai regne for a throwe, / God wole it schal ben overthrowe" (7.3263–64). By contrast, "Pite is thilke vertu blessed / Which nevere let his Maister falle (7.3260–61).

Pite here retains the meaning of the ancient Roman *pietas*, and it also expresses that *jus naturale* according to which like rejoice in like: it represents a natural devotion or kindness toward those connected by blood, and beyond that, toward an entire people or "realme." As a civil virtue, Pite is associated with *humanitas*.[10] For Gower, as for other medieval writers, a ruler loses none of his dignity in extending this affection: pity is indeed "a noble disposition of soul made ready to receive love, mercy, and other loving passions,"[11] and true *nobilitas* is nothing other than "a benignity in affection" or "a gentle [*generosus*] spirit."[12]

Without expressly tying together the threads of his earlier argument, Gower shifts perception from the temptation of *worschipe* or reverence and false *gentilesse* to the truer honor lodged in Pite and related virtues: tacitly, the poet cultivates a spiritualized reperception of the medieval topos that "pitee renneth soone in gentil herte" (KnT 1761). He surely recognizes that "Pite makth a king courteis / Bothe in his word and in his dede" (7.3120–21),[13] but beyond that, he also shows how pity, as a "vertu blessed," significantly transforms a king's office. Indeed, the poet's ideal of Pite is exemplified in the mystery of the Incarnation, in the high king who "in pite the world to rihte / Tok of the Maide fleissh and blod" (7.3110–11). A ruler's greatest dignity therefore rests not upon "tirannie" or self-generated lordship and might, but upon a Christ-like

10 For useful background on this *pietas* and *civilis benevolentia*, see Tolomeo of Lucca's continuation of Thomas Aquinas's De regimine principum [ad regem Cypri], 3.3–6, in Thomas Aquinas, Opera omnia (Parmae, 1865; rpt. New York, 1950), 16:252–55.
11 Dante, Convivio 2.11.6, trans. Katherine Hillard, The Banquet (London, 1889), p. 97; ed. Barbi, p. 182.
12 See Pierre Bersuire, Dictionarium, s. v. "nobilitas," 2: fol. 319v–320r.
13 Machaut provides a counterpart to this perception of the virtue in Voir-dit, when the lover, in a game within a dream, advises a player, "the king who does not lie," on his regal duties. He includes advice not only on truth, largess, and justice, but on pity: the king should be charitable; he should not oppress the weak or defenseless, thinking thereby to recover honor; he should love courtesy and hate villainy (4991, 5020–22, 5026–27, 5063–64).

humility. Three of Genius's exemplars in this section – Codrus, Trajan, and Pompey – display Pite in these terms. Codrus, for example, chooses to die in battle rather than live to see his people discomfited. With "Pite . . . parfit / Upon the point of his believe" (7.3196–97), he sacrifices himself for his people: "thurgh grace of his persone" (7.3177), he alone "Mai al the large realme save" (7.3179).

The analogy between this king and Christ, each of whom saves his people by the "grace of his persone," reinforces the point that Pite secures not only reverence or "worschipe," but love:

> in the lond where Pite fareth
> The king mai nevere faile of love,
> For Pite thurgh the grace above,
> So as the Philosophre affermeth,
> His regne in good astat confermeth.   7.3132–36

The opening of the soul to grace and Pite and the consequent expression of the virtue centrally require in the earthly ruler an awareness of his humanity. Pite becomes a concrete expression of Trouthe, discovered also through the "pointz" of Largesse and Justice: its premise is that all men, even those of eminence, are only men, and that premise underlies what otherwise might surprise us in a treatise on Pite, Gower's extended defense of taking counsel: the king who "wole his regne save" (7.3913), the poet argues, must be open to "Such conseil which is to believe" (7.3916). Gower may have found reason for including this statement in the precedent of the *Secretum secretorum*: "It sitteth to a kynge to have pite, . . . and no thynge to do with-out avisement, and resonably to know his errour, and wisely to revoke it."[14] His greater warrant, however, lies in his own treatment of the virtue: he has found a check to the weakness of human judgment in a Pite which in its great range and power, draws on the strength of others.

Gower's progress through the five points advances to a sharper definition of the weakness in humanity, and thence of a counterposed strength, the nobility or capacity which "is the gift of Divine grace to the soul fitted to receive it."[15] Dante, in describing this *nobilitas*, uses a metaphor that effectively describes the emerging pattern of argument in Book 7: this

> goodness of ours. . . descends upon us from the supreme and spiritual Virtue, in the same manner that virtue descends upon a [precious] stone, from a most noble celestial body.[16]

The need for grace becomes most apparent in relation to the final virtue, Chastete. Because man is a "natural" or fleshly creature,

---

14 "The 'Ashmole' Version," p. 36.
15 Dante, *Convivio* 4.20.7, trans. Hillard, p. 326; ed. Barbi, p. 271.
16 Ibid., trans. Hillard, p. 327; ed. Barbi, pp. 271–72.

> bot it be grace
> Above alle othre in special,
> Is non that chaste mai ben all.   7.4242–44

The dilemma of "political life" – that man cannot live "Out of his flessh" – obviously makes grace a necessity, a means to overcome the tyranny of "delyces of body," the pleasure that Boethius identifies as Fortune's fifth gift.

The chaste person, knowing his or her own frailty, fixes in "memoire" the image of a nature that lives "deyinge." Lust creates an illusion of power, of a freedom to do whatever one likes, perhaps even to escape mortality. Such pride is manifested in Genius's exemplum of the Lydians, a people who, tricked by Cyrus's feigned peace, "token eses manyfold" (7.4383), and "in idelschipe / . . . putten besinesse aweie / And token hem to daunce and pleie" (7.4390–92). Indulging "the likinges / Of fleysshly lust" (7.4394–95), they court disaster: precisely because "every man doth what him liste" (7.4397), Cyrus has no difficulty in overcoming them.

The unchaste lover, treating his fleshly weakness as his strength, sets himself apart, nurturing the "fool impression" (7.4271) that he is, for his love, most remarkable, most worthy of his lady's attention. About his passion, however, the lady "nothing knoweth" (7.4274) and "hath him nothing bounde" (7.4281); nor can she prevent or "lette the folie" (7.4283). His is a self-deceiving and self-isolating passion, yet another form of "passive" idolatry, or worship of the self.

In treating Chastete, Genius initially concentrates on virtuous exemplars. The tales of Sardanapalus, David, Cyrus, and Amalech variously show that "clennesse / Acordeth to the worthinesse / Of men of Armes overal" (7.4447–49). Even more important than these tests of chastity for "men of Armes," however, are the tests for a king:

> Bot most of alle in special
> This vertu to a king belongeth,
> For upon his fortune it hongeth
> Of that his lond schal spede or spille.   7.4450–53

Genius's principal instance of this point is fittingly chosen, for it shows an "ideal" king who, though he has built his career upon virtue and wisdom, remains vulnerable to fleshly pleasure. In earlier stories of this book, Solomon had displayed the wisdom given to him by God (7.3901–04), but in the tale about him in this section, all of that good comes to naught. Solomon falls to lust and "ydolatrie," and though his own pleasure is short-lived, his sin reaches through generations as, because of it, he bequeaths to his heirs a divided kingdom (7.4460–63).

Genius's key point in discussing chastity centers on a most difficult test of wisdom: finding a rule "of such mesure, / Which be to kinde sufficant, / And ek to reson acordant" (7.4562–64). The foil to Solomon, who has failed in this test, appears in the last exemplum in the sequence, the tale of Sara and Tobias.

Sara, like Lucrece and Virginia in the two stories preceding her own, is a virtuous character, but her tale, alone among the three, also makes the central male figure a positive exemplar: Thobie serves both "lawe" and "kinde" (see 7.5363, 5372–81). This tale celebrates "honeste" love, and in it Genius fittingly offers his most focused statement about *kinde*:

> For god the lawes hath assissed
> Als wel to reson as to kinde,
> Bot he the bestes wolde binde
> Only to lawes of nature,
> Bot to the mannes creature
> God yaf him reson forth withal,
> Wherof that he nature schal
> Upon the causes modefie,
> That he schal do no lecherie,
> And yit he schal hise lustes have.   7.5372–81

It is in modifying the causes of nature that one achieves honesty, or the *jus naturae* as natural reason, the judgment of reason, free will, or the power to choose good over evil.[17]

This "honesty" includes not only the *honestas* of chastity, but also the *honestum*, or truth to one's proper nature, represented in the other points as well. Genius thus enjoins the lover to reflect

> Noght only upon chastete,
> Bot upon alle honestete;
> Wherof a king himself mai taste,
> Hou trewe, hou large, hou joust, hou chaste
> Him oghte of reson forto be,
> Forth with the vertu of Pite,
> Thurgh which he mai gret thonk deserve
> Toward his godd.   7.5387–94

The "honestete" that embraces all five virtues of *policie* is the end-product of the highest natural law Genius knows, a "lawe of reson," and the priest, in so linking the virtues, represents wisdom, or the image of man "unified," strong enough to rule others and himself.

While each of the five points checks an unstable good of Fortune, what lends the greatest security to a single point is the complement of the other four.[18] Gower's sequence of gifts differs from that of Boethius, but more important than the order is the unity. For Boethius, "suffisaunce, power, noblesse,

---

[17] See the meanings of *jus naturale* listed, for example, in the *Summa Lipsiensis*, in the extracts printed by Lottin, p. 108.

[18] Gower thus reaffirms the common medieval doctrine that the virtues are interdependent; see, for example, Aegidius Romanus: "Qui vnam virtutem habet, omnes habet: & qui vna caret, omnibus caret" (*De regimine* 1.2.31, p. 139).

reverence, and gladnesse be oonly diverse by names, but hir substaunce hath no diversite."[19] For Gower, these are achieved respectively by justice, truth, largess, pity, and chastity. But as the five goals are of one substance, so too are these five points by which the king, or Amans, might achieve them.

Genius saves for Book 8 a tale that celebrates all five virtues together, specifically as embodied in Apollonius of Tyre. Book 7 presents the negative exemplar, a violator of the five points, in Aruns, the son of Tarquin. In his tale, more than in any other in the collection of stories in Book 7, we find a self-isolating tyranny that destroys others and the self. The first part of Aruns's tale recounts his treachery against the Gabiens, and here the priest hints that the entire narrative will invert all five points: by lies, flattery, greed, cruelty, and lechery, Aruns seeks, as his *summum bonum*, the immediate pleasure of doing whatever he likes. The account of Aruns's deception, injustice, cruelty, and "covoitise" in relation to the Gabiens does not involve the last vice of "lecherie," but it sets the stage for that especially horrifying reality in the second part of the story, which focuses on the rape of Lucrece. The earlier cruelties are now compounded in the violence of a "wylde man."

Unlike Aruns, Amans is a "gentil" man, and yet he too is deficient in all five points. He rejects Trouthe by persistently feigning a nature that is not his. He falls short of Largesse, Justice, and Pite by flattering himself, coveting his mistress, and resisting such counsel as might make his "regne stable." Finally, he has failed in Chastete, rejecting what the chaste person knows:

> The brihte Sonne be the morwe
> Beschyneth noght the derke nyht,
> The lusti youthe of mannes myht,
> In Age bot it stonde wel,
> Mistorneth at the laste whiel.   7.4464–68

Book 7 thus reorders the premises for judging Amans. The introduction of a Practique based upon "mannes free eleccion" follows in its distinction from the world of nature treated under Theorique a distinction between human and brute sensuality. The love of earthly and fleshly goods is, or should be, in man's power, and Genius, by the argument of this book, has set the terms for finding against Amans's willed abdication of reason and "free eleccion."

The excursus itself, however, is not in itself sufficient to free Amans, to effect his conversion or to bring his "querele" to resolution. Amans himself must step back into time, and specifically into his own history and confession; effectively, he must engage in a more radical re-creation of his past and by grace discover his true "noblesse" as a "gentil man." He will be helped in this task by another "distant" fiction, the tale of Apollonius, which differs from all those that have preceded it not merely in its length – it is the longest exemplum in the *Confessio* – but in its specific treatment of the virtues, of fortune, and of the

---

[19] *Bo* 3, pr. 9, 81–84.

ordering of time in memory. In this story, Genius presents a narrative foil to the tale of Nectanabus and also teaches something about wisdom and virtue that the idealizing structure of Book 7 could not provide. Finally, the narrative will set some of the key terms for Amans's greatest discovery.

CHAPTER EIGHTEEN

APOLLONIUS: INCEST, WISDOM, AND GRACE

The *ordinatio* of the *Confessio* is such that Book 8 should concern lechery, a vice which Gower in the *Mirour de l'Omme* had divided into five species: fornication, rape, adultery, incest, and vain delight.[1] Readers turning to Book 8 expecting a richly varied compilation of material on lechery will be surprised to find that the poet here deals exclusively with incest, tells few stories, and seems to limit his expository argument to a history and defense of laws of consanguinity. Book 8 will also surprise readers interested in the frame narrative. Lechery would seem to be the most important sin in this shrift because for Amans it holds the first place as the cause of all the others. For any confession to be complete, all seven sins must be introduced as topics, and thus Gower's choice of a Gregorian order for them, where lechery or *luxuria* appears last, seems perfectly suited to building, in a full confession, to Amans's most serious moral failing. But the lover, alas, is not guilty of incest, and we are therefore left with a topic and an order of questionable value, whether our interest is in the *genus peccati*, the strategies of compilation, or the course of Amans's confession.

The final book of the *Confessio* begins with an account of creation – "The myhti god, which unbegunne / Stant of himself and hath begunne / Alle othre things . . ." (8.1–3) – and with this statement, the work introduces a prospect reminiscent of the conclusion to Augustine's *Confessions*: questions about genesis, remembrance, and endings will become increasingly significant as Gower draws his own argument to a close. Initially, however, it appears that the poet's opening statement does no more than introduce an historical distinction regarding *cognatio* and marriage. As the marginal gloss at 8.1 suggests, the "legality" of a union of those related by blood has been variously determined over the course of time, in accordance with different principles: the *primordia nature*, the *racionis arbitrium*, and the *ecclesie legum imposicio*. In the earliest times, Genius argues,

> it was no Sinne
> The Soster forto take hire brother,
> Whan that ther was of chois non other.[2]   8.68–70

---

[1] The opening paragraphs of this chapter are adapted from my article, "Natural Law and Gower's *Confessio*," pp. 251–53.

[2] For a statement of this opinion among the Schoolmen, see, for example, John of la Rochelle: "Omne quod est contra legem naturalem semper est et fuit culpabile; sed non

Although this argument seems strangely irrelevant to the large issues of the *Confessio*, it helps to focus the concerns of the poem in a rather remarkable way. The terms of man's earliest history are fixed in Amans's mind: when the priest defends virginity in Book 5, the lover observes that he understands better the divine command to increase and multiply. In Book 8, incest comes to represent an analogous issue, and the discussion of it revises the premises of Amans's perception. Just as some legal authorities observe that the command to increase and multiply was a natural law especially appropriate before the earth was replenished,[3] so Genius notes that incest was permissible until the time of Abraham, when "The nede tho was overrunne, / For ther was poeple ynouh in londe" (8.100–01). Incest was permissible once, and it is encouraged in nature, but that does not mean that "nou adays" we are permitted to follow those "That taken wher thei take may" (8.152). This excursus into history thus identifies a moral, psychological issue. By natural law like things are drawn together. Clearly there can be no greater likeness in nature than likeness by *cognatio*, and incest therefore manifests particularly that law "quo similia in similibus gaudent." History now frames Gower's perception of this law: it is no longer the case that the incestuous can claim "ther was of chois non other": the only justification for such a claim is brute appetite.

Incest is an especially powerful exemplary species of lechery in the priest's argument because it reveals what it is like for a person to live without choice, as a "beste" limited to momentary sensual pleasure with those who live in closest proximity:

> as a cock among the Hennes
> Or as a Stalon in the Fennes,[4]
> Which goth amonges al the Stod,
> Riht so can he nomore good,
> Bot takth what thing comth next to honde.   8.159–63

As a desire for immediate and transitory self-gratification, incest exemplifies the shallowest human response to temporal experience.

Against this sin, Genius sets the "honestete" of Apollonius of Tyre. This ruler exemplifies honest love:

> Lo, what it is to be wel grounded:
> For he hath ferst his love founded
> Honesteliche as forto wedde,

---

semper fuit culpabilis coitus fratris cum sorore, sicut in principio; ergo non ex lege naturali est quod excipiatur frater et soror" (*Summa fratris Alexandri* 254 [Quaracchi, 1948], 4.2:359).

[3] See Philip the Chancellor, *Summa de bono*, and John of la Rochelle, *Summa de preceptis*, in the extracts printed by Lottin, pp. 112–13, 120.

[4] For especially relevant medieval background to Gower's image of the "Stalon in the Fennes," see V. A. Kolve, *Chaucer and the Imagery of Narrative: The First Five Canterbury Tales* (Stanford, Cal., 1984), pp. 236–51, 456–61.

> Honesteliche his love he spedde
> And hadde children with his wif,
> And as him liste he ladde his lif.   8.1993–98

Apollonius also exemplifies the other virtues of Policie: he is an ideal king, one who worthily rules himself and others, and the tale about him instantiates, in its outcome, the value of a regal education.

Whereas, in Alexander's education, the tales concerning Policie transvalu-ate the goods of Fortune into virtues, this tale pictures a king who, while he displays those virtues, is threatened, as the rulers portrayed in Book 7 are not, by the most adverse Fortune. Indeed, the "hap" of the represented action is part of the message of this wonderfully medieval tale. Chance or "aventure" tests all the characters of the tale, and Apollonius especially: he must flee the tyrant who threatens his life; he is driven from Tyre, and then from Tarsus; enduring a shipwreck, he is left "naked in a povere plit" (8.635); later, his young wife dies – or appears to have died – in childbirth, and even later he also loses his daughter. When the hero thinks his wife has died, he challenges Fortune: "Ha, thou fortune, I thee deffie. / Now hast thou do to me the werste" (8.1066–67). But the injustice of Fortune seems to lack bounds, for later Apollonius hears that his daughter has also died, and it is not surprising that he should then

> curseth and seith al the worste
> Unto fortune, as to the blinde,
> Which can no seker weie finde.   8.1584–86

We might suppose that a knowledge of "Aristotles lore" – or the wisdom derived from a comparable education – would be enough to fortify Apollonius against the worst Fortune. He knows those aspects of Theorique and Re-thorique that Genius had emphasized in Book 7:

> Of every naturel science,
> Which eny clerk him couthe teche,
> He couthe ynowh, and in his speche
> Of wordes he was eloquent.   8.390–93

By his knowledge not only in these fields, but, even more, in Practique, he should be empowered to rule himself.

The greatest test of Apollonius' wisdom occurs at the mid-point of the narrative, when he learns of his daughter's death. Crazed by this misfortune, he forsakes all human company and on his ship

> hath benethe his place nome,
> Wher he wepende al one lay,
> Ther as he sih no lyht of day.   8.1604–06

Having descended to a place "so derk" that "may no wiht sen his face," he refuses solace and offers "non ansuere" (8.1645) to those, including the lord of

Mitelene, Athenagoras, who seek to console him. Suffering from extreme "malencolie," he seems, with his descent in fortune, to have lost the wisdom he once possessed.

This sets the stage for what is perhaps the most poignant scene in the narrative, when the king is visited by the daughter he mourns. Apollonius is obviously not a wicked person; unlike some kings introduced in the treatise on Practique, he does not appear to serve Fortune or covet her goods, but rather resembles the persona Boethius in the *Consolation*. The scene with his daughter represents, in a curious way, a consolation of philosophy. In the relationship of its characters, that scene also comments on the history opening the entire narrative, the story of Antiochus' incest. "Withoute insihte of conscience," Antiochus rapes his own daughter:

> The fader so with lustes blente,
> That he caste al his hole entente
> His oghne doghter forto spille.   8.295–97

At the mid-point of the action, Apollonius faces the danger of similarly "un-kinde fare," and yet, though he is "blind," he is not blind "with lustes"; unlike Antiochus, he regains his sight, and significantly he does so through his daughter's agency.

The daughter who strives to console him, renamed Thaise from the Tharsia in the Latin prose version of this tale, suffers adversity of her own before she visits her father on the ship at Mitelene. Sent off by a jealous guardian to be killed, she is saved, but captured by pirates, and at Mitelene, sold to the brothel-keeper, Leonin. Manifestly unlike the harlot Thaise, her well-known namesake in medieval tradition, she displays a wonderful strength in resisting all the young men forced upon her in the brothel:

> Bot such a grace god hire sente,
> That for the sorwe which sche made
> Was non of hem which pouer hade
> To don hire eny vileinie.   8.1428–31

Eventually, Leonin realizes that he is losing trade because of her, and it is Thaise herself who offers a solution, proposing that she be freed to enter a religious house where "honeste wommen duelle"; there she will teach the daughters of nobles. Leonin accedes to her request because he will win the profits, but more important to the story is the knowledge Thaise eventually shares with these women:

> Sche can the wisdom of a clerk,
> Sche can of every lusti werk
> Which to a gentil womman longeth.   8.1483–85

In this school, she teaches music and the composition of proverbs and "deman-des slyhe"; indeed, no one "that science so wel tawhte," and it is no wonder that she can do so, given her own education:

> Sche was wel tawht, sche was wel boked,
> So wel sche spedde hir in hire youthe
> That sche of every wisdom couthe,
> That forto seche in every lond
> So wys an other noman fond,
> Ne so wel tawht at mannes yhe.   8.1328–33

No one in this story, not even Apollonius himself, is described so positively, and that will be significant for what this story implies.

Gower turns Thaise's gift at creating riddles to a purpose unlike the one described in the sources. In the *Gesta Romanorum*, Tharsia explains to Athenagoras that she proposes to remain a virgin by means of her liberal studies: she will use her skills in music and the casting and solving of riddles (*quaestiones*) to entertain people gathered in the forum.[5] Gower sees more: as in Book 7, the liberal studies ordered for Alexander ultimately teach chastity, so here, Thaise does not merely delight others to save herself; she dwells with "honeste" women and teaches honesty. Humbler and more "gentil" than the Tharsias in other versions of the legend, she helps herself by imparting wisdom.

Against that background, Gower rewrites the scene depicting Thaise's reunion with her father, and in doing so he also enlarges our perspective on what incest can mean. In the *Historia Apollonii regis Tyri*, Athenagoras promises to release Tharsia from the brothel if she successfully consoles Apollonius, leading him from where he sits, *in tenebris*, into light. She pays her visit, immediately announcing what kind of consolation she will not provide: "This is no prostitute who's come to comfort you, but an innocent girl who has kept her virginity intact even among the shipwrecks of other women's virtue."[6] In Gower's story, Thaise is perfectly secure in herself, and she betrays no need to make such an opening speech in defense of her honor. The danger to her and Apollonius is a much subtler one, as she follows Athenagoras' advice "To glade with this woful king" (8.1655).

Near the outset of the story, Apollonius, because he knows Antiochus's guilty secret, must flee the tyrant; he is shipwrecked, but then comes to land in Pentapolim and, despite his loses and grief, there courteously joins in the games of the people. For his worthiness, he is befriended by king Artestrathes, who, in his turn, introduces him to his daughter. As the hero grieves his loses while he recounts them, Artestrathes asks the princess, his daughter, to fetch "Hire harpe and don al that sche can / To glade with that sory man" (8.758–59). The princess sings, and Apollonius, drawn out of his grief, is inspired to teach her a "mesure" which "were a glad thing forto hiere" (8.770). When he sings, those gathered are so moved,

---

5 Ed. S. Singer, *Apollonius von Tyrus: Untersuchungen über das Fortleben des antiken Romans in späteren Zeiten* (Halle, 1895), p. 93.
6 *Historia Apollonii regis Tyri*, recension B, cap. 40, ed. G. A. A. Kortekaas, Mediaevalia Groningana, fasc. 3 (Groningen, 1984), p. 373; trans. Paul Turner, *Apollonius of Tyre* (London, 1956), p. 52.

> That as a vois celestial
> Hem thoghte it souneth in here Ere,
> As thogh that he an Angel were.   8.780–82

Thus begins an education of the princess, which leads eventually to a courtship and a marriage. The princess, for her part, has shifted Apollonius's attention from his sorrow to the deeper wisdom that is his, though it has been forgotten.

This scene of consolation anticipates the later one: Thaise, arriving on the ship at Mitelene "with hire Harpe on honde," tells Apollonius' men "that sche wolde fonde / Be alle weies that sche can, / To glade with this sory man" (8.1660–62). The characters encounter each other in the darkened room; they presumably have never met; neither is cognizant of the other's history. And yet the scene is devised to make us recall, through its tag-line, the scene out of Apollonius's past. In character Thaise is her mother's daughter, and this episode in which she must console Apollonius, hints, ever so subtly, at a re-enactment of that earlier scene: the characters are in a like "cas."

In a masterful revision of the traditional tale, Gower creates a whole series of circumstances which, in two less stable characters, might easily occasion a blind taking of what "comth next to honde." Thaise does not arrive on the ship directly from the brothel, but she carries that association in her history; coming "To glade with this sory man," she initially sets no rules; she does not enter the room proudly or timidly declaring that she is a virgin. Initially, the king might suppose that the pleasure or gladness she will afford is a sensual pleasure: the greater temptation to him, however, is one of reminiscence.

Thaise manifests the lost wisdom of her father, initially through her display of musical talent. To provide consolation, Thaise sings as her mother and father before her had sung: "sche harpeth many a lay / And lich an Angel sang withal" (8.1670–71). The issue represented in the episode of Antiochus, now transvaluated, is a concern of like rejoicing in like, but at a psychological level centered in remembrance.

The danger to Apollonius, we might suppose, is a nostalgic attraction to the "likeness" of an imagined past, or to the false consolation of the familiar. This mirrors an aspect of Amans's danger in looking for those who "were in [his] cas," effectively in letting time stand still, in seeking the image of what he merely wants to remember, based on an impulse of sensing and judging all things he desires to be good. This danger resides ultimately in the natural concupiscence that William of Conches associates with the god Genius, and which affects the way in which the confession itself is conducted. The threat extends to Gower as a compiler, in his resting content with what others have said, and to readers of the *compilatio*, in yielding to the "tirannie" of the familiar, in which "every man," with a license to do "what him liste," resists "thinges strange." The familiar is consolatory, of course, but it provides no more than the false comfort afforded by Boethius's harlot muses in the *Consolation*: it requires no change of perspective, no breaking out of oneself to discover one-self, no conversion: it is, in short, mere self-indulgence, finding a short-lived contentment or satisfaction in the proximate likeness. This is not a course to wisdom; it does not accommodate the "uncertein," give due regard to "danger" itself, or accept and adjust to things that may be otherwise than they seem or than one may wish them to be; ultimately, this course negates the human capacity to rule.

Thaise, in her actions, represents an antitype of Boethius' harlot muses. Her music does not feed Apollonius' passion. It is surely designed to please, and is in that sense consonant with an ideal presented in the treatise on Rethorique: "Whan wordes medlen with the song, / It doth plesance wel the more" (7.1586–87). In a gentle turn from the course we might expect, however, Apollonius finds no comfort in her song: "Bot he nomore than the wal / Tok hiede of eny thing he herde" (8.1672–73). As with Philosophy in the *Consolation*, however, so with Thaise in this epitome; the music is left for the rhetoric, the rhetoric for the thought:

> And whan sche sih that he so ferde,
> Sche falleth with him into wordes,
> And telleth him of sondri bordes,
> And axeth him demandes strange,
> Wherof sche made his herte change,
> And to hire speche his Ere he leide
> And hath merveile of that sche seide.   8.1674–80

Thaise's *demandes* win his attention, but no verbal response, and when he, "half in wraththe," dismisses her, Thaise courageously ventures forth: "in the derke forth sche goth, / Til sche him toucheth" (8.1691–92).

Apollonius is chaste, even as a depressed "madd man" (8.1687), and his response does not come entirely as a surprise: "and he wroth, / And after hire with his hond / He smot" (8.1692–94). A modern might read this as betraying a repressed desire, but Gower makes no such connection. While, a short time later, Apollonius will be naturally attracted to the daughter he does not recognize, that attraction is not one of taking superficial comfort in an irrecoverable past; the memory restored to Apollonius also embraces the present, and it holds the secret of a wisdom that can console.

What eventually calls Apollonius back to himself is Thaise's revelation of her name and history: this much is also in Gower's sources. Far more interesting and significant than that revelation, however, is the scene that precedes it. Thaise's response to the smiting is, against the backdrop of the sources, unexpected. In the prose *Historia* as well as the version of the story told by Godfrey of Viterbo, Tharsia expresses outrage at Fortune and the "ardua potestas celorum" for what they have caused her, an innocent, to suffer; her outrage is all the greater because, as she now reveals, she is "regis Apollonii filia."[7] Gower assigns speeches excoriating Fortune not to Thaise, but to Apollonius. He is

---

[7]   Godfrey, in the selection from the *Pantheon* ed. by Singer, p. 173; see also Godefredus Viterbiensis, *Pantheon, sive universitatis libri, qui chronici appellantur*, XX, pars 11

the one who succumbs to Fortune, whereas Thaise transcends it. In the present context, Thaise's speech is quieter than the expressions of outrage by her counterparts in tradition, and it becomes another mechanism for drawing the king back to himself, not merely to a recognition of his daughter, but to a realization of his forgotten character. We know from the earlier perception of Thaise's mother that Apollonius is a man of "gret gentilesse":

> Hise dedes ben therof witnesse
> Forth with the wisdom of his lore;
> It nedeth noght to seche more,
> He myhte noght have such manere,
> Of gentil blod bot if he were.   8.790–94

Thaise, whose nature is like Apollonius's own, draws that *gentilesse* out of him by means of a gentle rebuke. She now protests, courteously, that she is a virgin, but she does so because he has so manifestly made a wrong inference:

> and thus whan sche him fond
> Desesed, courtaisly sche saide,
> 'Avoi, mi lord, I am a Maide;
> And if ye wiste what I am,
> And out of what lignage I cam,
> Ye wolde noght be so salvage.'   8.1694–99

That statement beautifully prepares for the king's recovery. His response is entirely "kinde," but without a suggestion of desire:

> With that he sobreth his corage
> And put awey his hevy chiere.
> Bot of hem tuo a man mai liere
> What is to be so sibb of blod:
> Non wiste of other hou it stod,
> And yit the fader ate laste
> His herte upon this maide caste,
> That he hire loveth kindely,
> And yet he wiste nevere why.   8.1700–08

This is a remarkable reflection on the difference between incest and a kind but virtuous love of "what thing comth next to honde": the latter reflects a deeper truth to nature than does the blind, destructive power of Antiochus' will. Apollonius, even when he is mad, finds "no seker weie" to solace in the merely sensibly familiar or like; he responds not to the "touche," but instead to a deeper likeness of virtue, wisdom, and *gentilesse* in Thaise. Thaise's "demandes" inspire him to listen and thereby to discover a courtesy that sobers his "corage"

(Basle, 1559), col. 290; *Historia Apollonii regis Tyri*, recension B, cap. 44, ed. Kortekaas, p. 389.

and restores his own power to love "kindely," to manifest an "honeste" affection that is both natural and ordered.

In leading her "patient" back to himself, Thaise is a counterpart to Philosophia, and yet she lacks the stature of the Boethian figure. Her strategy is to proceed not by Boethian dialogue, but by posing her "demandes slyhe." In character she is less like Philosophia and more like the humble, courteous, gentle solver and master of riddles, Peronelle, in Gower's first tale celebrating a virtue in the *Confessio*. Thaise's display of a gentle nature, as well as Apollonius's recovery of his, help to tie this narrative to another external "text," Amans's own confession. Once again, the gentle idiom of the *Confessio* conduces to the lover's recovery of his "kindness" or *gentilesse* in the best sense: solace is found in a "philosophie" generated out of the "problemes" and "demandes" represented in and by Genius.

Amans, like Apollonius, cannot respond to the "soubtil" questions that his own gentle teacher has been posing during the course of the confession. His response, in the confessional dialogue that follows this narrative, echoes an intermediate stage in Apollonius' response to Thaise, when

> in proverbe and in probleme
> Sche spak, and bad he scholde deme
> In many soubtil question. 8.1681–83

Apollonius, however, "wolde noght o word ansuere" (8.1686), and at last "His heved wepende awey he caste, / And . . . he bad hire go" (8.1688–89).

The references to "demande," "probleme," and "soubtil question" fit Gower's *donnée*, for the Latin prose *Historia* begins with Apollonius' display of a talent at solving riddles, as he puzzles out Antiochus's dark secret; that same account, treating this later scene, has Tharsia present and Apollonius successfully respond to a series of ten riddles. Gower does not include this scene, and that may be due to the accident of his sources – the scene does not appear in Godfrey of Viterbo's *Pantheon* either, for example – but that exclusion, whatever its cause, leaves us with a deeply suggestive text whose import reaches far beyond Tharsia's ten riddles about physical things – ball, ladder, sea, mirror – to such riddles as presented to Peronelle in Book 1, and beyond them to the enigma of the universe represented in Book 7, and even farther, to the *demande* that comprises the entire poem.

In all versions of the story, Tharsia or Thaise's posing of riddles is an act of social integration, but the exercise itself need not always be so.[8] Often, as in

---

[8] For my general comments on the riddle, I am indebted to the following: Roger D. Abrahams, "The Literary Study of the Riddle," *Texas Studies in Language and Literature* 14 (1972): 177–97; Charles T. Scott, "Some Approaches to the Study of the Riddle," in *Studies in Language, Literature, and Culture of the Middle Ages and Later*, ed. E. Bagby Atwood and Archibald A. Hill (Austin, Texas, 1969), pp. 111–27; Andrew Welsh, *Roots of Lyric: Primitive Poetry and Modern Poetics* (Princeton, 1978), pp. 25–46; W. J. Pepicello and Thomas A. Green, *The Language of Riddles: New Perspectives* (Columbus, Ohio, 1984).

the case of Antiochus and even of the king in the story of Peronelle in Book 1 of the *Confessio*, the making of riddles can be a deadly game: it is a means of confusing, gaining control, and even destroying a rival or adversary: as such, it is a device of exclusion. For Apollonius' daughter in the various versions of this tale, it is a device of inclusion, a game designed to draw the respondent and the poser of the riddle together in shared knowledge. Just as "a grace god hire sente," so she, an initiate, bestows this "grace" on others, through her "demandes" leading them to wisdom.

Roger Abrahams has written that the riddle, by its "surface metaphor," prolongs the discovery process.[9] This is what Gower has sought to do on the grand scale in the *Confessio*: in a leisurely recreation, he is "bringing diverse elements of the world together" in a dialogue suggestive of a "technique by which the group rehearses its sense of order through the performance of devices which elicit collaboration, an intense community involvement in process."[10] These terms are not medieval, of course, but a like technique obtains in the medieval *demande* of the *Confessio*, whose richness depends on its capacity to prolong, and to engage participants in, the discovery process.

Like Apollonius, Amans does not respond directly to the "demandes" posed by his teacher, nor does he perceive the "soubtil question" lodged in Genius's very character and office. When, after this tale, Genius gets too close to the lover's condition, when he advises a course of action that is bound to enrage Amans, a "madd man," Amans does what we expect: he verbally "smites" his priest. Subsequently the lover earns a gentle rebuke not from one teacher, but from two. Neither rebuke by Genius or Venus "sobreth his corage" quite so quickly as does Thaise's rebuke sober Apollonius, but sober him each one does. From a world of projected false images, Amans will once again come to see reality, true likeness, and himself; he will recover his own *gentilesse*.

Thaise and Apollonius survive the trial on the ship at Mitelene, and henceforth the action of the narrative turns in favor of Apollonius and his family: "Fro this day forth fortune hath sworn / To sette him upward on the whiel" (8.1736–37). This reversal of fortune is, of course, in the *donnée*, but Genius's emphasis on the acts of Fortune throughout the story, and especially near the end, forces us to ask whether the tale, because of that turn, fully exemplifies the Boethian point that it is not the whim of Fortune, but the stability of moral character that makes a people "glade, / That sory hadden be toforn" (8.1734–35). Is it enough to say that Apollonius at his worst fortune "lacketh noght but worldes good," that he still transcends Fortune, that he therefore manifests "what it is to be wel grounded"?

Genius makes it very evident that Apollonius cannot save himself, that only an external agent can draw him out of his near-despair:

---

9   Abrahams, p. 178.
10 Ibid., pp. 182, 187.

> This king hath founde newe grace,
> So that out of his derke place
> He goth him up into the liht,
> And with him cam that swete wiht,
> His doghter Thaise. 8.1739–42

At the same time, Apollonius can regain the light because he is prepared to do so; he is a person who has cultivated wisdom and virtue. This is not a case of conversion in which a character, instantaneously, is wholly remade: preparation precedes sudden illumination.

The problem with Genius's perception is not that he fails to refer to grace, but that once again he appears to identify it merely with good luck. Even the Latin gloss at 8.1700 conveys more: "sicut deus destinauit, pater filiam inuentam recognouit" 'just as God destined, the father recognized his found daughter.' The priest understands that Fortune is unpredictable, but does not seem to comprehend the stability of theological grace, which, though it is "uncertein" to human perception, has restored Apollonius to himself, allowing him to recover his wisdom through the wisdom-in-likeness of Thaise.

At the close of this narrative, Genius again seems to encourage a dependence on Fortune as the provider of happiness. He argues that virtue brings good luck; "The mede arist of the servise" (8.2012) because Fortune, though she is unstable, at some time favors those who "ben of love trewe" (8.2015). It is therefore better to be good than wicked, for an evil act spells certain doom: "love ayein kinde," the priest summarizes, "makth sore a man to falle" (8.2018). This, of course, only has the effect of directing Amans's gaze outward once again to the grace he thinks properly his. The lover cannot cope with an uncertain fortune. On the one hand, he must fix blame on Danger, a surer villain (8.2041–43); he has never been "assoted" in his wits except "in that worthi place / Wher alle lust and alle grace / Is set, if that danger ne were" (8.2037–39). On the other hand, the same premise of desiring a world without danger leads him to hope for sure-fired advice on how to succeed in his *causa*. Even for his "thousand wordes on a rowe / Of suche as I best speke can" (8.2050–51), he has been rejected, and because Genius is a clerk, and he, the lover, is a "lewed man," he hopes the priest can show him "What is my beste, as for an ende" (8.2059).

Genius has not yet spoken about what is Amans's "beste." His advice throughout has been "uncertein," his surest counsel repeatedly qualified by references to chance; indeed, in the vagaries of his imagination, he himself seems to be an agent of Fortune, an endless source of "derk matiere." In what he compiles, it sometimes appears that "al is to him of o value" (8.2121); even his orthodoxies are often set loose from their foundation. As the confession now resumes, however, all of this will change: the priest comes to a *determinatio* or verdict regarding Amans's case.

CHAPTER NINETEEN

OLD AGE AND CONVERSION

During the course of the *Confessio*, Gower has not only compiled materials to fit his expressed topics, but also developed through a variety of structures an argument *ad motum*, designed to turn Amans to the good. The loose categories of this argument – the causes of good works – include the law of nature, reason, and grace.[1] Already appearing in various meanings and relationships in the course of the confession, they are now "corrected" to apply to the penitent's particular sickness as an aged lover.

Genius's task in his own "conclusioun final" (8.2070) is to persuade Amans to set his "herte under that lawe, / The which of reson is governed / And noght of will" (8.2134–36), and this "lawe" finds its measure in principles of delight, profit, and honesty. The lover has gained little pleasure from his "querele," and Genius shows him what he already fears, that pursuing it is useless: "Sinne mai no pris deserve," and in the lover's sin, Genius says, "I not what profit myhte availe" (8.2089, 2091). The priest stresses the folly of this profitless course – "Wher thou no profit hast ne pris, / Thou art toward thiself unwis" (8.2093–94) – and his premise is that Amans should have learned from this confession that "lust" is contingent and transitory: "Ensamples thou hast many on / Of now and ek of time gon, / That every lust is bot a whil" (8.2137–39). A sin can be committed for the sake of "delit" or "spede," but never for the sake of honesty.[2] As Genius now also shows, Amans's love, because its end is not "honeste," is bound to be lacking in delight and profit.

Genius is not content, however, merely to tell the lover to withdraw from "Sinne" or passion. Through his many tales, he has advanced to a defense of

---

1 See Hugh Ripelin of Strassburg: "Ad opera bona tria nos incitant, scilicet lex naturae, quae scripta est in corde hominis, dicens: *Quaecumque vultis ut faciant vobis homines, et vos facite illis*, etc. Ratio, quae dicit ea esse delectabilia, utilia et honesta. Gratia, quae dicit serviendum esse Deo, quia summe bonus: subveniendum proximo, quia Dei filius, quia imago Dei, quia in beatitudine socius. Gratia non datur ei, qui se non habilitat ad gratiam" (*Compendium theologicae veritatis* 5.2, in *Alberti Magni opera omnia*, ed. A. Borgnet [Paris, 1890–98], 34:154).

2 On this as a confessional standard for judging human behavior, see the "Statutes of Bishop Alexander of Stavensby for the Diocese of Coventry and Lichfield (1229–37)": "Solet autem triplex distingui finis, utile, honestum, delectabile. Multi committunt peccata propter utilitatem, multi propter delectationem; nullus potest committere peccatum propter honestatem" (*Councils and Synods*, ed. F. M. Powicke and C. R. Cheney [Oxford, 1964], 2.1: 224).

the "rihte weie" or "honestete" of a love that is sufficient to *kinde*, yet in accordance with *reson*. If, as David Benson has argued, Genius never succeeds in teaching Amans the "proper kind of human loving," it is not for Genius's want of trying.[3] Whatever his limitations, the confessor, often outside his order of announced topics, points the lover to that end through many of his stories, as well as in his final counsel. If Amans can come to accept "love where it mai noght faile" (8.2086), he will no longer retreat from life, but rather rejoice that he has found it, that he has become himself.

At the end of the confession proper, however, Amans cannot accept Genius's judgment, even though he recognizes its truth:

> Mi resoun understod him wel,
> And knew it was soth everydel
> That he hath seid, bot noght forthi
> Mi will hath nothing set therby.   8.2191–94

The lover has yet to change in the most important sense. Having coursed through the final "Debat and gret perplexete" (8.2189) with his priest, he falls into a gentler rhetoric, seeking accord through "wordes debonaire," but he still does so to the end of serving his will. His present wish is to gain for his "querele" a *status translationis*, to have it transferred from a jurisdiction of *reson* to one of *kinde*.

It is to this end that Amans appeals his case to Venus, first in the form of a "poetic" epistle and then in actual dialogue with the goddess. This appeal constitutes a return to the story framing the confession proper. Amans's complaint in Book 1 – that he has not received from Venus the "wele" he deserves – has a distant model in Boethius' complaint to Philosophy in Book 1 of the *Consolation*. In the *Consolation*, that grievance forms the great "perplexete" of the work, and over five books of dialogue Philosophy gradually and patiently resolves it. This Boethian pattern of resolution sets a standard for medieval writers. In Machaut's *Remede de Fortune*, for example, Esperance develops her argument within the lover's tolerance, slowing adapting Boethian doctrine to her own teaching about virtuous love-service (2403–816). The lover readily accepts what she says, and at the end he is fully prepared to write that "istoire" in his heart (2939–46). The argument of Gower's work is quite different. At the outset, Venus rebukes the lover, orders a confession, and vanishes. The initial "debate," including Venus's rather veiled complaint against "faitours," remains open until she returns to render her verdict.

The confession thereby forms an interlude – once again, a "recreation" – between this scene and the closing one, when the goddess reappears. Through the greater part of the shrift, Genius has been a genial and trusted *magister*, and it is only in Book 8 that he exceeds the lover's tolerance, prompting Amans to respond as a lover might, to one who claims to speak sense to a lover:

---

[3] Benson, "Incest in Gower's *Confessio*," pp. 107–08.

> The fielinge of a mannes Hiele
> Mai noght be likned to the Herte:
> I mai noght, thogh I wolde, asterte,
> And ye be fre from al the peine
> Of love, wherof I me pleigne.   8.2154–58

This prepares us for Venus's reappearance and yet another great perplexity.

Gower's decision to change the overall *ordinatio* of a traditional argument, moving toward conflict instead of away from it, has the advantage of "pointing" issues: by recompiling the elements of argument to that end, the poet gains greater reciprocal power in the relationship among his various statements about memory, time, and the *leges naturae*, about life and death, and about reason, "vertu moral," and grace. The interlude of the confession defines and redefines these terms and allows for that meaningful "pointing" in the conflict and resolution of the poem's final book. It is in the nature of this mode of argument that we, like one of the interlocutors in the fiction, may undergo shocks of recognition.

Amans's epistle to the goddess, written in rhyme royal, provides the only break in the pattern of octosyllabic couplets of the *Confessio*; as a *peroratio*, a poetic appeal designed to "excite" and set the heart of his judge "to pite," it forms the counterpart to the poem that concludes Boethius's opening self-defense in the *Consolation*. There Boethius argues that he has been singled out for unjust treatment, and so Amans here, very late in the poem, complains, "And thus, bot I, hath every kinde his blisse" (8.2230).

The power of Amans's petition, in this domain of *kinde*, is that it appropriates to itself certain terms that would appear to legitimize his plea that Cupid "yif me Salve such as I desire" (8.2290). The "Salve" is the lady, and Amans will have no other:

> For Service in thi Court withouten hyre
> To me, which evere yit have kept thin heste,
> Mai nevere be to loves lawe honeste.   8.2291–93

This claim of honesty of course renders Genius's earlier reasoned defense of "honeste love," of *honestas* and *honestum*, problematic. Amans thinks he is honest – faithful, chaste, obedient – but in that "honesty" he is false to his nature.[4] Once again, the use of a multi-valenced term in the argument of the *Confessio* prolongs the discovery process.

It is well and good that the priest has tried to lift Amans's perception to a truer honesty, but the lover persists in an attitude he again reveals at the end of his epistle, now in a plea to Venus: either "mi love aquite as I deserve, / Or elles

---

4 For a distinction between "vain" and "real" *honestas*, see Nicholas de Gorran, *Distinctiones*, s. v. "honestas," MS Bodley 427, fol. 80v. Pierre Bersuire makes a like distinction when he indicts those "qui si honesti sunt in verbis, tamen non in factis, in conversatione sed non in intentione, in gestu corporis non fructu operis" (*Dictionarium*, s. v. "honestas," 2: fol. 114v).

do me pleinly forto sterve" (8.2299–2300). Amans remains confused over his choices. Genius has instructed him to "ches if [he] wolt live or deie" (8.2148), but Amans has turned petulant. It is only after Venus, who allows in her retinue only "thing which is to kinde due" (8.2348), rejects him, that Amans will awaken to the wisdom that confers life.[5]

Whereas Genius, for his part, has defended a *reson* that frees, the goddess, for her part, now affirms a *kinde* that binds creatures to set courses. Amans knows that Venus, from the outset of her speech, is having a game with him, but he does not recognize it as designed to call him back to himself. Entirely on her own terms, the goddess will remove the fortune that has grieved him "manye daies" (8.2357): as she tells him, "be thou hol, it schal suffise" (8.2366), though her cure will not be not the one he desires:

> Mi medicine is noght to sieke
> For thee and for suche olde sieke,
> Noght al per chance as ye it wolden,
> Bot so as ye be reson scholden,
> Acordant unto loves kinde.   8.2367–71

The speech is important not merely because it associates Amans or "John Gower" with "olde sieke," but because it calls attention to the lover's seeking favor or medicine "al per chance." In his next speech, Amans turns this charge back on Venus herself, arguing that she, standing "withoute lawe / In noncertein" (8.2378–79), capriciously metes out favor:

> The trewe man fulofte aweie
> Sche put, which hath hir grace bede,
> And set an untrewe in his stede.   8.2382–84

This exchange thus reveals separate frames of perception in the two speakers. Amans supposes that he has done everything according to "reule"; though he has been a true lover, he has not been given the grace due him. Venus' principle of merit, because it does not fit his structure of values, seems to be merely capricious. Venus, of course, has her own set expectations, within which she deems Amans's wish fanciful.

In this natural jurisdiction, it is Venus who stands in "certein." As, according to Genius, Amans's love violates reason, so now, according to Venus, it violates *kinde*, and her conclusion is inescapable. Amans is too old to love, and he would do well to recognize his "fieble astat" before he begins "Thing wher [he] miht non ende winne" (8.2430). Venus thus concludes her opening counsel with pointed advice: "Remembre wel hou thou art old" (8.2439).

Were Amans's love pure or honest, one might suppose, such a judgment would not overwhelm him as this one does. The reminder causes a chill and swoon, and that it should matter quite so much to him is of course based on the

---

5   Cf. Prov. 8:35.

fact that this love, though he thinks it "honeste," is carnal. His suddenly catching cold is in a sense a coming into his status as an old man: "That erst was hete is thanne chele" (8.2857).[6]

As the lover suffers "chele," so have critics been chilled by this unexpected turn in the poem. John Burrow is not convinced by Donald Schueler's argument that Gower has prepared us for this discovery at the end.[7] The earlier hints of Amans's age are slight or unsure, and they do not keep the ending from coming as a surprise. Burrow is, I think, right, and yet one must still ask why Gower has chosen to defer his statement about Amans's age.

Burrow sees two problems in the poet's decision. The first is technical: "If the poet does not actually cheat, he comes very near to cheating." Given that weakness in the fabric of the narrative, however, Burrow then goes on to speculate about the poet's reasons for the decision: "for the greater part of the poem we have seen the affair from [Amans's] own point of view," and *senilis amor* "need not, after all, feel very different from the love of young people."[8]

Be that as it may, Gower's judgment remains troublesome. Burrow argues that "the cure of [Amans's] sickness lies not in the almost impossibly difficult transcending of Nature's law, but simply conforming to it."[9] Michael Cherniss takes this argument a step further: the poet "has abandoned his moral demands upon the individual in favor of a more 'naturalistic' solution to the problem of earthly desires."[10] Such a response, however, oversimplifies both the ending of the *Confessio* and the *jus naturae* that Gower has been so careful to expound. The human being is obligated not merely to conform to a nature that orders the progress of physical life from birth to death, but to follow natural reason and to "serve and glade" God, the source of every "beinge." Because a fallen nature is the species' inheritance, however, any of these "natural" tasks can be "almost impossibly difficult." Any of them – even accepting the simple fact of growing old – may require divine assistance.

That, however, raises another question. While Gower expresses an "optimistic trust in Providence (which created the natural order) to bring men to Reason and virtue," he does not at the same time hold that man thereby becomes less responsible or accountable for his actions, as Cherniss supposes.[11] Though no person, except by grace, can be entirely chaste, we are not thereby given the license to be unchaste. Gower's aim is not to exculpate the species; nor is it to encourage readers merely to let nature take its course: that is exactly what Amans, in his "lapsed" nature, has done.

Gower treats the issue of old age in Book 8 against a rich background of

---

6   See Papias: "Physici enim dicunt puerorum & senum aetates conuenire. In illis enim sanguis nondum calidus in istis iam frigidus" (*Vocabulista*, s. v. "senes," p. 313).
7   Donald Schueler, "The Age of the Lover in Gower's *Confessio Amantis*," *Medium Aevum* 36 (1967): 152–58; Burrow, "Portrayal," pp. 12–13.
8   Burrow, "Portrayal," pp. 14, 15.
9   Ibid., p. 17.
10   Cherniss, *Boethian Apocalypse*, p. 117.
11   Ibid., pp. 118, 117.

ancient and medieval writings on the subject. In this tradition, Seneca raises a
relevant question when he asks how much of the repose he experiences in his
old age "I owe to wisdom [sapientiae], and how much to my time of life [aeta-
ti]."[12] This question provides a useful caveat. For Gower, repose is never attributable to nature alone or to growing old merely; it originates in wisdom.
Throughout his poem, Gower is surely interested in the course of nature, as he
is interested in large questions of temporality. But to say that in drawing the
question of time of life into his final discussion, he effectively cancels his moral
demands on the individual, is to miss a very basic point in that ending, the
confession, and the poem itself.

All of Gower's various concerns in this work come together in a statement
that reassesses the passage of time. The age of Amans is a means by which the
poet fully articulates the issue not merely of growing old, or of letting nature
take its course, but of coming to understand one's own nature in every sense of
that very complex term. The problem of age and its resolution is centered in a
convergence of two senses of time and "ende": old age might betoken physical
corruption and mortality on the one hand, or the *telos* of a fulfilled nature, the
perfectio aetatis on the other.[13] In a larger setting, this distinction supposes two
perceptions of the ages or *aetates* of the individual, "the one of the body, which
is not in our power, but in the law of nature, the other of the soul, which is
properly situated in us." The latter "is in our power," and on its course, "if we
wish, we grow daily, even until we come to the end of life."[14] Gower uses a
recognition of the one sense to open out into a recognition of the other,
through a conversion that must take place in time. The figure of old age
provides a precise and focused way of talking about the moment when that
conversion occurs.

Venus undoubtedly understands old age only in the former sense – in the
sense of an age assigned "in lege naturae" – and unquestionably, the physical
age of Amans or "Gower" is a point that neither we, nor the narrator himself,
can now forget. But there is another sense in which the poet's deferring the
reference to Amans's age is perfectly timed, delayed as it is until Genius has
presented, in Book 7, a long excursus on *sapientia* that also concludes with an
extended tribute to chastity.

Ideally, old age represents wisdom.[15] When Venus argues that "loves lust and

---

12 Seneca, *Epistulae* 26.2–3, trans. Gummere, 1:186–89.
13 "Senectus est perfectio aetatis" (Conrad of Hirsau, *Dialogus super auctores* 958, ed.
Huygens, p. 102); "Senectus significat vitam perfectam, virtuosam & honestam"
(Pierre Bersuire, *Dictionarium*, s. v. "senex," 3: fol. 182v). For a different perspective on
medieval questions about the perfect age, see Mary Dove, *The Perfect Age of Man's Life*
(Cambridge, 1986); additional background may be found in Elizabeth Sears, *Ages of
Man: Medieval Interpretations of the Life Cycle* (Princeton, 1986), and J. A. Burrow, *The
Ages of Man: A Study in Medieval Writing and Thought* (Oxford, 1986).
14 Origen, *In Lucam*, hom. 20, Latin trans. Jerome, in *Die Homilien zu Lucas in der
Übersetzung des Hieronymus*, ed. Max Rauer, *Origines werke*, vol. 9, *Die griechischen
christlichen Schriftsteller der ersten drie Jahrhunderte*, vol. 49 (Berlin, 1959): 123–24.
15 "Quid fit amplissimum vite spacium: usque ad sapientiam venire" (John of Wales,

lockes hore / In chambre acorden neveremore" (8.2403–04), she means that old men are physically unfit for love. But because "wisdom is the gray hair unto men" (Wisd. 4:8), old men are also "unfit" for such love if they have attained the moral expectation for their age, if they possess the wisdom that Gower has set against unregulated sensual passion. Ernst Curtius notes in the language of the Fathers an association of " 'gray' (canus) and 'grayhairedness' (canities)" with wisdom: 'canities animae' (Ambrose); 'canities morum' (Augustine); 'canities sensum' (Cassianus)."[16] Medieval authors repeatedly argue, moreover, that this age should bring an honestas, chastity, or modestia wanting in youth; those whom "gray old age" – cana senectus – touches, Gower writes in a Latin epigram of this book, should practice chastity (8.3.9–10).[17]

Sapience and chastity are not properties exclusive to old age, of course; nor does being old prevent an Amans from being unchaste and foolish. Indeed, he represents the inversion of an ideal ancient and medieval figure, the puer senilis who, wise and vigorous, combines the best of both ages. Amans is a puerilis senex, a childish old man, a weary fool who acts on impulse. "Vieus d'aage et enfes de meurs," or "Senex tempore" and "Puer moribus," he is, in these terms of Brunetto and Aegidius,[18] the very antitype of the person who can rule himself.

This comically grotesque lover reverses history, clings to a youthful desire, and forsakes an "honeste" old age: "Old age is worthy [honesta], if it maintains its law. O glorious boon of age, if it does indeed free us from youth's most vicious fault!"[19] Bound to youthful pleasure, Amans obviously rejects a senectus that "moderates desire, increases wisdom, and provides mature counsel."[20] The excursus of Book 7 is aptly designed to nourish that kind of "old age," and in it Amans might appropriately have found consolation, a release from the vexation Cicero also sees in younger men:

> But how blessed it is for the soul, after having, as it were, finished its campaigns of lust . . . and of all the passions, to return within itself, and

Communiloquium, pars 3, dist. 2, cap. 6 [Strasbourg, 1518], fol. 61v); see also Robert Holkot, In librum Sapientiae, lect. 49, p. 175.

16 Ernst Robert Curtius, European Literature and the Latin Middle Ages, trans. Willard R. Trask (London, 1948), p. 100.

17 "Cessare enim debet in senectute, quidquid voluptatis, quidquid lasciuiae, quidquid illecebrae placuit in iuuentute" (Robert Holkot, In librum Sapientiae, lect. 49, p. 175); "Ergo servare debes in senectute tua castitatem" (Albertanus of Brescia, Liber de amore et dilectione Dei & proximi, tract. 2, lib. 1 [Coni, 1507], fol. 39r); "in moribus senectus quaedam honestas est" (John Balbus, Catholicon [Rouen, 1511], s. v. "senectus" [unfoliated]); "Senectus venerabilis est vita immaculata" (Pierre Bersuire, Dictionarium, s. v. "senex," vol. 3, fol. 182v).

18 Brunetto Latini, Tresor, 2.3.4, p. 177; Aegidius Romanus, De regimine principum, 1.1.6, p. 20.

19 Vincent of Beauvais, Speculum doctrinale 5.101, col. 461. Vincent's last sentence is taken from Cicero, De senectute 12.39, here trans. William Armistead Falconer, Loeb (London, 1927), p. 49.

20 Papias, s.v. "senectus," p. 313.

as the saying is, "to live apart"! And indeed if it has any provender, so to speak, of study and learning, nothing is more enjoyable than a leisured old age [*ociosa senectute*].[21]

A model of what the "forme of Aristotles lore" could have done for the aged lover is provided in the pseudo-Ovidian *De vetula*, a thirteenth-century work in which "Ovid," in exile, describes how, having left behind the amorous diversions of his youth and now "living apart," he looks for solace in philosophy.[22] He will dedicate his remaining days to studying the sciences and through them worshiping the Creator. He will ponder the heavens and the elements and the union of these in the "lesser world"; he will reflect on his soul, and be mindful, yet not fearful of death; for these tasks, and especially for the last, his exile has prepared him.[23]

This "Ovid" exemplifies the principle advocated by Cicero and wanting in Gower's *senex*. In Book 7, Amans is taken through an exercise, of which the pseudo-Ovid offers a rough epitome, before he is prepared to embark on it. Eager for a diversion, he has welcomed this instruction in Aristotle's lore, but at the end, he confesses, "The tales sounen in myn Ere, / Bot yit myn herte is elleswhere" (7.5411–12): this represents the pseudo-Ovid's exile in reverse. No lore, Amans argues, can make him "foryete" one point,

> That I my tydes ay ne kepte
> To thenke of love and of his lawe;
> That herte can I noght withdrawe.   7.5418–20

It is only after he has been forced to reflect upon his "tydes" at their source that he can ponder the tales that "sounen in [his] Ere," becoming what the confession is designed to make him, aged in the best sense, or prudent and morally wise.

The debates with his priest and Venus over reason and nature have prepared the lover for conversion, and fittingly, the actual change occurs in a vision, at another level of reality, before it occurs in waking life. Whereas the literal waking state of Amans has been a sleep, the literal swoon and trance effect a wakening from the temporal disquiet, ignorance, and dullness he suffers to a new, life-giving perception of himself.[24] This "grace" will eventuate in a new "disposition of mind" and "a healing from within of the sinner's will": it is, in figure, the grace by which the image of God in the soul, deformed through sin, is reformed, and it is formalized, in the fiction, by the priest's absolution.[25]

---

21 Cicero, *De senectute* 14.49, trans. Falconer, pp. 59, 61.

22 *The Pseudo-Ovidian De vetula*, 3.12–18, ed. Dorothy M. Robathan (Amsterdam, 1968), p. 108.

23 This portion of the work is so paraphrased in the *accessus, Introitus in librum Ovidii Nasonis de vetula*, ed. Robathan, pp. 45–46.

24 See Maurice of Provins, *Dictionarium*, s. v. "evigilatio," fol. 132v; on the sleep of carnal desire, see Pierre Bersuire, *Dictionarium*, s. v. "somnus, sopor," 3: fol. 179v.

25 Pierre Bersuire, *Dictionarium*, s. v. "gratia," 2: fol. 98r; to elucidate his statement about sanctifying grace (*gratia gratum faciens*), Bersuire uses the figure of a mirror, its

In his dream, Amans sees two companies of "gentil" lovers gathering before Cupid: these figures, many of them reintroduced from tales told earlier in the confession, are now grouped "naturally" according to their ages. In the "freissh" company of Youthe are those who "laghe and pleie, / And putten care out of the weie" (8.2491–92). As befits these young "gentils,"

> The moste matiere of her speche
> Was al of knyhthod and of Armes,
> And what it is to ligge in armes
> With love, whanne it is achieved.   8.2496–99

In this company Amans sees "ful many a bacheler / . . . / Forth with here loves glade and blithe" (8.2536, 2539). He sees those who complain of love, and he sees noble women, including those presented in the *Heroides*, and most importantly "foure wyves" – Penelope, Lucrece, Alceste, Alcyone – "Whos feith was proeved in her lyves," specifically "in essample of alle goode / With Mariage" (8.2616–18). Amans is doubly excluded from this first company by his natural *aetas* and his vitiated moral nature. Youth, carefree speech, a "mariage" where he might "welde his love at wille" – these are what he most desires, but never will attain.

He is placed, instead, in the second company, led by Elde. Its members, "of gret Age," also dance, but "A softe pas thei dance and trede" (8.2682); they smile "With sobre chier" but do not laugh, though, after their fashion, "thei weren glade" (8.2588). Here Amans sees kings, philosophers, poets: David, Solomon, Samson, Aristotle, Virgil, Sortes, Plato, and Ovid. If the first group embodies the lover's desire, the second one represents his excuse:

> I thoghte thanne how love is swete,
> Which hath so wise men reclamed,
> And was miself the lasse aschamed.   8.2720–22

"And thus," he tells us, "I lay in hope of grace" (8.2726). The old men pray to Venus for Amans's sake, and she asks Cupid, Amans reports, that he "thurgh his grace sende / Som confort, that I myhte amende" (8.2735–36). Even a few in the "yonge route" join in supporting this prayer, and the lovers – "most of hem that weren olde" (8.2756) – gather around Amans to see "what ende schal betyde / Upon the cure of my sotie" (8.2759–60).

The members of the gathered company engage in gentle "debat" over Amans's case: some argue that "for no riote / An old man scholde noght assote" (8.2765–66), but others claim "that the wylde loves rage / In mannes lif forberth non Age" (8.2773–74). These two opinions form the last of the poem's major *demandes*. At first it appears that the Latin glossator, presumably an

images, and what they reflect; at 8.2821 Gower has Venus give Amans a "wonder Mirour" in which he will see his natural likeness; on relevant background concerning sanctifying grace, see Heiko Oberman, *Forerunners of the Reformation: The Shape of Late Medieval Thought* (New York, 1966), pp. 123–36.

exemplar of wisdom, resolves it quietly by placing a "Nota" next to the second judgment. That decision is a curious one, however, for this is the reader of the text who is so concerned to side with Gower the *auctor* against the lover whom Gower feigns to be; here he appears to have shifted his allegiance to *Amans senex*. That gesture, whatever its intent, has the effect of presenting the debate as a legitimate *demande*: it raises the second opinion, with its premise that one cannot avoid love "Bot only if it be som seint, / Which god preserveth of his grace" (8.2778–79), to the level of the first one, the traditional and privileged notion that old age should represent *honestas* and chastity.

This conflict or *probleme* can only be resolved by external intervention, in this action by a Cupid who "wolde thanne yive / His grace" (8.2792–93). This action the lover did not seek, yet paradoxically asked for in his earlier petition, when he pleaded with Cupid either to give him his desired Salve or to heal him completely. The god, now taking the latter course, removes the "Dart brennende." The lover, presumably changed by this action, wakens, and the effects of that change become apparent after Venus applies an ointment to his wound, temples, and Reins, and gives him a "wonder Mirour" (8.2821) in which he is to behold himself.

In that mirror Amans sees himself "transformed," that is, as he really is, and his perception of his physical age carries with it the prospect of a greater *senectus*: a nature fulfilled, a *perfectio aetatis*. Amans now finds that his will "was tho to se nomore / Outwith, for ther was no plesance" (8.2832–33): the images that have nurtured his fantasy, including its setting of the "swote grene pleine," have disappeared, and he is able to draw into remembrance his "olde daies passed," making thereby a natural "liknesse of miselve / Unto the sondri Monthes twelve" (8.2837–38). In a passage of considerable power, he remarks on the resemblance between the periods of his life and the seasons:

> The Wynter wol no Somer knowe,
> The grene lef is overthrowe,
> The clothed erthe is thanne bare,
> Despuiled is the Somerfare.   8.2853–56

With that sight of himself as aged, Amans leaves his self-deception, the desire that seems but is not *kinde*, and returns to a life in which reason rejects "the sotie / Of thilke unwise fantasie" (8.2866–67). Now "mad sobre and hol ynowh" (8.2869), he can engage in an inverted catechism, where the proof of his "knowledge" is ignorance:

> Venus behield me than and lowh,
> And axeth, as it were in game,
> What love was. And I for schame
> Ne wiste what I scholde ansuere.   8.2870–72

Recognizing that he is "unbehovely" to serve in Venus' court, Amans asks to be excused from such service, receives absolution from Genius, and falls on his knees and receives from Venus beads *Por reposer*.

The sometime lover regrets, he now tells us, that "y hadde lore / My time" (8.2953–54), and yet, after the departure of Venus and the confessor,

> in my self y gan to smyle
> Thenkende uppon the bedis blake,
> And how they weren me betake,
> For that y schulde bidde and preie.   8.2958–61

This Gower, no longer suffering "debat" in himself, now goes "a softe pas," but to an entirely different destination than do the lovers pictured with Elde:

> Homward a softe pas y wente,
> Wher that with al myn hol entente
> Uppon the point that y am schryve
> I thenke bidde whil y live.   8.2967–70

Given the multiple senses of "game" in the *Confessio*, it is not surprising that the poem should now become a *ludus conscientiae*, a pastime of self-reflection, a searching out in conscience of whatever, hidden there, "might offend the eyes of divine majesty"; Pseudo-Vincent of Beauvais describes this exercise in terms drawn from Ecclus. 32:15:

> 'Be first to run home to thy house,' namely to the house of conscience,
> . . . 'And withdraw thyself,' that is, recall all the exterior senses to the
> innermost places of your heart, lest they wander idly.[26]

As Amans sees his "wittes straied," he "gan to clepe hem hom ayein" (8.2860–61), and Reason, hearing "That loves rage was aweie" (8.2863), returns to him "the rihte weie" (8.2864). The memory that Amans recovers "is not directed solely toward the past," but comprises "the entire width and depth of the mind which learns how to know itself and how to direct its will toward the right kind of love."[27] "John Gower" can now deal with time and "old age" in a much enlarged setting.

Cherniss complains that the resolution of the lover's problem "depends entirely upon the fact that Amans is old and so begs the question of what one is to do in Amans's situation if he is not old."[28] It is difficult to conceive of any literary text that might not be subjected to the same complaint: a character in a fiction must have features that are particular, historical, and contingent, and it is for that very reason that Gower cannot tell "every man his tale." In another sense, of course, the question of age is a universal. We ignore it, or questions regarding nature, time, and the course of life set for those "that duelle under the mone" (P.142), at our peril.

---

[26] Pseudo-Vincent of Beauvais, *Speculum morale* 3.8.4, col. 1361.
[27] Ladner, pp. 201–02, 201; Augustine, *De Trinitate* 14.11.14, PL 42:1048; *Confessiones* 13.5.6, ed. Skutella, pp. 331–32; *De Genesi ad litteram* 1.6, ed. Joseph Zycha, CSEL 28.1 (Prague, 1894): 10.
[28] Cherniss, p. 117.

Indeed, it is precisely the ignorance or rejection of such questions that has endangered not only Amans, but also the times about which Gower writes. A whole culture, he has suggested in the Prologue, seems to have forgotten its history and its very historicity. This concern also takes various forms elsewhere in the work. It is even presented metaphorically, for example, in the treatment of incest in Book 8, and not merely because that treatment involves an histori-cal reperception of the issue of *cognatio* and marriage: the analogy lies in the nearsightedness of the "regnes" described in the Prologue and the myopia of the incestuous, who only know the momentary gratification of taking what "comth next to honde."

Gower's linking of old age, history, and an awareness of one's place in an expanse of time is again enriched by tradition, including especially Augustine's treatment of old age as the sixth *aetas* of human life. Gerhard Ladner, in discussing that doctrine, introduces terms that also have a bearing on Gower's treatment of age, conversion, time, and confession. Generally, the Father char-acterizes this "age of man (old age) as a transition – later [he] will say reform – to that perfect form of man which was made in the image and likeness of God."[29] Ladner then introduces some of the relevant larger parallels developed by Augustine:

> To the ageing of individual man there corresponds his spiritual rene-wal, to the decline of the people of the Old Testament the coming of Christ, and above all to the creation of man on the last day of the six-day work his reform in the last age of world history.[30]

Gower presents these terms in various places in the confession: in Book 7, he celebrates man as "formed according to the image of God"; in his own short treatise *de vera religione* in Book 5, he shows that with the coming of Christ "our reformation becomes manifest, in newness of mind, according to the image of Him who created us."[31]

The teaching of Augustine centers on the distinction between "natural" ages specifically associated with the *vetus homo, et exterior, et terrenus,* and "spiritual" ages associated with the *novus homo, et interior, et coelestis.*[32] The old man is thus contrasted not with the young man, but with the new man, as in Col. 3:9–10: "Lie not one to another: stripping yourselves of the old man with his deeds, And putting on the new, him who is renewed in knowledge, accord-ing to the image of him that created him." In contrast to the old man, who "lives in the body and is bound by desires for temporal things," and whose old

---

[29] Ladner, p. 235; see Augustine, *De vera religione* 26.49, PL 34:143; idem, *Ennarationes in Psalmos* 92.1, CCSL 39:1291; idem, *In Iohannis Evangelium tractatus* 9.6, CCSL 36:93–94; also relevant is Ladner's discussion of the Pauline doctrine of reform, pp. 49–62.

[30] Ladner, p. 236.

[31] Augustine, *Contra Faustum Manichaeum* 12., ed. Joseph Zycha, CSEL 25.1 (Prague, 1891): 336; trans. Ladner, p. 236.

[32] Augustine, *De vera religione* 26.48, PL 34:143.

age "leads to death," the new man is reborn spiritually, and his old age is a "transformation into life eternal."[33] With "a total forgetfulness of temporal life" he passes into the perfect form that has been made in God's image. This is foreshadowed, of course, in the converted "John Gower," who has forgotten totally what venerean love is.

Although Gower does not enter into a discussion of the numerology so important to Augustine, he understands the rich correspondences evolved out of the distinction between *vetus homo* and *novus homo*. In relation to the history of the species as well as the individual lover, he also very powerfully conveys a sense of a world growing old, dying, a world in need of rebirth, of God's intervention. This has appeared in Book 5, for example, in his cyclical history of idolatries, in the decline of ancient religions and "the people of the Old Testament" before the birth of Christ, and in the subsequent return to idol-worship in "modern" instances.

An equally telling example of the world in decay has also appeared in the Prologue of the *Confessio*, in the history reflected in the statue of a man, the "wonder strange ymage" of Nebuchadnezzar's dream. A hint of the importance of that Old Testament episode for the *Confessio* is provided by the manuscripts; a good number of them contain only two illuminations, one of Amans kneeling before the priest, and another of Nebuchadnezzar asleep, with the image of a man, partitioned by colors representing the four metals, standing before his bed. Should a manuscript contain any illuminations at all, the picture of Amans is to be expected, but the one of Nebuchadnezzar and the statue gives the story a prominence that the text itself does not immediately seem to warrant. The picture is striking, especially in manuscripts such as British Library, MS Harley 3869, where it is spatially dominant: the figure of the king takes up the top third of the page (fol. 5r), and that of the human statue, the "wonder strange ymage," extends halfway down the right column.

This story is given this prominence on the page, indeed in the book, I think, because Gower wishes to convey something not merely about a specific *translatio imperii*, but about the history of the species in the type of man advancing through his ages. The "wonder strange ymage" undoubtedly reflects the wearing away, the progress of corruption with the passage of time, leading to "Thende of the world" (P.883): indeed, the image represents the world "That whilom was so magnefied, / And now is old and fieble and vil" (P.886–87). Gower obviously introduces the dream of the statue to remind the age of a history it has forgotten and to shake its misplaced confidence in itself: "whan men wene most upryht / To stonde," God in his might "schal hem overcaste" (P.655–57). For Daniel, the destruction of the "ymage" represents

33 Ibid., 26.48–49, PL 34:143–44, trans. John H. S. Burleigh, *On the True Religion*, in *Augustine: Earlier Writings*, The Library of Christian Classics, vol. 6 (London, 1953), pp. 248–49.

> of this world the laste,
> And thanne a newe schal beginne,
> Fro which a man schal nevere twinne;
> Or al to peine or al to pes
> That world schal lasten endeles.   P.658–62

The poet uses this analogy not only to reveal a threat to his times, however, but to frame his tale of Amans. The lover, as an aging man, mirrors the pattern of history figured in the statue; as a representation of man in his ages, he also embodies a traditional gloss on the story told in the book of Daniel.[34] The greater "wonder" of Amans is that he, in his own right, becomes a figure of this world; he becomes the "ymage." His story glosses Daniel's reading and "corrects" by its representation the category of the poet's judgment in the Prologue.

In the accounts of the ages of man and of Amans's age, the poet shows how one slips imperceptibly into a moral as well as natural status of being "old and fieble and vil." While in the Prologue the poet distinguishes empires by the metals of the statue, there is a curious sameness about the moral condition of those reigns. From the Golden Age, when the monarchy of "al the world in that partie / To Babiloyne was soubgit" (P.674–75), we pass to the "world of Selver" (P.688) when the Persians, coveting that entire Empire, put Babylon "under in subjeccioun / And tok it in possessioun" (P.683–84). This history of desire, subjection, and possession continues through the ages of Brass and Steel, where Greeks and Romans "here astat uplefte," and put those before them "under fote." The history conveys no real sense of the Golden Age – or of any other age – as a time apart in its moral rectitude.[35] Although, for Daniel, the gold betokens "A worthi world, a noble, a riche, / To which non after schal be liche" (P.633–34), subsequent worlds are simply "lasse worth." Subjection, desire, and possession, here manifested in all four ages, represent a post-lapsarian reality, and the distinction of ages in that sense becomes a matter of degree, not kind; it is a question of slippage.

The Golden Age, in this perceived "sameness" or likeness, thus comes "nexte to honde" and seems recoverable to those who "wene" they merit a world more "noble" and "riche." Analogously, through the greater part of the confession, Amans thinks of himself as standing "most upryht," as morally justified: the Golden Age or "Paradis" is deemed his, or at least not far out of reach, should justice be served. The Golden Age or projected "likeness" that he covets is, in a sense, the assumed "joie" of a youth he fails to accept he has lost.

But the tale of Amans also gives a turn to the history of ages outlined in the Prologue. The lover, at his end, anticipates a "newe" world precisely because he has come to recognize his history. The shocks in the debate of Book 8 force him

---

[34] See, for example, Pierre Bersuire, "Super Danielem," *Morale reductorium utriusque testamenti*, in *Opera omnia*, 6 vols. (Cologne, 1730), 2:169.
[35] See Anthony Farnham, "High Prosaic Seriousness," p. 170.

into accepting a separation of ages, duly reordered in human "psychological" time. Amans's discovery, a humbling, is that he is a creature of time, one who is spread out over seasons and "tydes."

Paradoxically, that awareness permits him to see himself as whole. After his conversion, he enters time as he had not done in the confession and thereby becomes a "Mirour of ensamplerie" between "the men and the godhiede" (P.496, 498). He has risen above his status as an "old man" – both *senex* and *vetus homo* – not only to see that status, but to glimpse his best nature and "image." Having so recompiled his life, he can ask for grace for England – "orat pro statu regni" – because he is free enough in his reformed nature to desire an enduring love and "joie" – a new world – for others as well as himself.

The new world Gower anticipates at the end of the work thus glosses Daniel's gloss. It is a figure of Creation itself, in a parallel that Augustine noted between the creation of man and the *aetas* of old age, wherein the former anticipates the latter, "the communal life of reformed man" brought about through Christ and the Church.[36] Thus Gower, in his prayer for England, invokes God in his power as Creator, who, through "his eternal providence," made the "large world forth with the hevene" (8.2972) and created man, setting him "Above alle erthli creature" (8.2978). The petition focuses on the work of recreation:

> His grace and mercy forto fonde
> Uppon my bare knes y preie,
> That he this lond in siker weie
> Wol sette uppon good governance.   8.2984–87

In this posture, the speaker transvaluates the kneeling imaged at the outset of the confession and captured in the other major illumination of the *Confessio* manuscripts. A "siker weie" for desire will emerge out of a reformed memory:

> For if men takyn remembrance
> What is to live in unite,
> Ther ys no staat in his degree
> That noughte to desire pes.   8.2988–91

This is the principle of communal life that Gower now seeks for the estates of the cleric, knight, man of law, merchant, laborer, and especially, since "stant it al in his power" (8.3062), the king. Peace, this book finally shows, depends on the law of nature "in lege et Evangelio," reason, and grace; it depends on a desire for "unite" that is present in the king who can "reule his owne astat" (8.3083) and wanting in the king who "takth his lust on every side" (8.3090); from the latter, a figure of *vetus homo*, God will "his grace caste aweie" (8.3092).

The old becomes new, in Gower's argument, at the point of entering time, of

---

36 Ladner, p. 238.

recognizing the uncertainty and precariousness of life in the "flesch." This is also a time of laying one's confession before God, and it forms the basis for Gower's final reflection in the poem, as he goes back over his entire project of undertaking "In englesch forto make a book / Which stant betwene ernest and game" (8.3107–09). His muse bids him, now that the book is finished,

> Fro this day forth to take reste,
> That y nomore of love make,
> Which many an herte hath overtake,
> And ovyrturnyd as the blynde
> Fro reson in to lawe of kynde
> Wher as the wisdom goth aweie
> And can nought se the ryhte weie
> How to governe his oghne estat. 8.3142–49

Amans has discovered and "John Gower" has regained "the ryhte weie" of this wisdom. The topos of governing one's "oghne estat" can never convey, however, the magnitude of the undertaking, or the joy of glimpsing its conclusion. Nor can it convey the fact that the process of discovery cannot end with the poem. The value of the confession, for "John Gower," is really lodged in the rereading, in entering the world of the shrift now that he has recovered his wits, in "reforming" its truths in structures that must, in temporal life, be ever-changing.

Gower has, through his fiction, been released from his status as *amans senex*, and yet, as he tells us at the very end, he is still an old man. He has written the *Confessio*

> So as siknesse it soffre wolde;
> And also for my daies olde,
> That y am feble and impotent,
> I wot nought how the world ys went. 8.3125–28

This conclusion is more than a topos: it is a confession of unsureness, of a *memoria labilis*, an unstable or slippery memory, and it thereby represents the Prologue's loose topic of the temporally "uncertein." Like Amans in relation to his beloved, the poet in relation to "my lordis alle" hopes to "stonden in here grace," but unlike Amans, he voices this desire "in myn age" and "the symplesse of my poverte." Under the governance of these lords he hopes "siker to abide" (8.3137), but also unlike Amans, he knows that true security can be achieved only "in thilke place / Wher resteth love and alle pes" (8.3170–71).

The aging of the lover and the aging of the poet together manifest the Augustinian point that "no one in this life can live as 'the new and heavenly man,' but must associate with the 'old man.' For he must begin there, and must so continue till death, though the old grows weaker and the new progresses."[37] Amans would like to think of himself as a "new and heavenly man," but he can

---

[37] Augustine, *On the True Religion*, 26.49–27.50, trans. Burleigh, p. 250; PL 34:144.

do so only through flawed images of "Paradis." This is exactly the problem that Cherniss introduces: Amans does not think he is in Amans's situation – that he is an old man.

By contrast, the reformed "John Gower," recognizing his "siknesse" and "daies olde," is able to glimpse the "rihte weie" to that place where "Oure joie mai ben endeles" (8.3172). Guided by doctrine and "feithe," he must repeatedly exercise his highest imaginative powers to internalize reform. Specifically, he must compile and recompile the elements of a "personal" and cultural past to discover a proper likeness of himself. The point of stressing Amans's old age, then, is not merely to call attention to what Venus thinks important: in more than a merely physical sense Amans has been one of those who "outward feignen youthe so / And ben withinne of pore assay" (8.2410–11). This entire exercise of confession has been directed to teaching him his capacity as an inner man; finally, to borrow words from the Apostle, it might lead him to rejoice that "though our outward man is corrupted, yet the inward man is renewed day by day" (2 Cor. 4:16).

Chapter Twenty

EPILOGUE

The problem set for Amans-"John Gower" with regard to memory and compiling a past is not unique in the tradition of late medieval court poetry. It appears in conventional form in Jean Froissart's Joli Buisson de Jonece, centrally a dream-vision in which the poet rediscovers his youth or Jonece.[1] The vision is framed on either side by scenes in which Froissart reflects on his past from the middle of his life. Knowing that he has lost his youth, he initially fears old age, in which "nothing is secure" (74), and in this melancholic state he doubts that he can continue to write. His thoughts, in the figure of "Philozophie," argue that his patrons expect and will continue to reward his verse, but he is overwhelmed by a sense of aging, of the passage of time: echoing biblical texts, he is upset that "Mes temps s'en fuit ensi q'uns ombres" (376), that his days have passed like a shadow, and he asks Philozophie to leave him alone so that he might reflect on his soul, repent the vanity of his life, and beseech God for mercy (385–90).

Philozophie seeks another palliative for him. She insists on the worth of Froissart's past endeavors as a poet, and urges him not to forsake his natural ability. Though he thinks he lacks a "nouviel" subject, he might find inspiration for a poem in a forgotten picture of the lady who, ten years earlier, had left him for another. Indeed, this portrait eventually inspires a "penser fresc et nouviel" (559) and the dream journey to the buisson; there Jonece becomes his companion-guide. In the pleasance of the dream, the narrator is startled not only to see his lady, but to see her unchanged; this, Jonece remarks, is a great thing about true love (2012), that to the lover, the beloved remains the same, unaffected by time. In this setting the poet also sees familiar allegorical figures such as Franchise and Plaisance, Dangier, and, as central to his dream-experience, Desir. His own ardor is rekindled as he engages once again in the conversation and various old and new games, dances, and songs of love, but nevertheless, he is not allowed to participate fully in these activities. When the members of the company he envisions finally engage in a contest of poetic skill,

---

[1] Jean Froissart, Le Joli Buisson de Jonece, ed. Anthime Fourrier (Geneva, 1975); for discussion, see Michelle A. Freeman, "Froissart's Le Joli Buisson de Jonece: A Farewell to Poetry?" in Machaut's World, ed. Cosman and Chandler, pp. 235–47; Peter F. Dembowski, Jean Froissart and His Meliador: Context, Craft, and Sense (Lexington, Ky., 1983), pp. 31–41.

he becomes their scribe, and when they depart to ask Love for his judgment, he wakens.

In this waking state, however, the poet experiences an even greater wonder; in what is now a winter scene, he comes to accept his distance from youth and the ardor it inspires. As he reviews once again the course of his life, he perceives the danger in carnal love and prays that in place of the flames of youthful desire, the grace of a "holy fire" be kindled in his heart. His prayer is a *lai*, a song to the Virgin, and it expresses a "nouviel sentement" (5195) distinct from that of the dream-vision. In it, the image of the *buisson* is transformed into the burning bush, paradoxically the "buisson sans flame" (5377) seen by Moses, commonly a figure of pure love in medieval tributes to the Virgin. Unlike the *buisson* of youth, which can fuel a ruinous passion, "li Buissons resplendissans" (5402) inspires a truly creative and pleasing love.

Gower describes a comparable growth of perception near the end of his *Mirour de l'Omme*, specifically as he shifts into a confessional mode, using the Biblical image of beam and mote to frame an inquiry into his past life. Admitting that he has formerly abandoned himself to *foldelit* and the writing of foolish love poems (27337–41), he promises to change, as guided by God's grace: "Ma conscience accuseray / Un autre chancon chanteray" (27246–47). This new song, which concludes the extant version of the poem, centrally includes a life of the Virgin and a hymn to her; poetically it displaces the earlier *fols ditz*, and, as a tribute to the purity of the Virgin's love, it signals the change of an affectus formerly ensnared in *foldelit*.[2]

When, in the *Confessio*, Gower leaves behind his earlier poetic efforts to write poetry in a new "Stile," he does so to an entirely different end. Because he is sick, perhaps even old, we might expect him to reject his *fols ditz* about love, but not his poems of "vertu moral." The latter are perfectly suited to his present time of life, to the study and reflection expected of a *senex*, a person who should have given up the sensual passion, folly, and rashness of "the budding-time of youth" for the sake of the wisdom and prudence that comes with "the harvest time of age."[3] Nevertheless, this harvest time, a time for gathering, perhaps even for *compilatio*, also requires leisure, which itself carries a risk to which Gower has apparently succumbed:

> The wise man rightly admonishes us that if we are to write words of wisdom we must have leisure; still we must be on our guard even against leisure itself. We must accordingly shun idleness, the mother of trifles, the step-mother of virtues.[4]

---

[2] On the different structures of conversion that Gower provides in this work, see my article, "The Cardinal Virtues and the Structure of John Gower's *Speculum Meditantis*," *Journal of Medieval and Renaissance Studies* 7 (1977): 113–48.
[3] Cicero *De senectute* 6.20, trans. Falconer, p. 29.
[4] Bernard of Clairvaux, *On Consideration* 2.13, trans. George Lewis (Oxford, 1908), p. 63; see Ecclus. 38:25: "The wisdom of a scribe cometh by his time of leisure: and he that is less in action, shall receive wisdom."

In this fiction, as author in his "daies olde," Gower has fallen snare to idleness and "pley," a dalliance. Genius perhaps says more than he knows at the end of the shrift when he promises, for the love of Amans, that he will now "unto the trouthe wende / . . . / And lete alle othre truffles be" (8.2060, 2062). For a poet, admittedly aged, to have devoted so much of his last major work to trifles seems especially unfitting if, as Genius testifies elsewhere, "Old age for the conseil serveth" (7.4137).

Old age should be a time for Gower to use his *honesta superior aetas*, as well as the status and authority he has gained as a poet, to natural advantage: "Surely old age, when crowned with public honours, enjoys an influence [*auctoritatem*] which is of more account than all the sensual pleasures of youth."[5] If it is the case that "The crown of old age is authority,"[6] however, Gower has boldly forsaken it – fictitiously – by casting himself in this role of an aged lover. Old age is a time when he might speak wisdom in his own distinctive style: "The style of speech that graces the old man is subdued and gentle, and very often the sedate and mild speaking of an eloquent old man wins itself a hearing."[7] In sum, various terms set forth by Cicero and others to describe *senectus* – prudence, a naturally "plain" style, a release from carnal desire, a time for leisure and study, for harvesting, a time to exercise one's *auctoritas* – all seem perfectly suited to what should come most naturally to this already moral poet.

Old Gower, in the *Confessio*, might well have followed a pattern set by Froissart, and even by a younger Gower. With a display of *ingenium*, however, the poet has reversed his career by casting himself as a lover in self-inflicted exile from the region of the very books he himself has written. His new "Stile" might have been a narrowly moral one, of course, if the author of the English text had been as clear about "feigning" as is the Latin glossator; in the fiction, however, the poet quickly settles into his role as Amans, falsely recovers his "youth," and relives a *foldelit* that he had formerly rejected. Of course this is not literally the case: it involves for Gower, as the marginal glossator knows, a rhetorical posturing; but it is a complete posturing whose "pleie" includes rather than excludes Gower in his role as *auctor*. Gower refuses to enter the story as a distinctly identifiable "confessional" author. He gives us no sense of "times" in the *Confessio* like those in Augustine's masterpiece, for example, where the Father can now see, as he formerly could not, "God present as a decisive force in the crucial junctures of life."[8] The English poem is not authorially "confessional," and that is one source of the impression that it lacks a secure center of meaning and a stability of moral style. The author of Ecclesiastes "was a sinner and a man of carnal desires," but Bonaventure can confidently argue that he wrote the book "when doing penance."[9] Gower gives us no hint,

---

5 Cicero, *De senectute* 17.61, trans. Falconer, pp. 74–75.
6 Ibid., 17.61, p. 73.
7 Ibid., 9.28, p. 37.
8 Heiko Oberman, "Forerunners," p. 128.
9 Bonaventure, *Commentarius in Ecclesiasten*, prooemium, q. 4, obj. 1 & rsp. 1, trans.

in the course of the shrift, that he, or Amans-"John Gower," is separated from the past of his narrative and is, in the present, actually repentant.

The poet's rejuvenation is not made a principal issue of the *Confessio*, and that is consistent with the absence of a distinction of times in the work. Unlike Froissart, who by the very invention of Jonece separates his older from his younger self, Gower conflates old age and youth without expressly acknowledging their difference. He does not think of himself as old, or even as middle-aged, as does the narrator of the *Joli Buisson*; he is presumably, until the end, a young man.

Froissart's self-consciousness about time, and about an older self, is evident not only in his re-creation of Jonece, but in his dream-perception of the lady. His amazement that the beloved he sees in the vision is unchanged from the *ymage* he possesses of her is based upon a realistic sense of time and difference. Gower's lover conveys no sense of change: the beloved is recalled from a past close at hand. This creates a clear impression, once we have finished reading, that this is because Amans has fallen in love late, as an aged man: neither he, nor his beloved, has a history extending over traditional periods of human life. In a special sense, then, the recreation of a youthful lover, or Gower's reluctance to make it appear categorically that his lover is old, makes the whole issue of memory a fabrication. Amans reinvents, recreates a non-existent youth through a fiction of being young.

Amans lives in this falsely imagined youthful past, but the real "past" he must recover is, paradoxically, his future, the age he will finally confess; in reality, he is feeble and old before he speaks to Genius. Not only because this work is a confession —where past images are recalled —but because Amans is so disoriented in his perception of time and his own history, the lady presented in Gower's own "joli buisson de jonece" is never separated, by time, from herself or her *ymage*. She is, for Amans, nothing more than her image; he does not see difference in her, and that is because he never sees change in himself. Indeed, rather than say that Amans before his conversion thinks of himself as young, we might more accurately say that he sees no age in himself. Unlike Froissart, in short, he is never conscious that in time he is a person who becomes different people, or who exists in different *personae*.

The "merveile" that Froissart experiences therefore becomes a very different kind of marvel in Gower's poem. In Venus's "wonder Mirour," Amans sees things as they are, not as he thought them to be; in that sense it offers no wonder, except to the lover who has previously forgotten who he is; it is, in effect, a mirror that does not enchant, but rather disenchants, calling Amans back to his status as "John Gower," to his existence in time, and to his different historical identities. The poet has captured, in this representation, a response to a thought voiced by Seneca:

Minnis and Scott, *Medieval Literary Theory*, pp. 232–33; S. *Bonaventurae opera omnia* (Quaracchi, 1882–1902), 6:8. See also Minnis, *Authorship*, pp. 103–106, 110–12, 189.

Nothing, Lucilius, is ours, except time. We were entrusted by nature with ownership of this single thing, so fleeting and slippery that anyone who will can oust us from possession.[10]

In recovering time, specifically at this time when "the mind should be entirely free for itself" and "should look backward in contemplation of itself,"[11] Gower has found the instrument of his renewal. Seeing himself as an old man *in lege naturae*, he can become a *homo renovatus*.

This event of recovering time underlies Gower's final transvaluation of *compilatio*. The point rests on an analogy which begins with the poet's tribute to books in the Prologue, but which might be reformulated according to terms laid out in the popular late medieval *Liber Pharetrae*:

At the earliest stage of my conversion, when for recreation of mind I would read the *auctoritates* of the saints and, in reading, would notice various corruptions, it pleased me to hasten back to the original source and, on account of its greater certitude, to gather it up mentally; afterward, I arranged what I knew so that in the same place things useful for meditation, preaching, or disputation could be found more easily.[12]

In the exercise either of compiling or of reading a *compilatio*, one returns to sources to gain greater certitude, storing and sorting whatever might prove useful. So in this work Gower returns to his genesis in multiple senses: to his love and its "querele," to "Paradis" and whatever has damaged his hope of attaining it, to his "tides" and his age and conversion. After his reform, Amans-"John Gower" will presumably be strong enough to see "varias corruptiones" in what he remembers of Genius's stories, as well as in his own earlier misreadings of his life; by mental re-creations, he will become strong enough to deal with "fleeting and slippery" time, to reorganize what he knows, to approximate the truth about himself and his culture. This, of course, is a recursive exercise, one that will be repeated in ever new *ordinationes*.

As a poet, Gower gathers stories and creates for them an order. As a narrator, he also gathers stories that he recollects from a "wonder hap" that has already occurred: he presumably knows the ending before he begins, and yet, though at the end he tells us he will reflect on the points of his shrift from the perspective of one who has forgotten what venerean love is, what he has forgotten as he narrates his experience is not venerean love, but his conversion. He thus goes through cycles of revision, a forgetting and remembering in which the mind is never fully present to itself. Yet, for all that, Gower seems to maintain that a mind so engaged – in creating "new" fictions within changing

---

[10] Seneca *Epistulae* 1.3, trans. Gummere, 1:5.

[11] Seneca, *Naturales quaestiones* 3. praef. 2, trans. Thomas H. Corcoran, Loeb (London and Cambridge, Mass., 1971), 1:201.

[12] *Liber Pharetrae*, praef., in *S. Bonaventurae opera omnia*, ed. A. C. Peltier (Paris, 1864–71), 7:3.

structures of conversion – is actually advancing toward wisdom. The sheer delight in hearing stories retold, in reading and writing *compilationes*, is part of becoming wise. Every time through the poem or the "life" it recounts, there will be a constant of Christian doctrine, and every time there will be a rewriting of structures for understanding that doctrine. Whatever in experience does not fit is, of course, the "uncertein"; for the time being only, it represents "the fortune of this worldes chance." Accepting contingency and such uncertainty is, however, the very starting-point of Gower's celebration of compilation; the structures, or figments, devised in response to these things prepare the mind for repeated conversions, and even more, for that status, which Gower perceives as conferred by grace, wherein the person and the culture are daily renewed.[13]

[13] For another medieval perspective on such renewal, see my article, "Poetic Invention and Chaucer's *Parlement of Foules*," *Modern Philology* 87 (1989): 13–35.

ABBREVIATIONS

AHDLMA	*Archives d'histoire doctrinale et littéraire du moyen âge.*
CCSL	*Corpus christianorum, series latina* (Turnhout, 1954–).
CSEL	*Corpus scriptorum ecclesiasticorum latinorum* (Vienna, 1866–).
EETS, os	Early English Text Society, original series.
EETS, es	Early English Text Society, extra series.
FC	Fathers of the Church.
Loeb	Loeb Classical Library.
PL	Migne, J.-P, ed. *Patrologiae cursus completus: series latina* (Paris, 1844–64).

BIBLIOGRAPHY

MANUSCRIPTS

Gower, John. *Confessio Amantis.*
    Cambridge, Cambridge University Library, MS Mm.2.21
    London, British Library, MS Harley 3869
    Oxford, Bodleian Library, MS Ashmole 35

Nicholas de Gorran. *Distinctiones.*
    Cambridge, Cambridge University Library, MS Gg.1.33
    Oxford, Bodleian Library, MS Bodley 427.

PRINTED SOURCES

Abelard, Peter. *Expositio in Epistolam S. Pauli ad Romanos.* PL 178:783–978.

———. *Peter Abelard's Ethics.* Ed. and trans. D. E. Luscombe. Oxford, 1971.

———. *Sic et non: A Critical Edition.* Ed. Blanche Boyer and Richard McKeon. Chicago, 1976–77.

Abrahams, Roger D. "The Literary Study of the Riddle." *Texas Studies in Language and Literature* 14 (1972): 177–97.

Accessus ad auctores; Bernard d'Utrecht; Conrad d'Hirsau, *Dialogus super auctores.* Ed. R. B. C. Huygens. Leiden, 1970.

Accursius. *In Institutiones.* Venice, 1499.

Aegidius Romanus. *Commentaria in rhetoricam Aristotelis.* Venice, 1515; rpt. Frankfurt am Main, 1968.

———. *De differentia rhetoricae, ethicae et politicae.* Ed. Gerardo Bruni. *New Scholasticism* 6 (1932): 1–18.

———. *De regimine principum.* Rome, 1607; rpt. Aalen, 1967.

Alan of Lille. *De planctu Naturae.* PL 210:429–82. Trans. James J. Sheridan. *The Plaint of Nature.* Toronto, 1980.

———. *Liber in distinctionibus dictionum theologicalium.* PL 210:685–1012.

———. *Liber sententiarum ac dictorum memorabilium.* PL 210:229–64.

———. *Summa de arte praedicatoria.* PL 210:109–98. Trans. Gillian R. Evans. *The Art of Preaching.* Kalamazoo, Mich., 1981.

Albericus de Rosate. *Vocabularius utriusque juris.* Paris, 1525.

Albertanus of Brescia. *Liber de amore et dilectione Dei & proximi.* Coni, 1507.

Alford, John A. "The Role of Quotations in *Piers Plowman.*" *Speculum* 52 (1977): 80–99.

Allen, Judson Boyce. "Langland's Reading and Writing: *Detractor* and the Pardon Passus." *Speculum* 59 (1984): 342–62.

———. *The Ethical Poetic of the Later Middle Ages: A Decorum of Convenient Distinction.* Toronto, 1982.

Allers, Rudolf. "Microcosmus from Anaximandros to Paracelsus." *Traditio* 2 (1944): 319–407.

Ambrose. *De officiis ministrorum*. PL 16:25–194.

André, Jean-Marie. *L'Otium dans la vie morale et intellectuelle romaine des origines à l'époque augustéenne*. Publications de la Faculté des Lettres et Sciences Humaines de Paris, Série "Recherches," vol. 30. Paris, 1966.

———. *Recherches sur l'otium romain*. Annales Littéraires de l'Université de Basançon, vol. 52. Paris, 1962.

Andreas Capellanus. *De amore*. Ed. and trans. P. G. Walsh. *On Love*. London, 1982.

Angelus, or *Allegoriae in universam sacram scripturam*. PL 112:849–1088.

Anselm of Laon. *Anselms von Laon systematische Sentenzen*. Ed. F. Bliemetzrieder. Münster, 1919.

Apuleius. *Liber de deo Socratis*. In *Apulei Platonici Madaurensis de philosophia libri*, ed. Paul Thomas. Leipzig, 1908. Trans. anon. *The God of Socrates*. In *The Works of Apuleius*. London, 1889.

Aquinas, Thomas. *De regno, ad regem Cypri*. Trans. Gerald B. Phelan, rev. I. Th. Eschmann. *On Kingship, to the King of Cyprus*. Toronto, 1949.

———. *In Aristotelis libros . . . posteriorum analyticorum expositio*. Ed. Raymund M. Spiazzi. 2d ed. Turin, 1964. Trans. F. R. Larcher. *Commentary on the Posterior Analytics of Aristotle*. Albany, N.Y., 1970.

———. *In Aristotelis libros de sensu et sensata de memoria et reminiscentia commentarium*. Ed. Raymund M. Spiazzi. 3d ed. Turin, 1973.

———. *In decem libros ethicorum Aristotelis ad Nicomachum expositio*. Ed. Raymund M. Spiazzi. 3d ed. Turin, 1964.

———. *In duodecim libros metaphysicorum Aristotelis expositio*. Ed. M. R. Cathala, rev. Raymund M. Spiazzi. Turin, 1971. Trans. John P. Rowan. *Commentary on the Metaphysics of Aristotle*. 2 vols. Chicago, 1961.

———. *Liber de veritate catholicae fidei contra errores infidelium seu "Summa contra gentiles."* Ed. L. C. Pera, P. Marc, and P. Caramello. 2 vols. Turin, 1961. Trans. Vernon J. Bourke. Notre Dame, Ind., 1975.

———. *Opera omnia*. 25 vols. Parmae, 1852–73; rpt. New York, 1950.

———. *Summa theologiae*. Blackfriars ed. and trans. 60 vols. London and New York, 1964–81.

Arderne, John. *Treatises of Fistula in Ano*. Ed. D'Arcy Power, EETS, os 139. London, 1910.

Aristotle. *The Basic Works of Aristotle*. Ed. Richard McKeon. New York, 1941.

Augustine. *Confessionum libri XIII*. Ed. Martin Skutella (1934), rev. H. Juergens and W. Schaub. Stuttgart, 1969. Trans. Vernon J. Bourke. *Confessions*. FC 21. Washington, D.C., 1953.

———. *Contra Faustum Manichaeum*. Ed. Joseph Zycha. CSEL 25.1. Prague, 1891.

———. *De bono conjugali*. PL 40:973–96. Trans. Charles T. Wilcox. *The Good of Marriage*. In *Treatises on Marriage and Other Subjects*. FC 27:9–51. Washington, D.C., 1955.

————. *De civitate Dei*. Ed. B Dombart. Leipzig, 1905–09. Trans. Marcus Dods. *The City of God*. New York, 1950.

————. *De diversis quaestionibus octoginta tribus*. Ed. PL 40:11–100. Trans. David L. Mosher. *Eighty-Three Different Questions*. FC 70. Washington, D.C., 1982.

————. *De doctrina christiana*. Ed. William M. Green. CSEL 80. Vienna, 1963. Trans. D. W. Robertson, Jr. *On Christian Doctrine*. New York, 1958.

————. *De Genesi ad litteram*. Ed. Joseph Zycha, CSEL 28.1. Prague, 1894.

————. *De libero arbitrio*. PL 32:1219–1310.

————. *De moribus ecclesiae*. PL 32:1309–44.

————. *De musica*. PL 32:1081–1194. Trans. Robert Catesby Taliaferro. *On Music*. FC 4:169–379. Washington, D. C., 1947.

————. *De ordine*. PL 32:977–1020. Trans. Robert P. Russell. *Divine Providence and the Problem of Evil*. FC 5. New York, 1948.

————. *De sermone Domini in monte*. PL 34:1229–1308. Trans. Denis J. Kavanagh. *Commentary on the Lord's Sermon on the Mount*. FC 11. Washington, D.C., 1951.

————. *De Trinitate*. PL 42:819–1098. Trans. Stephen McKenna. *The Trinity*. FC 45. Washington, D.C., 1963.

————. *De vera religione*. PL 34:121–72. Trans. John H. S. Burleigh. *On the True Religion*. In *Augustine: Earlier Writings*, pp. 225–83. Library of Christian Classics, vol. 6. London, 1953.

————. *Ennarationes in psalmos LI–C*. Ed. Eligius Dekkers and Jean Fraipont. CCSL 39. Turnhout, 1956.

————. *In Iohannis Evangelium tractatus CXXIV*. Ed. Radbodus Willems. CCSL 36. Turnhout, 1954.

Azo. *Summa institutionum*. Ed. F. W. Maitland. *Select Papers from the Works of Bracton and Azo*. Selden Society, 8. London, 1895.

Bacon, Roger. *Operis maioris pars septima seu moralis philosophia*. Ed. Eugenio Massa. Zurich, 1953.

Baker, Denise N. "The Priesthood of Genius: A Study of the Medieval Tradition." *Speculum* 50 (1976): 277–91.

Balbus, John. *Catholicon*. Rouen, 1511.

[John Damascene.] *Barlaam and Ioasaph*. Trans. G. R. Woodward and H. Mattingly. Loeb. London, 1967.

————. *Vita sanctorum Barlaam eremitae et Josaphat Indiae regis*. PL 73:443–604.

Bartholomaeus Anglicus. *De proprietatibus rerum*. Trans. John Trevisa. *On the Properties of Things*. Ed. M. C. Seymour et al. 2 vols. Oxford, 1975.

Bazelaire, L. de. "Connaissance de soi." *Dictionnaire de spiritualité*, fasc. 13 (Paris, 1950): 1511–43.

Bede. *In Matthaei Evangelium expositio*. PL 92:9–132.

————. *In Primam Epistolam S. Joannis*. PL 93:85–120.

Beidler, Peter, ed. *John Gower's Literary Transformations in the Confessio Amantis: Original Articles and Translations*. Washington, D.C., 1982.

————. "Diabolical Treachery in the Tale of Nectanabus." In *Gower's Literary Transformations*, ed. Beidler (supra), pp. 83–90.

Bennett, J. A. W. "Gower's 'Honeste Love.'" In *Patterns of Love and Courtesy*, ed. John Lawlor, pp. 107–21. London, 1966.

————. *Middle English Literature*. Ed. and completed by Douglas Gray. Oxford, 1986.

————. *The Parlement of Foules: An Interpretation*. Oxford, 1957.

Benson, C. David. "Incest and Moral Poetry in Gower's *Confessio Amantis*." *Chaucer Review* 19 (1984): 100–09.

Benton, John F. "Collaborative Approaches to Fantasy and Reality in the Literature of Champagne." In *Court and Poet*, ed. Burgess (infra), pp. 43–57.

Bernard of Clairvaux. *On the Song of Songs*. Trans. Killian Walsh (vol. 2); Irene Edmonds (vol. 4). Cistercian Fathers Series, 7, 40. Kalamazoo, Mich., 1976, 1980.

————. *On Consideration*. Trans. George Lewis. Oxford, 1908.

Bernardus Silvestris. *Cosmographia*. Ed. Peter Dronke. Leiden, 1978. Trans. Winthrop Wetherbee. *The Cosmographia of Berardus Silvestris*. New York, 1973.

Bersuire, Pierre. *Dictionarium, seu Repertorium morale*. 3 vols. Lyons, 1516–17.

————. *Opera omnia*. 6 vols. Cologne, 1730–31.

————. *Reductorium morale, liber XV: Ovidius moralizatus, cap. ii–xv, naar de Parijse druk van 1509*. Transcribed by D. Van Nes. Werkmateriaal-2. Utrecht, 1962.

————. *Reductorium morale, liber XV: Ovidius moralizatus, cap. i: De formis figurisque deorum, textus e codice Brux. Reg. 863–9 critice editus*. Ed. J. Engels. Werkmateriaal-3. Utrecht, 1966.

Bertola, E. "Il Socratismo Christiano nel XII secolo." *Rivista di Filosofia Neo-Scholastica* 51 (1959): 252–64.

Biblia sacra cum glossa ordinaria et postilla Nicolai Lyrani. 6 vols. Antwerp, 1634.

Biblia vulgata. Douay-Rheims translation.

Bloomfield, Morton. *Piers Plowman as a Fourteenth-Century Apocalypse*. New Brunswick, N.J., 1961.

Boccaccio, Giovanni. *Decameron*. Trans. John Payne, rev. Charles S. Singleton. 3 vols. Berkeley and Los Angeles, 1982.

————. *Il Filostrato*. Ed. Vincenzo Pernicone. Trans. Robert P. apRoberts and Anna Bruni Seldis. New York, 1986.

Boethius. *Consolation of Philosophy*. Trans. Richard Green. Indianapolis, 1962.

Bonaventure. *S. Bonaventurae opera omnia*. 11 vols. Quaracchi, 1882–1902.

————. *S. Bonaventurae opera omnia*. Ed. A. C. Peltier. 15 vols. Paris, 1864–71.

Born, Lester K. "The Perfect Prince: A Study in the Thirteenth- and Fourteenth-century Ideals." *Speculum* 3 (1928): 470–504.

Boullaye, Henry Pinard de la. "Conversion." *Dictionnaire de spiritualité*, fasc. 12 (Paris, 1949): 2224–65.

Bouyer, Louis. *The Meaning of the Monastic Life*. London, 1955.

Brito, William. *Summa Britonis sive Guillelmi Britonis expositiones vocabularum Biblie*. Ed. Lloyd W. Daly and Bernardine A. Daly. Thesaurus mundi, 15–16. Padua, 1975.

Bromyard, John. *Summa praedicantium*. 2 vols. Antwerp, 1614.

Brownlee, Kevin. *Poetic Identity in Guillaume de Machaut*. Madison, Wis. 1984.

Bryan, W. F., and Germaine Dempster, eds. *Sources and Analogues of Chaucer's Canterbury Tales*. Chicago, 1941.

Burgess, Glyn S., ed. *Court and Poet: Selected Proceedings of the Third Congress of the International Courtly Literature Society (Liverpool 1980)*. ARCA Classical and Medieval Texts, Papers, and Monographs 5. Liverpool, 1981.

Burnley, J. D. *Chaucer's Language and the Philosophers' Tradition*. Cambridge, 1979.

Burrow, J. A. "The Portrayal of Amans in 'Confessio Amantis.'" In *Gower's Confessio: Responses*, ed. Minnis (infra), pp. 5–24.

———. *Ricardian Poetry: Chaucer, Gower, Langland, and the Gawain Poet*. London, 1971.

———. *The Ages of Man: A Study in Medieval Writing and Thought*. Oxford, 1986.

Callahan, E. R., C. Williams, and G. F. Kirwin. "Conversion." *New Catholic Encyclopedia*, 4 (Washington, D.C., 1967): 286–92.

Censorinus. *De die natali liber*. Ed. Otto Jahn. 1845; rpt. Amsterdam, 1964.

Chalcidius. *Timaeus a Calcidio translatus commentarioque instructus*. Ed. J. H. Waszink. Corpus Platonicum Medii Aevi: Plato Latinus IV. 2d ed. London, 1975.

Chartier, Alain. *The Curial Made by Maystere Alain Charretier*. Trans. William Caxton, ed. Frederick J. Furnival. EETS, es 54. London, 1888.

Chaucer, Geoffrey. *The Riverside Chaucer*. Ed. Larry D. Benson et al. 3d ed. Boston, 1987.

Chenu, M.-D. "Auctor, actor, autor." *Archivum latinitatis medii aevi (Bulletin du Cange)* 3 (1927): 81–86.

———. *Toward Understanding Saint Thomas*. Trans. A.-M. Landry and D. Hughes. Chicago, 1964.

———. "*Imaginatio*: Note de lexicographie philosophique médiévale." *Miscellanea Giovanni Mercati II. Studi e Testi* 122 (1946): 593–602.

Cherniss, Michael D. *Boethian Apocalypse: Studies in Middle English Vision Poetry*. Norman, Okla., 1987.

Childs, Herbert Ellsworth, *A Study of the Unique Middle English Translation of the De regimine principum of Aegidius Romanus (MS. Digby 233)*. Ph.D. diss., University of Washington, 1932.

Christine de Pisan. *The Middle English Translation of Christine de Pisan's Livre du corps de policie*. Ed. Diane Bornstein. Middle English Texts, 7. Heidelberg, 1977.

Cicero. *De inventione, De optimo genere oratorum, Topica*. Trans. H. M. Hubbell. Loeb. London and Cambridge, Mass., 1961.

————. *De partitione oratoria*. Trans. H. Rackham. Loeb. London and Cambridge, Mass., 1960.

————. *De senectute, De amicitia, De divinatione*. Trans. William Armistead Falconer. Loeb. London and New York, 1927.

Cinus of Pistoia. *In Digesti Veteris libros commentaria*. Frankfurt am Main, 1578.

Congar, Y. M.-J. "The Idea of Conversion." *Thought* 32 (1958): 5–20.

Conrad of Hirsau. *Dialogus super auctores*. Ed. R. B. C. Huygens. Leiden, 1970.

Cortese, E. *La norma giuridica*. 2 vols. Milan, 1962.

Cosman, Madeleine Pelner, and Bruce Chandler, eds. *Machaut's World: Science and Art in the Fourteenth Century*. Annals of the New York Academy of Sciences, vol. 314. New York, 1978.

Courcelle, Pierre. " 'Nosce teipsum' du bas-empire au haut moyen âge: l'heritage profane et les developpements chrétiens." *Il Passagio dall' Antichita al Medioevo in Occidente*. Settimane di Studio del Centro Italiano sull' Alto Medioevo, 9 (Spoleto, 1962): 263–95.

————. "Répertoire des textes relatifs à la 'région de dissemblance' jusqu'au XIVe siècle." *AHDLMA* 24 (1957): 24–33.

————. "Témoins nouveaux de la 'région de la dissemblance.' " *Bibliothèque de l'École des Chartres* 118 (1960): 20–36.

————. "Tradition neo-platonicienne et traditions chrétiennes de la 'région de dissemblance' (Platon, *Politique*, 273d)." *AHDLMA* 24 (1957): 5–23.

Curtius, Ernst Robert. *European Literature and the Latin Middle Ages*. Trans. Willard R. Trask. London, 1948.

Daly, Lloyd W., and Betty A. Daly. "Some Techniques in Medieval Latin Lexicography." *Speculum* 39 (1964): 229–39.

Dante Alighieri. *Convivio*. Trans. Katherine Hillard. *The Banquet (Il Convito) of Dante Alighieri*. London, 1889.

————. *Le Opere di Dante, Testo Critico della Societa Dantesca Italiana*. Ed. M. Barbi et al. 2d ed. Florence, 1960.

————. *The Divine Comedy*. Ed. and trans. Charles S. Singleton. 3 vols., 6 parts. Princeton, 1970–75.

Dembowski, Peter F. *Jean Froissart and His Meliador: Context, Craft, and Sense*. Lexington, Ky., 1983.

Dickey, Mary. "Some Commentaries on the *De inventione* and *Ad Herennium* of the Eleventh and Early Twelfth Centuries." *Medieval and Renaissance Studies* 6 (1968): 1–41.

Dirksen, A. H. *The New Testament Concept of Metanoia*. Ph.D. diss., Catholic University of America, 1932.

Dove, Mary. *The Perfect Age of Man's Life*. Cambridge, 1986.

Doyle, A. I. "English Books In and Out of Court from Edward III to Henry VII." In *English Court Culture*, ed. Scattergood (infra) and Sherborne, pp. 163–81.

————, and M. B. Parkes, "The Production of Copies of the *Canterbury Tales* and the *Confessio Amantis* in the Early Fifteenth Century." In *Medieval*

Scribes, Manuscripts, & Libraries: Essays Presented to N. R. Ker, ed. M. B. Parkes and A. G. Watson, pp. 163–210. London, 1978.

Dumeige, Gervais. "Dissemblance." *Dictionnaire de spiritualité*, fasc. 3 (Paris, 1957): 1330–46.

Economou, George. "The Character *Genius* in Alain de Lille, Jean de Meun, and John Gower." *Chaucer Review* 4 (1970): 203–10;

Faral, Edmond. *Les Arts poétiques du XIIe et du XIIIe siècle* (Paris, 1924; rpt. 1962).

Farnham, Anthony E. "The Art of High Prosaic Seriousness: John Gower as Didactic Raconteur." In *The Learned and the Lewed: Studies in Chaucer and Medieval Literature*, ed. Larry D. Benson, pp. 161–73. Harvard English Studies 5. Cambridge, Mass., 1974.

Fisher, John H. *John Gower: Moral Philosopher and Friend of Chaucer*. New York, 1964.

Fison, Peter. "The Poet in John Gower." *Essays in Criticism* 8 (1958): 16–26.

Fleming, John V. *The Roman de la Rose: A Study in Allegory and Iconography*. Princeton, 1969.

Freeman, Michelle A. "Froissart's *Le Joli Buisson de Jonece*: A Farewell to Poetry?" In *Machaut's World*, ed. Cosman (supra) and Chandler, pp. 235–47.

Freyhan, R. "The Evolution of the *Caritas* Figure in the Thirteenth and Fourteenth Centuries." *Journal of the Warburg and Courtauld Institutes* 11 (1948): 68–86.

Froissart, Jean. *Le Joli Buisson de Jonece*. Ed. Anthime Fourrier. Geneva, 1975.

———. *Le Paradis d'Amour*. Ed. Peter F. Dembowski. Geneva, 1986.

———. *Oeuvres de Froissart: Poésies*. Ed. Auguste Scheler. 3 vols. Brussels, 1870–72.

———. *The Chronicle of Froissart*. Trans. Sir John Bourchier, Lord Berners. Ed. William Paton Ker. 6 vols. London, 1901–03.

Gallacher, Patrick J. *Love, the Word, and Mercury: A Reading of John Gower's Confessio Amantis*. Albuquerque, N. Mex., 1975.

Garner of St. Victor. *Gregorianum*. PL 193:23–462.

Gauvard, Claude. "Portrait du prince d'après l'oeuvre de Guillaume de Machaut: Étude sur les idées politiques du poète." In *Guillaume de Machaut: poète et compositeur*, Actes et colloques no. 23, Université de Reims (Paris, 1982): 23–39.

Ghisalberti, Fausto. "Giovanni del Virgilio espositore della *Metamorfosi*," *Il Giornale Dantesco* 34, n.s. 4 (1933 for 1931): 1–110.

Gilbert, Allan. "Notes on the Influence of the *Secretum Secretorum*," *Speculum* 2 (1928): 84–98.

Gilson, Etienne. "Regio dissimilitudinis de Platon à Saint Bernard." *Mediaeval Studies* 9 (1947): 103–30.

———. *History of Christian Philosophy in the Middle Ages*. New York, 1955.

———. *The Spirit of Mediaeval Philosophy*. Trans. A. H. C. Downes. New York, 1940.

Giuliani, Alessandro. "L'Élément 'juridique' dans la logique médiévale." In *La*

Théorie de l'argumentation: perspectives et applications, ed. Ch. Perelman, pp. 540–70. Louvain, 1963.

Gnilka, Christian. *Aetas Spiritalis: Die Uberwindung der natürlichen Altersstufen als Ideal frühchristlichen Lebens*. Bonn, 1972.

Godfrey of St. Victor. *Microcosmus*. Ed. Philippe Delhaye. *Le Microcosmos de Godefrey de Saint Victor*. Vol. 1. *Étude théologique*. Vol. 2. *Texte*. Lille, 1951.

Godfrey of Viterbo. *Pantheon, sive universitatis libri, qui chronici appellantur, XX.* Basle, 1559.

Gombrich, E. H. *Art and Illusion: A Study in the Psychology of Pictorial Representation*. 4th ed. London, 1972.

Gower, John. *The Complete Works of John Gower*. Ed. G. C. Macaulay. 4 vols. Oxford, 1899–1902.

———. *The English Works of John Gower*. Ed. G. C. Macaulay. EETS, es 81–82. Oxford, 1900–01.

Gratian. *Concordia discordantium canonum*. Ed. A. Friedberg. 2d ed. Leipzig, 1879.

Green, Richard Firth. "King Richard II's Books Revisited." *The Library*, 5th ser., 31 (1976): 235–39.

———. "The *Familia Regis* and the *Familia Cupidinis*." In *English Court Culture*, ed. Scattergood (infra) and Sherborne, pp. 87–108.

Gregory the Great. *Homiliae XL in Evangelia*. PL 76:1075–1312.

Grennen, Joseph E. "Chaucer's Man of Law and the Constancy of Justice." *Journal of English and Germanic Philology* 84 (1985): 498–514.

Guinizelli, Guido. *The Poetry of Guido Guinizelli*. Ed. and trans. Robert Edwards. New York, 1987.

Hamilton, George L. "Some Sources of the Seventh Book of Gower's *Confessio Amantis*." *Modern Philology* 9 (1911–12): 323–46.

Hayes, Zachary. *The General Doctrine of Creation in the Thirteenth Century, with Special Emphasis on Matthew of Aquasparta*. Munich, 1964.

Helinand de Froidmont. *De bono regimine principis*. PL 212:735–46.

Hieremias de Montagnone. *Epytoma sapientie* or *Compendium moralium notabilium*. Venice, 1505.

Historia Apollonii regis Tyri. Ed. G. A. A. Kortekaas, Mediaevalia Groningana, fasc. 3. Groningen, 1984. Trans. Paul Turner. *Apollonius of Tyre*. London, 1956.

Holkot, Robert. *In librum Sapientiae regis Salomonis praelectiones CCXIII*. Basle, 1586.

———. *Super librum Ecclesiastici*. Venice, 1509.

Honorius of Autun. *De animae exsilio et patria*. PL 172:1241–46.

———. *Speculum ecclesie*. PL 172:807–1108.

Hugh of St. Cher. *Opera omnia in universum Vetus et Novum Testamentum*. 8 vols. Cologne, 1621.

Hugh of St. Victor. *De sacramentis*. PL 176:173–618. Trans. Roy J. Deferrari. *On the Sacraments of the Christian Faith*. Cambridge, Mass., 1951.

———. *Didascalicon de studio legendi: A Critical Text*. Ed. Charles Henry

Buttimer. Ph.D. diss., Catholic University of America, 1939. Trans. Jerome Taylor. *The Didascalicon of Hugh of St. Victor.* New York, 1961.

———. *Epitome Dindimi in philosophiam.* In *Hugonis de Sancto Victore opera propaedeutica.* Ed. Roger Baron. Notre Dame, 1966.

Hugh Ripelin of Strassburg. *Compendium theologicae veritatis.* In *Alberti Magni opera omnia,* ed. A. Borgnet, 34:1–306. Paris, 1895.

Isidore of Seville. *Etymologiae.* Ed. W. M. Lindsay. 2 vols. Oxford, 1911.

Jacobus de Cessolis. *Liber de ludo scaccorum.* Trans. William Caxton. Ca. 1483; rpt. London, 1976.

Jacobus de Voragine. *Legenda aurea.* Ed. Th. Graesse. 3d ed. Breslau, 1890; rpt. Osnabrück, 1969.

Javelet, Robert. *Image et ressemblance au douzième siècle de Saint Anselme à Alain de Lille.* 2 vols. Paris, 1967.

Jeauneau, Edouard. "L'usage de la notion d'*integumentum* à travers les gloses de Guillaume de Conches." *AHDLMA* 32 (1957): 35–100.

Johannes Faber. *In Institutiones commentarii.* Lyon, 1557; rpt. Frankfurt am Main, 1969.

John Chrysostom. *Homiliae in Matthaeum.* In *Patrologia cursus completus, series graeca,* ed. J. P. Migne (Paris, 1857–66), 57, 58.

John of la Rochelle. *Summa fratris Alexandri,* vol. 4. Quaracchi, 1948.

John of Salisbury. *Metalogicon.* Ed. Clemens C. I. Webb. Oxford, 1929. Trans. Daniel D. McGarry. *The Metalogicon of John of Salisbury.* Berkeley and Los Angeles, Cal., 1962.

———. *Policratici siue De nugis curialium et vestigiis philosophorum.* Ed. Clemens C.I. Webb. 2 vols. Oxford, 1909. Trans. Joseph B. Pike. *Frivolities of Courtiers and Footprints of Philosophers: A Translation of Books I, II, and III, and selections from Books VII and VIII of the Policraticus of John of Salisbury.* Minneapolis, 1938.

John of Viterbo. *Liber de regimine civitatum.* Ed. Caietano Salvemini. Bibliotheca Iuridica Medii Aevi, 3. Bologna, 1901.

John of Wales. *Communiloquium.* Strasbourg, 1518.

Jordan, Robert. "Time and Contingency in St. Augustine." In *Augustine: A Collection of Critical Essays,* ed. R. A. Markus, pp. 260–62. Garden City, N.Y., 1972.

Josephus. *The Antiquities of the Jews.* In *The Works of Flavius Josephus,* trans. William Whiston, pp. 23–442. London, n.d.

Julius Valerius. "The Birth of Alexander." Trans. Edna S. deAngeli. In *Gower's Literary Transformations,* ed. Beidler (supra), pp. 119–41.

———. *Res gestae Alexandri Macedonis.* Ed. Bernard Kuebler. Leipzig, 1888.

Justinian. *Institutiones.* Ed. P. Krueger. Berlin, 1872.

Karnein, Alfred. "*Amor est passio* – A Definition of Courtly Love." In *Court and Poet,* ed. Burgess (supra), pp. 215–21.

Kelly, Douglas. *Medieval Imagination: Rhetoric and the Poetry of Courtly Love.* Madison, Wis., 1978.

Kelly, Henry Ansgar. *Love and Marriage in the Age of Chaucer*. Ithaca, N.Y., 1975.

Kilwardby, Robert. *De ortu scientiarum*. Ed. Albert G. Judy. Auctores Britannici Medii Aevi, vol. 4. Toronto, 1976.

Köhler, Erich. "Lea, Matelda und Oiseuse." *Zeitschrift für romanische Philologie* 78 (1962): 464–69.

Kolve, V. A. *Chaucer and the Imagery of Narrative: The First Five Canterbury Tales*. Stanford, Cal., 1984.

Ladner, Gerhart B. *The Idea of Reform: Its Impact on Christian Thought and Action in the Age of the Fathers*. Rev. ed. New York, 1967.

Langland, William. *Piers Plowman: The B Version. Will's Visions of Piers Plowman, Do-Well, Do-Better, and Do-Best*. Ed. George Kane and E. Talbot Donaldson. Rev. ed. London and Berkeley, Cal., 1988.

———. *The Vision of William concerning Piers the Plowman, in Three Parallel Texts*. Ed. W. W. Skeat. 2 vols. Oxford, 1886, rpt. 1968.

Latini, Brunetto. *Li Livres dou Tresor*. Ed. Francis J. Carmody. University of California Publications in Modern Philology, vol. 22. Berkeley and Los Angeles, Cal., 1948.

Leclercq, Jean. *Otia monastica: Études sur la vocabulaire de la contemplation au moyen âge*. Studia Anselmiana, fasc. 51. Rome, 1963.

———. *The Love of Learning and the Desire for God: A Study of Monastic Culture*. Trans. Catherine Misrahi. New York, 1960.

Lefevre, Jean. *La Vielle, ou les dernières amours d'Ovide*. Ed. Hippolyte Cocheris. Paris, 1861.

Lerner, Ralph, and Muhsin Mahdi, eds. *Medieval Political Philosophy: A Sourcebook*. New York, 1963.

Levy, Bernard S. "*Gentilesse* in Chaucer's Clerk's and Merchant's Tales." *Chaucer Review* 11 (1977):306–18.

———. "The Wife of Bath's *Queynte Fantasye*." *Chaucer Review* 4 (1969):106–22.

Lewis, C. S. *Allegory of Love: A Study in Medieval Tradition*. London, 1936.

Liber Pharetrae. In *S. Bonaventurae opera omnia*, ed. A. C. Peltier, 7:3–231. Paris, 1866.

Little, Lester K. "Pride Goes Before Avarice: Social Change and the Vices in Latin Christendom." *American Historical Review*, 76 (1971): 16–49.

Lombard, Peter. *In Epistolam ad Romanos*. PL 191:1301–1534.

Lorris, Guillaume de, and Jean de Meun. *Le Roman de la rose*. Ed. Félix Lecoy. 3 vols. Classiques français du moyen âge. Paris, 1970–1974. Trans. Charles Dahlberg. *The Romance of the Rose*. Princeton, 1971.

Lottin, Odon. *Le droit naturel chez Saint Thomas d'Aquin et ses prédécesseurs*. 2d ed. Bruges, 1931.

Lusignan, Serge. *Preface au 'Speculum Maius' de Vincent de Beauvais: réfraction et diffraction*. Cahiers d'Études Médiévales, vol. 5. Montreal, 1979.

Lynch, Kathryn L. *The High Medieval Dream Vision: Poetry, Philosophy, and Literary Form*. Stanford, 1988.

Machaut, Guillaume de. *Le Jugement dou Roy de Behaingne*. Ed. and trans. R. Barton Palmer. *The Judgment of the King of Bohemia*. New York, 1984.

———. *Oeuvres de Guillaume de Machaut*. Ed. Ernest Hoepffner. 3 vols. Société des anciens textes français. Paris, 1908–21.

———. *Le Livre du Voir-dit de Guillaume de Machaut*. Ed. Paulin Paris. Paris, 1875.

Macrobius. *Commentary on the Dream of Scipio*. Trans. W. H. Stahl. New York, 1952.

———. *Saturnalia*. Trans. Percival Vaughan Davies. New York, 1969.

Mainzer, Conrad. "John Gower's Use of the Medieval Ovid in the *Confessio Amantis*." *Medium Aevum* 41 (1972): 215–29.

Mandeville, Sir John. *Mandeville's Travels*. Ed. M. C. Seymour. Oxford, 1967.

Manzalaoui, M. A. " 'Noght in the Registre of Venus': Gower's English Mirror for Princes." In *Medieval Studies for J. A. W. Bennett: Aetatis Suae LXX*, ed. P. L. Heyworth, pp. 159–83. Oxford, 1981.

Marbode of Rennes. *De lapidibus*. Ed. John M. Riddle. Sudhoffs Archiv: Zeitschrift für Wissenschaftsgeschichte, Beiheft 20. Wiesbaden, 1977.

Martianus Capella. *De nuptiis Philologiae et Mercurii*. Ed. Adolf Dick. Stuttgart, 1969. Trans. William Harris Stahl and Richard Johnson, with E. L. Burge. *The Marriage of Philology and Mercury*. In *Martianus Capella and the Seven Liberal Arts*. 2 vols. New York, 1977.

Maurice of Provins. *Dictionarium Sacrae Scripturae Mauritii Hybernici*. Venice, 1603.

McKeon, Richard. "Rhetoric in the Middle Ages." In *Critics and Criticism, Ancient and Modern*, ed. R. S. Crane, pp. 260–96. Chicago, 1952.

———. *Thought Action and Passion*. Chicago, 1954.

Middle English Dictionary. Ed. Hans Kurath, Sherman M. Kuhn, Robert E. Lewis et al. Ann Arbor, 1952–.

Minnis, A. J. "Discussions of 'Authorial Role' and 'Literary Form' in Late-Medieval Scriptural Exegesis." *Beiträge zur Geschichte der deutschen Sprache und Literatur* 99 (1977): 37–65.

———. "John Gower, *Sapiens* in Ethics and Politics." *Medium Aevum* 49 (1980): 207–29.

———. "Late-Medieval Discussions of *Compilatio* and the Role of the *Compilator*." *Beiträge zur Geschichte der deutschen Sprache und Literatur* 101 (1979): 385–421.

———. "The Influence of Academic Prologues on the Prologues and Literary Attitudes of Late-Medieval English Writers." *Mediaeval Studies* 43 (1981): 342–83.

———, and A. B. Scott, eds., with the assistance of David Wallace. *Medieval Literary Theory c.1100–1375: The Commentary Tradition*. Oxford, 1988.

———. *Medieval Theory of Authorship: Scholastic Literary Attitudes in the Later Middle Ages*. 2d ed. Philadelphia, 1988.

———, ed. *Gower's Confessio Amantis: Responses and Reassessments*. Cambridge, 1983.

Moore, Philip S. *The Works of Peter of Poitiers: Master in Theology and Chancellor of Paris (1193–1205)*. Notre Dame, 1936.

Murphy, James J. "John Gower's *Confessio Amantis* and the First Discussion of Rhetoric in the English Language." *Philological Quarterly*, 41 (1962): 401–11.

Newhauser, Richard. "The Love of Money as Deadly Sin and Deadly Disease." In *Zusammenhänge, Einflüsse, Wirkungen: Kongressakten zum ersten Symposium des Mediävistenverbandes in Tübingen, 1984*. Ed. Joerg O. Fichte, Karl Heinz Göller, and Bernhard Schimmelpfennig (Berlin, 1986): 320–26.

Nitzsche, Jane Chance. *The Genius Figure in Antiquity and the Middle Ages*. New York, 1971.

Nock, A. D. *Conversion: The Old and the New in Religion from Alexander the Great to Augustine of Hippo*. Oxford, 1933.

O'Laughlin, Michael. *The Garlands of Repose: The Literary Celebration of Civic and Retired Leisure*. Chicago, 1978.

Oberman, Heiko. *Forerunners of the Reformation: The Shape of Late Medieval Thought*. New York, 1966.

Oculus pastoralis pascens officia. Ed. Dora Franceschi. Memorie dell' Accademia delle Scienze di Torino, 4th ser., no. 11. Turin, 1966.

Olson, Glending. *Literature as Recreation in the Later Middle Ages*. Ithaca, N.Y., 1982.

Olsson, Kurt. "Aspects of *Gentilesse* in John Gower's *Confessio Amantis*, Books III–V." In *John Gower: Recent Readings*, ed. R. F. Yeager, pp. 225–73. Kalamazoo, Mich., 1989.

———. "Grammar, Manhood, and Tears: The Curiosity of Chaucer's Monk." *Modern Philology* 76 (1978): 1–17.

———. "John Gower's *Vox Clamantis* and the Medieval Idea of Place." *Studies in Philology* 84 (1987): 134–58.

———. "Natural Law and John Gower's *Confessio Amantis*." *Medievalia et Humanistica*, n.s. 11 (1982): 229–61.

———. "Poetic Invention and Chaucer's *Parlement of Foules*." *Modern Philology* 87 (1989): 13–35.

———. "Rhetoric, John Gower, and the Late Medieval *Exemplum*." *Medievalia et Humanistica*, n.s. 8 (1977): 185–200.

———. "The Cardinal Virtues and the Structure of John Gower's *Speculum Meditantis*." *Journal of Medieval and Renaissance Studies* 7 (1977): 113–48.

Onclin, W. "Le droit naturel selon les Romanistes des XIIe et XIIIe siècles." In *Miscellanea moralia in honorem Arthur Janssen*, pp. 329–37. Louvain, 1949.

Origen. *In Lucam*. In *Die Homilien zu Lucas in der Übersetzung des Hieronymus*, ed. Max Rauer. *Origines werke*, vol. 9. *Die griechischen christlichen Schriftsteller der ersten drie Jahrhunderte*, vol. 49. Berlin, 1959.

Ovid. *Heroides and Amores*. Trans. Grant Showerman. Loeb. Cambridge, Mass., and London, 1921.

———. *Metamorphoses*. Trans. Frank Justus Miller. 2 vols. Loeb. 2d ed. London and New York, 1921–22.

———. *Remedia amoris*. Ed. E. J. Kenney. Oxford, 1961.

——. *The Art of Love*. Trans. Rolfe Humphries. Bloomington, Ind. 1957.

Ovide moralisé: Poème du commencement du quatorzième siècle. Ed. C. de Boer. 5 vols. Verhandelingen der Koninklijke Academie van Weterschappen te Amsterdam, Afdeeling Letterkunde Nieuwe Reeks, 15, 21, 30 no. 3, 37, 43. Amsterdam, 1915–38.

Oxford Latin Dictionary. Ed. P. G. W. Glare. Oxford, 1982.

Papias. *Vocabulista*. Venice, 1496; rpt. Turin, 1966.

Parkes, M. B. "The Influence of the Concepts of *Ordinatio* and *Compilatio* on the Development of the Book," in *Medieval Learning and Literature: Essays Presented to R. W. Hunt*, ed. J. J. G. Alexander and M. T. Gibson, pp. 115–41. Oxford, 1975.

Parvi flores. Ed. Jacqueline Hamesse. *Les Auctoritates Aristotelis: Un florilège médiéval, étude historique et édition critique*. Philosophes médiévaux, 17. Louvain, 1974.

Pearsall, Derek. "Gower's Narrative Art." *PMLA* 81 (1966): 475–84.

——. *Gower and Lydgate*. London, 1969.

——. *Old English and Middle English Poetry*. London, 1977.

Peck, Russell A. *Kingship and Common Profit in Gower's Confessio Amantis*. Carbondale, Ill., 1978.

Pelen, Marc M. "Machaut's Court of Love Narratives and Chaucer's *Book of the Duchess*." *Chaucer Review* 11 (1976): 128–55.

Pepicello, W. J., and Thomas A. Green. *The Language of Riddles: New Perspectives*. Columbus, Ohio, 1984.

Peraldus, William. *Summa virtutum ac vitiorum*. 2 vols. Mainz, 1618.

Peter of Blois. *De amicitia christiana*. Ed. E. De Boccard. *Un Traité de l'amour du XIIe siècle*. Paris, 1932.

Peter of Capua. *Rosa alphabetica seu Ars sermocinandi*, in extracts printed by J. B. Pitra, *Spicilegium Solesmense sanctorum patrum scriptorumque ecclesiasticorum*, (Paris, 1852–58), vols. 2 and 3, passim.

Pfander, H. G. "The Medieval Friars and Some Alphabetical Reference-Books for Sermons." *Medium Aevum* 3 (1934): 19–29.

Piaget, Arthur. "Un Manuscrit de la cour amoureuse de Charles VI." *Romania* 31 (1902): 597–603.

Pieper, Josef. *Leisure: The Basis of Culture*. Trans. Alexander Dru. New York, 1952.

Porter, Elizabeth. "Gower's Ethical Microcosm and Political Macrocosm." In *Gower's Confessio: Responses*, ed. Minnis (supra), pp. 135–62.

Post, Gaines. "The Naturalness of Society and the State." In *Studies in Medieval Legal Thought*, 494–561. Princeton, 1964.

Powicke, F. M., and C. R. Cheney, eds. *Councils and Synods, with Other Documents Relating to the English Church*. 2 vols. Oxford, 1964.

Prendiville, John G., S. J., "The Development of the Idea of Habit in the Thought of Saint Augustine." *Traditio* 28 (1972): 29–99.

Pseudo-Bede. *In Psalmorum librum exegesis*. PL 93:477–1098.

Pseudo-Hugh of St.Victor. *De bestiis et aliis rebus*. PL 177:9–164.

Pseudo-Ovid. *The Pseudo-Ovidian De vetula.* Ed. Dorothy M. Robathan. Amsterdam, 1968.

Quadlbauer, Franz. *Die antike Theorie der Genera dicendi im lateinischen Mittelalter.* Vienna, 1962.

Richard de Bury. *Philobiblon.* Text and trans. of E. C. Thomas, ed. Michael Maclagan. Oxford, 1970.

Richard of St.Victor. *Benjamin minor. PL* 196:1–64.

———. *In Apocalypsim Joannis. PL* 196:683–888.

Rickert, Edith. "King Richard II's Books," *The Library,* 4th ser., 13 (1932–33): 144–47.

Ridewall, John. *Fulgentius metaforalis: Ein Beitrag zur Geschichte der antiken Mythologie im Mittelalter.* Ed. Hans Liebeschütz. Studien der Bibliothek Warburg 4. Leipzig, 1926.

Robert, S. "Dialectic and Rhetoric: According to the First Latin Commentary on the Rhetoric of Aristotle." *New Scholasticism* 31 (1957): 484–98.

Robertson, D. W., Jr., ed. *The Literature of Medieval England.* New York, 1970.

———. *Preface to Chaucer: Studies in Medieval Perspectives.* Princeton, 1963.

———. *Chaucer's London.* New York, 1968.

Rochais, Henri-Marie, Philippe Delhaye, and Marcel Richard. "Florilèges spirituels." *Dictionnaire de spiritualité,* fasc. 5 (Paris, 1964): 435–512.

Rosarium theologiae. The Middle English Translation of the Rosarium theologie, a Selection. Ed. Christina Von Nolcken. Middle English Texts, 10. Heidelberg, 1979.

Rouse, Richard H., and Mary A. Rouse. "Biblical Distinctions in the Thirteenth Century." *AHDLMA* 41 (1974): 27–37.

———. "*Statim invenire*: Schools, Preachers and New Attitudes to the Page." In *Renaissance and Renewal in the Twelfth Century,* ed. Robert L. Benson and Giles Constable, pp. 201–25. Cambridge, Mass., 1982.

———. *Preachers, Florilegia and Sermons: Studies on the Manipulus florum of Thomas of Ireland.* Texts and Studies, vol. 47. Toronto, 1979.

Runacres, Charles. "Art and Ethics in the 'Exempla' of 'Confessio Amantis.' " In *Gower's Confessio: Responses,* ed. Minnis (supra), pp. 106–34.

Scattergood, V. J. "Literary Culture at the Court of Richard II." In *English Court Culture,* ed. Scattergood (infra) and Sherborne, pp. 29–43.

———, and J. W. Sherborne, eds. *English Court Culture in the Later Middle Ages.* London, 1983.

Schneider, Artur. "Der Gedanke der Erkenntnis des Gleichen durch Gleiches in antiker und patristischer Zeit." *Abhandlungen zur Geschichte der Philosophie des Mittelalters.* Beiträge zur Geschichte der Philosophie des Mittelalters, Texte und Untersuchungen Suppl. 2 (Münster, 1923): 49–77.

Schueler, Donald G. "Gower's Characterization of Genius in the *Confessio Amantis.*" *Modern Language Quarterly* 33 (1972): 240–56.

———. "The Age of the Lover in Gower's *Confessio Amantis. Medium Aevum* 36 (1967): 152–58.

Scott, Charles T. "Some Approaches to the Study of the Riddle." In *Studies in*

Language, Literature, and Culture of the Middle Ages and Later, ed. E. Bagby Atwood and Archibald A. Hill, pp. 111–27. Austin, Tex., 1969.

Sears, Elizabeth. *Ages of Man: Medieval Interpretations of the Life Cycle*. Princeton, 1986.

Secretum secretorum. "The 'Ashmole' Version: The Secrete of Secretes." In *Secretum Secretorum: Nine English Versions*, ed. M. A. Manzalaoui, pp. 18–113. EETS, os 276. Oxford, 1977.

———. Ed. Robert Steele. *Opera hactenus inedita Rogeri Baconi*, fasc. 5. Oxford, 1920.

———. *The Gouernaunce of Prynces, or Pryvete of Pryveteis*, trans. James Yonge. In *Three Prose Versions of the Secretum Secretorum*, ed. Robert Steele, pp. 121–248. EETS, es 74. London, 1898.

Seneca. *Ad Lucilium Epistulae morales*. Trans. Richard Gummere. Loeb. 3 vols. London and Cambridge, Mass., 1962–1967.

———. *Naturales quaestiones*. Trans. Thomas H. Corcoran. Loeb. 2 vols. London and Cambridge, Mass., 1971.

Shears, F. S. *Froissart: Chronicler and Poet*. London, 1930.

Silverstein, Theodore. "On the Genesis of De Monarchia II.v." *Speculum* 13 (1938): 326–49.

———. "The Fabulous Cosmogony of Bernardus Silvestris." *Modern Philology* 46 (1948): 92–116.

———. "The Wife of Bath and the Rhetoric of Enchantment: or How to Make a Hero See in the Dark." *Modern Philology* 58 (1961): 153–73.

Singer, S. *Apollonius von Tyrus: Untersuchungen über das Fortleben des antiken Romans in späteren Zeiten*. Halle, 1895.

Singleton, Charles. *Journey to Beatrice*. Dante Studies 2. Baltimore, 1958; rpt. 1977.

Souter, Alexander. *A Glossary of Later Latin to 600 A. D.* Oxford, 1949; rpt. 1964.

Stephan of Tournai. *Die Summa des Stephanus Tornacensis*. Ed. J. F. von Schulte. Giessen, 1921.

Stevens, John. *Music and Poetry in the Early Tudor Court*. Lincoln, Nebr., 1961.

Stock, Brian. *Myth and Science in the Twelfth Century: A Study of Bernard Silvester*. Princeton, 1972.

Summa Institutionum 'Iustiniani est in hoc opere.' Ed. Pierre Legendre. Frankfurt am Main, 1973.

Summa sententiarum. PL 176:41–174.

Summa Vindobonensis. Ed. J. B. Palmerius. Bonn, 1913–14.

The 'Demaundes off Love': A Middle English Prose Version (1487) of the French Game 'Au roy qui ne ment.' Ed. W. L. Braekman. Brussels, 1982.

The Book of Causes. Trans. Dennis J. Brand. 2nd ed. Milwaukee, 1984.

The Book of Vices and Virtues: A Fourteenth-Century English Translation of the Somme le Roi of Lorens d'Orléans. Ed. W. Nelson Francis. EETS, os 217. London, 1942; rpt. 1968.

Thomas Hibernicus. *Manipulus florum*, or *Flores doctorum pene omnium, tam Graecorum quam Latinorum.* Vienna, 1758.

Thomas of Kent. "Account of the Birth of Alexander." Trans. Patricia Inner-bichler De Bellis. In *Gower's Literary Transformations*, ed. Beidler (supra), pp. 91–117.

————. *La Romanz de tute chevalerie.* In *Alexandre le Grand dans la littérature française du moyen âge*, 2 vols., ed. Paul Meyer, 1:177–235. Paris, 1886; rpt. Geneva, 1970.

Trimpi, Wesley. "The Quality of Fiction: The Rhetorical Transmission of Literary Theory." *Traditio* 30 (1974): 1–118.

Uitti, Karl D. "*Clerc* to *Poète*: The Relevance of the *Romance of the Rose* to Machaut's World." In *Machaut's World*, ed. Cosman (supra) and Chandler, pp. 209–16.

Valerius Maximus. *Factorum et dictorum memorabilium libri novem.* Ed. Carolus Kempf. Stuttgart, 1966.

Verbeke, G. "Introductory Conference: Peter Abelard and the Concept of Subjectivity." In *Peter Abelard: Proceedings of the International Conference, Louvain, May 10–12, 1971*, ed. E. M. Buytaert, pp. 1–11. Louvain, 1974.

Verducci, Florence. *Ovid's Toyshop of the Heart: Epistulae Heroidum.* Princeton, 1985.

Vincent of Beauvais. "Apologia totius operis." Ed. Anna-Dorothee v. den Brincken. "Geschichtsbetrachtung bei Vincenz von Beauvais: Die Apologia Actoris zum Speculum Maius." *Deutsches Archiv für Erforschung des Mittelalters* 34 (1978): 465–99.

————. *De morali principis institutione.* Rostock, ca. 1476.

————. *Speculum quadruplex: naturale, doctrinale, morale, historiale.* 4 vols. Douay, 1624; rpt. Graz, 1965.

Voorbij, J. B. "The *Speculum Historiale*: Some Aspects of Its Genesis and Manuscript Tradition." In *Vincent of Beauvais and Alexander the Great: Studies on the Speculum Maius and Its Translations into Medieval Vernaculars*, ed. W. J. Aerts et al., 11–55. Medievalia Groningana, fasc. 7. Groningen, 1986.

Wack, Mary Frances. "The *Liber de heros morbo* of Johannes Afflacius and Its Implications for Medieval Love Conventions." *Speculum* 62 (1987): 324–44.

Welsh, Andrew. *Roots of Lyric: Primitive Poetry and Modern Poetics.* Princeton, 1978.

Wenzel, Siegfried. "Dante's Rationale for the Seven Deadly Sins ('*Purgatorio*' XVII)." *Modern Language Review* 60 (1965): 529–33.

————. "The Seven Deadly Sins: Some Problems of Research." *Speculum* 43 (1968): 1–22.

————. *The Sin of Sloth: Acedia in Medieval Thought and Literature.* Chapel Hill, N.C., 1967.

Wetherbee, Winthrop. "Genius and Interpretation in the 'Confessio Amantis.'" In *Magister Regis: Studies in Honor of Robert Earl Kaske*, ed. Arthur Groos, pp. 241–60. New York, 1986.

————. "The Theme of Imagination in Medieval Poetry and the Allegorical Figure of 'Genius.' " *Medievalia et Humanistica*, n.s. 7 (1976): 45–64.

————. *Platonism and Poetry in the Twelfth Century: The Literary Influence of the School of Chartres*. Princeton, 1972.

Wilkins, David, ed. *Concilia Magnae Britanniae et Hiberniae*. 4 vols. London, 1737.

William of Auxerre. *Summa aurea in quattuor libros sententiarum*. Paris, 1500–1501; rpt. Frankfurt am Main, 1964.

William of Conches. *Glosae super Platonem*. Ed. E. Jeauneau. Paris, 1965.

William of St.Thierry. *De natura corporis et animae. PL* 180:695–726.

————. *De natura et dignitate amoris. PL* 184:379–408.

Wilmart, André. "Un répertoire d'exégèse composé en Engleterre vers le début du XIIIe siècle," *Mémorial Lagrange* (Paris 1940), pp. 307–46, especially "Note sur les plus anciens recueils de distinctions bibliques," pp. 335–46.

Wittig, Joseph S. " 'Piers Plowman' B, Passus IX–XII: Elements in the Design of the Inward Journey." *Traditio* 28 (1972): 211–80.

Woolf, Rosemary. "Moral Chaucer and Kindly Gower." In *J. R. R. Tolkien, Scholar and Storyteller: Essays in Memoriam*, ed. Mary Salu and Robert T. Farrell, pp. 221–45. Ithaca, N.Y., 1979.

Yeager, R. F. "Aspects of Gluttony in Chaucer and Gower." *Studies in Philology* 81 (1984): 42–55.

————. "*Pax Poetica*: On the Pacifism of Chaucer and Gower." *Studies in the Age of Chaucer* 9 (1987): 97–108.

————. "John Gower and the Uses of Allusion." *Res Publica Litterarum* 7 (1984): 201–13.

Ysagoge in theologiam. In *Écrits théologiques de l'école d'Abelard*, ed. Artur Landgraf, pp. 61–285. Louvain, 1934.

INDEX